THE WORLD'S CLASSICS

NORTHANGER ABBEY, LADY SUSAN, THE WATSONS, AND SANDITON

JANE AUSTEN was born at Steventon, Hampshire, in 1775, the daughter of a clergyman. At the age of nine she was sent to school at Reading with her elder sister Cassandra, who was her lifelong friend and confidante, but she was largely taught by her father. She began to write for recreation while still in her teens. In 1801 the family moved to Bath, the scene of so many episodes in her books and, after the death of her father in 1805, to Southampton and then to the village of Chawton, near Alton in Hampshire. Here she lived uneventfully until May 1817, when the family moved to Winchester seeking skilled medical attention for her ill-health, but she died two months later. She is buried in Winchester Cathedral.

Her best-known novels are *Sense and Sensibility* (1811), *Pride and Prejudice* (1813), *Mansfield Park* (1814), *Emma* (1816), and *Northanger Abbey* and *Persuasion*, both published posthumously in 1818.

JOHN DAVIE is Senior Lecturer in English at Trent Polytechnic. His main academic interests are in eighteenth- and nineteenth-century literature, and he has researched on authors as diverse as Jane Austen and Browning.

THE WORLD'S CLASSICS

JANE AUSTEN

Northanger Abbey, Lady Susan, The Watsons, and Sanditon

Edited by
JOHN DAVIE

Oxford New York
OXFORD UNIVERSITY PRESS

Oxford University Press, Walton Street, Oxford OX2 6DP

Oxford New York Toronto
Delhi Bombay Calcutta Madras Karachi
Petaling Jaya Singapore Hong Kong Tokyo
Nairobi Dar es Salaam Cape Town
Melbourne Auckland

and associated companies in
Beirut Berlin Ibadan Nicosia

Bibliography, Chronology, Introduction and Notes to Northanger Abbey
© Oxford University Press 1971
Introduction and Notes to Lady Susan, The Watsons, Sanditon © John Davie 1980

First published by Oxford University Press 1971
First issued as a World's Classics paperback
and in a hardback edition 1980
Paperback reprinted 1985, 1987

British Library Cataloguing in Publication Data

Austen, Jane
Northanger Abbey; and Lady Susan; and
The Watsons; and, Sanditon. – (Oxford classics).
I. Title   II. Kinsley, James
III. Davie, John   IV. Series
823'.7   PR4031.5   80–40257
ISBN 0–19–281525–3

Printed in Great Britain by
Hazell Watson & Viney Limited
Aylesbury, Bucks

CONTENTS

———

CONTENTS

INTRODUCTION

NONE of the work in this volume appeared in print in Jane
Austen's lifetime. *Northanger Abbey* was published together
with *Persuasion* in four volumes by John Murray in 1818;[1] *Lady
Susan* was first printed, rather inaccurately, in the 1871 edition
of J. E. Austen-Leigh's *A Memoir of Jane Austen*, which also
included *The Watsons*[2] and an account with some extracts of
what he called 'The Last Work' but which has become known
as *Sanditon*, and which was not published in full until R. W.
Chapman's edition of 1925.

The history of the manuscript of *Northanger Abbey* (which,
like those of Jane Austen's other major novels, does not survive)[3]
gives an interesting insight into the possible problems and
hazards facing an unknown novelist seeking publication in the
early nineteenth century. The work was probably written in
1798 and 1799: this is the date given in Cassandra Austen's
memorandum and, though that memorandum was not itself
written until 1817, there is no external evidence to dispute the
dating, which accords well with the known composition dates of
the other early novels. Some revision of the work took place
before it was sold, with the title *Susan*, to the publisher Crosby
in 1803 for £10. As Jane Austen wrote in the 'Advertisement, by
the Authoress' which appeared in the eventual publication, the
book was actually advertised but for some reason did not appear.

---

[1] This is the date on the title-page. Publication had, however, been announced in the *Morning Chronicle* for 19 and 20 December 1817.

[2] The titles *Lady Susan* and *The Watsons* were given by J. E. Austen-
Leigh: neither manuscript has a title. On the title of *Sanditon* see below
p. xviii.

[3] With the exception of the manuscript of two cancelled chapters of
Persuasion, now in the British Library.

She wrote under a pseudonym to Crosby in 1809 in an effort to spur him to publication, indicating that if he did not publ.sh the book, of which she could supply another copy, she would feel free to make arrangements elsewhere. His reply[1] merely threatened to 'take proceedings to stop the sale' in the event of publication by anyone else, and offered to return the manuscript for the original £10. The matter apparently rested there until 1816 when, after four of Jane Austen's novels had been published, Henry Austen bought back the manuscript and the copyright and enjoyed then telling Crosby that the work was by the author of *Pride and Prejudice*. However, publication was further delayed, for in a letter to Fanny Knight, Jane Austen wrote that 'Miss Catherine is put upon the Shelve for the present, and I do not know that she will ever come out'.[2] (The change of the heroine's name may be due to the publication in 1809 of an anonymous novel entitled *Susan*.) In the event, *Northanger Abbey* and *Persuasion* were seen through the press by Henry Austen, who wrote an accompanying Biographical Notice of his sister. He may well also be responsible for naming at least the first novel: *Northanger Abbey* as a title seems to promise the Gothic vein which the book in part satirizes, and perhaps accounts for the *Morning Chronicle's* heralding it as a 'Romance' while describing *Persuasion* as a novel. But it is worth remembering that Jane Austen's other abbey, Donwell in *Emma*, is not intended to give rise to thoughts of terror or even of antiquity, except in so far as it is a place which befits the long-established gentility of the Knightleys.[3]

The generally accepted details in the foregoing account of the composition of *Northanger Abbey* have been challenged in two articles by Mr. C. S. Emden,[4] who suggests that Jane Austen wrote 'a light satire of manners comprising occasional

---

[1] Printed with Jane Austen's letter in *Letters*, pp. 263-4.

[2] *Letters*, p. 484.

[3] *Emma*, ed. David Lodge, World's Classics (1980), p. 323.

[4] '*Northanger Abbey* Re-Dated?', *Notes and Queries*, cxcv (1950), and 'The Composition of *Northanger Abbey*', *The Review of English Studies* xix (1968).

burlesque of the silly sentimental novel' about 1794 and rather clumsily added the Gothic element in 1798, introducing a few passages about *The Mysteries of Udolpho*[1] into the early part of the book as preparation for Henry Tilney's parody of the Gothic novel[2] and Catherine's adventures at Northanger. Since this argument is based on a critical observation about the novel, it must remain only a hypothesis, suspect in my view because it suggests that Jane Austen here worked in a technically crude way foreign to her usual practice – very different for example from the kind of recasting which she must have done to turn the epistolary *Elinor and Marianne* into *Sense and Sensibility*. But the argument is useful in raising the pertinent critical questions about the book's structure and the role of literary satire and burlesque in it.

The main unifying force of *Northanger Abbey*, as of all Jane Austen's novels, is its heroine. Catherine Morland is presented initially in such a way that Jane Austen can bring within her own and the reader's easy view most of the conventions of the fiction of the late eighteenth century. Here, in the matter of the character and portrayal of heroines, it would be artificial and mistaken to attempt a rigid distinction between the novel of sensibility and the Gothic novel: Mrs. Radcliffe's Emily is as sensitive and cultivated as any of the tribe of 'Julias and Louisas' of the sentimental novels of the 1770s which Henry Tilney has presumably also read.[3] Jane Austen also draws on the theme, familiar to readers of Fanny Burney, of the young lady's entry into society with all the real and felt dangers and rewards involved in that process which the intricacies of etiquette and the ingenuities of plot can supply. In addition to these, the early part of *Northanger Abbey* makes plain its satire on certain clichés of the novel, such as the 'lucky overturn to introduce them to the hero'[4] which does *not* happen on Catherine's journey to Bath with the Allens. In this way Jane Austen can make intermittent direct or indirect references to the fact that she is presenting Catherine in a novel – a form which, in an often-

[1] By Mrs. Radcliffe; ed. Bonamy Dobrée, Oxford English Novels (1966).
[2] pp. 124–6.   [3] p. 83.   [4] p. 6.

quoted passage,[1] she seems deliberately to over-extol as a humorous foil to the frequently implied ridicule of extravagant contrivances in the popular novel. This gently mocking preoccupation with the way in which she tells her story is a device which Jane Austen might have learned from Fielding, or even from Sterne, though her tone and manner remain her own. Mischievously but characteristically she uses it to make fun not only of the Gothic or the sentimental novel, but also of the overtly moral narrative of which there were many examples in the late eighteenth and early nineteenth centuries; for at the end of *Northanger Abbey* Jane Austen points to the immediate causes of her happy ending and declares:

I leave it to be settled by whomsoever it may concern, whether the tendency of this work be altogether to recommend parental tyranny, or reward filial disobedience.[2]

The wide range of Jane Austen's awareness of contemporary fiction in *Northanger Abbey* is what one would expect from a knowledge of her sprightly and often miniature juvenilia; and indeed the book perpetuates some features of those early works such as the use of family jokes° and the tendency to give an epigrammatic expression of a real state of affairs brought about by actions which the characters themselves would present in a different light, as when Isabella (consciously) and Catherine (unconsciously) 'set off immediately as fast as they could walk, in pursuit of the two young men'.[4] It is also possible that Jane Austen did some actual reworking from her more ambitious early works: Mrs. Stanley, for example, in 'Catharine, or the Bower' speaks with a kind of ponderous emptiness[5] which is not unlike some of Mrs. Allen's remarks, and there are other similarities between the same story and some conversations or situations in *Northanger Abbey*.

What was a new venture for Jane Austen in writing *Northanger Abbey* – and it is a characteristic which equally marks the

---

[1] p. 22.   [2] p. 205.
[3] See the explanatory notes to pp. 1, 83 (n. 2).
[4] p. 27.
[5] *Minor Works*, ed. R. W. Chapman, p. 201.

work off from such parody as Barrett's *The Heroine*, which Jane
Austen in 1814 found 'a delightful burlesque, particularly on
the Radcliffe style'[1] – was the attempt to weave together the
literary burlesque and a serious story leading to the marriage of
Catherine Morland and Henry Tilney. It is important for the
success of this attempt that Catherine's head should not be
completely turned for a long, unbroken part of the narrative by
her fondness for reading Gothic novels. Indeed, one may remark
that the references to Catherine's actually reading Gothic novels
are more sparing than might at first be supposed,[2] and that she
mistakes the names of both the Lady Laurentini and M. St.
Aubert[3] from *The Mysteries of Udolpho*. In any case a girl who
has already found *Sir Charles Grandison* 'very entertaining'[4] is
unlikely to have her literary taste vitiated for long: if Catherine
is to enjoy Gothic novels it must eventually be, appropriately
enough, with something like Henry's ardent suspension of dis-
belief. As it is, the attractions of the Gothic strike her most
forcibly when the circumstances of her rapidly enlarging experience seem at Northanger to resemble the world of the
Gothic novel – if not in the abbey's setting,[5] at least in her room
on the first night of her stay[6] (a ludicrous episode which is a fine
set-piece with a possible antecedent in Mrs. Radcliffe's *Romance
of the Forest*),[7] and again in the mystery which appears to sur-
round General Tilney's relationship with his wife.[8]

The suspicions which Catherine weaves around the General's
aversion to going to his late wife's room, and around the fact
that when Mrs. Tilney died Eleanor was away from home, are of
course the very stuff of the sensational novel. Either the General
has been responsible for his wife's death, or she is secretly
imprisoned, 'receiving from the pitiless hands of her husband a
nightly supply of coarse food'[9] – even the idiom and rhythm of
the words prompted by Catherine's imagination here suggest

---

[1] *Letters*, pp. 376–7.

[2] Though in retrospect Catherine does blame her Bath reading for her
delusion (p. 160).

[3] See pp. 23, 25, 26, 62.   [4] p. 25.   [5] p. 127.   [6] pp. 133–6.

[7] See *Persuasion*, ed. R. W. Chapman, pp. 307–12.

[8] pp. 143–4.   [9] p. 150.

Gothic cliché. (What she suspects is no more melodramatic than Mr. Rochester's secret in *Jane Eyre*, which shows how long the Gothic element endured in English fiction.) In Henry's absence from Northanger, Catherine allows her mind to become feverishly possessed by her wild speculations – she tacitly leaps to the conclusion that all the General's children must have been away from home when Mrs. Tilney died or was imprisoned, and in mistakenly treating this assumption as fact she finds her theory further supported. She is eventually driven by her excitement to explore the fateful apartments on her own, so committing the only breach of etiquette of which she was really (as opposed to apparently) guilty in the novel. (In Bath the decent common sense of Catherine's upbringing had made her more sensitive to such matters than were the guardian Allens.) Her previous adventures with the chest and the laundry bill had ended only in bathos and the reflection 'Heaven forbid that Henry Tilney should ever know her folly!'[1] This of course is the kind of unobtrusive proleptic irony which Jane Austen habitually uses and which makes the rereading of her novels so rich in discovery. The scene in which Henry discovers her greater, her culpable folly is at once the climax of the literary burlesque – Henry's 'swift steps' on the stairs could in Radcliffian fashion so easily have been those of the General or of a menacing stranger – and of the courtship story. The scene which follows, as R. W. Chapman pointed out, 'vibrates with passion',[2] largely because of Jane Austen's unfailingly dramatic sense of dialogue. It also leads into the culmination of Henry's role as the mentor-hero of the novel; for he, now and in the succeding chapter in which she receives her brother's letter, not merely (as he had done in Bath) shows Catherine a far greater knowledge of the world than she herself possesses, but, moderating his high-spirited address with something of Eleanor's tact, leads her to a greater understanding of herself. Jane Austen may have taken over the mentor-hero figure from Fanny Burney, who used him in *Evelina, Cecilia*, and *Camilla*, but in Henry Tilney she improves on her predecessor in several ways. His instruction is witty, whereas in

[1] p. 137. [2] *Jane Austen: Facts and Problems* (1948), p. 193.

Fanny Burney wit (of different kinds) is possessed only by the heroines and the vulgar; he acts from a feeling curiosity about Catherine's developing personality at least as much as from any dutiful chivalry, and is therefore a much more satisfactory and credible lover; he influences the character and not merely the circumstances of the heroine. Most significantly of all, he changes without inconsistency, his development as a character being intimately linked in Jane Austen's characteristic and skilful manner to Catherine's perception of him which (another improvement on Fanny Burney) grows as she discovers her love.

The core of the book, the relationship between Catherine and Henry, is thus surely executed and neatly integrated with the pattern of literary burlesque, and if the novel as a whole were on the same artistic level it would command even greater critical esteem. Jane Austen is less successful in the narrative structure, since, with the brilliant exception of Isabella's letter,[1] there is a loss of immediacy in the treatment of events concerning the Thorpes once Bath has been left behind. Less successful too is the handling of certain characters in relation to each other and to the plot: it is hard to accept that John Thorpe could seriously influence General Tilney, and even that Isabella should captivate the colourless and rather conventional James. The friendship between Catherine and Eleanor is well contrasted with that between Catherine and Isabella, the latter being the kind of sentimental acquaintance, a contract of mutual folly, which courtesy-book writers such as Hester Chapone and Hannah More warned against; it is, then, the more unsatisfactory to find Eleanor so lightly given in marriage to the noble writer of the laundry bill.[2] We appreciate the mockery of the over-tidy denouement; but Eleanor is not a figure for burlesque, and when Jane Austen goes on to attribute the General's consent to Henry's marriage to his satisfaction at Eleanor's, she comes perilously close to undermining her serious characters with the kind of contrivance she elsewhere parodies.

*

[1] pp. 174-5.   [2] p. 204.

Jane Austen's readers have never wished that she had written less. Those who are familiar only with the six completed full-length novels are likely, therefore, to turn to her minor works with eager curiosity. Collectively, *Lady Susan*, *The Watsons*, and *Sanditon* tell us a good deal about the development of her art, confirming some of our impressions from the major novels, but hinting also of other possibilities in both techniques and themes; individually, each has its own points of particular interest.

The manuscript of *Lady Susan* exists in a fair copy, containing few alterations, made on paper with a watermark of 1805, but on the evidence (both internal and external) convincingly marshalled by Mr. B. C. Southam,[1] the actual composition – except perhaps for the Conclusion – was much earlier, probably in 1793–4. The maturity of conception, style, and narrative control are remarkable in an author merely eighteen or nineteen years old, but not more remarkable than familiarity with Jane Austen's even earlier work would have led one to expect.[2] And in two ways at least *Lady Susan* is paradoxically both characteristic of Jane Austen and yet unique in her work as we can now see it. She is interested in the consciousness of a guilty and dangerous woman elsewhere, but only in the creation of Lady Susan does she show us so complete a self-revelation of so complete a villain – a self-revelation indeed which forms the pitiless heart of the story. She experimented elsewhere too in writing epistolary fiction, but *Lady Susan* is the only example which has survived of her serious and completed attempts at the form.

Epistolary novels are capable of a curious effect, which can be experienced in reading *Lady Susan*. Correspondence in fiction, as in real life, combines intimacy with distance – a disconcerting pairing, and one which affects our response to Lady Susan herself. On the one hand we are given a clear insight into her ruthlessness, more memorably through her own letters than in the conventionally worded protests of Mrs. Vernon; on the

[1] *Jane Austen's Literary Manuscripts* (1964) pp. 45–7.
[2] See R. W. Chapman ed., *Minor Works*, (1954), rev. B. C. Southam (1975).

other hand, we can never be required to make the more complex acts of judgement when witnessing conduct that are required of us, for example, when considering Mary Crawford in *Mansfield Park*. This intrinsic limitation in the form, cutting Jane Austen off from what was to become one of her greatest and most distinctive strengths as a novelist, may well have played its part in her evident decision to round off the narrative rather peremptorily. The tone of her entry as narrator in the Conclusion mingles irony, impatience, and a sense of release.

There are other weaknesses. Those characters whose business is to receive letters rather than send them inevitably remain rather shadowy, or stock types of eighteenth-century satire. The fact that Frederica, Lady Susan's ill-used daughter, can write only one desperate letter provides pathos at the cost of precluding significant development or exploration of her interesting situation. But it would be unjust to dwell on shortcomings in *Lady Susan* when these are outweighed by strengths. The characterization of the brilliantly deceptive Lady Susan is subtle enough for her to add at least one twentieth-century critic to the specially pleading advocates she attracts within the story.[1] More remarkable still is the technical advance made by Jane Austen's handling of the epistolary form over that of many of her eighteenth-century predecessors. Whereas they often allow the epistolary novel to become much more like a diary-novel, in which the bulk of the letters are the confessional outpouring of a central character, Jane Austen uses the web-like nature of correspondence to reinforce the reader's interest in the timing and manœuvrings of the plot, and to heighten both suspense and irony. In short, *Lady Susan* shows great skill in construction. I think, though this admittedly is the kind of assertion which it is almost impossible to prove, that this deftness of construction is in part at least the result of Jane Austen's successful adaptation for the novel of what she had learned from eighteenth-century drama.

---

[1] Marvin Mudrick, *Jane Austen. Irony as Defense and Discovery* (1952), p. 138.

Finally, as always in Jane Austen, there is the quiet triumph of her realism. Each reader will have his own sense of what this entails, but, in keeping with what has been said about the authenticity of the handling of correspondence in *Lady Susan*, one may point to the range of styles (from Frederica's artlessness tinged with melodrama to Sir Reginald De Courcy's remonstrance with his son in tones echoed from Lord Chesterfield) and also to the sparing use of direct speech except in the climactic Letter 24. In her later fiction, Jane Austen avoids the limitations imposed by a complete commitment to the epistolary form while retaining to excellent effect the occasional use of self-revealing letters from the pen of a Lucy Steele or a Frank Churchill.

If *Lady Susan* was brought somewhat artificially to an end, *The Watsons* and *Sanditon* were both set aside, though for different reasons, while still incomplete. The former was begun in 1804 and abandoned apparently in the low period following the death of Jane Austen's father in January 1805; her own final illness compelled her to stop work on *Sanditon* in March 1817 after just two months of fairly rapid composition.

The Watsons, with its heroine called Emma and her ailing father, has sometimes been seen as a kind of prototype for *Emma*. But it is nearer the mark to say that it has rather obvious points of similarity with all of Jane Austen's completed novels: the work is so characteristic that if the manuscript had simply appeared from nowhere there would have been no doubt of its authorship.

Like all of Jane Austen's heroines at some stage or another, Emma Watson is both surrounded by people and yet in a sense very much alone. Her separateness does not come from any introspective insecurities, however; she is quite free from any private need to fashion a change in perspective of herself or the world. In the sentence with which the fragment breaks off we are told that 'Emma was of course un-influenced' by an argument put to her in her own interest, and this is the keynote of her character. Unlike almost all the other figures in the novel, she is consistently uninfluenced by considerations of selfishness or snobbery or habit or predetermined motive. In other words

she is one of those good people in Jane Austen's world who are
not miserable even when their circumstances are pitiable, who
exist – though without priggishness – as a force for the improvement of others, and who are destined to be led through the
dance of the plot to a deservedly happy fulfilment.

So much might in principle have been said of the heroines
created by many novelists who were roughly contemporary
with Jane Austen. In practice, Jane Austen typically excels in
her ability to transmit such ideals through memorable little
incidents or exchanges of dialogue. *The Watsons* has its share of
these, for example in the scene in which Emma offers to dance
with the ten-year-old Charles Blake,[1] or the conversation in
which she tells Lord Osborne that 'Female Economy will do a
great deal my Lord, but it cannot turn a small income into a
large one' and incidentally improves his manner by the sober
justice of her remarks.[2] In both instances Emma is promptly
guided by her honest assessment of things as they really are – a
principle simple to understand but difficult to follow, and almost
a definition of the way of life to which Jane Austen's heroines
aspire.

Jane Austen's sister Cassandra told her nieces something of
the intended outcome of *The Watsons*: Emma was 'to decline an
offer of marriage from Lord Osborne, and much of the interest
of the tale was to arise from Lady Osborne's love for Mr.
Howard, and his counter affection for Emma, whom he was
finally to marry.[3] Readers have often assumed that 'Lady
Osborne' here means Miss Osborne, and this would fit the
usual pattern of Jane Austen's plots very well, leaving the
middle-aged Lady Osborne perhaps to play an interfering role
like that of Lady Catherine de Bourgh in *Pride and Prejudice*.
But it is possible that the names are not confused and that the
'very handsome' Lady Osborne was to use 'all the Dignity of
Rank'[4] to attempt to secure the semi-dependent Mr. Howard.
The recent completion of *The Watsons* by 'Another' follows
this assumption, though without attempting to bring it to the
foreground of the novel.

[1] pp. 289–90   [2] p. 303.   [3] *Minor Works* p. 363.   [4] p. 288.

In style, as well as in plot and characterization, it seems likely that *The Watsons* would have stood comparison with Jane Austen's other novels if she had finished it. It is true that there are some passages of rather tired writing between the high points of incident and dialogue, but the manuscript shows that the work was being thoroughly revised and improved during composition, and there are examples of the happiest kind of conjunction between Jane Austen's powers of observation and phrasing. Most readers will recall Nanny's bustling preparations for the Watsons' unfashionably early dinner, and will delight in such gently satiric touches as Tom Musgrave's prospect of being 'famously snug' with a 'Barrel of Oysters' and the old mare's halting the carriage by force of habit at the milliner's.[1]

That *The Watsons* is unfinished is at least a loss to Jane Austen's admirers, but that *Sanditon* is unfinished is a major loss to English fiction as a whole. Its destination seems as mysterious as that of *The Watsons* seems settled, but what are unmistakable and exciting are the signs of fresh developments in Jane Austen's work. E. M. Forster was perhaps the first to point out a new kind of focus when he wrote that 'Sanditon gives out an atmosphere, and also exists as a geographic and economic force'.[2] Our sense of this has been sharpened by the adoption of *Sanditon* as the title – an accidental sharpening in one way, because the family tradition is that Jane Austen was going to call the novel *The Brothers*, but not so accidental if you take the view that it was clearly the stress on the resort and its development which suggested *Sanditon* as an appropriate title to later members of the Austen family.

The promotion of seaside resorts, especially on grounds of health, gathered momentum during the eighteenth century, but development on the south coast ('Sanditon' is in Sussex) reached a new and feverish peak in Regency England. Jane Austen perfectly catches the complex of attitudes and activities involved in this – the financial speculation, the aesthetics of property

[1] pp. 302-4, 294, 281.

[2] In a review of *Sanditon* in *Nation*, xxxvi (1925), reprinted in *Abinger Harvest* (1936).

development, the spirited patriotism engendered by the defeat of Napoleon, the zeal for the organization of leisure, the language and strategy of advertising. If *Sanditon* had been finished, the English novel might not have had to wait until the early Victorian period for a significant extension of the work begun in *Mansfield Park* of diagnosing major forces and movements in society as it reflected the spirit of the age.

Yet the signs too are that Jane Austen was achieving this without abandoning the tried and known strengths of her work. There would have been – there already is – a highly skilful grafting of the new on to the old. The carriage accident with which the novel opens, for example, is consistent with Jane Austen's habitual verisimilitude, but provides an impulsive headlong start to the narrative which fits the brisk mood of the enthusiastic Mr. Parker and which invests the scene with at least the potential of being seen as a symbol for his risk-taking in the development of Sanditon.[1] Financially as well as physically, he might be expected to sustain injuries but to survive.

There is Jane Austen's customary use of distinctive idiom to indicate character, most obviously in Sir Edward Denham with his sensibility paraded in the latest extravagant inkhorn terms,[2] but present too in Lady Denham's curiously starched informality and in the fussing of the little clutch of hypochondriac Parkers.

There is characteristically ample ground for moral reflection and debate, notably between the claims of the traditional rural way of life of the Heywoods and the modern commercial spirit of Mr. Parker. This spirit may or (more probably) may not be able to join forces successfully with the financial world of the Denhams, more conscious of inheritance than of investment. Finally there is the satisfying way in which the domestic and social side of the novel is linked with the theme of Sanditon's

---

[1] It is suggestive that the first sentence of the manuscript shows that Jane Austen replaced the colourless 'on quitting' with 'being induced by Business to quit'.

[2] Though further revision may have toned down Sir Edward's speech. It would be uncharacteristic of Jane Austen, for example, to retain two uses of the phrase 'illimitable ardour' in such proximity (pp. 352, 357).

development: Mrs. Parker, like George Eliot's Mrs. Tulliver in *The Mill on the Floss*, is clearly a hostage to the outcome of her husband's financial dealings, and there is a neat irony whereby the Parkers' status in society is dependent on the operations of business while these in turn are dependent on the operations of society, with its network for recommendations of Sanditon and its lodgings.

Some of the characters seem immutably fixed, in Jane Austen's best early caricature manner, though the roles in the plot of, say, Sir Edward Denham and Arthur Parker remain open. But other characters are more complex and have ample potential for further development and revelation. Clara Brereton is potentially at least as interesting as Jane Fairfax in *Emma*, and as with Jane Fairfax the reader could be kept guessing for many more chapters yet about what kind of explicable whole could bind together the puzzling fragments of our glimpses of her. And Charlotte Heywood seems admirably fitted to be one of Jane Austen's heroines: we do not learn enough to feel sure of the precise course of her future, but we can see that she has a many-sided receptivity to experience and a compulsion to interiorize it in a way which involves making and remaking judgments about both her world and herself. Taken together, these qualities guarantee that her further development by Jane Austen would have been of absorbing interest.

Then there is the style of *Sanditon*, bracing and impressionistic, with new accents to sound. It is true that the effect of this partly depends on some idiosyncrasies in Jane Austen's manuscript, especially in her punctuation and her use of contractions, and that many of these would presumably have disappeared in a final printed version; but even after allowance has been made for this, one is left with the sense of a new adventurousness in Jane Austen's style which is bent on exploring the possibilities of giving features of syntax, rhythm and image a telling and dramatic appropriateness to characterization and theme.[1]

[1] For some detailed analysis of the style of *Sanditon*, see R. W. Chapman, *Jane Austen: Facts and Problems* (1948) p. 209 and B. C. Southam, *Jane Austen's Literary Manuscripts* (1964) pp. 124–9.

How all this would have appeared in the end it is tempting, if tantalizing, to guess. Indeed in its capacity to invite speculations from both critic and general reader alike, *Sanditon* the novel is as hospitable as Sanditon the place set out to be.

J.N.D.

NOTE ON THE TEXT

THE text of *Northanger Abbey* presents few problems for the editor. Jane Austen's manuscript does not survive, and the sole authority is the first edition, which was posthumously published (see Introduction, p. vii). Although the proofs were not corrected by Jane Austen herself, the edition contains few detectable errors. The text in the present edition is that prepared by Professor James Kinsley for the Oxford English Novels series; this in turn was based on the treatment of the text of the first edition in R. W. Chapman's Oxford Illustrated Jane Austen (1923; revised by Mary Lascelles 1965, 1969), and incorporated a reconsideration of Chapman's few emendations. The details are readily available to scholars in those editions, but none of the departures from the text of the first edition raises significant questions for either the general reader or the literary critic in his reading of *Northanger Abbey*.

It is less simple to determine the best procedure in editing the 'Minor Works' which are here included. Whereas for *Northanger Abbey* there is an authoritative early edition but no manuscript, for *Lady Susan, The Watsons*, and *Sanditon* there are manuscripts but no early printed texts. An ideal version of all three works would of course consist of the text which Jane Austen would have sanctioned if she had seen them into print, and the problems for the editor arise out of the impossibility of constructing such an ideal version. The manuscript of *Lady Susan* was a fair copy and therefore reasonably near to what might have been expected in print, but *The Watsons* and *Sanditon* exist in first drafts which bear many signs of work still at a provisional stage.

Four editorial approaches are possible in such a situation. One is to publish a facsimile, as in B. C. Southam's 1975 edition of *Sanditon* (see the Select Bibliography): this is valuable for scholars and critics, but is hardly the form in which the general reader wants a text. A second method is to attempt a printed version which represents as faithfully as possible what appear to be the latest readings of the manuscript – this again, if skilfully done, yields a text which is reliable for the scholar, and it is the procedure which was followed in the Oxford Illustrated Jane Austen, Volume VI of which includes these and other 'Minor Works'. But, as will be seen presently, there are idiosyncrasies in Jane Austen's manuscripts which mean that this editorial method cannot guarantee the smooth and fluent experience of ordinary reading. A third method seeks by contrast to provide this by normalizing the text along lines which the editor presumes would have been followed in publication: this clearly aims at the kind of ideal version envisaged above, but in practice to normalize the 'Minor Works' to this extent involves guesswork and runs the risk of departing from Jane Austen's intentions in some points of substance.

The fourth approach, which has been followed in this edition, is a fairly conservative compromise which confines its modernization of Jane Austen's manuscript to changes of a kind which, on the evidence of the other novels, would certainly have been made in publication and which can be consistently applied to all parallel examples in the text. These are:

1. the expansion of a few obvious and standard abbreviations except for abbreviated signatures in *Lady Susan*, e.g. 'Lord' from 'L^d', 'could' from 'c^d', 'morning' from 'morn^g';

2. the replacement of '&' by 'and';

3. the replacement of figures by words, not involving times of day;

4. the use of single speech marks ('   ') throughout, and the insertion of these in a few instances where the manuscript omits to close or re-open them.

Some further changes which would have been made in publication have been refrained from here, because they could not be applied to all instances without the risk of losing, in at least a minority of instances, effects which Jane Austen would have retained in print. The most important examples of this kind are:

1. the abbreviations (not involving superior contractions) of names, such as 'Mr. P.' for 'Mr. Parker' (readers of *Emma* will recall that Mrs. Elton affectedly refers to her husband as 'Mr. E.');

2. the use of capitals where they would not be expected by rule e.g. 'a match for every Disorder, of the Stomach, the Lungs or the Blood';

3. misspellings (it is sometimes hard to distinguish between a mistake and a possible period spelling).

J.N.D.

SELECT BIBLIOGRAPHY

———

Northanger Abbey was published with *Persuasion* by John Murray in December 1817 (title-page 1818) in a four-volume edition of 2,500 copies. The first American editions (1,250 copies each) were published by Carey and Lea of Philadelphia in 1832–3. Mme Isabelle de Montolieu translated *Persuasion* as *La Famille Elliot* (1821, 1828); *L'Abbaye de Northanger* appeared in 1824. All six novels were included in Bentley's cheap Standard Novels series (6s. a volume) in 1833 (often reprinted). The Everyman edition (1892) was revised by Mary Lascelles in 1963.

COLLECTED EDITIONS. See above, Carey and Lea, Bentley, Everyman's Library, World's Classics. The standard edition of the novels is R. W. Chapman's, illustr., 6 vols. (Oxford, 1923–54; revised by Mary Lascelles, 1965–7), the texts are based on collation of the early editions, with invaluable commentaries and appendices.

BIBLIOGRAPHY. Geoffrey Keynes, *Jane Austen: A Bibliography* (1929) is important for the early editions of the novels. R. W. Chapman's *Critical Bibliography* (1953) was revised in 1955. See also *The New Cambridge Bibliography of English Literature* (Vol. III, 1969) and the *Annual Bibliography of English Language and Literature* (Modern Humanities Research Association, 1919–   ).

BIOGRAPHY AND CRITICISM. The primary sources are *Jane Austen's Letters to her Sister Cassandra and Others*, ed. R. W. Chapman, 2 vols. (1932; 1 vol., 1952), superseding Lord Brabourne's edition, 1884 (note also Chapman's *Letters 1796–1817*, World's Classics, 1955); the 'Biographical Notice of the Author' by her brother Henry, prefixed to *Northanger Abbey* (1818; expanded in Bentley's edition, 1833, and reprinted in Chapman's edition of the novels, vol. v); the *Memoir* by her nephew J. E. Austen-Leigh (1870; 1871 edn. containing fragments and minor works – see Chapman, vol. vi), ed. Chapman

(1926, 1951); William and Richard Austen-Leigh, *Life and Letters of J. A.* (1913). Modern biographies include Mary Austen-Leigh, *Personal Aspects of J. A.* (1920); C. Linklater Thomson, *J. A., A Survey* (1929); Mona Wilson, *J. A. and Some Contemporaries* (1938); Elizabeth Jenkins, *J. A. A Biography* (1938; revised edn., 1948); R. W. Chapman, *J. A.: Facts and Problems* (1948); Clark Lectures; W. A. Craik, *J. A. in her Time* (1969); Marghanita Laski, *J. A. and her World* (1969); Lord David Cecil, *A Portrait of J. A.* (1978); and Brian Wilks, *J. A.* (1978).

The early criticism is collected and surveyed in B. C. Southam, *J. A.: The Critical Heritage* (1968). F. M. Link, 'The Reputation of J. A. in the Twentieth Century' (unpublished doctoral dissertation, Boston University, 1958). Modern studies: Virginia Woolf in *The Common Reader* (1925); H. W. Garrod, 'J. A.: A Depreciation', and Chapman's refutation, in *Essays by Divers Hands* (Royal Society of Literature), viii (1928) and x (1931); Lord David Cecil's Leslie Stephen Lecture (1935); E. M. Forster in *Abinger Harvest* (1936); Mary Lascelles, *Jane Austen and her Art* (1939, 1941; paperback 1963); Q. D. Leavis, 'A Critical Theory of J. A.'s Writings', *Scrutiny*, x (1942) and xii (1944) reprinted in F. R. Leavis, *A Selection from Scrutiny*, vol. II (1968) – see also B. C. Southam in *Nineteenth-Century Fiction*, xvii (1962); Sheila Kaye-Smith and G. B. Stern, *Talking of J. A.* (1943) and *More Talk of J. A.* (1950); F. W. Bradbrook in the *Cambridge Journal*, iv (1951); Marvin Mudrick, *J. A.: Irony as Defense and Discovery* (1952); A. H. Wright, *J. A.'s Novels: A Study in Structure* (1953; 1962); C. S. Lewis in *Essays in Criticism*, iv (1954); Irène Simon in *English Studies*, xliii (1962); H. S. Babb, *J. A.'s Novels: The Fabric of Dialogue* (1962); W. L. Renwick in *English Literature 1789–1815* (1963); Ian Watt (ed.), *J. A.: A Collection of Critical Essays* (1963); B. C. Southam, *J. A.'s Literary Manuscripts. A Study of the Novelist's Development* (1964); W. A. Craik, *J. A.: The Six Novels* (1965); A. W. Litz, *J. A.: A Study of her Artistic Development* (1965); F. W. Bradbrook, *J. A. and her Predecessors* (1966); Norman Sherry, *J. A.* (1966); Kenneth L. Moler, *J. A.'s Art of Allusion* (1968); Yasmine Gooneratne, *J. A.* (1970); Alistair M. Duckworth, *The Improvement of the Estate: A Study of J. A.'s Novels* (1971); K. C. Phillipps, *J. A.'s English* (1971); Norman Page, *The Language of J. A.* (1972); Darrel Mansell, *The Novels of J. A.: An Interpretation* (1973); F. B. Pinion, *A J. A. Companion* (1973); Stuart M. Tave,

Some Words of J. A. (1973); Christopher Gillie, *A Preface to J. A.* (1974); Douglas Bush, *J. A.* (1975); Marilyn Butler, *J. A. and the War of Ideas* (1975); John Halperin (ed.), *J. A. Bicentenary Essays* (1975); Barbara Hardy, *A Reading of J. A.* (1975).

Northanger Abbey. There are editions by Olivia Manning (1968) and Anne Henry Ehrenpreis (1972). M. Sadleir, 'The Northanger Novels', English Association Pamphlet No. 68 (1927); A. D. McKillop, 'Critical Realism in *Northanger Abbey*' in R. C. Rathburn and M. Steinmann, Jr. (eds.), *From Jane Austen to Joseph Conrad* (1958); Avrom Fleishman, 'The Socialization of Catherine Morland', *ELH*, xli (1974).

Lady Susan, The Watsons, and *Sanditon.* Many of the critical books on Jane Austen listed above give little or no attention to these works, though valuable discussion will be found in the studies by Mary Lascelles, Marvin Mudrick, B. C. Southam, A. W. Litz and Douglas Bush. The three texts have been edited in one volume by Margaret Drabble (1974) and a facsimile of the manuscript of *Sanditon* is published in B. C. Southam (ed.), *Sanditon. An Unfinished Novel by Jane Austen* (1975). There are recent attempts at completing the two unfinished novels: *The Watsons. A Novel by Jane Austen and Another* (1977) and *Sanditon. A Novel by Jane Austen and Another Lady* (1975). In addition, see J. A. Levine, 'Lady Susan: Jane Austen's Character of the Merry Widow', *Studies in English Literature*, i (1961) and J. Lauber, ' "Sanditon" – the kingdom of folly', *Studies in the Novel*, iv (1972).

A CHRONOLOGY OF JANE AUSTEN*

━━━

* For a detailed chronology, see R. W. Chapman, *Jane Austen: Facts and Problems* (1948), pp. 175–83.

ADVERTISEMENT,

BY THE AUTHORESS,

TO

NORTHANGER ABBEY

―――

THIS little work was finished in the year 1803, and intended for immediate publication. It was disposed of to a bookseller, it was even advertised, and why the business proceeded no farther, the author has never been able to learn. That any bookseller should think it worth while to purchase what he did not think it worth while to publish seems extraordinary. But with this, neither the author nor the public have any other concern than as some observation is necessary upon those parts of the work which thirteen years have made comparatively obsolete. The public are entreated to bear in mind that thirteen years have passed since it was finished, many more since it was begun, and that during that period, places, manners, books, and opinions have undergone considerable changes.

NORTHANGER ABBEY

───

VOLUME I

───

CHAPTER I

No one who had ever seen Catherine Morland in her infancy, would have supposed her born to be an heroine. Her situation in life, the character of her father and mother, her own person and disposition, were all equally against her. Her father was a clergyman, without being neglected, or poor, and a very respectable man, though his name was Richard[1] - and he had never been handsome. He had a considerable independence, besides two good livings - and he was not in the least addicted to locking up his daughters. Her mother was a woman of useful plain sense, with a good temper, and, what is more remarkable, with a good constitution. She had three sons before Catherine was born; and instead of dying in bringing the latter into the world, as any body might expect, she still lived on - lived to have six children more - to see them growing up around her, and to enjoy excellent health herself. A family of ten children will be always called a fine family, where there are heads and arms and legs enough for the number; but the Morlands had little other right to the word, for they were in general very plain, and Catherine, for many years of her life, as plain as any. She had a thin awkward figure, a sallow skin without colour, dark lank hair, and strong features; - so much for her person; - and not less unpropitious for heroism seemed her mind. She was

fond of all boys' plays, and greatly preferred cricket not merely
to dolls, but to the more heroic enjoyments of infancy, nursing a
dormouse, feeding a canary-bird, or watering a rose-bush.
Indeed she had no taste for a garden; and if she gathered flowers
at all, it was chiefly for the pleasure of mischief - at least so it
was conjectured from her always preferring those which she was
forbidden to take. - Such were her propensities - her abilities
were quite as extraordinary. She never could learn or understand
any thing before she was taught; and sometimes not even then,
for she was often inattentive, and occasionally stupid. Her
mother was three months in teaching her only to repeat the
'Beggar's Petition;'[1] and after all, her next sister, Sally, could
say it better than she did. Not that Catherine was always
stupid, - by no means; she learnt the fable of 'The Hare and
many Friends,'[2] as quickly as any girl in England. Her mother
wished her to learn music; and Catherine was sure she should
like it, for she was very fond of tinkling the keys of the old forlorn spinnet; so, at eight years old she began. She learnt a year,
and could not bear it; - and Mrs. Morland, who did not insist
on her daughters being accomplished in spite of incapacity or
distaste, allowed her to leave off. The day which dismissed the
music-master was one of the happiest of Catherine's life. Her
taste for drawing was not superior; though whenever she could
obtain the outside of a letter[3] from her mother, or seize upon any
other odd piece of paper, she did what she could in that way, by
drawing houses and trees, hens and chickens, all very much like
one another. - Writing and accounts she was taught by her
father; French by her mother: her proficiency in either was not
remarkable, and she shirked her lessons in both whenever she
could. What a strange, unaccountable character! - for with all
these symptoms of profligacy at ten years old, she had neither a
bad heart nor a bad temper; was seldom stubborn, scarcely ever
quarrelsome, and very kind to the little ones, with few inter-
ruptions of tyranny; she was moreover noisy and wild, hated
confinement and cleanliness, and loved nothing so well in the
world as rolling down the green slope at the back of the house.

Such was Catherine Morland at ten. At fifteen, appearances

were mending; she began to curl her hair and long for balls; her complexion improved, her features were softened by plumpness and colour, her eyes gained more animation, and her figure more consequence. Her love of dirt gave way to an inclination for finery, and she grew clean as she grew smart; she had now the pleasure of sometimes hearing her father and mother remark on her personal improvement. 'Catherine grows quite a good-looking girl, - she is almost pretty to day,' were words which caught her ears now and then; and how welcome were the sounds! To look *almost* pretty, is an acquisition of higher delight to a girl who has been looking plain the first fifteen years of her life, than a beauty from her cradle can ever receive.

Mrs. Morland was a very good woman, and wished to see her children every thing they ought to be; but her time was so much occupied in lying-in and teaching the little ones, that her elder daughters were inevitably left to shift for themselves, and it was not very wonderful that Catherine, who had by nature nothing heroic about her, should prefer cricket, base ball,[1] riding on horseback, and running about the country at the age of fourteen, to books - or at least books of information - for, provided that nothing like useful knowledge could be gained from them, provided they were all story and no reflection, she had never any objection to books at all. But from fifteen to seventeen she was in training for a heroine; she read all such works as heroines must read to supply their memories with those quotations which are so serviceable and so soothing in the vicissitudes of their eventful lives.

From Pope, she learnt to censure those who

'bear about the mockery of woe.'

From Gray, that

'Many a flower is born to blush unseen,
'And waste its fragrance on the desert air.'

From Thompson, that

— 'It is a delightful task
'To teach the young idea how to shoot.'[2]

And from Shakspeare[1] she gained a great store of information
– amongst the rest, that

> — 'Trifles light as air,
> 'Are, to the jealous, confirmation strong,
> 'As proofs of Holy Writ.'

That

> 'The poor beetle, which we tread upon,
> 'In corporal sufferance feels a pang as great
> 'As when a giant dies.'

And that a young woman in love always looks

> — 'like Patience on a monument
> 'Smiling at Grief.'

So far her improvement was sufficient – and in many other
points she came on exceedingly well; for though she could not
write sonnets, she brought herself to read them; and though
there seemed no chance of her throwing a whole party into
raptures by a prelude on the pianoforte, of her own composition,
she could listen to other people's performance with very little
fatigue. Her greatest deficiency was in the pencil – she had no
notion of drawing – not enough even to attempt a sketch of her
lover's profile,[2] that she might be detected in the design. There
she fell miserably short of the true heroic height. At present she
did not know her own poverty, for she had no lover to pourtray.
She had reached the age of seventeen, without having seen one
amiable youth[3] who could call forth her sensibility; without
having inspired one real passion, and without having excited
even any admiration but what was very moderate and very
transient. This was strange indeed! But strange things may be
generally accounted for if their cause be fairly searched out.
There was not one lord in the neighbourhood; no – not even a
baronet. There was not one family among their acquaintance
who had reared and supported a boy accidentally found at their
door – not one young man whose origin was unknown. Her
father had no ward, and the squire of the parish no children.

But when a young lady is to be a heroine, the perverseness of forty surrounding families cannot prevent her. Something must and will happen to throw a hero in her way.

Mr. Allen, who owned the chief of the property about Fullerton, the village in Wiltshire where the Morlands lived, was ordered to Bath for the benefit of a gouty constitution; – and his lady, a good-humoured woman, fond of Miss Morland, and probably aware that if adventures will not befal a young lady in her own village, she must seek them abroad, invited her to go with them. Mr. and Mrs. Morland were all compliance, and Catherine all happiness.

CHAPTER II

IN addition to what has been already said of Catherine Morland's personal and mental endowments, when about to be launched into all the difficulties and dangers of a six weeks' residence in Bath, it may be stated, for the reader's more certain information, lest the following pages should otherwise fail of giving any idea of what her character is meant to be; that her heart was affectionate, her disposition cheerful and open, without conceit or affectation of any kind – her manners just removed from the awkwardness and shyness of a girl; her person pleasing, and, when in good looks, pretty – and her mind about as ignorant and uninformed as the female mind at seventeen usually is.

When the hour of departure drew near, the maternal anxiety of Mrs. Morland will be naturally supposed to be most severe. A thousand alarming presentiments of evil to her beloved Catherine from this terrific separation must oppress her heart with sadness, and drown her in tears for the last day or two of their being together; and advice of the most important and applicable nature must of course flow from her wise lips in their parting conference in her closet. Cautions against the violence of such noblemen and baronets as delight in forcing young ladies away to some remote farm-house, must, at such a moment, relieve the fulness of her heart. Who would not think so? But Mrs. Morland knew so little of lords and baronets, that she entertained no notion of their general mischievousness, and was wholly un-suspicious of danger to her daughter from their machinations. Her cautions were confined to the following points. 'I beg, Catherine, you will always wrap yourself up very warm about the throat, when you come from the Rooms at night; and I wish you would try to keep some account of the money you spend; – I will give you this little book on purpose.'

Sally, or rather Sarah, (for what young lady of common gentility will reach the age of sixteen without altering her name[1] as far as she can?) must from situation be at this time the in-timate friend and confidante of her sister. It is remarkable, however, that she neither insisted on Catherine's writing by every post, nor exacted her promise of transmitting the character of every new acquaintance, nor a detail of every interesting conversation that Bath might produce. Every thing indeed relative to this important journey was done, on the part of the Morlands, with a degree of moderation and composure, which seemed rather consistent with the common feelings of common life, than with the refined susceptibilities, the tender emotions which the first separation of a heroine from her family ought always to excite. Her father, instead of giving her an unlimited order on his banker, or even putting an hundred pounds bank-bill into her hands, gave her only ten guineas, and promised her more when she wanted it.

Under these unpromising auspices, the parting took place, and the journey began. It was performed with suitable quietness and uneventful safety. Neither robbers nor tempests befriended them, nor one lucky overturn to introduce them to the hero. Nothing more alarming occurred than a fear on Mrs. Allen's side, of having once left her clogs behind her at an inn, and that fortunately proved to be groundless.

They arrived at Bath. Catherine was all eager delight; – her eyes were here, there, every where, as they approached its fine and striking environs, and afterwards drove through those streets which conducted them to the hotel. She was come to be happy, and she felt happy already.

They were soon settled in comfortable lodgings in Pulteney-street.

It is now expedient to give some description of Mrs. Allen, that the reader may be able to judge, in what manner her actions will hereafter tend to promote the general distress of the work, and how she will, probably, contribute to reduce poor Catherine to all the desperate wretchedness of which a last volume is capable - whether by her imprudence, vulgarity, or jealousy - whether by intercepting her letters, ruining her character, or turning her out of doors.

Mrs. Allen was one of that numerous class of females, whose society can raise no other emotion than surprise at there being any men in the world who could like them well enough to marry them. She had neither beauty, genius, accomplishment, nor manner. The air of a gentlewoman, a great deal of quiet, inactive good temper, and a trifling turn of mind, were all that could account for her being the choice of a sensible, intelligent man, like Mr. Allen. In one respect she was admirably fitted to introduce a young lady into public, being as fond of going every where and seeing every thing herself as any young lady could be. Dress was her passion. She had a most harmless delight in being fine; and our heroine's entrée into life could not take place till after three or four days had been spent in learning what was mostly worn, and her chaperon was provided with a dress of the newest fashion. Catherine too made some purchases herself, and when all these matters were arranged, the important evening came which was to usher her into the Upper Rooms.[1] Her hair was cut and dressed by the best hand, her clothes put on with care, and both Mrs. Allen and her maid declared she looked quite as she should do. With such encouragement, Catherine hoped at least to pass uncensured through the crowd. As for admiration, it was always very welcome when it came, but she did not depend on it.

Mrs. Allen was so long in dressing, that they did not enter the ball-room till late. The season was full, the room crowded, and the two ladies squeezed in as well as they could. As for Mr. Allen, he repaired directly to the card-room, and left them to

enjoy a mob by themselves. With more care for the safety of her
new gown than for the comfort of her protegée, Mrs. Allen
made her way through the throng of men by the door, as swiftly
as the necessary caution would allow; Catherine, however, kept
close at her side, and linked her arm too firmly within her
friend's to be torn asunder by any common effort of a struggling
assembly. But to her utter amazement she found that to proceed
along the room was by no means the way to disengage themselves from the crowd; it seemed rather to increase as they went
on, whereas she had imagined that when once fairly within the
door, they should easily find seats and be able to watch the
dances with perfect convenience. But this was far from being
case, and though by unwearied diligence they gained even the
top of the room, their situation was just the same; they saw
nothing of the dancers but the high feathers of some of the
ladies. Still they moved on – something better was yet in view;
and by a continued exertion of strength and ingenuity they
found themselves at last in the passage behind the highest
bench. Here there was something less of crowd than below; and
hence Miss Morland had a comprehensive view of all the company beneath her, and of all the dangers of her late passage
through them. It was a splendid sight, and she began, for the
first time that evening, to feel herself at a ball: she longed to
dance, but she had not an acquaintance in the room. Mrs. Allen
did all that she could do in such a case by saying very placidly,
every now and then, 'I wish you could dance, my dear, – I wish
you could get a partner.' For some time her young friend felt
obliged to her for these wishes; but they were repeated so often,
and proved so totally ineffectual, that Catherine grew tired at
last, and would thank her no more.

They were not long able, however, to enjoy the repose of the
eminence they had so laboriously gained. – Every body was
shortly in motion for tea, and they must squeeze out like the
rest. Catherine began to feel something of disappointment – she
was tired of being continually pressed against by people, the
generality of whose faces possessed nothing to interest, and with
all of whom she was so wholly unacquainted, that she could not

relieve the irksomeness of imprisonment by the exchange of a
syllable with any of her fellow captives; and when at last arrived
in the tea-room, she felt yet more the awkwardness of having no
party to join, no acquaintance to claim, no gentleman to assist
them. – They saw nothing of Mr. Allen; and after looking about
them in vain for a more eligible situation, were obliged to sit
down at the end of a table, at which a large party were already
placed, without having any thing to do there, or any body to
speak to, except each other.

Mrs. Allen congratulated herself, as soon as they were seated,
on having preserved her gown from injury. 'It would have been
very shocking to have it torn,' said she, 'would not it? – It is
such a delicate muslin. – For my part I have not seen any thing I
like so well in the whole room, I assure you.'

'How uncomfortable it is,' whispered Catherine, 'not to have
a single acquaintance here!'

'Yes, my dear,' replied Mrs. Allen, with perfect serenity,
'it is very uncomfortable indeed.'

'What shall we do? – The gentlemen and ladies at this table
look as if they wondered why we came here – we seem forcing
ourselves into their party.'

'Aye, so we do. – That is very disagreeable. I wish we had a
large acquaintance here.'

'I wish we had *any*; – it would be somebody to go to.'

'Very true, my dear; and if we knew anybody we would join
them directly. The Skinners were here last year – I wish they
were here now.'

'Had not we better go away as it is? – Here are no tea things
for us, you see.'

'No more there are, indeed. – How very provoking! But I
think we had better sit still, for one gets so tumbled in such a
crowd! How is my head,[1] my dear? – Somebody gave me a push
that has hurt it I am afraid.'

'No, indeed, it looks very nice. – But, dear Mrs Allen, are you
sure there is nobody you know in all this multitude of people? I
think you *must* know somebody.'

'I don't upon my word – I wish I did. I wish I had a large

acquaintance here with all my heart, and then I should get you a partner. - I should be so glad to have you dance. There goes a strange-looking woman! What an odd gown she has got on! - How old fashioned it is! Look at the back.'

After some time they received an offer of tea from one of their neighbours; it was thankfully accepted, and this introduced a light conversation with the gentleman who offered it, which was the only time that any body spoke to them during the evening, till they were discovered and joined by Mr. Allen when the dance was over.

'Well, Miss Morland,' said he, directly, 'I hope you have had an agreeable ball.'

'Very agreeable indeed,' she replied, vainly endeavouring to hide a great yawn.

'I wish she had been able to dance,' said his wife, 'I wish we could have got a partner for her. - I have been saying how glad I should be if the Skinners were here this winter instead of last; or if the Parrys had come, as they talked of once, she might have danced with George Parry. I am so sorry she has not had a partner!'

'We shall do better another evening I hope,' was Mr. Allen's consolation.

The company began to disperse when the dancing was over - enough to leave space for the remainder to walk about in some comfort; and now was the time for a heroine, who had not yet played a very distinguished part in the events of the evening, to be noticed and admired. Every five minutes, by removing some of the crowd, gave greater openings for her charms. She was now seen by many young men who had not been near her before. Not one, however, started with rapturous wonder on beholding her, no whisper of eager inquiry ran round the room, nor was she once called a divinity[1] by any body. Yet Catherine was in very good looks, and had the company only seen her three years before, they would *now* have thought her exceedingly hand-some.

She *was* looked at however, and with some admiration; for, in her own hearing, two gentlemen pronounced her to be a pretty girl. Such words had their due effect; she immediately thought the evening pleasanter than she had found it before – her humble vanity was contented – she felt more obliged to the two young men for this simple praise than a true quality heroine would have been for fifteen sonnets in celebration of her charms, and went to her chair in good humour with every body, and perfectly satisfied with her share of public attention.

CHAPTER III

EVERY morning now brought its regular duties; – shops were to be visited; some new part of the town to be looked at; and the Pump-room to be attended, where they paraded up and down for an hour, looking at every body and speaking to no one. The wish of a numerous acquaintance in Bath was still uppermost with Mrs. Allen, and she repeated it after every fresh proof, which every morning brought, of her knowing nobody at all.

They made their appearance in the Lower Rooms; and here fortune was more favourable to our heroine. The master of the ceremonies introduced to her a very gentlemanlike young man as a partner; – his name was Tilney. He seemed to be about four or five and twenty, was rather tall, had pleasing countenance, a very intelligent and lively eye, and, if not quite handsome, was very near it. His address was good, and Catherine felt herself in high luck. There was little leisure for speaking while they danced; but when they were seated at tea, she found him as agreeable as she had already given him credit for being. He talked with fluency and spirit – and there was an archness and pleasantry in his manner which interested, though it was hardly understood by her. After chatting some time on such matters as naturally arose from the objects around them, he suddenly addressed her with – 'I have hitherto been very remiss, madam, in the proper attentions of a partner here; I have not yet asked you how long you have been in Bath; whether you were ever here before; whether you have been at the Upper Rooms, the theatre, and the concert; and how you like the place altogether. I have been very negligent – but are you now at leisure to satisfy me in these particulars? If you are I will begin directly.'

'You need not give yourself that trouble, sir.'

'No trouble I assure you, madam.' Then forming his features into a set smile, and affectedly softening his voice, he added, with a simpering air, 'Have you been long in Bath, madam?'

'About a week, sir,' replied Catherine, trying not to laugh.

'Really!' with affected astonishment.

'Why should you be surprized, sir?'

'Why, indeed!' said he, in his natural tone – 'but some emotion must appear to be raised by your reply, and surprize is more easily assumed, and not less reasonable than any other. – Now let us go on. Were you never here before, madam?'

'Never, sir.'

'Indeed! Have you yet honoured the Upper Rooms?'

'Yes, sir, I was there last Monday.'

'Have you been to the theatre?'

'Yes, sir, I was at the play on Tuesday.'

'To the concert?'

'Yes, sir, on Wednesday.'

'And are you altogether pleased with Bath?'

'Yes – I like it very well.'

'Now I must give one smirk, and then we may be rational again.'

Catherine turned away her head, not knowing whether she might venture to laugh.

'I see what you think of me,' said he gravely – 'I shall make but a poor figure in your journal to-morrow.'

'My journal!'

'Yes, I know exactly what you will say: Friday, went to the Lower Rooms; wore my sprigged muslin robe with blue trimmings – plain black shoes – appeared to much advantage; but was strangely harassed by a queer, half-witted man, who would make me dance with him, and distressed me by his nonsense.'

'Indeed I shall say no such thing.'

'Shall I tell you what you ought to say?'

'If you please.'

'I danced with a very agreeable young man, introduced by Mr. King;[1] had a great deal of conversation with him – seems a most extraordinary genius – hope I may know more of him. *That*, madam, is what I *wish* you to say.'

'But, perhaps, I keep no journal.'

'Perhaps you are not sitting in this room, and I am not sitting by you. These are points in which a doubt is equally possible. Not keep a journal! How are your absent cousins to understand the tenour of your life in Bath without one? How are the civilities and compliments of every day to be related as they ought to be, unless noted down every evening in a journal? How are your various dresses to be remembered, and the particular state of your complexion, and curl of your hair to be described in all their diversities, without having constant recourse to a journal? – My dear madam, I am not so ignorant of young ladies' ways as you wish to believe me; it is this delightful habit of journalizing which largely contributes to form the easy style of writing for which ladies are so generally celebrated. Every body allows that the talent of writing agreeable letters is peculiarly female. Nature may have done something, but I am sure it must be essentially assisted by the practice of keeping a journal.'

'I have sometimes thought,' said Catherine, doubtingly, 'whether ladies do write so much better letters than gentlemen! That is – I should not think the superiority was always on our side.'

'As far as I have had opportunity of judging, it appears to me that the usual style of letter-writing among women is faultless, except in three particulars.'

'And what are they?'

'A general deficiency of subject, a total inattention to stops, and a very frequent ignorance of grammar.'

'Upon my word! I need not have been afraid of disclaiming the compliment. You do not think too highly of us in that way.'

'I should no more lay it down as a general rule that women write better letters than men, than that they sing better duets, or draw better landscapes. In every power, of which taste is the foundation, excellence is pretty fairly divided between the sexes.'

They were interrupted by Mrs. Allen: – 'My dear Catherine,' said she, 'do take this pin out of my sleeve; I am afraid it has torn a hole already; I shall be quite sorry if it has, for this is a favourite gown, though it cost but nine shillings a yard.'

'That is exactly what I should have guessed it, madam,' said Mr. Tilney, looking at the muslin.

'Do you understand muslins, sir?'

'Particularly well; I always buy my own cravats, and am allowed to be an excellent judge; and my sister has often trusted me in the choice of a gown. I bought one for her the other day, and it was pronounced to be a prodigious bargain by every lady who saw it. I gave but five shillings a yard for it, and a true Indian muslin.'

Mrs. Allen was quite struck by his genius. 'Men commonly take so little notice of those things,' said she: 'I can never get Mr. Allen to know one of my gowns from another. You must be a great comfort to your sister, sir.'

'I hope I am, madam.'

'And pray, sir, what do you think of Miss Morland's gown?'

'It is very pretty, madam,' said he, gravely examining it; 'but I do not think it will wash well; I am afraid it will fray.'

'How can you,' said Catherine, laughing, 'be so—' she had almost said, strange.

'I am quite of your opinion, sir,' replied Mrs. Allen: 'and so I told Miss Morland when she bought it.'

'But then you know, madam, muslin always turns to some account or other; Miss Morland will get enough out of it for a handkerchief, or a cap, or a cloak. – Muslin can never be said to be wasted. I have heard my sister say so forty times, when she has been extravagant in buying more than she wanted, or careless in cutting it to pieces.'

'Bath is a charming place, sir; there are so many good shops here. – We are sadly off in the country; not but what we have very good shops in Salisbury, but it is so far to go; – eight miles is a long way; Mr. Allen says it is nine, measured nine; but I am sure it cannot be more than eight; and it is such a fag – I come back tired to death. Now here one can step out of doors and get a thing in five minutes.'

Mr. Tilney was polite enough to seem interested in what she said; and she kept him on the subject of muslins till the dancing recommenced. Catherine feared, as she listened to their discourse, that he indulged himself a little too much with the foibles of others. – 'What are you thinking of so earnestly?' said he, as they walked back to the ball-room; – 'not of your partner, I hope, for, by that shake of the head, your meditations are not satisfactory.'

Catherine coloured, and said, 'I was not thinking of any thing.'

'That is artful and deep, to be sure; but I had rather be told at once that you will not tell me.'

'Well then, I will not.'

'Thank you; for now we shall soon be acquainted, as I am authorized to tease you on this subject whenever we meet, and nothing in the world advances intimacy so much.'

They danced again; and, when the assembly closed, parted, on the lady's side at least, with a strong inclination for continuing the acquaintance. Whether she thought of him so much, while she drank her warm wine and water, and prepared herself for bed, as to dream of him when there, cannot be ascertained; but I hope it was no more than in a slight slumber, or a morning doze at most; for if it be true, as a celebrated writer has maintained, that no young lady can be justified in falling in love before the gentleman's love is declared,[1]* it must be very improper that a young lady should dream of a gentleman before the gentleman is first known to have dreamt of her. How proper Mr. Tilney might be as a dreamer or a lover, had not yet perhaps entered Mr. Allen's head, but that he was not objectionable as a common acquaintance for his young charge he was on inquiry satisfied; for he had early in the evening taken pains to know who her partner was, and had been assured of Mr. Tilney's being a clergyman, and of a very respectable family in Gloucestershire.

* Vide a letter from Mr. Richardson, No. 97, vol. ii. Rambler.

CHAPTER IV

WITH more than usual eagerness did Catherine hasten to the Pump-room the next day, secure within herself of seeing Mr. Tilney there before the morning were over, and ready to meet him with a smile: – but no smile was demanded – Mr. Tilney did not appear. Every creature in Bath, except himself, was to be seen in the room at different periods of the fashionable hours; crowds of people were every moment passing in and out, up the steps and down; people whom nobody cared about, and nobody wanted to see; and he only was absent. 'What a delightful place Bath is,' said Mrs. Allen, as they sat down near the great clock, after parading the room till they were tired; 'and how pleasant it would be if we had any acquaintance here.'

This sentiment had been uttered so often in vain, that Mrs. Allen had no particular reason to hope it would be followed with more advantage now; but we are told to 'despair of nothing we would attain,' as 'unwearied diligence our point would gain;'[1] and the unwearied diligence with which she had every day wished for the same thing was at length to have its just reward, for hardly had she been seated ten minutes before a lady of about her own age, who was sitting by her, and had been looking at her attentively for several minutes, addressed her with great complaisance in these words: – 'I think, madam, I cannot be mistaken; it is a long time since I had the pleasure of seeing you, but is not your name Allen?' This question answered, as it readily was, the stranger pronounced her's to be Thorpe; and Mrs. Allen immediately recognized the features of a former school-fellow and intimate, whom she had seen only once since their respective marriages, and that many years ago. Their joy on this meeting was very great, as well it might since they had been contented to know nothing of each other for the last fifteen years. Compliments on good looks now passed; and, after observing how time had slipped away since they were last together, how little they had thought of meeting in Bath, and what a pleasure it was to see an old friend, they proceeded to make inquiries and give intelligence as to their families, sisters, and cousins, talking both together, far more ready to give than to receive information, and each hearing very little of what the other said. Mrs. Thorpe, however, had one great advantage as a talker, over Mrs. Allen, in a family of children; and when she expatiated on the talents of her sons, and the beauty of her daughters, – when she related their different situations and views, – that John was at Oxford, Edward at Merchant-Taylors', and William at sea, – and all of them more beloved and respected in their different stations than any other three beings ever were, Mrs. Allen had no similar information to give, no similar triumphs to press on the unwilling and unbelieving ear of her friend, and was forced to sit and appear to listen to all these maternal effusions, consoling herself, however, with the discovery, which her keen eye soon made, that the lace on Mrs. Thorpe's pelisse was not half so handsome as that on her own.

'Here come my dear girls,' cried Mrs. Thorpe, pointing at three smart looking females, who, arm in arm, were then moving towards her. 'My dear Mrs. Allen, I long to introduce them; they will be so delighted to see you: the tallest is Isabella, my eldest; is not she a fine young woman? The others are very much admired too, but I believe Isabella is the handsomest.'

The Miss Thorpes were introduced; and Miss Morland, who had been for a short time forgotten, was introduced likewise. The name seemed to strike them all; and, after speaking to her with great civility, the eldest young lady observed aloud to the rest, 'How excessively like her brother Miss Morland is!'

'The very picture of him indeed!' cried the mother – and 'I should have known her any where for his sister!' was repeated by them all, two or three times over. For a moment Catherine was surprized; but Mrs. Thorpe and her daughters had scarcely begun the history of their acquaintance with Mr. James Morland, before she remembered that her eldest brother had lately formed an intimacy with a young man of his own college, of the name of Thorpe; and that he had spent the last week of the Christmas vacation with his family, near London.

The whole being explained, many obliging things were said

by the Miss Thorpes of their wish of being better acquainted with her; of being considered as already friends, through the friendship of their brothers, &c. which Catherine heard with pleasure, and answered with all the pretty expressions she could command; and, as the first proof of amity, she was soon invited to accept an arm of the eldest Miss Thorpe, and take a turn with her about the room. Catherine was delighted with this extension of her Bath acquaintance, and almost forgot Mr. Tilney while she talked to Miss Thorpe. Friendship is certainly the finest balm for the pangs of disappointed love.

Their conversation turned upon those subjects, of which the free discussion has generally much to do in perfecting a sudden intimacy between two young ladies; such as dress, balls, flirtations, and quizzes. Miss Thorpe, however, being four years older than Miss Morland, and at least four years better informed, had a very decided advantage in discussing such points; she could compare the balls of Bath with those of Tunbridge; its fashions with the fashions of London; could rectify the opinions of her new friend in many articles of tasteful attire; could discover a flirtation between any gentleman and lady who only smiled on each other; and point out a quiz through the thickness of a crowd. These powers received due admiration from Catherine, to whom they were entirely new; and the respect which they naturally inspired might have been too great for familiarity, had not the easy gaiety of Miss Thorpe's manners, and her frequent expressions of delight on this acquaintance with her, softened down every feeling of awe, and left nothing but tender affection. Their increasing attachment was not to be satisfied with half a dozen turns in the Pump-room, but required, when they all quitted it together, that Miss Thorpe should accompany Miss Morland to the very door of Mr. Allen's house; and that they should there part with a most affectionate and lengthened shake of hands, after learning, to their mutual relief, that they should see each other across the theatre at night, and say their prayers in the same chapel the next morning. Catherine then ran directly up stairs, and watched Miss Thorpe's progress down the street from the drawing-room window; admired the graceful spirit of her walk, the fashionable air of her figure and dress, and felt grateful, as well she might, for the chance which had procured her such a friend.

Mrs. Thorpe was a widow, and not a very rich one; she was a good-humoured, well-meaning woman, and a very indulgent mother. Her eldest daughter had great personal beauty, and the younger ones, by pretending to be as handsome as their sister, imitating her air, and dressing in the same style, did very well.

This brief account of the family is intended to supersede the necessity of a long and minute detail from Mrs. Thorpe herself, of her past adventures and sufferings, which might otherwise be expected to occupy the three or four following chapters; in which the worthlessness of lords and attornies[1] might be set forth, and conversations, which had passed twenty years before, be minutely repeated.

CHAPTER V

CATHERINE was not so much engaged at the theatre that evening, in returning the nods and smiles of Miss Thorpe, though they certainly claimed much of her leisure, as to forget to look with an inquiring eye for Mr. Tilney in every box which her eye could reach; but she looked in vain. Mr. Tilney was no fonder of the play than the Pump-room. She hoped to be more fortunate the next day; and when her wishes for fine weather were answered by seeing a beautiful morning, she hardly felt a doubt of it; for a fine Sunday in Bath empties every house of its inhabitants, and all the world appears on such an occasion to walk about and tell their acquaintance what a charming day it is.

As soon as divine service was over, the Thorpes and Allens eagerly joined each other; and after staying long enough in the Pump-room to discover that the crowd was insupportable, and that there was not a genteel face to be seen, which every body discovers every Sunday throughout the season, they hastened away to the Crescent, to breathe the fresh air of better company.

Here Catherine and Isabella, arm in arm, again tasted the sweets of friendship in an unreserved conversation; – they talked much, and with much enjoyment; but again was Catherine disappointed in her hope of re-seeing her partner. He was no where to be met with; every search for him was equally unsuccessful, in morning lounges or evening assemblies; neither at the upper nor lower rooms, at dressed or undressed balls, was he perceivable; nor among the walkers, the horsemen, or the curricle-drivers of the morning. His name was not in the Pump-room book, and curiosity could do no more. He must be gone from Bath. Yet he had not mentioned that his stay would be so short! This sort of mysteriousness, which is always so becoming in a hero, threw a fresh grace in Catherine's imagination around his person and manners, and increased her anxiety to know more of him. From the Thorpes she could learn nothing, for they had been only two days in Bath before they met with Mrs. Allen. It was a subject, however, in which she often indulged with her fair friend, from whom she received every possible encourage-ment to continue to think of him; and his impression on her fancy was not suffered therefore to weaken. Isabella was very sure that he must be a charming young man; and was equally sure that he must have been delighted with her dear Catherine, and would therefore shortly return. She liked him the better for being a clergyman, 'for she must confess herself very partial to the profession;' and something like a sigh escaped her as she said it. Perhaps Catherine was wrong in not demanding the cause of that gentle emotion – but she was not experienced enough in the finesse of love, or the duties of friendship, to know when delicate raillery was properly called for, or when a confidence should be forced.

Mrs. Allen was now quite happy – quite satisfied with Bath. She had found some acquaintance, had been so lucky too as to find in them the family of a most worthy old friend; and, as the completion of good fortune, had found these friends by no means so expensively dressed as herself. Her daily expressions were no longer, 'I wish we had some acquaintance in Bath!' They were changed into – 'How glad I am we have met with

Mrs. Thorpe!' – and she was as eager in promoting the inter-course of the two families, as her young charge and Isabella themselves could be; never satisfied with the day unless she spent the chief of it by the side of Mrs. Thorpe, in what they called conversation, but in which there was scarcely ever any exchange of opinion, and not often any resemblance of subject, for Mrs. Thorpe talked chiefly of her children, and Mrs. Allen of her gowns.

The progress of the friendship between Catherine and Isabella was quick as its beginning had been warm, and they passed so rapidly through every gradation of increasing tenderness, that there was shortly no fresh proof of it to be given to their friends or themselves. They called each other by their Christian name, were always arm in arm when they walked, pinned up each other's train for the dance, and were not to be divided in the set; and if a rainy morning deprived them of other enjoyments, they were still resolute in meeting in defiance of wet and dirt, and shut themselves up, to read novels together. Yes, novels; – for I will not adopt that ungenerous and impolitic custom so common with novel writers, of degrading by their contemptuous censure the very performances, to the number of which they are them-selves adding – joining with their greatest enemies in bestowing the harshest epithets on such works, and scarcely ever permitting them to be read by their own heroine, who, if she accidentally take up a novel, is sure to turn over its insipid pages with dis-gust. Alas! if the heroine of one novel be not patronized by the heroine of another, from whom can she expect protection and regard? I cannot approve of it. Let us leave it to the Reviewers to abuse such effusions of fancy at their leisure, and over every new novel to talk in threadbare strains of the trash with which the press now groans. Let us not desert one another; we are an injured body. Although our productions have afforded more extensive and unaffected pleasure than those of any other literary corporation in the world, no species of composition has been so much decried. From pride, ignorance, or fashion, our foes are almost as many as our readers. And while the abilities of the nine-hundredth abridger of the History of England,[1] or of the man who collects and publishes in a volume some dozen lines of Milton, Pope, and Prior, with a paper from the Spectator, and a chapter from Sterne, are eulogized by a thousand pens, – there seems almost a general wish of decrying the capacity and under-valuing the labour of the novelist, and of slighting the per-formances which have only genius, wit, and taste to recommend them. 'I am no novel reader – I seldom look into novels – Do not imagine that *I* often read novels – It is really very well for a novel.' – Such is the common cant. – 'And what are you reading, Miss—?' 'Oh! it is only a novel!' replies the young lady; while she lays down her book with affected indifference, or momentary shame. – 'It is only Cecilia, or Camilla, or Belinda;'[1] or, in short, only some work in which the greatest powers of the mind are displayed, in which the most thorough knowledge of human nature, the happiest delineation of its varieties, the liveliest effusions of wit and humour are conveyed to the world in the best chosen language. Now, had the same young lady been en-gaged with a volume of the Spectator, instead of such a work, how proudly would she have produced the book, and told its name; though the chances must be against her being occupied by any part of that voluminous publication, of which either the matter or manner would not disgust a young person of taste: the substance of its papers so often consisting in the statement of improbable circumstances, unnatural characters, and topics of conversation, which no longer concern any one living; and their language, too, frequently so coarse as to give no very favourable idea of the age that could endure it.

CHAPTER VI

THE following conversation, which took place between the two friends in the Pump-room one morning, after an acquaintance of eight or nine days, is given as a specimen of their very warm attachment, and of the delicacy, discretion, originality of thought, and literary taste which marked the reasonableness of that attachment.

They met by appointment; and as Isabella had arrived nearly five minutes before her friend, her first address naturally was – 'My dearest creature, what can have made you so late? I have been waiting for you at least this age!'

'Have you, indeed! – I am very sorry for it; but really I thought I was in very good time. It is but just one. I hope you have not been here long?'

'Oh! these ten ages at least. I am sure I have been here this half hour. But now, let us go and sit down at the other end of the room, and enjoy ourselves. I have an hundred things to say to you. In the first place, I was so afraid it would rain this morning, just as I wanted to set off; it looked very showery, and that would have thrown me into agonies! Do you know, I saw the prettiest hat you can imagine, in a shop window in Milsom-street just now – very like yours, only with coquelicot[1] ribbons instead of green; I quite longed for it. But, my dearest Catherine, what have you been doing with yourself all this morning? – Have you gone on with Udolpho?'

'Yes, I have been reading it ever since I woke; and I am got to the black veil.'

'Are you, indeed? How delightful! Oh! I would not tell you what is behind the black veil for the world! Are not you wild to know?'

'Oh! yes, quite; what can it be? – But do not tell me – I would not be told upon any account. I know it must be a skeleton, I am sure it is Laurentina's skeleton. Oh! I am delighted with the book! I should like to spend my whole life in reading it. I assure you, if it had not been to meet you, I would not have come away from it for all the world.'

'Dear creature! how much I am obliged to you; and when you have finished Udolpho, we will read the Italian[2] together; and I have made out a list of ten or twelve more of the same kind for you.'

'Have you, indeed! How glad I am! – What are they all?'

'I will read you their names directly; here they are, in my

pocket-book. Castle of Wolfenbach, Clermont, Mysterious Warnings, Necromancer of the Black Forest, Midnight Bell, Orphan of the Rhine, and Horrid Mysteries.[1] Those will last us some time.'

'Yes, pretty well; but are they all horrid, are you sure they are all horrid?'

'Yes, quite sure; for a particular friend of mine, a Miss Andrews, a sweet girl, one of the sweetest creatures in the world, has read every one of them. I wish you knew Miss Andrews, you would be delighted with her. She is netting herself the sweetest cloak you can conceive. I think her as beautiful as an angel, and I am so vexed with the men for not admiring her! – I scold them all amazingly about it.'

'Scold them! Do you scold them for not admiring her?'

'Yes, that I do. There is nothing I would not do for those who are really my friends. I have no notion of loving people by halves, it is not my nature. My attachments are always excessively strong. I told Capt. Hunt at one of our assemblies this winter, that if he was to tease me all night, I would not dance with him, unless he would allow Miss Andrews to be as beautiful as an angel. The men think us incapable of real friendship you know, and I am determined to shew them the difference. Now, if I were to hear any body speak slightingly of you, I should fire up in a moment: – but that is not at all likely, for *you* are just the kind of girl to be a great favourite with the men.'

'Oh! dear,' cried Catherine, colouring, 'how can you say so?'

'I know you very well; you have so much animation, which is exactly what Miss Andrews wants, for I must confess there is something amazingly insipid about her. Oh! I must tell you, that just after we parted yesterday, I saw a young man looking at you so earnestly – I am sure he is in love with you.' Catherine coloured, and disclaimed again. Isabella laughed. 'It is very true, upon my honour, but I see how it is; you are indifferent to every body's admiration, except that of one gentleman, who shall be nameless. Nay, I cannot blame you – (speaking more seriously) – your feelings are easily understood. Where the heart is really attached, I know very well how little one can be pleased with the attention of any body else. Every thing is so insipid, so uninteresting, that does not relate to the beloved object! I can perfectly comprehend your feelings.'

'But you should not persuade me that I think so very much about Mr. Tilney, for perhaps I may never see him again.'

'Not see him again! My dearest creature, do not talk of it. I am sure you would be miserable if you thought so.'

'No, indeed, I should not. I do not pretend to say that I was not very much pleased with him; but while I have Udolpho to read, I feel as if nobody could make me miserable. Oh! the dreadful black veil! My dear Isabella, I am sure there must be Laurentina's skeleton behind it.'

'It is so odd to me, that you should never have read Udolpho before; but I suppose Mrs. Morland objects to novels.'

'No, she does not. She very often reads Sir Charles Grandison herself; but new books do not fall in our way.'

'Sir Charles Grandison! That is an amazing horrid book, is it not? – I remember Miss Andrews could not get through the first volume.'

'It is not like Udolpho at all; but yet I think it is very entertaining.'

'Do you indeed! – you surprize me; I thought it had not been readable. But, my dearest Catherine, have you settled what to wear on your head to-night? I am determined at all events to be dressed exactly like you. The men take notice of *that* sometimes you know.'

'But it does not signify if they do;' said Catherine, very innocently.

'Signify! Oh, heavens! I make it a rule never to mind what they say. They are very often amazingly impertinent if you do not treat them with spirit, and make them keep their distance.'

'Are they? – Well, I never observed *that*. They always behave very well to me.'

'Oh! they give themselves such airs. They are the most conceited creatures in the world, and think themselves of so much importance! – By the bye, though I have thought of it a hundred times, I have always forgot to ask you what is your favourite complexion in a man. Do you like them best dark or fair?'

'I hardly know. I never much thought about it. Something between both, I think. Brown – not fair, and not very dark.'

'Very well, Catherine. That is exactly he. I have not forgot your description of Mr. Tilney; – "a brown skin, with dark eyes, and rather dark hair." – Well, my taste is different. I prefer light eyes, and as to complexion – do you know – I like a sallow better than any other. You must not betray me, if you should ever meet with one of your acquaintance answering that description.'

'Betray you! – What do you mean?'

'Nay, do not distress me. I believe I have said too much. Let us drop the subject.'

Catherine, in some amazement, complied; and after remaining a few moments silent, was on the point of reverting to what interested her at that time rather more than any thing else in the world, Laurentina's skeleton; when her friend prevented her, by saying, – 'For Heaven's sake! let us move away from this end of the room. Do you know, there are two odious young men who have been staring at me this half hour. They really put me quite out of countenance. Let us go and look at the arrivals. They will hardly follow us there.'

Away they walked to the book; and while Isabella examined the names, it was Catherine's employment to watch the proceedings of these alarming young men.

'They are not coming this way, are they? I hope they are not so impertinent as to follow us. Pray let me know if they are coming. I am determined I will not look up.'

In a few moments Catherine, with unaffected pleasure, assured her that she need not be longer uneasy, as the gentlemen had just left the Pump-room.

'And which way are they gone?' said Isabella, turning hastily round. 'One was a very good-looking young man.'

'They went towards the churchyard.'

'Well, I am amazingly glad I have got rid of them! And now, what say you to going to Edgar's Buildings with me, and looking at my new hat? You said you should like to see it.'

Catherine readily agreed. 'Only,' she added, 'perhaps we may overtake the two young men.'

'Oh! never mind that. If we make haste, we shall pass by them presently, and I am dying to shew you my hat.'

'But if we only wait a few minutes, there will be no danger of our seeing them at all.'

'I shall not pay them any such compliment, I assure you. I have no notion of treating men with such respect. *That* is the way to spoil them.'

Catherine had nothing to oppose against such reasoning; and therefore, to shew the independence of Miss Thorpe, and her resolution of humbling the sex, they set off immediately as fast as they could walk, in pursuit of the two young men.

CHAPTER VII

HALF a minute conducted them through the Pump-yard to the archway, opposite Union-passage;[1] but here they were stopped. Every body acquainted with Bath may remember the difficulties of crossing Cheap-street at this point; it is indeed a street of so impertinent a nature, so unfortunately connected with the great London and Oxford roads, and the principal inn of the city, that a day never passes in which parties of ladies, however important their business, whether in quest of pastry, millinery, or even (as in the present case) of young men, are not detained on one side or other by carriages, horsemen, or carts. This evil had been felt and lamented, at least three times a day, by Isabella since her residence in Bath; and she was now fated to feel and lament it once more, for at the very moment of coming opposite to Union-passage, and within view of the two gentlemen who were proceeding through the crowds, and threading the gutters of that interesting alley, they were prevented crossing by the approach of a gig, driven along on bad pavement by a most knowing-looking coachman with all the vehemence that could most fitly endanger the lives of himself, his companion, and his horse.

'Oh, these odious gigs!' said Isabella, looking up, 'how I detest them.' But this detestation, though so just, was of short duration, for she looked again and exclaimed, 'Delightful! Mr. Morland and my brother!'

'Good heaven! 'tis James!' was uttered at the same moment by Catherine; and, on catching the young men's eyes, the horse was immediately checked with a violence which almost threw him on his haunches, and the servant having now scampered up, the gentlemen jumped out, and the equipage was delivered to his care.

Catherine, by whom this meeting was wholly unexpected, received her brother with the liveliest pleasure; and he, being of a very amiable disposition, and sincerely attached to her, gave every proof on his side of equal satisfaction, which he could have leisure to do, while the bright eyes of Miss Thorpe were incessantly challenging his notice; and to her his devoirs were speedily paid, with a mixture of joy and embarrassment which might have informed Catherine, had she been more expert in the development of other people's feelings, and less simply engrossed by her own, that her brother thought her friend quite as pretty as she could do herself.

John Thorpe, who in the mean time had been giving orders about the horses, soon joined them, and from him she directly received the amends which were her due; for while he slightly and carelessly touched the hand of Isabella, on her he bestowed a whole scrape[1] and half a short bow. He was a stout young man of middling height, who, with a plain face and ungraceful form, seemed fearful of being too handsome unless he wore the dress of a groom, and too much like a gentleman unless he were easy where he ought to be civil, and impudent where he might be allowed to be easy. He took out his watch: 'How long do you think we have been running it from Tetbury, Miss Morland?'

'I do not know the distance.' Her brother told her that it was twenty-three miles.

'*Three*-and-twenty!' cried Thorpe; 'five-and-twenty if it is an inch.' Morland remonstrated, pleaded the authority of road-books, innkeepers, and milestones; but his friend disregarded them all; he had a surer test of distance. 'I know it must be five-and-twenty,' said he, 'by the time we have been doing it. It is now half after one; we drove out of the inn-yard at Tetbury as the town-clock struck eleven; and I defy any man in England to make my horse go less than ten miles an hour in harness; that makes it exactly twenty-five.'

'You have lost an hour,' said Morland; 'it was only ten o'clock when we came from Tetbury.'

'Ten o'clock! it was eleven, upon my soul! I counted every stroke. This brother of yours would persuade me out of my senses, Miss Morland; do but look at my horse; did you ever see an animal so made for speed in your life?' (The servant had just mounted the carriage and was driving off.) 'Such true blood! Three hours and a half indeed coming only three-and-twenty miles! look at that creature, and suppose it possible if you can.'

'He *does* look very hot to be sure.'

'Hot! he had not turned a hair till we came to Walcot Church: but look at his forehead;[1] look at his loins; only see how he moves; that horse *cannot* go less than ten miles an hour: tie his legs and he will get on. What do you think of my gig, Miss Morland? a neat one, is not it? Well hung; town built; I have not had it a month. It was built for a Christchurch man, a friend of mine, a very good sort of fellow; he ran it a few weeks, till, I believe, it was convenient to have done with it. I happened just then to be looking out for some light thing of the kind, though I had pretty well determined on a curricle too; but I chanced to meet him on Magdalen Bridge, as he was driving into Oxford, last term: "Ah! Thorpe," said he, "do you happen to want such a little thing as this? it is a capital one of the kind, but I am cursed tired of it." "Oh! d—," said I, "I am your man; what do you ask?" And how much do you think he did, Miss Morland?'

'I am sure I cannot guess at all.'

'Curricle-hung you see; seat, trunk, sword-case, splashing-board,[1] lamps, silver moulding, all you see complete; the iron-work as good as new, or better. He asked fifty guineas; I closed with him directly, threw down the money, and the carriage was mine.'

'And I am sure,' said Catherine, 'I know so little of such things that I cannot judge whether it was cheap or dear.'

'Neither one nor t'other; I might have got it for less I dare say; but I hate haggling, and poor Freeman wanted cash.'

'That was very good-natured of you,' said Catherine, quite pleased.

'Oh! d— it, when one has the means of doing a kind thing by a friend, I hate to be pitiful.'

An inquiry now took place into the intended movements of the young ladies; and, on finding whither they were going, it was decided that the gentlemen should accompany them to Edgar's Buildings, and pay their respects to Mrs. Thorpe. James and Isabella led the way; and so well satisfied was the latter with her lot, so contentedly was she endeavouring to ensure a pleasant walk to him who brought the double recommendation of being her brother's friend, and her friend's brother, so pure and uncoquettish were her feelings, that, though they overtook and passed the two offending young men in Milsom-street, she was so far from seeking to attract their notice, that she looked back at them only three times.

John Thorpe kept of course with Catherine, and, after a few minutes' silence, renewed the conversation about his gig – 'You will find, however, Miss Morland, it would be reckoned a cheap thing by some people, for I might have sold it for ten guineas more the next day; Jackson, of Oriel, bid me sixty at once; Morland was with me at the time.'

'Yes,' said Morland, who overheard this; 'but you forget that your horse was included.'

'My horse! oh, d— it! I would not sell my horse for a hundred. Are you fond of an open carriage, Miss Morland?'

'Yes, very; I have hardly ever an opportunity of being in one; but I am particularly fond of it.'

'I am glad of it; I will drive you out in mine every day.'

'Thank you,' said Catherine, in some distress, from a doubt of the propriety of accepting such an offer.

'I will drive you up Lansdown Hill to-morrow.'

'Thank you; but will not your horse want rest?'

'Rest! he has only come three-and-twenty miles to-day; all nonsense; nothing ruins horses so much as rest; nothing knocks them up so soon. No, no; I shall exercise mine at the average of four hours every day while I am here.'

'Shall you indeed!' said Catherine very seriously, 'that will be forty miles a day.'

'Forty! aye fifty, for what I care. Well, I will drive you up Lansdown to-morrow; mind, I am engaged.'

'How delightful that will be!' cried Isabella, turning round; 'my dearest Catherine, I quite envy you; but I am afraid, brother, you will not have room for a third.'

'A third indeed! no, no; I did not come to Bath to drive my sisters about; that would be a good joke, faith! Morland must take care of you.'

This brought on a dialogue of civilities between the other two; but Catherine heard neither the particulars nor the result. Her companion's discourse now sunk from its hitherto animated pitch, to nothing more than a short decisive sentence of praise or condemnation on the face of every woman they met; and Catherine, after listening and agreeing as long as she could, with all the civility and deference of the youthful female mind, fearful of hazarding an opinion of its own in opposition to that of a self-assured man, especially where the beauty of her own sex is concerned, ventured at length to vary the subject by a question which had been long uppermost in her thoughts; it was, 'Have you ever read Udolpho, Mr. Thorpe?'

'Udolpho! Oh, Lord! not I; I never read novels; I have something else to do.'

Catherine, humbled and ashamed, was going to apologize for her question, but he prevented her by saying, 'Novels are all so full of nonsense and stuff; there has not been a tolerably decent one come out since Tom Jones, except the Monk;[1] I read that t'other day; but as for all the others, they are the stupidest things in creation.'

'I think you must like Udolpho, if you were to read it; it is so very interesting.'

'Not I, faith! No, if I read any, it shall be Mrs. Radcliff's; her novels are amusing enough; they are worth reading; some fun and nature in *them*.'

'Udolpho was written by Mrs. Radcliff,' said Catherine, with some hesitation, from the fear of mortifying him.

'No sure; was it? Aye, I remember, so it was; I was thinking of that other stupid book, written by that woman they make such a fuss about, she who married the French emigrant.'

'I suppose you mean Camilla?'

'Yes, that's the book; such unnatural stuff! – An old man playing at see-saw! I took up the first volume once, and looked it over, but I soon found it would not do; indeed I guessed what sort of stuff it must be before I saw it: as soon as I heard she had married an emigrant, I was sure I should never be able to get through it.'

'I have never read it.'

'You had no loss I assure you; it is the horridest nonsense you can imagine; there is nothing in the world in it but an old man's playing at see-saw and learning Latin;[2] upon my soul there is not.'

This critique, the justness of which was unfortunately lost on poor Catherine, brought them to the door of Mrs. Thorpe's lodgings, and the feelings of the discerning and unprejudiced reader of Camilla gave way to the feelings of the dutiful and affectionate son, as they met Mrs. Thorpe, who had descried them from above, in the passage. 'Ah, mother! how do you do?' said he, giving her a hearty shake of the hand: 'where did you get that quiz of a hat, it makes you look like an old witch? Here is Morland and I come to stay a few days with you, so you must look out for a couple of good beds some where near.' And this address seemed to satisfy all the fondest wishes of the mother's heart, for she received him with the most delighted and exulting affection. On his two younger sisters he then bestowed an equal portion of his fraternal tenderness, for he asked each of them how they did, and observed that they both looked very ugly.

These manners did not please Catherine; but he was James's friend and Isabella's brother; and her judgment was further bought off by Isabella's assuring her, when they withdrew to see the new hat, that John thought her the most charming girl in the world, and by John's engaging her before they parted to dance with him that evening. Had she been older or vainer, such attacks might have done little; but, where youth and diffidence are united, it requires uncommon steadiness of reason to resist the attraction of being called the most charming girl in the world, and of being so very early engaged as a partner; and the consequence was, that, when the two Morlands, after sitting an hour with the Thorpes, set off to walk together to Mr. Allen's, and James, as the door was closed on them, said, 'Well, Catherine, how do you like my friend Thorpe?' instead of answering, as she probably would have done, had there been no friendship and no flattery in the case, 'I do not like him at all;' she directly replied, 'I like him very much; he seems very agreeable.'

'He is as good-natured a fellow as ever lived; a little of a rattle; but that will recommend him to your sex I believe: and how do you like the rest of the family?'

'Very, very much indeed: Isabella particularly.'

'I am very glad to hear you say so; she is just the kind of young woman I could wish to see you attached to; she has so much good sense, and is so thoroughly unaffected and amiable; I always wanted you to know her; and she seems very fond of you. She said the highest things in your praise that could possibly be; and the praise of such a girl as Miss Thorpe even you, Catherine,' taking her hand with affection, 'may be proud of.'

'Indeed I am,' she replied; 'I love her exceedingly, and am delighted to find that you like her too. You hardly mentioned any thing of her, when you wrote to me after your visit there.'

'Because I thought I should soon see you myself. I hope you will be a great deal together while you are in Bath. She is a most amiable girl; such a superior understanding! How fond all the family are of her; she is evidently the general favourite; and how much she must be admired in such a place as this – is not she?'

'Yes, very much indeed, I fancy; Mr. Allen thinks her the prettiest girl in Bath.'

'I dare say he does; and I do not know any man who is a better judge of beauty than Mr. Allen. I need not ask you whether you are happy here, my dear Catherine; with such a companion and friend as Isabella Thorpe, it would be impossible for you to be otherwise; and the Allens I am sure are very kind to you?'

'Yes, very kind; I never was so happy before; and now you are come it will be more delightful than ever; how good it is of you to come so far on purpose to see *me*.'

James accepted this tribute of gratitude, and qualified his conscience for accepting it too, by saying with perfect sincerity, 'Indeed, Catherine, I love you dearly.'

Inquiries and communications concerning brothers and sisters, the situation of some, the growth of the rest, and other family matters, now passed between them, and continued, with only one small digression on James's part, in praise of Miss Thorpe, till they reached Pulteney-street, where he was welcomed with great kindness by Mr. and Mrs. Allen, invited by the former to dine with them, and summoned by the latter to guess the price and weigh the merits of a new muff and tippet. A pre-engagement in Edgar's Buildings prevented his accepting the invitation of one friend, and obliged him to hurry away as soon as he had satisfied the demands of the other. The time of the two parties uniting in the Octagon Room[1] being correctly adjusted, Catherine was then left to the luxury of a raised, restless, and frightened imagination over the pages of Udolpho, lost from all worldly concerns of dressing and dinner, incapable of soothing Mrs. Allen's fears on the delay of an expected dressmaker, and having only one minute in sixty to bestow even on the reflection of her own felicity, in being already engaged for the evening.

CHAPTER VIII

In spite of Udolpho and the dress-maker, however, the party from Pulteney-street reached the Upper-rooms in very good time. The Thorpes and James Morland were there only two minutes before them; and Isabella having gone through the usual ceremonial of meeting her friend with the most smiling and affectionate haste, of admiring the set of her gown, and envying the curl of her hair, they followed their chaperons, arm in arm, into the ball-room, whispering to each other whenever a thought occurred, and supplying the place of many ideas by a squeeze of the hand or a smile of affection.

The dancing began within a few minutes after they were seated; and James, who had been engaged quite as long as his sister, was very importunate with Isabella to stand up; but John was gone into the card-room to speak to a friend, and nothing, she declared, should induce her to join the set before her dear Catherine could join it too: 'I assure you,' said she, 'I would not stand up without your dear sister for all the world; for if I did we should certainly be separated the whole evening.' Catherine accepted this kindness with gratitude, and they continued as they were for three minutes longer, when Isabella, who had been talking to James on the other side of her, turned again to his sister and whispered, 'My dear creature, I am afraid I must leave you, your brother is so amazingly impatient to begin; I know you will not mind my going away, and I dare say John will be back in a moment, and then you may easily find me out.' Catherine, though a little disappointed, had too much good-nature to make any opposition, and the others rising up, Isabella had only time to press her friend's hand and say, 'Good bye, my dear love,' before they hurried off. The younger Miss Thorpes being also dancing, Catherine was left to the mercy of Mrs. Thorpe and Mrs. Allen, between whom she now remained. She could not help being vexed at the non-appearance of Mr. Thorpe, for she not only longed to be dancing, but was likewise aware that, as the real dignity of her situation could not be known, she was sharing with the scores of other young ladies still sitting down all the discredit of wanting a partner. To be disgraced in the eye of the world, to wear the appearance of infamy while her heart is all purity, her actions all innocence, and the misconduct of another the true source of her debasement, is one of those circumstances which peculiarly belong to the heroine's life, and her fortitude under it what particularly dignifies her character. Catherine had fortitude too; she suffered, but no murmur passed her lips.

From this state of humiliation, she was roused, at the end of ten minutes, to a pleasanter feeling, by seeing, not Mr. Thorpe, but Mr. Tilney, within three yards of the place where they sat; he seemed to be moving that way, but he did not see her, and therefore the smile and the blush, which his sudden reappearance raised in Catherine, passed away without sullying her heroic importance. He looked as handsome and as lively as ever, and was talking with interest to a fashionable and pleasing-looking young woman, who leant on his arm, and whom Catherine immediately guessed to be his sister; thus unthinkingly throwing away a fair opportunity of considering him lost to her for ever, by being married already. But guided only by what was simple and probable, it had never entered her head that Mr. Tilney could be married; he had not behaved, he had not talked, like the married men to whom she had been used; he had never mentioned a wife, and he had acknowledged a sister. From these circumstances sprang the instant conclusion of his sister's now being by his side; and therefore, instead of turning of a deathlike paleness, and falling in a fit on Mrs. Allen's bosom, Catherine sat erect, in the perfect use of her senses, and with cheeks only a little redder than usual.

Mr. Tilney and his companion, who continued, though slowly, to approach, were immediately preceded by a lady, an acquaintance of Mrs. Thorpe; and this lady stopping to speak to her, they, as belonging to her, stopped likewise, and Catherine, catching Mr. Tilney's eye, instantly received from him the smiling tribute of recognition. She returned it with pleasure, and then advancing still nearer, he spoke both to her and Mrs.

Allen, by whom he was very civilly acknowledged. 'I am very happy to see you again, sir, indeed; I was afraid you had left Bath.' He thanked her for her fears, and said that he had quitted it for a week, on the very morning after his having had the pleasure of seeing her.

'Well, sir, and I dare say you are not sorry to be back again, for it is just the place for young people – and indeed for every body else too. I tell Mr. Allen, when he talks of being sick of it, that I am sure he should not complain, for it is so very agreeable a place, that it is much better to be here than at home at this dull time of year. I tell him he is quite in luck to be sent here for his health.'

'And I hope, madam, that Mr. Allen will be obliged to like the place, from finding it of service to him.'

'Thank you, sir. I have no doubt that he will. – A neighbour of ours, Dr. Skinner, was here for his health last winter, and came away quite stout.'

'That circumstance must give great encouragement.'

'Yes, sir – and Dr. Skinner and his family were here three months; so I tell Mr. Allen he must not be in a hurry to get away.'

Here they were interrupted by a request from Mrs. Thorpe to Mrs. Allen, that she would move a little to accommodate Mrs. Hughes and Miss Tilney with seats, as they had agreed to join their party. This was accordingly done, Mr. Tilney still continuing standing before them; and after a few minutes consideration, he asked Catherine to dance with him. This compliment, delightful as it was, produced severe mortification to the lady; and in giving her denial, she expressed her sorrow on the occasion so very much as if she really felt it, that had Thorpe, who joined her just afterwards, been half a minute earlier, he might have thought her sufferings rather too acute. The very easy manner in which he then told her that he had kept her waiting, did not by any means reconcile her more to her lot; nor did the particulars which he entered into while they were standing up, of the horses and dogs of the friend whom he had just left, and of a proposed exchange of terriers between them, interest her so much as to prevent her looking very often towards that part of the room where she had left Mr. Tilney. Of her dear Isabella, to whom she particularly longed to point out that gentleman, she could see nothing. They were in different sets. She was separated from all her party, and away from all her acquaintance; – one mortification succeeded another, and from the whole she deduced this useful lesson, that to go previously engaged to a ball, does not necessarily increase either the dignity or enjoyment of a young lady. From such a moralizing strain as this, she was suddenly roused by a touch on the shoulder, and turning round, perceived Mrs. Hughes directly behind her, attended by Miss Tilney and a gentleman. 'I beg your pardon, Miss Morland,' said she, 'for this liberty, – but I cannot any how get to Miss Thorpe, and Mrs. Thorpe said she was sure you would not have the least objection to letting in this young lady by you.' Mrs. Hughes could not have applied to any creature in the room more happy to oblige her than Catherine. The young ladies were introduced to each other, Miss Tilney expressing a proper sense of such goodness, Miss Morland with the real delicacy of a generous mind making light of the obligation; and Mrs. Hughes, satisfied with having so respectably settled her young charge, returned to her party.

Miss Tilney had a good figure, a pretty face, and a very agreeable countenance; and her air, though it had not all the decided pretension, the resolute stilishness of Miss Thorpe's, had more real elegance. Her manners shewed good sense and good breeding; they were neither shy, nor affectedly open; and she seemed capable of being young, attractive, and at a ball, without wanting to fix the attention of every man near her, and without exaggerated feelings of extatic delight or inconceivable vexation on every little trifling occurrence. Catherine, interested at once by her appearance and her relationship to Mr. Tilney, was desirous of being acquainted with her, and readily talked therefore whenever she could think of any thing to say, and had courage and leisure for saying it. But the hindrance thrown in the way of a very speedy intimacy, by the frequent want of one or more of these requisites, prevented their doing more than going through the first rudiments of an acquaintance, by informing themselves how well the other liked Bath, how much she admired its buildings and surrounding country, whether she drew, or played or sang, and whether she was fond of riding on horseback.

The two dances were scarcely concluded before Catherine found her arm gently seized by her faithful Isabella, who in great spirits exclaimed – 'At last I have got you. My dearest creature, I have been looking for you this hour. What could induce you to come into this set, when you knew I was in the other? I have been quite wretched without you.'

'My dear Isabella, how was it possible for me to get at you? I could not even see where you were.'

'So I told your brother all the time – but he would not believe me. Do go and see for her, Mr. Morland, said I – but all in vain – he would not stir an inch. Was not it so, Mr. Morland? But you men are all so immoderately lazy! I have been scolding him to such a degree, my dear Catherine, you would be quite amazed. – You know I never stand upon ceremony with such people.'

'Look at that young lady with the white beads round her head,' whispered Catherine, detaching her friend from James – 'It is Mr. Tilney's sister.'

'Oh! heavens! You don't say so! Let me look at her this moment. What a delightful girl! I never saw any thing half so beautiful! But where is her all-conquering brother? Is he in the room? Point him out to me this instant, if he is. I die to see him. Mr. Morland, you are not to listen. We are not talking about you.'

'But what is all this whispering about? What is going on?'

'There now, I knew how it would be. You men have such restless curiosity! Talk of the curiosity of women, indeed! – 'tis nothing. But be satisfied, for you are not to know any thing at all of the matter.'

'And is that likely to satisfy me, do you think?'

'Well, I declare I never knew any thing like you. What can it signify to you, what we are talking of? Perhaps we are talking about you, therefore I would advise you not to listen, or you may happen to hear something not very agreeable.'

In this common-place chatter, which lasted some time, the

original subject seemed entirely forgotten; and though Catherine
was very well pleased to have it dropped for a while, she could
not avoid a little suspicion at the total suspension of all Isabella's
impatient desire to see Mr. Tilney. When the orchestra struck
up a fresh dance, James would have led his fair partner away,
but she resisted. 'I tell you, Mr. Morland,' she cried, 'I would
not do such a thing for all the world. How can you be so teasing;
only conceive, my dear Catherine, what your brother wants me
to do. He wants me to dance with him again, though I tell him
that it is a most improper thing, and entirely against the rules. It
would make us the talk of the place, if we were not to change
partners.'

'Upon my honour,' said James, 'in these public assemblies,
it is as often done as not.'

'Nonsense, how can you say so? But when you men have a
point to carry, you never stick at any thing. My sweet Catherine,
do support me, persuade your brother how impossible it is.
Tell him, that it would quite shock you to see me do such a
thing; now would not it?'

'No, not at all; but if you think it wrong, you had much
better change.'

'There,' cried Isabella, 'you hear what your sister says, and
yet you will not mind her. Well, remember that it is not my
fault, if we set all the old ladies in Bath in a bustle. Come along,
my dearest Catherine, for heaven's sake, and stand by me.'
And off they went, to regain their former place. John Thorpe,
in the meanwhile, had walked away; and Catherine, ever willing
to give Mr. Tilney an opportunity of repeating the agreeable
request which had already flattered her once, made her way to
Mrs. Allen and Mrs. Thorpe as fast as she could, in the hope of
finding him still with them – a hope which, when it proved to be
fruitless, she felt to have been highly unreasonable. 'Well, my
dear,' said Mrs. Thorpe, impatient for praise of her son, 'I hope
you have had an agreeable partner.'

'Very agreeable, madam.'

'I am glad of it. John has charming spirits, has not he?'

'Did you meet Mr. Tilney, my dear?' said Mrs. Allen.

'No, where is he?'

'He was with us just now, and said he was so tired of lounging about, that he was resolved to go and dance; so I thought perhaps he would ask you, if he met with you.'

'Where can he be?' said Catherine, looking round; but she had not looked round long before she saw him leading a young lady to the dance.

'Ah! he has got a partner, I wish he had asked *you*,' said Mrs. Allen; and after a short silence, she added, 'he is a very agreeable young man.'

'Indeed he is, Mrs. Allen,' said Mrs. Thorpe, smiling complacently; 'I must say it, though I *am* his mother, that there is not a more agreeable young man in the world.'

This inapplicable answer might have been too much for the comprehension of many; but it did not puzzle Mrs. Allen, for after only a moment's consideration, she said, in a whisper to Catherine, 'I dare say she thought I was speaking of her son.'

Catherine was disappointed and vexed. She seemed to have missed by so little the very object she had had in view; and this persuasion did not incline her to a very gracious reply, when John Thorpe came up to her soon afterwards, and said, 'Well, Miss Morland, I suppose you and I are to stand up and jig it together again.'

'Oh, no; I am much obliged to you, our two dances are over; and, besides, I am tired, and do not mean to dance any more.'

'Do not you? – then let us walk about and quiz people. Come along with me, and I will shew you the four greatest quizzes in the room; my two younger sisters and their partners. I have been laughing at them this half hour.'

Again Catherine excused herself; and at last he walked off to quiz his sisters by himself. The rest of the evening she found very dull; Mr. Tilney was drawn away from their party at tea, to attend that of his partner; Miss Tilney, though belonging to it, did not sit near her, and James and Isabella were so much engaged in conversing together, that the latter had no leisure to bestow more on her friend than one smile, one squeeze, and one 'dearest Catherine.'

CHAPTER IX

THE progress of Catherine's unhappiness from the events of the evening, was as follows. It appeared first in a general dissatisfaction with every body about her, while she remained in the rooms, which speedily brought on considerable weariness and a violent desire to go home. This, on arriving in Pulteney-street, took the direction of extraordinary hunger, and when that was appeased, changed into an earnest longing to be in bed; such was the extreme point of her distress; for when there she immediately fell into a sound sleep which lasted nine hours, and from which she awoke perfectly revived, in excellent spirits, with fresh hopes and fresh schemes. The first wish of her heart was to improve her acquaintance with Miss Tilney, and almost her first resolution, to seek her for that purpose, in the Pump-room at noon.[1] In the Pump-room, one so newly arrived in Bath must be met with, and that building she had already found so favourable for the discovery of female excellence, and the completion of female intimacy, so admirably adapted for secret discourses and unlimited confidence, that she was most reasonably encouraged to expect another friend from within its walls. Her plan for the morning thus settled, she sat quietly down to her book after breakfast, resolving to remain in the same place and the same employment till the clock struck one; and from habitude very little incommoded by the remarks and ejaculations of Mrs. Allen, whose vacancy of mind and incapacity for thinking were such, that as she never talked a great deal, so she could never be entirely silent; and, therefore, while she sat at her work, if she lost her needle or broke her thread, if she heard a carriage in the street, or saw a speck upon her gown, she must observe it aloud, whether there were any one at leisure to answer her or not. At about half past twelve, a remarkably loud rap drew her in haste to the window, and scarcely had she time to inform Catherine of there being two open carriages at the door, in the first only a servant, her brother driving Miss Thorpe in the second, before John Thorpe came running up stairs, calling out, 'Well, Miss

Morland, here I am. Have you been waiting long? We could not come before; the old devil of a coachmaker was such an eternity finding out a thing fit to be got into, and now it is ten thousand to one, but they break down before we are out of the street. How do you do, Mrs. Allen? a famous ball last night, was not it? Come, Miss Morland, be quick, for the others are in a confounded hurry to be off. They want to get their tumble over.'

'What do you mean?' said Catherine, 'where are you all going to?'

'Going to? why, you have not forgot our engagement! Did not we agree together to take a drive this morning? What a head you have! We are going up Claverton Down.'

'Something was said about it, I remember,' said Catherine, looking at Mrs. Allen for her opinion; 'but really I did not expect you.'

'Not expect me! that's a good one! And what a dust you would have made, if I had not come.'

Catherine's silent appeal to her friend, meanwhile, was entirely thrown away, for Mrs. Allen, not being at all in the habit of conveying any expression herself by a look, was not aware of its being ever intended by any body else; and Catherine, whose desire of seeing Miss Tilney again could at that moment bear a short delay in favour of a drive, and who thought there could be no impropriety in her going with Mr. Thorpe, as Isabella was going at the same time with James, was therefore obliged to speak plainer. 'Well, ma'am, what do you say to it? Can you spare me for an hour or two? shall I go?'

'Do just as you please, my dear,' replied Mrs. Allen, with the most placid indifference. Catherine took the advice, and ran off to get ready. In a very few minutes she re-appeared, having scarcely allowed the two others time enough to get through a few short sentences in her praise, after Thorpe had procured Mrs. Allen's admiration of his gig; and then receiving her friend's parting good wishes, they both hurried down stairs. 'My dearest creature,' cried Isabella, to whom the duty of friendship immediately called her before she could get into the carriage, 'you have been at least three hours getting ready. I was afraid you were ill. What a delightful ball we had last night. I have a thousand things to say to you; but make haste and get in, for I long to be off.'

Catherine followed her orders and turned away, but not too soon to hear her friend exclaim aloud to James, 'What a sweet girl she is! I quite doat on her.'

'You will not be frightened, Miss Morland,' said Thorpe, as he handed her in, 'if my horse should dance about a little at first setting off. He will, most likely, give a plunge or two, and perhaps take the rest for a minute; but he will soon know his master. He is full of spirits, playful as can be, but there is no vice in him.'

Catherine did not think the portrait a very inviting one, but it was too late to retreat, and she was too young to own herself frightened; so, resigning herself to her fate, and trusting to the animal's boasted knowledge of its owner, she sat peaceably down, and saw Thorpe sit down by her. Every thing being then arranged, the servant who stood at the horse's head was bid in an important voice 'to let him go,' and off they went in the quietest manner imaginable, without a plunge or a caper, or any thing like one. Catherine, delighted at so happy an escape, spoke her pleasure aloud with grateful surprize; and her companion immediately made the matter perfectly simple by assuring her that it was entirely owing to the peculiarly judicious manner in which he had then held the reins, and the singular discernment and dexterity with which he had directed his whip. Catherine, though she could not help wondering that with such perfect command of his horse, he should think it necessary to alarm her with a relation of its tricks, congratulated herself sincerely on being under the care of so excellent a coachman; and perceiving that the animal continued to go on in the same quiet manner, without shewing the smallest propensity towards any unpleasant vivacity, and (considering its inevitable pace was ten miles an hour) by no means alarmingly fast, gave herself up to all the enjoyment of air and exercise of the most invigorating kind, in a fine mild day of February, with the consciousness of safety. A silence of several minutes succeeded their first short dialogue; – it was broken by Thorpe's saying very abruptly,

'Old Allen is as rich as a Jew – is not he?' Catherine did not understand him – and he repeated his question, adding in explanation, 'Old Allen, the man you are with.'

'Oh! Mr. Allen, you mean. Yes, I believe, he is very rich.'

'And no children at all?'

'No – not any.'

'A famous thing for his next heirs. He is *your* godfather, is not he?'

'My godfather! – no.'

'But you are always very much with them.'

'Yes, very much.'

'Aye, that is what I meant. He seems a good kind of old fellow enough, and has lived very well in his time, I dare say; he is not gouty for nothing. Does he drink his bottle a-day now?'

'His bottle a-day! – no. Why should you think of such a thing? He is a very temperate man, and you could not fancy him in liquor last night?'

'Lord help you! – You women are always thinking of men's being in liquor. Why you do not suppose a man is overset by a bottle? I am sure of *this* – that if every body was to drink their bottle a-day, there would not be half the disorders in the world there are now. It would be a famous good thing for us all.'

'I cannot believe it.'

'Oh! lord, it would be the saving of thousands. There is not the hundredth part of the wine consumed in this kingdom, that there ought to be. Our foggy climate wants help.'

'And yet I have heard that there is a great deal of wine drank in Oxford.'

'Oxford! There is no drinking at Oxford now, I assure you. Nobody drinks there. You would hardly meet with a man who goes beyond his four pints at the utmost. Now, for instance, it was reckoned a remarkable thing at the last party in my rooms, that upon an average we cleared about five pints a head. It was looked upon as something out of the common way. *Mine* is famous good stuff to be sure. You would not often meet with any thing like it in Oxford – and that may account for it. But this will just give you a notion of the general rate of drinking there.'

'Yes, it does give a notion,' said Catherine, warmly, 'and that is, that you all drink a great deal more wine than I thought you did. However, I am sure James does not drink so much.'

This declaration brought on a loud and overpowering reply, of which no part was very distinct, except the frequent exclamations, amounting almost to oaths, which adorned it, and Catherine was left, when it ended, with rather a strengthened belief of there being a great deal of wine drank in Oxford, and the same happy conviction of her brother's comparative sobriety.

Thorpe's ideas then all reverted to the merits of his own equipage, and she was called on to admire the spirit and freedom with which his horse moved along, and the ease which his paces, as well as the excellence of the springs, gave the motion of the carriage. She followed him in all his admiration as well as she could. To go before, or beyond him was impossible. His knowledge and her ignorance of the subject, his rapidity of expression, and her diffidence of herself put that out of her power; she could strike out nothing new in commendation, but she readily echoed whatever he chose to assert, and it was finally settled between them without any difficulty, that his equipage was altogether the most complete of its kind in England, his carriage the neatest, his horse the best goer, and himself the best coachman. – 'You do not really think, Mr. Thorpe,' said Catherine, venturing after some time to consider the matter as entirely decided, and to offer some little variation on the subject, 'that James's gig will break down?'

'Break down! Oh! lord! Did you ever see such a little tittuppy[1] thing in your life! There is not a sound piece of iron about it. The wheels have been fairly worn out these ten years at least – and as for the body! Upon my soul, you might shake it to pieces yourself with a touch. It is the most devilish little ricketty business I ever beheld! – Thank God! we have got a better. I would not be bound to go two miles in it for fifty thousand pounds.'

'Good heavens!' cried Catherine, quite frightened, 'then

pray let us turn back; they will certainly meet with an accident if we go on. Do let us turn back, Mr. Thorpe; stop and speak to my brother, and tell him how very unsafe it is.'

'Unsafe! Oh, lord! what is there in that? they will only get a roll if it does break down; and there is plenty of dirt, it will be excellent falling. Oh, curse it! the carriage is safe enough, if a man knows how to drive it; a thing of that sort in good hands will last above twenty years after it is fairly worn out. Lord bless you! I would undertake for five pounds to drive it to York and back again, without losing a nail.'

Catherine listened with astonishment; she knew not how to reconcile two such very different accounts of the same thing; for she had not been brought up to understand the propensities of a rattle, nor to know to how many idle assertions and impudent falsehoods the excess of vanity will lead. Her own family were plain matter-of-fact people, who seldom aimed at wit of any kind; her father, at the utmost, being contented with a pun, and her mother with a proverb; they were not in the habit therefore of telling lies to increase their importance, or of asserting at one moment what they would contradict the next. She reflected on the affair for some time in much perplexity, and was more than once on the point of requesting from Mr. Thorpe a clearer insight into his real opinion on the subject; but she checked herself, because it appeared to her that he did not excel in giving those clearer insights, in making those things plain which he had before made ambiguous; and, joining to this, the consideration, that he would not really suffer his sister and his friend to be exposed to a danger from which he might easily preserve them, she concluded at last, that he must know the carriage to be in fact perfectly safe, and therefore would alarm herself no longer. By him the whole matter seemed entirely forgotten; and all the rest of his conversation, or rather talk, began and ended with himself and his own concerns. He told her of horses which he had bought for a trifle and sold for incredible sums; of racing matches, in which his judgment had infallibly foretold the winner; of shooting parties, in which he had killed more birds (though without having one good shot) than all his companions together; and described to her some famous day's sport, with the foxhounds, in which his foresight and skill in directing the dogs had repaired the mistakes of the most experienced huntsman, and in which the boldness of his riding, though it had never endangered his own life for a moment, had been constantly leading others into difficulties, which he calmly concluded had broken the necks of many.

Little as Catherine was in the habit of judging for herself, and unfixed as were her general notions of what men ought to be, she could not entirely repress a doubt, while she bore with the effusions of his endless conceit, of his being altogether completely agreeable. It was a bold surmise, for he was Isabella's brother; and she had been assured by James, that his manners would recommend him to all her sex; but in spite of this, the extreme weariness of his company, which crept over her before they had been out an hour, and which continued unceasingly to increase till they stopped in Pulteney-street again, induced her, in some small degree, to resist such high authority, and to distrust his powers of giving universal pleasure.

When they arrived at Mrs. Allen's door, the astonishment of Isabella was hardly to be expressed, on finding that it was too late in the day for them to attend her friend into the house: – 'Past three o'clock!' it was inconceivable, incredible, impossible! and she would neither believe her own watch, nor her brother's, nor the servant's; she would believe no assurance of it founded on reason or reality, till Morland produced his watch, and ascertained the fact; to have doubted a moment longer *then*, would have been equally inconceivable, incredible, and impossible; and she could only protest, over and over again, that no two hours and a half had ever gone off so swiftly before, as Catherine was called on to confirm; Catherine could not tell a falsehood even to please Isabella; but the latter was spared the misery of her friend's dissenting voice, by not waiting for her answer. Her own feelings entirely engrossed her; her wretchedness was most acute on finding herself obliged to go directly home. – It was ages since she had had a moment's conversation with her dearest Catherine; and, though she had such thousands of things to say to her, it appeared as if they were never to be together again; so, with smiles of most exquisite misery, and the laughing eye of utter despondency, she bade her friend adieu and went on.

Catherine found Mrs. Allen just returned from all the busy idleness of the morning, and was immediately greeted with, 'Well, my dear, here you are;' a truth which she had no greater inclination than power to dispute; 'and I hope you have had a pleasant airing?'

'Yes, ma'am, I thank you; we could not have had a nicer day.'

'So Mrs. Thorpe said; she was vastly pleased at your all going.'

'You have seen Mrs. Thorpe then?'

'Yes, I went to the Pump-room as soon as you were gone, and there I met her, and we had a great deal of talk together. She says there was hardly any veal to be got at market this morning, it is so uncommonly scarce.'

'Did you see any body else of our acquaintance?'

'Yes; we agreed to take a turn in the Crescent, and there we met Mrs. Hughes, and Mr. and Miss Tilney walking with her.'

'Did you indeed? and did they speak to you?'

'Yes, we walked along the Crescent together for half an hour. They seem very agreeable people. Miss Tilney was in a very pretty spotted muslin, and I fancy, by what I can learn, that she always dresses very handsomely. Mrs. Hughes talked to me a great deal about the family.'

'And what did she tell you of them?'

'Oh! a vast deal indeed; she hardly talked of any thing else.'

'Did she tell you what part of Gloucestershire they come from?'

'Yes, she did; but I cannot recollect now. But they are very good kind of people, and very rich. Mrs. Tilney was a Miss Drummond, and she and Mrs. Hughes were school-fellows; and Miss Drummond had a very large fortune; and, when she married, her father gave her twenty thousand pounds, and five hundred to buy wedding-clothes. Mrs. Hughes saw all the clothes after they came from the warehouse.'

'And are Mr. and Mrs. Tilney in Bath?'

'Yes, I fancy they are, but I am not quite certain. Upon recollection, however, I have a notion they are both dead; at least the mother is; yes, I am sure Mrs. Tilney is dead, because Mrs. Hughes told me there was a very beautiful set of pearls that Mr. Drummond gave his daughter on her wedding-day and that Miss Tilney has got now, for they were put by for her when her mother died.'

'And is Mr. Tilney, my partner, the only son?'

'I cannot be quite positive about that, my dear; I have some idea he is; but however, he is a very fine young man Mrs. Hughes says, and likely to do very well.'

Catherine inquired no further; she had heard enough to feel that Mrs. Allen had no real intelligence to give, and that she was most particularly unfortunate herself in having missed such a meeting with both brother and sister. Could she have foreseen such a circumstance, nothing should have persuaded her to go out with the others; and, as it was, she could only lament her ill-luck, and think over what she had lost, till it was clear to her, that the drive had by no means been very pleasant and that John Thorpe himself was quite disagreeable.

CHAPTER X

THE Allens, Thorpes, and Morlands, all met in the evening at the theatre; and, as Catherine and Isabella sat together, there was then an opportunity for the latter to utter some few of the many thousand things which had been collecting within her for communication, in the immeasurable length of time which had divided them. – 'Oh, heavens! my beloved Catherine, have I got you at last?' was her address on Catherine's entering the box and sitting by her. 'Now, Mr. Morland,' for he was close to her on the other side, 'I shall not speak another word to you all the rest of the evening; so I charge you not to expect it. My sweetest Catherine, how have you been this long age? but I need not ask you, for you look delightfully. You really have done your hair in a more heavenly style than ever: you mischievous creature, do you want to attract every body? I assure you, my brother is quite in love with you already; and as for Mr. Tilney – but *that* is a settled thing – even *your* modesty cannot doubt his attachment now; his coming back to Bath makes it too plain. Oh! what would not I give to see him! I really am quite wild with impatience. My mother says he is the most delightful young man in the world; she saw him this morning you know: you must introduce him to me. Is he in the house now? – Look about for heaven's sake! I assure you, I can hardly exist till I see him.'

'No,' said Catherine, 'he is not here; I cannot see him any where.'

'Oh, horrid! am I never to be acquainted with him? How do you like my gown? I think it does not look amiss; the sleeves were entirely my own thought. Do you know I get so immoderately sick of Bath; your brother and I were agreeing this morning that, though it is vastly well to be here for a few weeks, we would not live here for millions. We soon found out that our tastes were exactly alike in preferring the country to every other place; really, our opinions were so exactly the same, it was quite ridiculous! There was not a single point in which we differed; I would not have had you by for the world; you are such a sly thing, I am sure you would have made some droll remark or other about it.'

'No, indeed I should not.'

'Oh, yes you would indeed; I know you better than you know yourself. You would have told us that we seemed born for each other, or some nonsense of that kind, which would have distressed me beyond conception; my cheeks would have been as red as your roses; I would not have had you by for the world.'

'Indeed you do me injustice; I would not have made so improper a remark upon any account; and besides, I am sure it would never have entered my head.'

Isabella smiled incredulously, and talked the rest of the evening to James.

Catherine's resolution of endeavouring to meet Miss Tilney

again continued in full force the next morning; and till the usual moment of going to the Pump-room, she felt some alarm from the dread of a second prevention. But nothing of that kind occurred, no visitors appeared to delay them, and they all three set off in good time for the Pump-room, where the ordinary course of events and conversation took place; Mr. Allen, after drinking his glass of water, joined some gentlemen to talk over the politics of the day and compare the accounts of their newspapers; and the ladies walked about together, noticing every new face, and almost every new bonnet in the room. The female part of the Thorpe family, attended by James Morland, appeared among the crowd in less than a quarter of an hour, and Catherine immediately took her usual place by the side of her friend. James, who was now in constant attendance, maintained a similar position, and separating themselves from the rest of their party, they walked in that manner for some time, till Catherine began to doubt the happiness of a situation which confining her entirely to her friend and brother, gave her very little share in the notice of either. They were always engaged in some sentimental discussion or lively dispute, but their sentiment was conveyed in such whispering voices, and their vivacity attended with so much laughter, that though Catherine's supporting opinion was not unfrequently called for by one or the other, she was never able to give any, from not having heard a word of the subject. At length however she was empowered to disengage herself from her friend, by the avowed necessity of speaking to Miss Tilney, whom she most joyfully saw just entering the room with Mrs. Hughes, and whom she instantly joined, with a firmer determination to be acquainted, than she might have had courage to command, had she not been urged by the disappointment of the day before. Miss Tilney met her with great civility, returned her advances with equal good will, and they continued talking together as long as both parties remained in the room; and though in all probability not an observation was made, nor an expression used by either which had not been made and used some thousands of times before, under that roof, in every Bath season, yet the merit of their being spoken with simplicity and truth, and without personal conceit, might be something uncommon.—

'How well your brother dances!' was an artless exclamation of Catherine's towards the close of their conversation, which at once surprized and amused her companion.

'Henry!' she replied with a smile. 'Yes, he does dance very well.'

'He must have thought it very odd to hear me say I was engaged the other evening, when he saw me sitting down. But I really had been engaged the whole day to Mr. Thorpe.' Miss Tilney could only bow. 'You cannot think,' added Catherine after a moment's silence, 'how surprized I was to see him again. I felt so sure of his being quite gone away.'

'When Henry had the pleasure of seeing you before, he was in Bath but for a couple of days. He came only to engage lodgings for us.'

'*That* never occurred to me; and of course, not seeing him any where, I thought he must be gone. Was not the young lady he danced with on Monday a Miss Smith?'

'Yes, an acquaintance of Mrs. Hughes.'

'I dare say she was very glad to dance. Do you think her pretty?'

'Not very.'

'He never comes to the Pump-room, I suppose?'

'Yes, sometimes; but he has rid out this morning with my father.'

Mrs. Hughes now joined them, and asked Miss Tilney if she was ready to go. 'I hope I shall have the pleasure of seeing you again soon,' said Catherine. 'Shall you be at the cotillion ball to-morrow?'

'Perhaps we— yes, I think we certainly shall.'

'I am glad of it, for we shall all be there.' – This civility was duly returned; and they parted – on Miss Tilney's side with some knowledge of her new acquaintance's feelings, and on Catherine's, without the smallest consciousness of having explained them.

She went home very happy. The morning had answered all

her hopes, and the evening of the following day was now the object of expectation, the future good. What gown and what head-dress she should wear on the occasion became her chief concern. She cannot be justified in it. Dress is at all times a frivolous distinction, and excessive solicitude about it often destroys its own aim. Catherine knew all this very well; her great aunt had read her a lecture on the subject only the Christmas before; and yet she lay awake ten minutes on Wednesday night debating between her spotted and her tamboured[1] muslin, and nothing but the shortness of the time prevented her buying a new one for the evening. This would have been an error in judgment, great though not uncommon, from which one of the other sex rather than her own, a brother rather than a great aunt might have warned her, for man only can be aware of the insensibility of man towards a new gown. It would be mortifying to the feelings of many ladies, could they be made to understand how little the heart of man is affected by what is costly or new in their attire; how little it is biassed by the texture of their muslin, and how unsusceptible of peculiar tenderness towards the spotted, the sprigged, the mull or the jackonet.[2] Woman is fine for her own satisfaction alone. No man will admire her the more, no woman will like her the better for it. Neatness and fashion are enough for the former, and a something of shabbiness or impropriety will be most endearing to the latter. – But not one of these grave reflections troubled the tranquillity of Catherine.

She entered the rooms on Thursday evening with feelings very different from what had attended her thither the Monday before. She had then been exulting in her engagement to Thorpe, and was now chiefly anxious to avoid his sight, lest he should engage her again; for though she could not, dared not expect that Mr. Tilney should ask her a third time to dance, her wishes, hopes and plans all centered in nothing less. Every young lady may feel for my heroine in this critical moment, for every young lady has at some time or other known the same agitation. All have been, or at least all have believed themselves to be, in danger from the pursuit of some one whom they wished to avoid; and all have been anxious for the attentions of some one whom they wished to please. As soon as they were joined by the Thorpes, Catherine's agony began; she fidgetted about if John Thorpe came towards her, hid herself as much as possible from his view, and when he spoke to her pretended not to hear him. The cotillions were over, the country-dancing beginning, and she saw nothing of the Tilneys. 'Do not be frightened, my dear Catherine,' whispered Isabella, 'but I am really going to dance with your brother again. I declare positively it is quite shocking. I tell him he ought to be ashamed of himself, but you and John must keep us in countenance. Make haste, my dear creature, and come to us. John is just walked off, but he will be back in a moment.'

Catherine had neither time nor inclination to answer. The others walked away, John Thorpe was still in view, and she gave herself up for lost. That she might not appear, however, to observe or expect him, she kept her eyes intently fixed on her fan; and a self-condemnation for her folly, in supposing that among such a crowd they should even meet with the Tilneys in any reasonable time, had just passed through her mind, when she suddenly found herself addressed and again solicited to dance, by Mr. Tilney himself. With what sparkling eyes and ready motion she granted his request, and with how pleasing a flutter of heart she went with him to the set, may be easily imagined. To escape, and, as she believed, so narrowly escape John Thorpe, and to be asked, so immediately on his joining her, asked by Mr. Tilney, as if he had sought her on purpose! – it did not appear to her that life could supply any greater felicity.

Scarcely had they worked themselves into the quiet possession of a place, however, when her attention was claimed by John Thorpe, who stood behind her. 'Hey-day, Miss Morland!' said he, 'what is the meaning of this? – I thought you and I were to dance together.'

'I wonder you should think so, for you never asked me.'
'That is a good one, by Jove! – I asked you as soon as I came into the room, and I was just going to ask you again, but when I turned round, you were gone! – this is a cursed shabby trick! I

only came for the sake of dancing with *you*, and I firmly believe you were engaged to me ever since Monday. Yes; I remember, I asked you while you were waiting in the lobby for your cloak. And here have I been telling all my acquaintance that I was going to dance with the prettiest girl in the room; and when they see you standing up with somebody else, they will quiz me famously.'

'Oh, no; they will never think of *me*, after such a description as that.'

'By heavens, if they do not, I will kick them out of the room for blockheads. What chap have you there?' Catherine satisfied his curiosity. 'Tilney,' he repeated, 'Hum – I do not know him. A good figure of a man; well put together. – Does he want a horse? – Here is a friend of mine, Sam Fletcher, has got one to sell that would suit any body. A famous clever animal for the road – only forty guineas. I had fifty minds to buy it myself, for it is one of my maxims always to buy a good horse when I meet with one; but it would not answer my purpose, it would not do for the field. I would give any money for a real good hunter. I have three now, the best that ever were back'd. I would not take eight hundred guineas for them. Fletcher and I mean to get a house in Leicestershire, against the next season. It is so d— uncomfortable, living at an inn.'

This was the last sentence by which he could weary Catherine's attention, for he was just then born off by the resistless pressure of a long string of passing ladies. Her partner now drew near, and said, 'That gentleman would have put me out of patience, had he staid with you half a minute longer. He has no business to withdraw the attention of my partner from me. We have entered into a contract of mutual agreeableness for the space of an evening, and all our agreeableness belongs solely to each other for that time. Nobody can fasten themselves on the notice of one, without injuring the rights of the other. I consider a country-dance as an emblem of marriage. Fidelity and complaisance are the principal duties of both; and those men who do not chuse to dance or marry themselves, have no business with the partners or wives of their neighbours.'

'But they are such very different things!—'

'—That you think they cannot be compared together.'

'To be sure not. People that marry can never part, but must go and keep house together. People that dance, only stand opposite each other in a long room for half an hour.'

'And such is your definition of matrimony and dancing. Taken in that light certainly, their resemblance is not striking; but I think I could place them in such a view. – You will allow, that in both, man has the advantage of choice, woman only the power of refusal; that in both, it is an engagement between man and woman, formed for the advantage of each; and that when once entered into, they belong exclusively to each other till the moment of its dissolution; that it is their duty, each to endeavour to give the other no cause for wishing that he or she had bestowed themselves elsewhere, and their best interest to keep their own imaginations from wandering towards the perfections of their neighbours, or fancying that they should have been better off with any one else. You will allow all this?'

'Yes, to be sure, as you state it, all this sounds very well; but still they are so very different. – I cannot look upon them at all in the same light, nor think the same duties belong to them.'

'In one respect, there certainly is a difference. In marriage, the man is supposed to provide for the support of the woman; the woman to make the home agreeable to the man; he is to purvey, and she is to smile. But in dancing, their duties are exactly changed; the agreeableness, the compliance are expected from him, while she furnishes the fan and the lavender water. *That*, I suppose, was the difference of duties which struck you, as rendering the conditions incapable of comparison.'

'No, indeed, I never thought of that.'

'Then I am quite at a loss. One thing, however, I must observe. This disposition on your side is rather alarming. You totally disallow any similarity in the obligations; and may I not thence infer, that your notions of the duties of the dancing state are not so strict as your partner might wish? Have I not reason to fear, that if the gentleman who spoke to you just now were to return, or if any other gentleman were to address you, there would be nothing to restrain you from conversing with him as long as you chose?'

'Mr. Thorpe is such a very particular friend of my brother's, that if he talks to me, I must talk to him again; but there are hardly three young men in the room besides him, that I have any acquaintance with.'

'And is that to be my only security? alas, alas!'

'Nay, I am sure you cannot have a better; for if I do not know any body, it is impossible for me to talk to them; and, besides, I do not *want* to talk to any body.'

'Now you have given me a security worth having; and I shall proceed with courage. Do you find Bath as agreeable as when I had the honour of making the inquiry before?'

'Yes, quite – more so, indeed.'

'More so! – Take care, or you will forget to be tired of it at the proper time. – You ought to be tired at the end of six weeks.'

'I do not think I should be tired, if I were to stay here six months.'

'Bath, compared with London, has little variety, and so every body finds out every year. "For six weeks, I allow Bath is pleasant enough; but beyond *that*, it is the most tiresome place in the world." You would be told so by people of all descriptions, who come regularly every winter, lengthen their six weeks into ten or twelve, and go away at last because they can afford to stay no longer.'

'Well, other people must judge for themselves, and those who go to London may think nothing of Bath. But I, who live in a small retired village in the country, can never find greater sameness in such a place as this, than in my own home; for here are a variety of amusements, a variety of things to be seen and done all day long, which I can know nothing of there.'

'You are not fond of the country.'

'Yes, I am. I have always lived there, and always been very happy. But certainly there is much more sameness in a country life than in a Bath life. One day in the country is exactly like another.'

'But then you spend your time so much more rationally in the country.'

'Do I?'

'Do you not?'

'I do not believe there is much difference.'

'Here you are in pursuit only of amusement all day long.'

'And so I am at home – only I do not find so much of it. I walk about here, and so I do there; – but here I see a variety of people in every street, and there I can only go and call on Mrs. Allen.'

Mr. Tilney was very much amused. 'Only go and call on Mrs. Allen!' he repeated. 'What a picture of intellectual poverty! However, when you sink into this abyss again, you will have more to say. You will be able to talk of Bath, and of all that you did here.'

'Oh! yes. I shall never be in want of something to talk of again to Mrs. Allen, or any body else. I really believe I shall always be talking of Bath, when I am at home again – I *do* like it so very much. If I could but have papa and mamma, and the rest of them here, I suppose I should be too happy! James's coming (my eldest brother) is quite delightful – and especially as it turns out, that the very family we are just got so intimate with, are his intimate friends already. Oh! who can ever be tired of Bath?'

'Not those who bring such fresh feelings of every sort to it, as you do. But papas and mammas, and brothers and intimate friends are a good deal gone by, to most of the frequenters of Bath – and the honest relish of balls and plays, and every-day sights, is past with them.'

Here their conversation closed; the demands of the dance becoming now too importunate for a divided attention.

Soon after their reaching the bottom of the set, Catherine perceived herself to be earnestly regarded by a gentleman who stood among the lookers-on, immediately behind her partner. He was a very handsome man, of a commanding aspect, past the bloom, but not past the vigour of life; and with his eye still directed towards her, she saw him presently address Mr. Tilney in a familiar whisper. Confused by his notice, and blushing from the fear of its being excited by something wrong in her appearance, she turned away her head. But while she did so, the gentleman retreated, and her partner coming nearer, said, 'I see that you guess what I have just been asked. That gentleman knows your name, and you have a right to know his. It is General Tilney, my father.'

Catherine's answer was only 'Oh!' – but it was an 'Oh!' expressing every thing needful; attention to his words, and perfect reliance on their truth. With real interest and strong admiration did her eye now follow the General, as he moved through the crowd, and 'How handsome a family they are!' was her secret remark.

In chatting with Miss Tilney before the evening concluded, a new source of felicity arose to her. She had never taken a country walk since her arrival in Bath. Miss Tilney, to whom all the commonly-frequented environs were familiar, spoke of them in terms which made her all eagerness to know them too; and on her openly fearing that she might find nobody to go with her, it was proposed by the brother and sister that they should join in a walk, some morning or other. 'I shall like it,' she cried, 'beyond any thing in the world; and do not let us put it off – let us go to-morrow.' This was readily agreed to, with only a proviso of Miss Tilney's, that it did not rain, which Catherine was sure it would not. At twelve o'clock, they were to call for her in Pulteney-street – and 'remember – twelve o'clock,' was her parting speech to her new friend. Of her other, her older, her more established friend, Isabella, of whose fidelity and worth she had enjoyed a fortnight's experience, she scarcely saw any thing during the evening. Yet, though longing to make her acquainted with her happiness, she cheerfully submitted to the wish of Mr. Allen, which took them rather early away, and her spirits danced within her, as she danced in her chair all the way home.

CHAPTER XI

THE morrow brought a very sober looking morning; the sun making only a few efforts to appear; and Catherine augured from it, every thing most favourable to her wishes. A bright morning so early in the year, she allowed would generally turn to rain, but a cloudy one foretold improvement as the day advanced. She applied to Mr. Allen for confirmation of her hopes, but Mr. Allen not having his own skies and barometer about him, declined giving any absolute promise of sunshine. She applied to Mrs. Allen, and Mrs. Allen's opinion was more positive. 'She had no doubt in the world of its being a very fine day, if the clouds would only go off, and the sun keep out.'

At about eleven o'clock however, a few specks of small rain upon the windows caught Catherine's watchful eye, and 'Oh! dear, I do believe it will be wet,' broke from her in a most desponding tone.

'I thought how it would be,' said Mrs. Allen.

'No walk for me to-day,' sighed Catherine; – 'but perhaps it may come to nothing, or it may hold up before twelve.'

'Perhaps it may, but then, my dear, it will be so dirty.'

'Oh! that will not signify; I never mind dirt.'

'No,' replied her friend very placidly, 'I know you never mind dirt.'

After a short pause, 'It comes on faster and faster!' said Catherine, as she stood watching at a window.

'So it does indeed. If it keeps raining, the streets will be very wet.'

'There are four umbrellas up already. How I hate the sight of an umbrella!'

'They are disagreeable things to carry. I would much rather take a chair at any time.'

'It was such a nice looking morning! I felt so convinced it would be dry!'

'Any body would have thought so indeed. There will be very few people in the Pump-room, if it rains all the morning. I hope Mr. Allen will put on his great coat when he goes, but I dare say he will not, for he had rather do any thing in the world than walk out in a great coat; I wonder he should dislike it, it must be so comfortable.'

The rain continued – fast, though not heavy. Catherine went every five minutes to the clock, threatening on each return that, if it still kept on raining another five minutes, she would give up the matter as hopeless. The clock struck twelve, and it still rained. – 'You will not be able to go, my dear.'

'I do not quite despair yet. I shall not give it up till a quarter after twelve. This is just the time of day for it to clear up, and I do think it looks a little lighter. There, it is twenty minutes after twelve, and now I *shall* give it up entirely. Oh! that we had such weather here as they had at Udolpho, or at least in Tuscany and the South of France! – the night that poor St. Aubin died![1] – such beautiful weather!'

At half past twelve, when Catherine's anxious attention to the weather was over, and she could no longer claim any merit from its amendment, the sky began voluntarily to clear. A gleam of sunshine took her quite by surprize; she looked round; the clouds were parting, and she instantly returned to the window to watch over and encourage the happy appearance. Ten minutes more made it certain that a bright afternoon would succeed, and justified the opinion of Mrs. Allen, who had 'always thought it would clear up.' But whether Catherine might still expect her friends, whether there had not been too much rain for Miss Tilney to venture, must yet be a question.

It was too dirty for Mrs. Allen to accompany her husband to the Pump-room; he accordingly set off by himself, and Catherine had barely watched him down the street, when her notice was claimed by the approach of the same two open carriages, containing the same three people that had surprized her so much a few mornings back.

'Isabella, my brother, and Mr. Thorpe, I declare! They are coming for me perhaps – but I shall not go – I cannot go indeed, for you know Miss Tilney may still call.' Mrs. Allen agreed to it. John Thorpe was soon with them, and his voice was with them yet sooner, for on the stairs he was calling out to Miss Morland to be quick. 'Make haste! make haste!' as he threw open the door – 'put on your hat this moment – there is no time to be lost – we are going to Bristol. – How d'ye do, Mrs. Allen?'

'To Bristol! Is not that a great way off? – But, however, I cannot go with you to-day, because I am engaged; I expect

some friends every moment.' This was of course vehemently
talked down as no reason at all; Mrs. Allen was called on to
second him, and the two others walked in, to give their assistance.
'My sweetest Catherine, is not this delightful? We shall have a
most heavenly drive. You are to thank your brother and me for
the scheme; it darted into our heads at breakfast-time, I verily
belive at the same instant; and we should have been off two
hours ago if it had not been for this detestable rain. But it does
not signify, the nights are moonlight, and we shall do delightfully.
Oh: I am in such extasies at the thoughts of a little country air
and quiet! – so much better than going to the Lower Rooms. We
shall drive directly to Clifton and dine there; and, as soon as
dinner is over, if there is time for it, go on to Kingsweston.'

'I doubt our being able to do so much,' said Morland.

'You croaking fellow!' cried Thorpe, 'we shall be able to do
ten times more. Kingsweston! aye, and Blaize Castle too, and
any thing else we can hear of; but here is your sister says she will
not go.'

'Blaize Castle!' cried Catherine; 'what is that?'

'The finest place in England – worth going fifty miles at any
time to see.'

'What, is it really a castle, an old castle?'

'The oldest in the kingdom.'

'But is it like what one reads of?'

'Exactly – the very same.'

'But now really – are there towers and long galleries?'

'By dozens.'

'Then I should like to see it; but I cannot—I cannot go.'

'Not go! – my beloved creature, what do you mean?'

'I cannot go, because'—(looking down as she spoke, fearful of
Isabella's smile) 'I expect Miss Tilney and her brother to call
on me to take a country walk. They promised to come at twelve,
only it rained; but now, as it is so fine, I dare say they will be
here soon.'

'Not they indeed,' cried Thorpe; 'for, as we turned into
Broad-street, I saw them – does he not drive a phaeton with
bright chesnuts?'

'I do not know indeed.'

'Yes, I know he does; I saw him. You are talking of the man you danced with last night, are not you?'

'Yes.'

'Well, I saw him at that moment turn up the Lansdown Road, – driving a smart-looking girl.'

'Did you indeed?'

'Did upon my soul; knew him again directly, and he seemed to have got some very pretty cattle too.'

'It is very odd! but I suppose they thought it would be too dirty for a walk.'

'And well they might, for I never saw so much dirt in my life. Walk! you could no more walk than you could fly! it has not been so dirty the whole winter; it is ancle-deep every where.'

Isabella corroborated it: – 'My dearest Catherine, you cannot form an idea of the dirt; come, you must go; you cannot refuse going now.'

'I should like to see the castle; but may we go all over it? may we go up every staircase, and into every suite of rooms?'

'Yes, yes, every hole and corner.'

'But then, – if they should only be gone out for an hour till it is drier, and call by and bye?'

'Make yourself easy, there is no danger of that, for I heard Tilney hallooing to a man who was just passing by on horseback, that they were going as far as Wick Rocks.'

'Then I will. Shall I go, Mrs. Allen?'

'Just as you please, my dear.'

'Mrs. Allen, you must persuade her to go,' was the general cry. Mrs. Allen was not inattentive to it: – 'Well, my dear,' said she, 'suppose you go.' – And in two minutes they were off.

Catherine's feelings, as she got into the carriage, were in a very unsettled state; divided between regret for the loss of one great pleasure, and the hope of soon enjoying another, almost its equal in degree, however unlike in kind. She could not think the Tilneys had acted quite well by her, in so readily giving up their engagement, without sending her any message of excuse. It was now but an hour later than the time fixed on for the beginning

of their walk; and, in spite of what she had heard of the prodigious accumulation of dirt in the course of that hour, she could
not from her own observation help thinking, that they might have
gone with very little inconvenience. To feel herself slighted by
them was very painful. On the other hand, the delight of exploring an edifice like Udolpho, as her fancy represented Blaize
Castle to be, was such a counterpoise of good, as might console
her for almost any thing.

They passed briskly down Pulteney-street, and through
Laura-place, without the exchange of many words. Thorpe
talked to his horse, and she meditated, by turns, on broken
promises and broken arches, phaetons and false hangings,
Tilneys and trap-doors. As they entered Argyle-buildings,
however, she was roused by this address from her companion,
'Who is that girl who looked at you so hard as she went by?'

'Who? – where?'

'On the right-hand pavement – she must be almost out of
sight now.' Catherine looked round and saw Miss Tilney leaning on her brother's arm, walking slowly down the street. She
saw them both looking back at her. 'Stop, stop, Mr. Thorpe,'
she impatiently cried, 'it is Miss Tilney; it is indeed. – How
could you tell me they were gone? – Stop, stop, I will get out
this moment and go to them.' But to what purpose did she
speak? – Thorpe only lashed his horse into a brisker trot; the
Tilneys, who had soon ceased to look after her, were in a
moment out of sight round the corner of Laura-place, and in
another moment she was herself whisked into the Market-
place. Still, however, and during the length of another street, she
intreated him to stop. 'Pray, pray stop, Mr. Thorpe. – I cannot
go on. – I will not go on. – I must go back to Miss Tilney.' But
Mr. Thorpe only laughed, smacked his whip, encouraged his
horse, made odd noises, and drove on; and Catherine, angry
and vexed as she was, having no power of getting away, was
obliged to give up the point and submit. Her reproaches, however, were not spared. 'How could you deceive me so, Mr.
Thorpe? – How could you say, that you saw them driving up
the Lansdown-road? – I would not have had it happen so for the

world. – They must think it so strange; so rude of me! to go by them, too, without saying a word! You do not know how vexed I am. – I shall have no pleasure at Clifton, nor in any thing else. I had rather, ten thousand times rather get out now, and walk back to them. How could you say, you saw them driving out in a phaeton?' Thorpe defended himself very stoutly, declared he had never seen two men so much alike in his life, and would hardly give up the point of its having been Tilney himself.

Their drive, even when this subject was over, was not likely to be very agreeable. Catherine's complaisance was no longer what it had been in their former airing. She listened reluctantly, and her replies were short. Blaize Castle remained her only comfort; towards *that*, she still looked at intervals with pleasure; though rather than be disappointed of the promised walk, and especially rather than be thought ill of by the Tilneys, she would willingly have given up all the happiness which its walls could supply – the happiness of a progress through a long suite of lofty rooms, exhibiting the remains of magnificent furniture, though now for many years deserted – the happiness of being stopped in their way along narrow, winding vaults, by a low, grated door; or even of having their lamp, their only lamp, extinguished by a sudden gust of wind, and of being left in total darkness. In the meanwhile, they proceeded on their journey without any mischance; and were within view of the town of Keynsham, when a halloo from Morland, who was behind them, made his friend pull up, to know what was the matter. The others then came close enough for conversation, and Morland said, 'We had better go back, Thorpe; it is too late to go on to-day; your sister thinks so as well as I. We have been exactly an hour coming from Pulteney-street, very little more than seven miles; and, I suppose, we have at least eight more to go. It will never do. We set out a great deal too late. We had much better put it off till another day, and turn round.'

'It is all one to me,' replied Thorpe rather angrily; and instantly turning his horse, they were on their way back to Bath.

'If your brother had not got such a d— beast to drive,' said he soon afterwards, 'we might have done it very well. My horse would have trotted to Clifton within the hour, if left to himself, and I have almost broke my arm with pulling him in to that cursed broken-winded jade's pace. Morland is a fool for not keeping a horse and gig of his own.'

'No, he is not,' said Catherine warmly, 'for I am sure he could not afford it.'

'And why cannot he afford it?'

'Because he has not money enough.'

'And whose fault is that?'

'Nobody's, that I know of.' Thorpe then said something in the loud, incoherent way to which he had often recourse, about its being a d— thing to be miserly; and that if people who rolled in money could not afford things, he did not know who could; which Catherine did not even endeavour to understand. Disappointed of what was to have been the consolation for her first disappointment, she was less and less disposed either to be agreeable herself, or to find her companion so; and they returned to Pulteney-street without her speaking twenty words.

As she entered the house, the footman told her, that a gentleman and lady had called and inquired for her a few minutes after her setting off; that, when he told them she was gone out with Mr. Thorpe, the lady had asked whether any message had been left for her; and on his saying no, had felt for a card, but said she had none about her, and went away. Pondering over these heart-rending tidings, Catherine walked slowly up stairs. At the head of them she was met by Mr. Allen, who, on hearing the reason of their speedy return, said, 'I am glad your brother had so much sense; I am glad you are come back. It was a strange, wild scheme.'

They all spent the evening together at Thorpe's. Catherine was disturbed and out of spirits; but Isabella seemed to find a pool of commerce,[1] in the fate of which she shared, by private partnership with Morland, a very good equivalent for the quiet and country air of an inn at Clifton. Her satisfaction, too, in not being at the Lower Rooms, was spoken more than once. 'How I pity the poor creatures that are going there! How glad I am that I am not amongst them! I wonder whether it will be a full ball or not! They have not begun dancing yet. I would not be there for all the world. It is so delightful to have an evening now and then to oneself. I dare say it will not be a very good ball. I know the Mitchells will not be there. I am sure I pity every body that is. But I dare say, Mr. Morland, you long to be at it, do not you? I am sure you do. Well, pray do not let any body here be a restraint on you. I dare say we could do very well without you; but you men think yourselves of such consequence.'

Catherine could almost have accused Isabella of being wanting in tenderness towards herself and her sorrows; so very little did they appear to dwell on her mind, and so very inadequate was the comfort she offered. 'Do not be so dull, my dearest creature,' she whispered. 'You will quite break my heart. It was amazingly shocking to be sure; but the Tilney's were entirely to blame. Why were not they more punctual? It was dirty, indeed, but what did that signify? I am sure John and I should not have minded it. I never mind going through any thing, where a friend is concerned; that is my disposition, and John is just the same; he has amazing strong feelings. Good heavens! what a delightful hand you have got! Kings, I vow! I never was so happy in my life! I would fifty times rather you should have them than myself.'

And now I may dismiss my heroine to the sleepless couch, which is the true heroine's portion; to a pillow strewed with thorns and wet with tears. And lucky may she think herself, if she get another good night's rest in the course of the next three months.

CHAPTER XII

'MRS. ALLEN,' said Catherine the next morning, 'will there be any harm in my calling on Miss Tilney to-day? I shall not be easy till I have explained every thing.'

'Go by all means, my dear; only put on a white gown; Miss Tilney always wears white.'

Catherine cheerfully complied; and being properly equipped, was more impatient than ever to be at the Pump-room, that she might inform herself of General Tilney's lodgings, for though she believed they were in Milsom-street, she was not certain of the house, and Mrs. Allen's wavering convictions only made it more doubtful. To Milsom-street she was directed; and having made herself perfect in the number, hastened away with eager steps and a beating heart to pay her visit, explain her conduct, and be forgiven; tripping lightly through the church-yard, and resolutely turning away her eyes, that she might not be obliged to see her beloved Isabella and her dear family, who, she had reason to believe, were in a shop hard by. She reached the house without any impediment, looked at the number, knocked at the door, and inquired for Miss Tilney. The man believed Miss Tilney to be at home, but was not quite certain. Would she be pleased to send up her name? She gave her card. In a few minutes the servant returned, and with a look which did not quite confirm his words, said he had been mistaken, for that Miss Tilney was walked out. Catherine, with a blush of mortification, left the house. She felt almost persuaded that Miss Tilney *was* at home, and too much offended to admit her; and as she retired down the street, could not withhold one glance at the drawing-room windows, in expectation of seeing her there, but no one appeared at them. At the bottom of the street, however, she looked back again, and then, not at a window, but issuing from the door, she saw Miss Tilney herself. She was followed by a gentleman, whom Catherine believed to be her father, and they turned up towards Edgar's-buildings. Catherine, in deep mortification, proceeded on her way. She could almost be angry herself at such angry incivility; but she checked the resentful sensation; she remembered her own ignorance. She knew not how such an offence as her's might be classed by the laws of worldly politeness, to what a degree of unforgivingness it might with propriety lead, nor to what rigours of rudeness in return it might justly make her amenable.

Dejected and humbled, she had even some thoughts of not going with the others to the theatre that night; but it must be

confessed that they were not of long continuance: for she soon
recollected, in the first place, that she was without any excuse
for staying at home; and, in the second, that it was a play she
wanted very much to see. To the theatre accordingly they all
went; no Tilneys appeared to plague or please her; she feared
that, amongst the many perfections of the family, a fondness
for plays was not to be ranked; but perhaps it was because they
were habituated to the finer performances of the London stage,
which she knew, on Isabella's authority, rendered every thing
else of the kind 'quite horrid.' She was not deceived in her own
expectation of pleasure; the comedy so well suspended her care,
that no one, observing her during the first four acts, would have
supposed she had any wretchedness about her. On the beginning of the fifth, however, the sudden view of Mr. Henry Tilney
and his father, joining a party in the opposite box, recalled her to
anxiety and distress. The stage could no longer excite genuine
merriment – no longer keep her whole attention. Every other
look upon an average was directed towards the opposite box;
and, for the space of two entire scenes, did she thus watch Henry
Tilney, without being once able to catch his eye. No longer
could he be suspected of indifference for a play; his notice was
never withdrawn from the stage during two whole scenes. At
length, however, he did look towards her, and he bowed – but
such a bow! no smile, no continued observance attended it;
his eyes were immediately returned to their former direction.
Catherine was restlessly miserable; she could almost have run
round to the box in which he sat, and forced him to hear her
explanation. Feelings rather natural than heroic possessed her;
instead of considering her own dignity injured by this ready
condemnation – instead of proudly resolving, in conscious
innocence, to shew her resentment towards him who could
harbour a doubt of it, to leave to him all the trouble of seeking
an explanation, and to enlighten him on the past only by avoiding
his sight, or flirting with somebody else, she took to herself all
the shame of misconduct, or at least of its appearance, and was
only eager for an opportunity of explaining its cause.

The play concluded – the curtain fell – Henry Tilney was no

longer to be seen where he had hitherto sat, but his father remained, and perhaps he might be now coming round to their box. She was right; in a few minutes he appeared, and, making his way through the then thinning rows, spoke with like calm politeness to Mrs. Allen and her friend. – Not with such calmness was he answered by the latter: 'Oh! Mr. Tilney, I have been quite wild to speak to you, and make my apologies. You must have thought me so rude; but indeed it was not my own fault, – was it, Mrs. Allen? Did not they tell me that Mr. Tilney and his sister were gone out in a phaeton together? and then what could I do? But I had ten thousand times rather have been with you; now had not I, Mrs. Allen?'

'My dear, you tumble my gown,' was Mrs. Allen's reply.

Her assurance, however, standing sole as it did, was not thrown away; it brought a more cordial, more natural smile into his countenance, and he replied in a tone which retained only a little affected reserve: – 'We were much obliged to you at any rate for wishing us a pleasant walk after our passing you in Argyle-street: you were so kind as to look back on purpose.'

'But indeed I did not wish you a pleasant walk; I never thought of such a thing; but I begged Mr. Thorpe so earnestly to stop; I called out to him as soon as ever I saw you; now, Mrs. Allen, did not—Oh! you were not there; but indeed I did; and, if Mr. Thorpe would only have stopped, I would have jumped out and run after you.'

Is there a Henry in the world who could be insensible to such a declaration? Henry Tilney at least was not. With a yet sweeter smile, he said every thing that need be said of his sister's concern, regret, and dependence on Catherine's honour. – 'Oh! do not say Miss Tilney was not angry,' cried Catherine, 'because I know she was; for she would not see me this morning when I called; I saw her walk out of the house the next minute after my leaving it; I was hurt, but I was not affronted. Perhaps you did not know I had been there.'

'I was not within at the time; but I heard of it from Eleanor, and she has been wishing ever since to see you, to explain the reason of such incivility; but perhaps I can do it as well. It was nothing more than that my father – they were just preparing to walk out, and he being hurried for time, and not caring to have it put off, made a point of her being denied. That was all, I do assure you. She was very much vexed, and meant to make her apology as soon as possible.'

Catherine's mind was greatly eased by this information, yet a something of solicitude remained, from which sprang the following question, thoroughly artless in itself, though rather distressing to the gentleman: – 'But, Mr. Tilney, why were *you* less generous than your sister? If she felt such confidence in my good intentions, and could suppose it to be only a mistake, why should *you* be so ready to take offence?'

'Me! – I take offence!'

'Nay, I am sure by your look, when you came into the box, you were angry.'

'I angry! I could have no right.'

'Well, nobody would have thought you had no right who saw your face.' He replied by asking her to make room for him, and talking of the play.

He remained with them some time, and was only too agreeable for Catherine to be contented when he went away. Before they parted, however, it was agreed that the projected walk should be taken as soon as possible; and, setting aside the misery of his quitting their box, she was, upon the whole, left one of the happiest creatures in the world.

While talking to each other, she had observed with some surprize, that John Thorpe, who was never in the same part of the house for ten minutes together, was engaged in conversation with General Tilney; and she felt something more than surprize, when she thought she could perceive herself the object of their attention and discourse. What could they have to say of her? She feared General Tilney did not like her appearance: she found it was implied in his preventing her admittance to his daughter, rather than postpone his own walk a few minutes. 'How came Mr. Thorpe to know your father?' was her anxious inquiry, as she pointed them out to her companion. He knew nothing about it; but his father, like every military man, had a very large acquaintance.

When the entertainment was over, Thorpe came to assist them in getting out. Catherine was the immediate object of his gallantry; and, while they waited in the lobby for a chair, he prevented the inquiry which had travelled from her heart almost to the tip of her tongue, by asking, in a consequential manner, whether she had seen him talking with General Tilney: – 'He is a fine old fellow, upon my soul! – stout, active, – looks as young as his son. I have a great regard for him, I assure you: a gentleman-like, good sort of fellow as ever lived.'

'But how came you to know him?'

'Know him! – There are few people much about town that I do not know. I have met him for ever at the Bedford;[1] and I knew his face again to-day the moment he came into the billiard-room. One of the best players we have, by the bye; and we had a little touch[2] together, though I was almost afraid of him at first: the odds were five to four against me; and, if I had not made one of the cleanest strokes that perhaps ever was made in this world – I took his ball exactly – but I could not make you under-stand it without a table; – however I *did* beat him. A very fine fellow; as rich as a Jew. I should like to dine with him; I dare say he gives famous dinners. But what do you think we have been talking of? – You. Yes, by heavens! – and the General thinks you the finest girl in Bath.'

'Oh! nonsense! how can you say so?'

'And what do you think I said?' (lowering his voice) 'Well done, General, said I, I am quite of your mind.'

Here, Catherine, who was much less gratified by his admira-tion than by General Tilney's, was not sorry to be called away by Mr. Allen. Thorpe, however, would see her to her chair, and, till she entered it, continued the same kind of delicate flattery, in spite of her entreating him to have done.

That General Tilney, instead of disliking, should admire her, was very delightful; and she joyfully thought, that there was not one of the family whom she need now fear to meet. – The evening had done more, much more, for her, than could have been expected.

CHAPTER XIII

MONDAY, Tuesday, Wednesday, Thursday, Friday and Saturday have now passed in review before the reader; the events of each day, its hopes and fears, mortifications and pleasures have been separately stated, and the pangs of Sunday only now remain to be described, and close the week. The Clifton scheme had been deferred, not relinquished, and on the afternoon's Crescent of this day, it was brought forward again. In a private consultation between Isabella and James, the former of whom had particularly set her heart upon going, and the latter no less anxiously placed his upon pleasing her, it was agreed that, provided the weather were fair, the party should take place on the following morning; and they were to set off very early, in order to be at home in good time. The affair thus determined, and Thorpe's approbation secured, Catherine only remained to be apprized of it. She had left them for a few minutes to speak to Miss Tilney. In that interval the plan was completed, and as soon as she came again, her agreement was demanded; but instead of the gay acquiescence expected by Isabella, Catherine looked grave, was very sorry, but could not go. The engagement which ought to have kept her from joining in the former attempt, would make it impossible for her to accompany them now. She had that moment settled with Miss Tilney to take their promised walk to-morrow; it was quite determined, and she would not, upon any account, retract. But that she *must* and *should* retract, was instantly the eager cry of both the Thorpes; they must go to Clifton to-morrow, they would not go without her, it would be nothing to put off a mere walk for one day longer, and they would not hear of a refusal. Catherine was distressed, but not subdued. 'Do not urge me, Isabella. I am engaged to Miss Tilney. I cannot go.' This availed nothing. The same arguments assailed her again; she must go, she should go, and they would not hear of a refusal. 'It would be so easy to tell Miss Tilney that you had just been reminded of a prior engagement, and must only beg to put off the walk till Tuesday.'

'No, it would not be easy. I could not do it. There has been no prior engagement.' But Isabella became only more and more urgent; calling on her in the most affectionate manner; addressing her by the most endearing names. She was sure her dearest, sweetest Catherine would not seriously refuse such a trifling request to a friend who loved her so dearly. She knew her beloved Catherine to have so feeling a heart, so sweet a temper, to be so easily persuaded by those she loved. But all in vain; Catherine felt herself to be in the right, and though pained by such tender, such flattering supplication, could not allow it to influence her. Isabella then tried another method. She reproached her with having more affection for Miss Tilney, though she had known her so little a while, than for her best and oldest friends; with being grown cold and indifferent, in short, towards herself. 'I cannot help being jealous, Catherine, when I see myself slighted for strangers, I, who love you so excessively! When once my affections are placed, it is not in the power of any thing to change them. But I believe my feelings are stronger than any body's; I am sure they are too strong for my own peace; and to see myself supplanted in your friendship by strangers, does cut me to the quick, I own. These Tilneys seem to swallow up every thing else.'

Catherine thought this reproach equally strange and unkind. Was it the part of a friend thus to expose her feelings to the notice of others? Isabella appeared to her ungenerous and selfish, regardless of every thing but her own gratification. These painful ideas crossed her mind, though she said nothing. Isabella, in the meanwhile, had applied her handkerchief to her eyes, and Morland, miserable at such a sight, could not help saying, 'Nay, Catherine. I think you cannot stand out any longer now. The sacrifice is not much; and to oblige such a friend – I shall think you quite unkind, if you still refuse.'

This was the first time of her brother's openly siding against her, and anxious to avoid his displeasure, she proposed a compromise. If they would only put off their scheme till Tuesday, which they might easily do, as it depended only on themselves, she could go with them, and every body might then be satisfied.

But 'No, no, no!' was the immediate answer; 'that could not be, for Thorpe did not know that he might not go to town on Tuesday.' Catherine was sorry, but could do no more; and a short silence ensued, which was broken by Isabella; who in a voice of cold resentment said, 'Very well, then there is an end of the party. If Catherine does not go, I cannot be the only woman. I would not, upon any account in the world, do so improper a thing.'

'Catherine, you must go,' said James.

'But why cannot Mr. Thorpe drive one of his other sisters? I dare say either of them would like to go.'

'Thank ye,' cried Thorpe, 'but I did not come to Bath to drive my sisters about, and look like a fool. No, if you do not go, d— me if I do. I only go for the sake of driving you.'

'That is a compliment which gives me no pleasure.' But her words were lost on Thorpe, who had turned abruptly away.

The three others still continued together, walking in a most uncomfortable manner to poor Catherine; some times not a word was said, sometimes she was again attacked with supplications or reproaches, and her arm was still linked within Isabella's, though their hearts were at war. At one moment she was softened, at another irritated; always distressed, but always steady.

'I did not think you had been so obstinate, Catherine,' said James; 'you were not used to be so hard to persuade; you once were the kindest, best-tempered of my sisters.'

'I hope I am not less so now,' she replied, very feelingly; 'but indeed I cannot go. If I am wrong, I am doing what I believe to be right.'

'I suspect,' said Isabella, in a low voice, 'there is no great struggle.'

Catherine's heart swelled; she drew away her arm, and Isabella made no opposition. Thus passed a long ten minutes, till they were again joined by Thorpe, who coming to them with a gayer look, said, 'Well, I have settled the matter, and now we may all go to-morrow with a safe conscience. I have been to Miss Tilney, and made your excuses.'

'You have not!' cried Catherine.

'I have, upon my soul. Left her this moment. Told her you had sent me to say, that having just recollected a prior engagement of going to Clifton with us to-morrow, you could not have the pleasure of walking with her till Tuesday. She said very well, Tuesday was just as convenient to her; so there is an end of all our difficulties. – A pretty good thought of mine – hey?'

Isabella's countenance was once more all smiles and good-humour, and James too looked happy again.

'A most heavenly thought indeed! Now, my sweet Catherine, all our distresses are over; you are honourably acquitted, and we shall have a most delightful party.'

'This will not do,' said Catherine; 'I cannot submit to this. I must run after Miss Tilney directly and set her right.'

Isabella, however, caught hold of one hand; Thorpe of the other; and remonstrances poured in from all three. Even James was quite angry. When every thing was settled, when Miss Tilney herself said that Tuesday would suit her as well, it was quite ridiculous, quite absurd to make any further objection.

'I do not care. Mr. Thorpe had no business to invent any such message. If I had thought it right to put it off, I could have spoken to Miss Tilney myself. This is only doing it in a ruder way; and how do I know that Mr. Thorpe has – he may be mistaken again perhaps; he led me into one act of rudeness by his mistake on Friday. Let me go, Mr. Thorpe; Isabella, do not hold me.'

Thorpe told her it would be in vain to go after the Tilneys; they were turning the corner into Brock-street, when he had overtaken them, and were at home by this time.

'Then I will go after them,' said Catherine; 'wherever they are I will go after them. It does not signify talking. If I could not be persuaded into doing what I thought wrong, I never will be tricked into it.' And with these words she broke away and hurried off. Thorpe would have darted after her, but Morland withheld him. 'Let her go, let her go, if she will go.'

'She is as obstinate as—'

Thorpe never finished the simile, for it could hardly have been a proper one.

Away walked Catherine in great agitation, as fast as the crowd would permit her, fearful of being pursued, yet determined to persevere. As she walked, she reflected on what had passed. It was painful to her to disappoint and displease them, particularly to displease her brother, but she could not repent her resistance. Setting her own inclination apart, to have failed a second time in her engagement to Miss Tilney, to have retracted a promise voluntarily made only five minutes before, and on a false pretence too, must have been wrong. She had not been withstanding them on selfish principles alone, she had not consulted merely her own gratification; *that* might have been ensured in some degree by the excursion itself, by seeing Blaize Castle; no, she had attended to what was due to others, and to her own character in their opinion. Her conviction of being right however was not enough to restore her composure, till she had spoken to Miss Tilney she could not be at ease; and quickening her pace when she got clear of the Crescent, she almost ran over the remaining ground till she gained the top of Milsom-street. So rapid had been her movements, that in spite of the Tilneys' advantage in the outset, they were but just turning into their lodgings as she came within view of them; and the servant still remaining at the open door, she used only the ceremony of saying that she must speak with Miss Tilney that moment, and hurrying by him proceeded up stairs. Then, opening the first door before her, which happened to be the right, she immediately found herself in the drawing-room with General Tilney, his son and daughter. Her explanation, defective only in being – from her irritation of nerves and shortness of breath – no explanation at all, was instantly given. 'I am come in a great hurry – It was all a mistake – I never promised to go – I told them from the first I could not go. – I ran away in a great hurry to explain it. – I did not care what you thought of me. – I would not stay for the servant.'

The business however, though not perfectly elucidated by this speech, soon ceased to be a puzzle. Catherine found that John Thorpe *had* given the message; and Miss Tilney had no scruple in owning herself greatly surprized by it. But whether

her brother had still exceeded her in resentment, Catherine, though she instinctively addressed herself as much to one as to the other in her vindication, had no means of knowing. Whatever might have been felt before her arrival, her eager declarations immediately made every look and sentence as friendly as she could desire.

The affair thus happily settled, she was introduced by Miss Tilney to her father, and received by him with such ready, such solicitous politeness as recalled Thorpe's information to her mind, and made her think with pleasure that he might be sometimes depended on. To such anxious attention was the general's civility carried, that not aware of her extraordinary swiftness in entering the house, he was quite angry with the servant whose neglect had reduced her to open the door of the apartment herself. 'What did William mean by it? He should make a point of inquiring into the matter.' And if Catherine had not most warmly asserted his innocence, it seemed likely that William would lose the favour of his master for ever, if not his place, by her rapidity.

After sitting with them a quarter of an hour,[1] she rose to take leave, and was then most agreeably surprized by General Tilney's asking her if she would do his daughter the honour of dining and spending the rest of the day with her. Miss Tilney added her own wishes. Catherine was greatly obliged; but it was quite out of her power. Mr. and Mrs. Allen would expect her back every moment. The general declared he could say no more; the claims of Mr. and Mrs. Allen were not to be superseded; but on some other day he trusted, when longer notice could be given, they would not refuse to spare her to her friend. 'Oh, no; Catherine was sure they would not have the least objection, and she should have great pleasure in coming.' The general attended her himself to the street-door, saying every thing gallant as they went down stairs, admiring the elasticity of her walk, which corresponded exactly with the spirit of her dancing and making her one of the most graceful bows she had ever beheld, when they parted.

Catherine, delighted by all that had passed, proceeded gaily to Pulteney-street; walking, as she concluded, with great elasticity, though she had never thought of it before. She reached home without seeing any thing more of the offended party; and now that she had been triumphant throughout, had carried her point and was secure of her walk, she began (as the flutter of her spirits subsided) to doubt whether she had been perfectly right. A sacrifice was always noble; and if she had given way to their entreaties, she should have been spared the distressing idea of a friend displeased, a brother angry, and a scheme of great happiness to both destroyed, perhaps through her means. To ease her mind, and ascertain by the opinion of an unprejudiced person what her own conduct had really been, she took occasion to mention before Mr. Allen the half-settled scheme of her brother and the Thorpes for the following day. Mr. Allen caught at it directly. 'Well,' said he, 'and do you think of going too?'

'No; I had just engaged myself to walk with Miss Tilney before they told me of it; and therefore you know I could not go with them, could I?'

'No certainly not; and I am glad you do not think of it. These schemes are not at all the thing. Young men and women driving about the country in open carriages! Now and then it is very well; but going to inns and public places together! It is not right; and I wonder Mrs. Thorpe should alllow it. I am glad you do not think of going; I am sure Mrs. Morland would not be pleased. Mrs. Allen, are not you of my way of thinking? Do not you think these kind of projects objectionable?'

'Yes, very much so indeed. Open carriages are nasty things. A clean gown is not five minutes wear in them. You are splashed getting in and getting out; and the wind takes your hair and your bonnet in every direction. I hate an open carriage myself.'

'I know you do; but that is not the question. Do not you think it has an odd appearance, if young ladies are frequently driven about in them by young men, to whom they are not even related?'

'Yes, my dear, a very odd appearance indeed. I cannot bear to see it.'

'Dear madam,' cried Catherine, 'then why did not you tell

me so before? I am sure if I had known it to be improper, I would not have gone with Mr. Thorpe at all; but I always hoped you would tell me, if you thought I was doing wrong.'

'And so I should, my dear, you may depend on it; for as I told Mrs. Morland at parting, I would always do the best for you in my power. But one must not be over particular. Young people *will* be young people, as your good mother says herself. You know I wanted you, when we first came, not to buy that sprigged muslin, but you would. Young people do not like to be always thwarted.'

'But this was something of real consequence; and I do not think you would have found me hard to persuade.'

'As far as it has gone hitherto, there is no harm done,' said Mr. Allen; 'and I would only advise you, my dear, not to go out with Mr. Thorpe any more.'

'That is just what I was going to say,' added his wife.

Catherine, relieved for herself, felt uneasy for Isabella; and after a moment's thought, asked Mr. Allen whether it would not be both proper and kind in her to write to Miss Thorpe, and explain the indecorum of which she must be as insensible as herself; for she considered that Isabella might otherwise perhaps be going to Clifton the next day, in spite of what had passed. Mr. Allen however discouraged her from doing any such thing. 'You had better leave her alone, my dear, she is old enough to know what she is about; and if not, has a mother to advise her. Mrs. Thorpe is too indulgent beyond a doubt; but however you had better not interfere. She and your brother chuse to go, and you will be only getting ill-will.'

Catherine submitted; and though sorry to think that Isabella should be doing wrong, felt greatly relieved by Mr. Allen's approbation of her own conduct, and truly rejoiced to be preserved by his advice from the danger of falling into such an error herself. Her escape from being one of the party to Clifton was now an escape indeed; for what would the Tilneys have thought of her, if she had broken her promise to them in order to do what was wrong in itself? if she had been guilty of one breach of propriety, only to enable her to be guilty of another?

CHAPTER XIV

THE next morning was fair, and Catherine almost expected another attack from the assembled party. With Mr. Allen to support her, she felt no dread of the event: but she would gladly be spared a contest, where victory itself was painful; and was heartily rejoiced therefore at neither seeing nor hearing any thing of them. The Tilneys called for her at the appointed time; and no new difficulty arising, no sudden recollection, no unexpected summons, no impertinent intrusion to disconcert their measures, my heroine was most unnaturally able to fulfil her engagement, though it was made with the hero himself. They determined on walking round Beechen Cliff, that noble hill, whose beautiful verdure and hanging coppice render it so striking an object from almost every opening in Bath.

'I never look at it,' said Catherine, as they walked along the side of the river, 'without thinking of the south of France.'

'You have been abroad then?' said Henry, a little surprized.

'Oh! no, I only mean what I have read about. It always puts me in mind of the country that Emily and her father travelled through, in the "Mysteries of Udolpho." But you never read novels, I dare say?'

'Why not?'

'Because they are not clever enough for you – gentlemen read better books.'

'The person, be it gentleman or lady, who has not pleasure in a good novel, must be intolerably stupid. I have read all Mrs. Radcliffe's works, and most of them with great pleasure. The Mysteries of Udolpho, when I had once begun it, I could not lay down again; – I remember finishing it in two days – my hair standing on end the whole time.'

'Yes,' added Miss Tilney, 'and I remember that you undertook to read it aloud to me, and that when I was called away for only five minutes to answer a note, instead of waiting for me, you took the volume into the Hermitage-walk, and I was obliged to stay till you had finished it.'

'Thank you, Eleanor; – a most honourable testimony. You see, Miss Morland, the injustice of your suspicions. Here was I, in my eagerness to get on, refusing to wait only five minutes for my sister; breaking the promise I had made of reading it aloud, and keeping her in suspense at a most interesting part, by running away with the volume, which, you are to observe, was her own, particularly her own. I am proud when I reflect on it, and I think it must establish me in your good opinion.'

'I am very glad to hear it indeed, and now I shall never be ashamed of liking Udolpho myself. But I really thought before, young men despised novels amazingly.'

'It is *amazingly*; it may well suggest *amazement* if they do – for they read nearly as many as women. I myself have read hundreds and hundreds. Do not imagine that you can cope with me in a knowledge of Julias and Louisas.[1] If we proceed to particulars, and engage in the never-ceasing inquiry of "Have you read this?" and "Have you read that?" I shall soon leave you as far behind me as – what shall I say? – I want an appropriate simile; – as far as your friend Emily herself left poor Valancourt when she went with her aunt into Italy. Consider how many years I have had the start of you. I had entered on my studies at Oxford, while you were a good little girl working your sampler at home!'

'Not very good I am afraid. But now really, do not you think Udolpho the nicest book in the world?'

'The nicest;[2] – by which I suppose you mean the neatest. That must depend upon the binding.'

'Henry,' said Miss Tilney, 'you are very impertinent. Miss Morland, he is treating you exactly as he does his sister. He is for ever finding fault with me, for some incorrectness of language, and now he is taking the same liberty with you. The word "nicest," as you used it, did not suit him; and you had better change it as soon as you can, or we shall be overpowered with Johnson and Blair[3] all the rest of the way.'

'I am sure,' cried Catherine, 'I did not mean to say any thing wrong; but it *is* a nice book, and why should not I call it so?'

'Very true,' said Henry, 'and this is a very nice day, and

we are taking a very nice walk, and you are two very nice young ladies. Oh! it is a very nice word indeed! – it does for every thing. Originally perhaps it was applied only to express neatness, propriety, delicacy, or refinement; – people were nice in their dress, in their sentiments, or their choice. But now every commendation on every subject is comprised in that one word.'

'While, in fact,' cried his sister, 'it ought only to be applied to you, without any commendation at all. You are more nice than wise. Come, Miss Morland, let us leave him to meditate over our faults in the utmost propriety of diction, while we praise Udolpho in whatever terms we like best. It is a most interesting work. You are fond of that kind of reading?'

'To say the truth, I do not much like any other.'

'Indeed!'

'That is, I can read poetry and plays, and things of that sort, and do not dislike travels. But history, real solemn history, I cannot be interested in. Can you?'

'Yes, I am fond of history.'

'I wish I were too. I read it a little as a duty, but it tells me nothing that does not either vex or weary me. The quarrels of popes and kings, with wars or pestilences, in every page; the men all so good for nothing, and hardly any women at all – it is very tiresome: and yet I often think it odd that it should be so dull, for a great deal of it must be invention. The speeches that are put into the heroes' mouths, their thoughts and designs – the chief of all this must be invention, and invention is what delights me in other books.'

'Historians, you think,' said Miss Tilney, 'are not happy in their flights of fancy. They display imagination without raising interest. I am fond of history – and am very well contented to take the false with the true. In the principal facts they have sources of intelligence in former histories and records, which may be as much depended on, I conclude, as any thing that does not actually pass under one's own observation; and as for the little embellishments you speak of, they are embellishments, and I like them as such. If a speech be well drawn up, I read it with pleasure, by whomsoever it may be made – and probably with much greater, if the production of Mr. Hume or Mr. Robertson,[1] than if the genuine words of Caractacus, Agricola, or Alfred the Great.'

'You are fond of history! – and so are Mr. Allen and my father; and I have two brothers who do not dislike it. So many instances within my small circle of friends is remarkable! At this rate, I shall not pity the writers of history any longer. If people like to read their books, it is all very well, but to be at so much trouble in filling great volumes, which, as I used to think, nobody would willingly ever look into, to be labouring only for the torment of little boys and girls, always struck me as a hard fate; and though I know it is all very right and necessary, I have often wondered at the person's courage that could sit down on purpose to do it.'

'That little boys and girls should be tormented,' said Henry, 'is what no one at all acquainted with human nature in a civilized state can deny; but in behalf of our most distinguished historians, I must observe, that they might well be offended at being supposed to have no higher aim; and that by their method and style, they are perfectly well qualified to torment readers of the most advanced reason and mature time of life. I use the verb "to torment," as I observed to be your own method, instead of "to instruct," supposing them to be now admitted as synonimous.'

'You think me foolish to call instruction a torment, but if you had been as much used as myself to hear poor little children first learning their letters and then learning to spell, if you had ever seen how stupid they can be for a whole morning together, and how tired my poor mother is at the end of it, as I am in the habit of seeing almost every day of my life at home, you would allow that to *torment* and to *instruct* might sometimes be used as synonimous words.'

'Very probably. But historians are not accountable for the difficulty of learning to read; and even you yourself, who do not altogether seem particularly friendly to very severe, very intense application, may perhaps be brought to acknowledge that it is very well worth while to be tormented for two or three years of one's life, for the sake of being able to read all the rest of it.

Consider – if reading had not been taught, Mrs. Radcliffe would have written in vain – or perhaps might not have written at all.'

Catherine assented – and a very warm panegyric from her on that lady's merits, closed the subject. – The Tilneys were soon engaged in another on which she had nothing to say. They were viewing the country with the eyes of persons accustomed to drawing, and decided on its capability of being formed into pictures, with all the eagerness of real taste. Here Catherine was quite lost. She knew nothing of drawing – nothing of taste: – and she listened to them with an attention which brought her little profit, for they talked in phrases which conveyed scarcely any idea to her. The little which she could understand however appeared to contradict the very few notions she had entertained on the matter before. It seemed as if a good view were no longer to be taken from the top of an high hill, and that a clear blue sky was no longer a proof of a fine day. She was heartily ashamed of her ignorance. A misplaced shame. Where people wish to attach, they should always be ignorant. To come with a well-informed mind, is to come with an inability of administering to the vanity of others, which a sensible person would always wish to avoid. A woman especially, if she have the misfortune of knowing any thing, should conceal it as well as she can.

The advantages of natural folly in a beautiful girl have been already set forth by the capital pen of a sister author;[1] – and to her treatment of the subject I will only add in justice to men, that though to the larger and more trifling part of the sex, imbecility in females is a great enhancement of their personal charms, there is a portion of them too reasonable and too well informed themselves to desire any thing more in woman than ignorance. But Catherine did not know her own advantages – did not know that a good-looking girl, with an affectionate heart and a very ignorant mind, cannot fail of attracting a clever young man, unless circumstances are particularly untoward. In the present instance, she confessed and lamented her want of knowledge: declared that she would give any thing in the world to be able to draw; and a lecture on the picturesque immediately followed, in which his instructions were so clear that she soon began to see beauty in every thing admired by him, and her attention was so earnest, that he became perfectly satisfied of her having a great deal of natural taste. He talked of fore-grounds, distances, and second distances – side-screens and perspectives – lights and shades;[1] – and Catherine was so hopeful a scholar, that when they gained the top of Beechen Cliff, she voluntarily rejected the whole city of Bath, as unworthy to make part of a landscape. Delighted with her progress, and fearful of wearying her with too much wisdom at once, Henry suffered the subject to decline, and by an easy transition from a piece of rocky fragment and the withered oak which he had placed near its summit, to oaks in general, to forests, the inclosure of them, waste lands, crown lands and government, he shortly found himself arrived at politics; and from politics, it was an easy step to silence. The general pause which succeeded his short disquisition on the state of the nation, was put an end to by Catherine, who, in rather a solemn tone of voice, uttered these words, 'I have heard that something very shocking indeed, will soon come out in London.'

Miss Tilney, to whom this was chiefly addressed, was startled, and hastily replied, 'Indeed! – and of what nature?'

'That I do not know, nor who is the author. I have only heard that it is to be more horrible than any thing we have met with yet.'

'Good heaven! – Where could you hear of such a thing?'

'A particular friend of mine had an account of it in a letter from London yesterday. It is to be uncommonly dreadful. I shall expect murder and every thing of the kind.'

'You speak with astonishing composure! But I hope your friend's accounts have been exaggerated; – and if such a design is known beforehand, proper measures will undoubtedly be taken by government to prevent its coming to effect.'

'Government,' said Henry, endeavouring not to smile, 'neither desires nor dares to interfere in such matters. There must be murder; and government cares not how much.'

The ladies stared. He laughed, and added, 'Come, shall I

make you understand each other, or leave you to puzzle out an explanation as you can? No – I will be noble. I will prove myself a man, no less by the generosity of my soul than the clearness of my head. I have no patience with such of my sex as disdain to let themselves sometimes down to the comprehension of yours. Perhaps the abilities of women are neither sound nor acute – neither vigorous nor keen. Perhaps they may want observation, discernment, judgment, fire, genius, and wit.'

'Miss Morland, do not mind what he says; – but have the goodness to satisfy me as to this dreadful riot.'

'Riot! – what riot?'

'My dear Eleanor, the riot is only in your own brain. The confusion there is scandalous. Miss Morland has been talking of nothing more dreadful than a new publication which is shortly to come out, in three duodecimo volumes, two hundred and seventy-six pages in each, with a frontispiece to the first, of two tombstones and a lantern – do you understand? – And you, Miss Morland – my stupid sister has mistaken all your clearest expressions. You talked of expected horrors in London – and instead of instantly conceiving, as any rational creature would have done, that such words could relate only to a circulating library, she immediately pictured to herself a mob of three thousand men assembling in St. George's Fields;[1] the Bank attacked, the Tower threatened, the streets of London flowing with blood, a detachment of the 12th Light Dragoons, (the hopes of the nation,) called up from Northampton[2] to quell the insurgents, and the gallant Capt. Frederick Tilney, in the moment of charging at the head of his troop, knocked off his horse by a brickbat from an upper window. Forgive her stupidity. The fears of the sister have added to the weakness of the woman; but she is by no means a simpleton in general.'

Catherine looked grave. 'And now, Henry,' said Miss Tilney, 'that you have made us understand each other, you may as well make Miss Morland understand yourself – unless you mean to have her think you intolerably rude to your sister, and a great brute in your opinion of women in general. Miss Morland is not used to your odd ways.'

'I shall be most happy to make her better acquainted with them.'

'No doubt; – but that is no explanation of the present.'

'What am I to do?'

'You know what you ought to do. Clear your character hand-somely before her. Tell her that you think very highly of the understanding of women.'

'Miss Morland, I think very highly of the understanding of all the women in the world – especially of those – whoever they may be – with whom I happen to be in company.'

'That is not enough. Be more serious.'

'Miss Morland, no one can think more highly of the under-standing of women than I do. In my opinion, nature has given them so much, that they never find it necessary to use more than half.'

'We shall get nothing more serious from him now, Miss Morland. He is not in a sober mood. But I do assure you that he must be entirely misunderstood, if he can ever appear to say an unjust thing of any woman at all, or an unkind one of me.'

It was no effort to Catherine to believe that Henry Tilney could never be wrong. His manner might sometimes surprize, but his meaning must always be just: – and what she did not understand, she was almost as ready to admire, as what she did. The whole walk was delightful, and though it ended too soon, its conclusion was delightful too; – her friends attended her into the house, and Miss Tilney, before they parted, addressing her-self with respectful form, as much to Mrs. Allen as to Catherine, petitioned for the pleasure of her company to dinner on the day after the next. No difficulty was made on Mrs. Allen's side – and the only difficulty on Catherine's was in concealing the excess of her pleasure.

The morning had passed away so charmingly as to banish all her friendship and natural affection; for no thought of Isabella or James had crossed her during their walk. When the Tilneys were gone, she became amiable again, but she was amiable for some time to little effect; Mrs. Allen had no intel-ligence to give that could relieve her anxiety, she had heard nothing of any of them. Towards the end of the morning however, Catherine having occasion for some indispensable yard of ribbon which must be bought without a moment's delay, walked out into the town, and in Bond-street overtook the second Miss Thorpe, as she was loitering towards Edgar's Buildings between two of the sweetest girls in the world, who had been her dear friends all the morning. From her, she soon learned that the party to Clifton had taken place. 'They set off at eight this morning,' said Miss Anne, 'and I am sure I do not envy them their drive. I think you and I are very well off to be out of the scrape. – It must be the dullest thing in the world, for there is not a soul at Clifton at this time of year. Belle went with your brother, and John drove Maria.'

Catherine spoke the pleasure she really felt on hearing this part of the arrangement.

'Oh! yes,' rejoined the other, 'Maria is gone. She was quite wild to go. She thought it would be something very fine. I cannot say I admire her taste; and for my part I was determined from the first not to go, if they pressed me ever so much.'

Catherine, a little doubtful of this, could not help answering, 'I wish you could have gone too. It is a pity you could not all go.'

'Thank you; but it is quite a matter of indifference to me. Indeed, I would not have gone on any account. I was saying so to Emily and Sophia when you overtook us.'

Catherine was still unconvinced; but glad that Anne should have the friendship of an Emily and a Sophia to console her, she bade her adieu without much uneasiness, and returned home, pleased that the party had not been prevented by her refusing to join it, and very heartily wishing that it might be too pleasant to allow either James or Isabella to resent her resistance any longer.

CHAPTER XV

EARLY the next day, a note from Isabella, speaking peace and tenderness in every line, and entreating the immediate presence of her friend on a matter of the utmost importance, hastened Catherine, in the happiest state of confidence and curiosity, to Edgar's Buildings. – The two youngest Miss Thorpes were by themselves in the parlour; and, on Anne's quitting it to call her sister, Catherine took the opportunity of asking the other for some particulars of their yesterday's party. Maria desired no greater pleasure than to speak of it; and Catherine immediately learnt that it had been altogether the most delightful scheme in the world; that nobody could imagine how charming it had been, and that it had been more delightful than any body could conceive. Such was the information of the first five minutes; the second unfolded thus much in detail, – that they had driven directly to the York Hotel, ate some soup, and bespoke an early dinner, walked down to the Pump-room, tasted the water, and laid out some shillings in purses and spars;[1] thence adjourned to eat ice at a pastry-cook's, and hurrying back to the Hotel, swallowed their dinner in haste, to prevent being in the dark; and then had a delightful drive back, only the moon was not up, and it rained a little, and Mr. Morland's horse was so tired he could hardly get it along.

Catherine listened with heartfelt satisfaction. It appeared that Blaize Castle had never been thought of; and, as for all the rest, there was nothing to regret for half an instant. – Maria's intelligence concluded with a tender effusion of pity for her sister Anne, whom she represented as insupportably cross, from being excluded the party.

'She will never forgive me, I am sure; but, you know, how could I help it? John would have me go, for he vowed he would not drive her, because she had such thick ancles. I dare say she will not be in good humour again this month; but I am determined I will not be cross; it is not a little matter that puts me out of temper.'

Isabella now entered the room with so eager a step, and a look of such happy importance, as engaged all her friend's notice. Maria was without ceremony sent away, and Isabella, embracing Catherine, thus began: – 'Yes, my dear Catherine, it is so indeed; your penetration has not deceived you. – Oh! that arch eye of yours! – It sees through every thing.'

Catherine replied only by a look of wondering ignorance.

'Nay, my beloved, sweetest friend,' continued the other, 'compose yourself. – I am amazingly agitated, as you perceive. Let us sit down and talk in comfort. Well, and so you guessed it the moment you had my note? – Sly creature! – Oh! my dear Catherine, you alone who know my heart can judge of my present happiness. Your brother is the most charming of men. I only wish I were more worthy of him. – But what will your excellent father and mother say? – Oh! heavens! when I think of them I am so agitated!'

Catherine's understanding began to awake: an idea of the truth suddenly darted into her mind; and, with the natural blush of so new an emotion, she cried out, 'Good heaven! – my dear Isabella, what do you mean? Can you – can you really be in love with James?'

This bold surmise, however, she soon learnt comprehended but half the fact. The anxious affection, which she was accused of having continually watched in Isabella's every look and action, had, in the course of their yesterday's party, received the delightful confession of an equal love. Her heart and faith were alike engaged to James. – Never had Catherine listened to any thing so full of interest, wonder, and joy. Her brother and her friend engaged! – New to such circumstances, the importance of it appeared unspeakably great, and she contemplated it as one of those grand events, of which the ordinary course of life can hardly afford a return. The strength of her feelings she could not express; the nature of them, however, contented her friend. The happiness of having such a sister was their first effusion, and the fair ladies mingled in embraces and tears of joy.

Delighting, however, as Catherine sincerely did in the prospect of the connexion, it must be acknowledged that Isabella far surpassed her in tender anticipations. – 'You will be so infinitely dearer to me, my Catherine, than either Anne or Maria: I feel that I shall be so much more attached to my dear Morland's family than to my own.'

This was a pitch of friendship beyond Catherine.

'You are so like your dear brother,' continued Isabella, 'that I quite doated on you the first moment I saw you. But so it always is with me; the first moment settles every thing. The very first day that Morland came to us last Christmas – the very first moment I beheld him – my heart was irrecoverably gone. I remember I wore my yellow gown, with my hair done up in braids; and when I came into the drawing-room, and John introduced him, I thought I never saw any body so handsome before.'

Here Catherine secretly acknowledged the power of love; for, though exceedingly fond of her brother, and partial to all his endowments, she had never in her life thought him handsome.

'I remember too, Miss Andrews drank tea with us that evening, and wore her puce-coloured sarsenet;[1] and she looked so heavenly, that I thought your brother must certainly fall in love with her; I could not sleep a wink all night for thinking of it. Oh! Catherine, the many sleepless nights I have had on your brother's account! – I would not have you suffer half what I have done! I am grown wretchedly thin I know; but I will not pain you by describing my anxiety; you have seen enough of it. I feel that I have betrayed myself perpetually; – so unguarded in speaking of my partiality for the church! – But my secret I was always sure would be safe with *you*.'

Catherine felt that nothing could have been safer; but ashamed of an ignorance little expected, she dared no longer contest the point, nor refuse to have been as full of arch penetration and affectionate sympathy as Isabella chose to consider her. Her brother she found was preparing to set off with all speed to Fullerton, to make known his situation and ask consent; and here was a source of some real agitation to the mind of Isabella. Catherine endeavoured to persuade her, as she was herself persuaded, that her father and mother would never oppose their son's wishes. – 'It is impossible,' said she, 'for parents to be more kind, or more desirous of their children's happiness; I have no doubt of their consenting immediately.'

'Morland says exactly the same,' replied Isabella; 'and yet I dare not expect it; my fortune will be so small; they never can consent to it. Your brother, who might marry any body!'

Here Catherine again discerned the force of love.

'Indeed, Isabella, you are too humble. – The difference of fortune can be nothing to signify.'

'Oh! my sweet Catherine, in *your* generous heart I know it would signify nothing; but we must not expect such disinterestedness in many. As for myself, I am sure I only wish our situations were reversed. Had I the command of millions, were I mistress of the whole world, your brother would be my only choice.'

This charming sentiment, recommended as much by sense as novelty, gave Catherine a most pleasing remembrance of all the heroines of her acquaintance; and she thought her friend never looked more lovely than in uttering the grand idea. – 'I am sure they will consent,' was her frequent declaration; 'I am sure they will be delighted with you.'

'For my own part,' said Isabella, 'my wishes are so moderate, that the smallest income in nature would be enough for me. Where people are really attached, poverty itself is wealth: grandeur I detest: I would not settle in London for the universe. A cottage in some retired village would be extasy. There are some charming little villas about Richmond.'

'Richmond!' cried Catherine. – 'You must settle near Fullerton. You must be near us.'

'I am sure I shall be miserable if we do not. If I can but be near *you*, I shall be satisfied. But this is idle talking! I will not allow myself to think of such things, till we have your father's answer. Morland says that by sending it to-night to Salisbury, we may have it to-morrow. – To-morrow? – I know I shall never have courage to open the letter. I know it will be the death of me.'

A reverie succeeded this conviction – and when Isabella spoke again, it was to resolve on the quality of her wedding-gown.

Their conference was put an end to by the anxious young lover himself, who came to breathe his parting sigh before he set off for Wiltshire. Catherine wished to congratulate him, but knew not what to say, and her eloquence was only in her eyes. From them however the eight parts of speech shone out most expressively, and James could combine them with ease. Impatient for the realization of all that he hoped at home, his adieus were not long; and they would have been yet shorter, had he not been frequently detained by the urgent entreaties of his fair one that he would go. Twice was he called almost from the door by her eagerness to have him gone. 'Indeed, Morland, I must drive you away. Consider how far you have to ride. I cannot bear to see you linger so. For Heaven's sake, waste no more time. There, go, go – I insist on it.'

The two friends, with hearts now more united than ever, were inseparable for the day; and in schemes of sisterly happiness the hours flew along. Mrs. Thorpe and her son, who were acquainted with every thing, and who seemed only to want Mr. Morland's consent, to consider Isabella's engagement as the most fortunate circumstance imaginable for their family, were allowed to join their counsels, and add their quota of significant looks and mysterious expressions to fill up the measure of curiosity to be raised in the unprivileged younger sisters. To Catherine's simple feelings, this odd sort of reserve seemed neither kindly meant, nor consistently supported; and its unkindness she would hardly have forborn pointing out, had its inconsistency been less their friend; – but Anne and Maria soon set her heart at ease by the sagacity of their 'I know what;' and the evening was spent in a sort of war of wit, a display of family ingenuity; on one side in the mystery of an affected secret, on the other of undefined discovery, all equally acute.

Catherine was with her friend again the next day, endeavouring to support her spirits, and while away the many tedious hours before the delivery of the letters; a needful exertion, for as the time of reasonable expectation drew near, Isabella became more and more desponding, and before the letter arrived, had worked herself into a state of real distress. But when it did come, where could distress be found? 'I have had no difficulty in gaining the consent of my kind parents, and am promised that every thing in their power shall be done to forward my happiness,' were the first three lines, and in one moment all was joyful security. The brightest glow was instantly spread over Isabella's features, all care and anxiety seemed removed, her spirits became almost too high for controul, and she called herself without scruple the happiest of mortals.

Mrs. Thorpe, with tears of joy, embraced her daughter, her son, her visitor, and could have embraced half the inhabitants of Bath with satisfaction. Her heart was overflowing with tenderness. It was 'dear John,' and 'dear Catherine' at every word; – 'dear Anne and dear Maria' must immediately be made sharers in their felicity; and two 'dears' at once before the name of Isabella were not more than that beloved child had now well earned. John himself was no skulker in joy. He not only bestowed on Mr. Morland the high commendation of being one of the finest fellows in the world, but swore off many sentences in his praise.

The letter, whence sprang all this felicity, was short, containing little more than this assurance of success; and every particular was deferred till James could write again. But for particulars Isabella could well afford to wait. The needful was comprised in Mr. Morland's promise; his honour was pledged to make every thing easy; and by what means their income was to be formed, whether landed property were to be resigned, or funded money made over, was a matter in which her disinterested spirit took no concern. She knew enough to feel secure of an honourable and speedy establishment, and her imagination took a rapid flight over its attendant felicities. She saw herself at the end of a few weeks, the gaze and admiration of every new acquaintance at Fullerton, the envy of every valued old friend in Putney, with a carriage at her command, a new name on her tickets,[1] and a brilliant exhibition of hoop rings[2] on her finger.

When the contents of the letter were ascertained, John Thorpe, who had only waited its arrival to begin his journey to London, prepared to set off. 'Well, Miss Morland,' said he, on finding her alone in the parlour, 'I am come to bid you good bye.' Catherine wished him a good journey. Without appearing to hear her, he walked to the window, fidgetted about, hummed a tune, and seemed wholly self-occupied.

'Shall not you be late at Devizes?'[1] said Catherine. He made no answer; but after a minute's silence burst out with, 'A famous good thing this marrying scheme, upon my soul! A clever fancy of Morland's and Belle's. What do you think of it, Miss Morland? *I* say it is no bad notion.'

'I am sure I think it a very good one.'

'Do you? – that's honest, by heavens! I am glad you are no enemy to matrimony however. Did you ever hear the old song, "Going to one wedding brings on another?" I say, you will come to Belle's wedding, I hope.'

'Yes; I have promised your sister to be with her, if possible.'

'And then you know' – twisting himself about and forcing a foolish laugh – 'I say, then you know, we may try the truth of this same old song.'

'May we? – but I never sing. Well, I wish you a good journey. I dine with Miss Tilney to-day, and must now be going home.'

'Nay, but there is no such confounded hurry. – Who knows when we may be together again? – Not but that I shall be down again by the end of a fortnight, and a devilish long fort-night it will appear to me.'

'Then why do you stay away so long?' replied Catherine – finding that he waited for an answer.

'That is kind of you, however – kind and good-natured. – I shall not forget it in a hurry. – But you have more good-nature and all that, than any body living I believe. A monstrous deal of good-nature, and it is not only good-nature, but you have so much, so much of every thing; and then you have such – upon my soul I do not know any body like you.'

'Oh! dear, there are a great many people like me, I dare say, only a great deal better. Good morning to you.'

'But I say, Miss Morland, I shall come and pay my respects at Fullerton before it is long, if not disagreeable.'

'Pray do. – My father and mother will be very glad to see you.'

'And I hope – I hope, Miss Morland, *you* will not be sorry to see me.'

'Oh! dear, not at all. There are very few people I am sorry to see. Company is always cheerful.'

'That is just my way of thinking. Give me but a little cheerful company, let me only have the company of the people I love, let me only be where I like and with whom I like, and the devil take the rest, say I. – And I am hearily glad to hear you say the same. But I have a notion, Miss Morland, you and I think pretty much alike upon most matters.'

'Perhaps we may; but it is more than I ever thought of. And as to *most matters*, to say the truth, there are not many that I know my own mind about.'

'By Jove, no more do I. It is not my way to bother my brains with what does not concern me. My notion of things is simple enough. Let me only have the girl I like, say I, with a comfortable house over my head, and what care I for all the rest? Fortune is nothing. I am sure of a good income of my own; and if she had not a penny, why so much the better.'

'Very true. I think like you there. If there is a good fortune on one side, there can be no occasion for any on the other. No matter which has it, so that there is enough. I hate the idea of one great fortune looking out for another.[1] And to marry for money I think the wickedest thing in existence. – Good day. – We shall be very glad to see you at Fullerton, whenever it is convenient.' And away she went. It was not in the power of all his gallantry to detain her longer. With such news to communicate, and such a visit to prepare for, her departure was not to be delayed by any thing in his nature to urge; and she hurried away, leaving him to the undivided consciousness of his own happy address, and her explicit encouragement.

The agitation which she had herself experienced on first learning her brother's engagement, made her expect to raise no inconsiderable emotion in Mr. and Mrs. Allen, by the communication of the wonderful event. How great was her disappointment! The important affair, which many words of preparation ushered in, had been foreseen by them both ever since her brother's arrival; and all that they felt on the occasion was comprehended in a wish for the young people's happiness, with a remark, on the gentleman's side, in favour of Isabella's beauty, and on the lady's, of her great good luck. It was to Catherine the most surprizing insensibility. The disclosure however of the great secret of James's going to Fullerton the day before, did raise some emotion in Mrs. Allen. She could not listen to that with perfect calmness; but repeatedly regretted the necessity of its concealment, wished she could have known his intention, wished she could have seen him before he went, as she should certainly have troubled him with her best regards to his father and mother, and her kind compliments to all the Skinners.

VOLUME II

CHAPTER I

CATHERINE'S expectations of pleasure from her visit in Milsom-street were so very high, that disappointment was inevitable; and accordingly, though she was most politely received by General Tilney, and kindly welcomed by his daughter, though Henry was at home, and no one else of the party, she found, on her return, without spending many hours in the examination of her feelings, that she had gone to her appointment preparing for happiness which it had not afforded. Instead of finding herself improved in acquaintance with Miss Tilney, from the inter-course of the day, she seemed hardly so intimate with her as before; instead of seeing Henry Tilney to greater advantage than ever, in the ease of a family party, he had never said so little, nor been so little agreeable; and, in spite of their father's great civilities to her – in spite of his thanks, invitations, and compliments – it had been a release to get away from him. It puzzled her to account for all this. It could not be General Tilney's fault. That he was perfectly agreeable and good-natured, and altogether a very charming man, did not admit of a doubt, for he was tall and handsome, and Henry's father. *He* could not be accountable for his children's want of spirits, or for her want of enjoyment in his company. The former she hoped at last might have been accidental, and the latter she could only attri-bute to her own stupidity. Isabella, on hearing the particulars of the visit, gave a different explanation: 'It was all pride, pride, insufferable haughtiness and pride! She had long suspected the family to be very high, and this made it certain. Such insolence of behaviour as Miss Tilney's she had never heard of in her life!

Not to do the honours of her house with common good-breeding!
– To behave to her guest with such superciliousness! – Hardly
even to speak to her!'

'But it was not so bad as that, Isabella; there was no superciliousness; she was very civil.'

'Oh! don't defend her! And then the brother, he, who had
appeared so attached to you! Good heavens! well, some people's
feelings are incomprehensible. And so he hardly looked once at
you the whole day?'

'I do not say so: but he did not seem in good spirits.'

'How contemptible! Of all things in the world inconstancy is
my aversion. Let me entreat you never to think of him again,
my dear Catherine; indeed he is unworthy of you.'

'Unworthy! I do not suppose he ever thinks of me.'

'That is exactly what I say; he never thinks of you. – Such
fickleness! Oh! how different to your brother and to mine!
I really believe John has the most constant heart.'

'But as for General Tilney, I assure you it would be impossible for any body to behave to me with greater civility and
attention; it seemed to be his only care to entertain and make me
happy.'

'Oh! I know no harm of him; I do not suspect him of pride. I
believe he is a very gentleman-like man. John thinks very well
of him, and John's judgment—'

'Well, I shall see how they behave to me this evening; we
shall meet them at the rooms.'

'And must I go?'

'Do not you intend it? I thought it was all settled.'

'Nay, since you make such a point of it, I can refuse you
nothing. But do not insist upon my being very agreeable, for my
heart, you know, will be some forty miles off. And as for dancing,
do not mention it I beg; *that* is quite out of the question. Charles
Hodges will plague me to death I dare say; but I shall cut him
very short. Ten to one but he guesses the reason, and that is
exactly what I want to avoid, so I shall insist on his keeping his
conjecture to himself.'

Isabella's opinion of the Tilneys did not influence her friend;

she was sure there had been no insolence in the manners either
of brother or sister; and she did not credit there being any pride
in their hearts. The evening rewarded her confidence; she was
met by one with the same kindness, and by the other with the
same attention as heretofore: Miss Tilney took pains to be near
her, and Henry asked her to dance.

Having heard the day before in Milsom-street, that their
elder brother, Captain Tilney, was expected almost every hour,
she was at no loss for the name of a very fashionable-looking,
handsome young man, whom she had never seen before, and
who now evidently belonged to their party. She looked at him
with great admiration, and even supposed it possible, that some
people might think him handsomer than his brother, though, in
her eyes, his air was more assuming, and his countenance less
prepossessing. His taste and manners were beyond a doubt
decidedly inferior; for, within her hearing, he not only protested
against every thought of dancing himself, but even laughed
openly at Henry for finding it possible. From the latter circumstance it may be presumed, that, whatever might be our heroine's
opinion of him, his admiration of her was not of a very dangerous
kind; not likely to produce animosities between the brothers,
nor persecutions to the lady. *He* cannot be the instigator of the
three villains in horsemen's great coats, by whom she will
hereafter be forced into a travelling-chaise and four, which will
drive off with incredible speed. Catherine, meanwhile, undisturbed by presentiments of such an evil, or of any evil at all,
except that of having but a short set to dance down, enjoyed her
usual happiness with Henry Tilney, listening with sparkling
eyes to every thing he said; and, in finding him irresistible,
becoming so herself.

At the end of the first dance, Captain Tilney came towards
them again, and, much to Catherine's dissatisfaction, pulled his
brother away. They retired whispering together; and, though
her delicate sensibility did not take immediate alarm, and lay it
down as fact, that Captain Tilney must have heard some mal-
evolent misrepresentation of her, which he now hastened to
communicate to his brother, in the hope of separating them for

ever, she could not have her partner conveyed from her sight without very uneasy sensations. Her suspense was of full five minutes' duration; and she was beginning to think it a very long quarter of an hour, when they both returned, and an explanation was given, by Henry's requesting to know, if she thought her friend, Miss Thorpe, would have any objection to dancing, as his brother would be most happy to be introduced to her. Catherine, without hesitation, replied, that she was very sure Miss Thorpe did not mean to dance at all. The cruel reply was passed on to the other, and he immediately walked away.

'Your brother will not mind it I know,' said she, 'because I heard him say before, that he hated dancing; but it was very good-natured in him to think of it. I suppose he saw Isabella sitting down, and fancied she might wish for a partner; but he is quite mistaken, for she would not dance upon any account in the world.'

Henry smiled, and said, 'How very little trouble it can give you to understand the motive of other people's actions.'

'Why? – What do you mean?'

'With you, it is not, How is such a one likely to be influenced? What is the inducement most likely to act upon such a person's feelings, age, situation, and probable habits of life considered? – but, how should *I* be influenced, what would be *my* inducement in acting so and so?'

'I do not understand you.'

'Then we are on very unequal terms, for I understand you perfectly well.'

'Me? – yes; I cannot speak well enough to be unintelligible.'[1]

'Bravo! – an excellent satire on modern language.'

'But pray tell me what you mean.'

'Shall I indeed? – Do you really desire it? – But you are not aware of the consequences; it will involve you in a very cruel embarrassment, and certainly bring on a disagreement between us.'

'No, no; it shall not do either; I am not afraid.'

'Well then, I only meant that your attributing my brother's wish of dancing with Miss Thorpe to good-nature alone, convinced me of your being superior in good-nature yourself to all the rest of the world.'

Catherine blushed and disclaimed, and the gentleman's predictions were verified. There was a something, however, in his words which repaid her for the pain of confusion; and that something occupied her mind so much, that she drew back for some time, forgetting to speak or to listen, and almost forgetting where she was; till, roused by the voice of Isabella, she looked up and saw her with Captain Tilney preparing to give them hands across.

Isabella shrugged her shoulders and smiled, the only explanation of this extraordinary change which could at that time be given; but as it was not quite enough for Catherine's comprehension, she spoke her astonishment in very plain terms to her partner.

'I cannot think how it could happen! Isabella was so determined not to dance.'

'And did Isabella never change her mind before?'

'Oh! but, because – and your brother! – After what you told him from me, how could he think of going to ask her?'

'I cannot take surprize to myself on that head. You bid me be surprized on your friend's account, and therefore I am; but as for my brother, his conduct in the business, I must own, has been no more than I believed him perfectly equal to. The fairness of your friend was an open attraction; her firmness, you know, could only be understood by yourself.'

'You are laughing; but I assure you, Isabella is very firm in general.'

'It is as much as should be said of any one. To be always firm must be to be often obstinate. When properly to relax is the trial of judgment; and, without reference to my brother, I really think Miss Thorpe has by no means chosen ill in fixing on the present hour.'

The friends were not able to get together for any confidential discourse till all the dancing was over; but then, as they walked about the room arm in arm, Isabella thus explained herself: – 'I do not wonder at your surprize; and I am really fatigued to death. He is such a rattle! – Amusing enough, if my mind had been disengaged; but I would have given the world to sit still.'

'Then why did not you?'

'Oh! my dear! it would have looked so particular; and you know how I abhor doing that. I refused him as long as I possibly could, but he would take no denial. You have no idea how he pressed me. I begged him to excuse me, and get some other partner – but no, not he; after aspiring to my hand, there was nobody else in the room he could bear to think of; and it was not that he wanted merely to dance, he wanted to be with *me*. Oh! such nonsense! – I told him he had taken a very unlikely way to prevail upon me; for, of all things in the world, I hated fine speeches and compliments; – and so—and so then I found there would be no peace if I did not stand up. Besides, I thought Mrs. Hughes, who introduced him, might take it ill if I did not: and your dear brother, I am sure he would have been miserable if I had sat down the whole evening. I am so glad it is over! My spirits are quite jaded with listening to his nonsense: and then, – being such a smart young fellow, I saw every eye was upon us.'

'He is very handsome indeed.'

'Handsome! – Yes, I suppose he may. I dare say people would admire him in general; but he is not at all in my style of beauty. I hate a florid complexion and dark eyes in a man. However, he is very well. Amazingly conceited, I am sure. I took him down several times you know in my way.'

When the young ladies next met, they had a far more interesting subject to discuss. James Morland's second letter was then received, and the kind intentions of his father fully explained. A living, of which Mr. Morland was himself patron and incumbent, of about four hundred pounds yearly value, was to be resigned to his son as soon as he should be old enough to take it; no trifling deduction from the family income, no niggardly assignment to one of ten children. An estate of at least equal value, moreover, was assured as his future inheritance.

James expressed himself on the occasion with becoming gratitude; and the necessity of waiting between two and three years before they could marry, being, however unwelcome, no more than he had expected, was born by him without discontent. Catherine, whose expectations had been as unfixed as her ideas of her father's income, and whose judgment was now entirely led by her brother, felt equally well satisfied, and heartily congratulated Isabella on having every thing so pleasantly settled.

'It is very charming indeed,' said Isabella, with a grave face. 'Mr. Morland has behaved vastly handsome indeed,' said the gentle Mrs. Thorpe, looking anxiously at her daughter. 'I only wish I could do as much. One could not expect more from him you know. If he finds he *can* do more by and bye, I dare say he will, for I am sure he must be an excellent good hearted man. Four hundred is but a small income to begin on indeed, but your wishes, my dear Isabella, are so moderate, you do not consider how little you ever want, my dear.'

'It is not on my own account I wish for more; but I cannot bear to be the means of injuring my dear Morland, making him sit down upon an income hardly enough to find one in the common necessaries of life. For myself, it is nothing; I never think of myself.'

'I know you never do, my dear; and you will always find your reward in the affection it makes every body feel for you. There never was a young woman so beloved as you are by every body that knows you; and I dare say when Mr. Morland sees you, my dear child – but do not let us distress our dear Catherine by talking of such things. Mr. Morland has behaved so very hand-some you know. I always heard he was a most excellent man; and you know, my dear, we are not to suppose but what, if you had had a suitable fortune, he would have come down with some-thing more, for I am sure he must be a most liberal-minded man.'

'Nobody can think better of Mr. Morland than I do, I am sure. But every body has their failing you know, and every body has a right to do what they like with their own money.' Catherine was hurt by these insinuations. 'I am very sure,' said she, 'that my father has promised to do as much as he can afford.'

Isabella recollected herself. 'As to that, my sweet Catherine, there cannot be a doubt, and you know me well enough to be sure that a much smaller income would satisfy me. It is not the want of more money that makes me just at present a little out of spirits; I hate money; and if our union could take place now upon only fifty pounds a year, I should not have a wish unsatisfied. Ah! my Catherine, you have found me out. There's the sting. The long, long, endless two years and half that are to pass before your brother can hold the living.'

'Yes, yes, my darling Isabella,' said Mrs. Thorpe, 'we perfectly see into your heart. You have no disguise. We perfectly understand the present vexation; and every body must love you the better for such a noble honest affection.'

Catherine's uncomfortable feelings began to lessen. She endeavoured to believe that the delay of the marriage was the only source of Isabella's regret; and when she saw her at their next interview as cheerful and amiable as ever, endeavoured to forget that she had for a minute thought otherwise. James soon followed his letter, and was received with the most gratifying kindness.

CHAPTER II

THE Allens had now entered on the sixth week of their stay in Bath; and whether it should be the last, was for some time a question, to which Catherine listened with a beating heart. To have her acquaintance with the Tilneys end so soon, was an evil which nothing could counterbalance. Her whole happiness seemed at stake, while the affair was in suspense, and every thing secured when it was determined that the lodgings should be taken for another fortnight. What this additional fortnight was to produce to her beyond the pleasure of sometimes seeing Henry Tilney, made but a small part of Catherine's speculation. Once or twice indeed, since James's engagement had taught her what *could* be done, she had got so far as to indulge in a secret 'perhaps,' but in general the felicity of being with him for the present bounded her views: the present was now comprised in another three weeks, and her happiness being certain for that period, the rest of her life was at such a distance as to excite but little interest. In the course of the morning which saw this business arranged, she visited Miss Tilney, and poured forth her joyful feelings. It was doomed to be a day of trial. No sooner had she expressed her delight in Mr. Allen's lengthened stay, than Miss Tilney told her of her father's having just determined upon quitting Bath by the end of another week. Here was a blow! The past suspense of the morning had been ease and quiet to the present disappointment. Catherine's countenance fell, and in a voice of most sincere concern she echoed Miss Tilney's concluding words, 'By the end of another week!'

'Yes, my father can seldom be prevailed on to give the waters what I think a fair trial. He has been disappointed of some friends' arrival whom he expected to meet here, and as he is now pretty well, is in a hurry to get home.'

'I am very sorry for it,' said Catherine dejectedly, 'if I had known this before—'

'Perhaps,' said Miss Tilney in an embarrassed manner, 'you would be so good – it would make me very happy if—'

The entrance of her father put a stop to the civility, which Catherine was beginning to hope might introduce a desire of their corresponding. After addressing her with his usual politeness, he turned to his daughter and said, 'Well, Eleanor, may I congratulate you on being successful in your application to your fair friend?'

'I was just beginning to make the request, sir, as you came in.'

'Well, proceed by all means. I know how much your heart is in it. My daughter, Miss Morland,' he continued, without leaving his daughter time to speak, 'has been forming a very bold wish. We leave Bath, as she has perhaps told you, on Saturday se'nnight. A letter from my steward tells me that my presence is wanted at home; and being disappointed in my hope of seeing the Marquis of Longtown and General Courteney here, some of my very old friends, there is nothing to detain me longer in Bath. And could we carry our selfish point with you, we should leave it without a single regret. Can you, in short, be prevailed on to quit this scene of public triumph and oblige your friend Eleanor with your company in Gloucestershire? I am almost ashamed to make the request, though its presumption would certainly appear greater to every creature in Bath than yourself. Modesty such as your's – but not for the world would I pain it by open praise. If you can be induced to honour us with a visit, you will make us happy beyond expression. 'Tis true, we can offer you nothing like the gaieties of this lively place; we can tempt you neither by amusement nor splendour, for our mode of living, as you see, is plain and unpretending; yet no endeavours shall be wanting on our side to make Northanger Abbey not wholly disagreeable.'

Northanger Abbey! – These were thrilling words, and wound up Catherine's feelings to the highest point of extasy. Her grateful and gratified heart could hardly restrain its expressions within the language of tolerable calmness. To receive so flattering an invitation! To have her company so warmly solicited! Every thing honourable and soothing, every present enjoyment, and every future hope was contained in it; and her acceptance, with only the saving clause of papa and mamma's approbation, was eagerly given. – 'I will write home directly,' said she, 'and if they do not object, as I dare say they will not'—

General Tilney was not less sanguine, having already waited on her excellent friends in Pulteney-street, and obtained their sanction of his wishes. 'Since they can consent to part with you,' said he, 'we may expect philosophy from all the world.'

Miss Tilney was earnest, though gentle, in her secondary civilities, and the affair became in a few minutes as nearly settled, as this necessary reference to Fullerton would allow.

The circumstances of the morning had led Catherine's feelings through the varieties of suspense, security, and disappointment; but they were now safely lodged in perfect bliss; and with spirits elated to rapture, with Henry at her heart, and Northanger Abbey on her lips, she hurried home to write her letter. Mr. and Mrs. Morland, relying on the discretion of the friends to whom they had already entrusted their daughter, felt no doubt of the propriety of an acquaintance which had been formed under their eye, and sent therefore by return of post their ready consent to her visit in Gloucestershire. This indulgence, though not more than Catherine had hoped for, completed her conviction of being favoured beyond every other human creature, in friends and fortune, circumstance and chance. Every thing seemed to co-operate for her advantage. By the kindness of her first friends the Allens, she had been introduced into scenes, where pleasures of every kind had met her. Her feelings, her preferences had each known the happiness of a return. Wherever she felt attachment, she had been able to create it. The affection of Isabella was to be secured to her in a sister. The Tilneys, they, by whom above all, she desired to be favourably thought of, out-stripped even her wishes in the flattering measures by which their intimacy was to be continued. She was to be their chosen visitor, she was to be for weeks under the same roof with the person whose society she mostly prized – and, in addition to all the rest, this roof was to be the roof of an abbey! – Her passion for ancient edifices was next in degree to her passion for Henry Tilney – and castles and abbies made usually the charm of those reveries which his image did not fill. To see and explore either the ramparts and keep of the one, or the cloisters of the other, had been for many weeks a darling wish, though to be more than the visitor of an hour, had seemed too nearly impossible for desire. And yet, this was to happen. With all the chances against her of house, hall, place, park, court, and cottage, Northanger turned up an abbey, and she was to be its inhabitant. Its long, damp passages, its narrow cells and ruined chapel, were to be within her daily reach, and she could not entirely subdue the hope of some traditional legends, some awful memorials of an injured and ill-fated nun.

It was wonderful that her friends should seem so little elated by the possession of such a home; that the consciousness of it should be so meekly born. The power of early habit only could account for it. A distinction to which they had been born gave no pride. Their superiority of abode was no more to them than their superiority of person.

Many were the inquiries she was eager to make of Miss Tilney; but so active were her thoughts, that when these inquiries were answered, she was hardly more assured than before, of Northanger Abbey having been a richly-endowed convent at the time of the Reformation, of its having fallen into the hands of an ancestor of the Tilneys on its dissolution, of a large portion of the ancient building still making a part of the present dwelling although the rest was decayed, or of its standing low in a valley, sheltered from the north and east by rising woods of oak.

CHAPTER III

WITH a mind thus full of happiness, Catherine was hardly aware that two or three days had passed away, without her seeing Isabella for more than a few minutes together. She began first to be sensible of this, and to sigh for her conversation, as she walked along the Pump-room one morning, by Mrs. Allen's side, without any thing to say or to hear; and scarcely had she felt a five minutes' longing of friendship, before the object of it appeared, and inviting her to a secret conference, led the way to a seat. 'This is my favourite place,' said she, as they sat down on a bench between the doors, which commanded a tolerable view of every body entering at either, 'it is so out of the way.'

Catherine, observing that Isabella's eyes were continually bent towards one door or the other, as in eager expectation, and remembering how often she had been falsely accused of being arch, thought the present a fine opportunity for being really so; and therefore gaily said, 'Do not be uneasy, Isabella. James will soon be here.'

'Psha! my dear creature,' she replied, 'do not think me such a simpleton as to be always wanting to confine him to my elbow. It would be hideous to be always together; we should be the jest of the place. And so you are going to Northanger! – I am amazingly glad of it. It is one of the finest old places in England, I understand. I shall depend upon a most particular description of it.'

'You shall certainly have the best in my power to give. But

who are you looking for? Are your sisters coming?'

'I am not looking for any body. One's eyes must be some-where, and you know what a foolish trick I have of fixing mine, when my thoughts are an hundred miles off. I am amazingly absent; I believe I am the most absent creature in the world. Tilney says it is always the case with minds of a certain stamp.'

'But I thought, Isabella, you had something in particular to tell me?'

'Oh! yes, and so I have. But here is a proof of what I was saying. My poor head! I had quite forgot it. Well, the thing is this, I have just had a letter from John; – you can guess the contents.'

'No, indeed, I cannot.'

'My sweet love, do not be so abominably affected. What can he write about but yourself? You know he is over head and ears in love with you.'

'With *me*, dear Isabella!'

'Nay, my sweetest Catherine, this is being quite absurd! Modesty, and all that, is very well in its way, but really a little common honesty is sometimes quite as becoming. I have no idea of being so overstrained! It is fishing for compliments. His attentions were such as a child must have noticed. And it was but half an hour before he left Bath, that you gave him the most positive encouragement. He says so in this letter, says that he as good as made you an offer, and that you received his advances in the kindest way; and now he wants me to urge his suit, and say all manner of pretty things to you. So it is in vain to affect ignorance.'

Catherine, with all the earnestness of truth, expressed her astonishment at such a charge, protesting her innocence of every thought of Mr. Thorpe's being in love with her, and the con-sequent impossibility of her having ever intended to encourage him. 'As to any attentions on his side, I do declare, upon my honour, I never was sensible of them for a moment – except just his asking me to dance the first day of his coming. And as to making me an offer, or any thing like it, there must be some unaccountable mistake. I could not have misunderstood a thing of that kind, you know! – and, as I ever wish to be believed, I solemnly protest that no syllable of such a nature ever passed between us. The last half hour before he went away! – It must be all and completely a mistake – for I did not see him once that whole morning.'

'But *that* you certainly did, for you spent the whole morning in Edgar's Buildings – it was the day your father's consent came – and I am pretty sure that you and John were alone in the parlour, some time before you left the house.'

'Are you? – Well, if you say it, it was so, I dare say – but for the life of me, I cannot recollect it. – I *do* remember now being with you, and seeing him as well as the rest – but that we were ever alone for five minutes – However, it is not worth arguing about, for whatever might pass on his side, you must be convinced, by my having no recollection of it, that I never thought, nor expected, nor wished for any thing of the kind from him. I am excessively concerned that he should have any regard for me – but indeed it has been quite unintentional on my side, I never had the smallest idea of it. Pray undeceive him as soon as you can, and tell him I beg his pardon – that is – I do not know what I ought to say – but make him understand what I mean, in the properest way. I would not speak disrespectfully of a brother of your's, Isabella, I am sure; but you know very well that if I could think of one man more than another – *he* is not the person.' Isabella was silent. 'My dear friend, you must not be angry with me. I cannot suppose your brother cares so very much about me. And, you know, we shall still be sisters.'

'Yes, yes,' (with a blush) 'there are more ways than one of our being sisters. – But where am I wandering to?[1] – Well, my dear Catherine, the case seems to be, that you are determined against poor John – is not it so?'

'I certainly cannot return his affection, and as certainly never meant to encourage it.'

'Since that is the case, I am sure I shall not tease you any further. John desired me to speak to you on the subject, and therefore I have. But I confess, as soon as I read his letter, I thought it a very foolish, imprudent business, and not likely to promote the good of either; for what were you to live upon, supposing you came together? You have both of you something to be sure, but it is not a trifle that will support a family now-a-days; and after all that romancers may say, there is no doing without money. I only wonder John could think of it; he could not have received my last.'

'You *do* acquit me then of any thing wrong? – You are convinced that I never meant to deceive your brother, never suspected him of liking me till this moment?'

'Oh! as to that,' answered Isabella laughingly, 'I do not pretend to determine what your thoughts and designs in time past may have been. All that is best known to yourself. A little harmless flirtation or so will occur, and one is often drawn on to give more encouragement than one wishes to stand by. But you may be assured that I am the last person in the world to judge you severely. All those things should be allowed for in youth and high spirits. What one means one day, you know, one may not mean the next. Circumstances change, opinions alter.'

'But my opinion of your brother never did alter; it was always the same. You are describing what never happened.'

'My dearest Catherine,' continued the other without at all listening to her, 'I would not for all the world be the means of hurrying you into an engagement before you knew what you were about. I do not think any thing would justify me in wishing you to sacrifice all your happiness merely to oblige my brother, because he is my brother, and who perhaps after all, you know, might be just as happy without you, for people seldom know what they would be at, young men especially, they are so amazingly changeable and inconstant. What I say is, why should a brother's happiness be dearer to me than a friend's? You know I carry my notions of friendship pretty high. But, above all things, my dear Catherine, do not be in a hurry. Take my word for it, that if you are in too great a hurry, you will certainly live to repent it. Tilney says, there is nothing people are so often deceived in, as the state of their own affections, and I believe he is very right. Ah! here he comes; never mind, he will not see us, I am sure.'

Catherine, looking up, perceived Captain Tilney; and Isabella, earnestly fixing her eye on him as she spoke, soon caught his notice. He approached immediately, and took the seat to which her movements invited him. His first address made Catherine start. Though spoken low, she could distinguish, 'What! always to be watched, in person or by proxy!'

'Psha, nonsense!' was Isabella's answer in the same half whisper. 'Why do you put such things into my head? If I could believe it – my spirit, you know, is pretty independent.'

'I wish your heart were independent. That would be enough for me.'

'My heart, indeed! What can you have to do with hearts? You men have none of you any hearts.'

'If we have not hearts, we have eyes; and they give us torment enough.'

'Do they? I am sorry for it; I am sorry they find any thing so disagreeable in me. I will look another way. I hope this pleases you, (turning her back on him,) I hope your eyes are not tormented now.'

'Never more so; for the edge of a blooming cheek is still in view – at once too much and too little.'

Catherine heard all this, and quite out of countenance could listen no longer. Amazed that Isabella could endure it, and jealous for her brother, she rose up, and saying she should join Mrs. Allen, proposed their walking. But for this Isabella shewed no inclination. She was so amazingly tired, and it was so odious to parade about the Pump-room; and if she moved from her seat she should miss her sisters, she was expecting her sisters every moment; so that her dearest Catherine must excuse her, and must sit quietly down again. But Catherine could be stubborn too; and Mrs. Allen just then coming up to propose their returning home, she joined her and walked out of the Pump-room, leaving Isabella still sitting with Captain Tilney. With much uneasiness did she thus leave them. It seemed to her that Captain Tilney was falling in love with Isabella, and Isabella unconsciously encouraging him; unconsciously it must be, for Isabella's attachment to James was as certain and well acknowledged as her engagement. To doubt her truth or good intentions was impossible; and yet, during the whole of their conversation her manner had been odd. She wished Isabella had talked more like her usual self, and not so much about money; and had not looked so well pleased at the sight of Captain Tilney. How strange that she should not perceive his admiration! Catherine longed to give her a hint of it, to put her on her guard, and prevent all the pain which her too lively behaviour might otherwise create both for him and her brother.

The compliment of John Thorpe's affection did not make amends for this thoughtlessness in his sister. She was almost as far from believing as from wishing it to be sincere; for she had not forgotten that he could mistake, and his assertion of the offer and of her encouragement convinced her that his mistakes could sometimes be very egregious. In vanity therefore she gained but little, her chief profit was in wonder. That he should think it worth his while to fancy himself in love with her, was a matter of lively astonishment. Isabella talked of his attentions; *she* had never been sensible of any; but Isabella had said many things which she hoped had been spoken in haste, and would never be said again; and upon this she was glad to rest altogether for present ease and comfort.

CHAPTER IV

A few days passed away, and Catherine, though not allowing herself to suspect her friend, could not help watching her closely. The result of her observations was not agreeable. Isabella seemed an altered creature. When she saw her indeed surrounded only by their immediate friends in Edgar's Buildings or Pulteney-street, her change of manners was so trifling that, had it gone no farther, it might have passed unnoticed. A something of languid indifference, or of that boasted absence of mind which Catherine had never heard of before, would occasionally come across her; but had nothing worse appeared, *that* might only have spread a new grace and inspired a warmer interest. But when Catherine saw her in public, admitting Captain Tilney's attentions as readily as they were offered, and allowing him almost an equal share with James in her notice and smiles, the alteration became too positive to be past over. What could be meant by such unsteady conduct, what her friend could be at, was beyond her comprehension. Isabella could not be aware of the pain she was inflicting; but it was a degree of wilful thoughtlessness which Catherine could not but resent. James was the sufferer. She saw him grave and uneasy; and however careless of his present comfort the woman might be who had given him her heart, to *her* it was always an object. For poor Captain Tilney too she was greatly concerned. Though his looks did not please her, his name was a passport to her good will, and she thought with sincere compassion of his approaching disappointment; for, in spite of what she had believed herself to overhear in the Pump-room, his behaviour was so incompatible with a knowledge of Isabella's engagement, that she could not, upon reflection, imagine him aware of it. He might be jealous of her brother as a rival, but if more had seemed implied, the fault must have been in her misapprehension. She wished, by a gentle remonstrance, to remind Isabella of her situation, and make her aware of this double unkindness; but for remonstrance, either opportunity or comprehension was always against her. If able to suggest a hint, Isabella could never understand it. In this distress, the intended departure of the Tilney family became her chief consolation; their journey into Gloucestershire was to take place within a few days, and Captain Tilney's removal would at least restore peace to every heart but his own. But Captain Tilney had at present no intention of removing; he was not to be of the party to Northanger, he was to continue at Bath. When Catherine knew this, her resolution was directly made. She spoke to Henry Tilney on the subject, regretting his brother's evident partiality for Miss Thorpe, and entreating him to make known her prior engagement.

'My brother does know it,' was Henry's answer.

'Does he? – then why does he stay here?'

He made no reply, and was beginning to talk of something

else; but she eagerly continued, 'Why do not you persuade him to go away? The longer he stays, the worse it will be for him at last. Pray advise him for his own sake, and for every body's sake, to leave Bath directly. Absence will in time make him comfortable again; but he can have no hope here, and it is only staying to be miserable.' Henry smiled and said, 'I am sure my brother would not wish to do that.'

'Then you will persuade him to go away?'

'Persuasion is not at command; but pardon me, if I cannot even endeavour to persuade him. I have myself told him that Miss Thorpe is engaged. He knows what he is about, and must be his own master.'

'No, he does not know what he is about,' cried Catherine; 'he does not know the pain he is giving my brother. Not that James has ever told me so, but I am sure he is very uncomfortable.'

'And are you sure it is my brother's doing?'

'Yes, very sure.'

'Is it my brother's attentions to Miss Thorpe, or Miss Thorpe's admission of them, that gives the pain?'

'Is not it the same thing?'

'I think Mr. Morland would acknowledge a difference. No man is offended by another man's admiration of the woman he loves; it is the woman only who can make it a torment.'

Catherine blushed for her friend, and said, 'Isabella is wrong. But I am sure she cannot mean to torment, for she is very much attached to my brother. She has been in love with him ever since they first met, and while my father's consent was uncertain, she fretted herself almost into a fever. You know she must be attached to him.'

'I understand: she is in love with James, and flirts with Frederick.'

'Oh! no, not flirts. A woman in love with one man cannot flirt with another.'

'It is probable that she will neither love so well, nor flirt so well, as she might do either singly. The gentlemen must each give up a little.'

After a short pause, Catherine resumed with 'Then you do not believe Isabella so very much attached to my brother?'

'I can have no opinion on that subject.'

'But what can your brother mean? If he knows her engagement, what can he mean by his behaviour?'

'You are a very close questioner.'

'Am I? – I only ask what I want to be told.'

'But do you only ask what I can be expected to tell?'

'Yes, I think so; for you must know your brother's heart.'

'My brother's heart, as you term it, on the present occasion, I assure you I can only guess at.'

'Well?'

'Well! – Nay, if it is to be guess-work, let us all guess for ourselves. To be guided by second-hand conjecture is pitiful. The premises are before you. My brother is a lively, and perhaps sometimes a thoughtless young man; he has had about a week's acquaintance with your friend, and he has known her engagement almost as long as he has known her.'

'Well,' said Catherine, after some moments' consideration, '*you* may be able to guess at your brother's intentions from all this; but I am sure I cannot. But is not your father uncomfortable about it? – Does not he want Captain Tilney to go away? – Sure, if your father were to speak to him, he would go.'

'My dear Miss Morland,' said Henry, 'in this amiable solicitude for your brother's comfort, may you not be a little mistaken? Are you not carried a little too far? Would he thank you, either on his own account or Miss Thorpe's, for supposing that her affection, or at least her good-behaviour, is only to be secured by her seeing nothing of Captain Tilney? Is he safe only in solitude? – or, is her heart constant to him only when unsolicited by any one else? – He cannot think this – and you may be sure that he would not have you think it. I will not say, "Do not be uneasy," because I know that you are so, at this moment; but be as little uneasy as you can. You have no doubt of the mutual attachment of your brother and your friend; depend upon it therefore, that real jealousy never can exist between them; depend upon it that no disagreement between them can be of any duration. Their hearts are open to each other, as neither heart can be to you; they know exactly what is required and what can be borne; and you may be certain, that one will never tease the other beyond what is known to be pleasant.'

Perceiving her still to look doubtful and grave, he added, 'Though Frederick does not leave Bath with us, he will probably remain but a very short time, perhaps only a few days behind us. His leave of absence will soon expire, and he must return to his regiment. – And what will then be their acquaintance? – The mess-room will drink Isabella Thorpe for a fortnight, and she will laugh with your brother over poor Tilney's passion for a month.'

Catherine would contend no longer against comfort. She had resisted its approaches during the whole length of a speech, but it now carried her captive. Henry Tilney must know best. She blamed herself for the extent of her fears, and resolved never to think so seriously on the subject again.

Her resolution was supported by Isabella's behaviour in their parting interview. The Thorpes spent the last evening of Catherine's stay in Pulteney-street, and nothing passed between the lovers to excite her uneasiness, or make her quit them in apprehension. James was in excellent spirits, and Isabella most engagingly placid. Her tenderness for her friend seemed rather the first feeling of her heart; but that at such a moment was allowable; and once she gave her lover a flat contradiction, and once she drew back her hand; but Catherine remembered Henry's instructions, and placed it all to judicious affection. The embraces, tears, and promises of the parting fair ones may be fancied.

CHAPTER V

MR. and Mrs. Allen were sorry to lose their young friend, whose good-humour and cheerfulness had made her a valuable companion, and in the promotion of whose enjoyment their own had been gently increased. Her happiness in going with

Miss Tilney, however, prevented their wishing it otherwise; and, as they were to remain only one more week in Bath themselves, her quitting them now would not long be felt. Mr. Allen attended her to Milsom-street, where she was to breakfast, and saw her seated with the kindest welcome among her new friends; but so great was her agitation in finding herself as one of the family, and so fearful was she of not doing exactly what was right, and of not being able to preserve their good opinion, that, in the embarrassment of the first five minutes, she could almost have wished to return with him to Pulteney-street.

Miss Tilney's manners and Henry's smile soon did away some of her unpleasant feelings; but still she was far from being being at ease; nor could the incessant attentions of the General himself entirely reassure her. Nay, perverse as it seemed, she doubted whether she might not have felt less, had she been less attended to. His anxiety for her comfort – his continual solicitations that she would eat, and his often-expressed fears of her seeing nothing to her taste – though never in her life before had she beheld half such variety on a breakfast-table – made it impossible for her to forget for a moment that she was a visitor. She felt utterly unworthy of such respect, and knew not how to reply to it. Her tranquillity was not improved by the General's impatience for the appearance of his eldest son, nor by the displeasure he expressed at his laziness when Captain Tilney at last came down. She was quite pained by the severity of his father's reproof, which seemed disproportionate to the offence; and much was her concern increased, when she found herself the principal cause of the lecture; and that his tardiness was chiefly resented from being disrespectful to her. This was placing her in a very uncomfortable situation, and she felt great compassion for Captain Tilney, without being able to hope for his good-will.

He listened to his father in silence, and attempted not any defence, which confirmed her in fearing, that the inquietude of his mind, on Isabella's account, might, by keeping him long sleepless, have been the real cause of his rising late. – It was the first time of her being decidedly in his company, and she had hoped to be now able to form her opinion of him; but she scarcely heard his voice while his father remained in the room; and even afterwards, so much were his spirits affected, she could distinguish nothing but these words, in a whisper to Eleanor, 'How glad I shall be when you are all off.'

The bustle of going was not pleasant. – The clock struck ten while the trunks were carrying down, and the General had fixed to be out of Milsom-street by that hour. His great coat, instead of being brought for him to put on directly, was spread out in the curricle in which he was to accompany his son. The middle seat of the chaise was not drawn out, though there were three people to go in it, and his daughter's maid had so crowded it with parcels, that Miss Morland would not have room to sit; and, so much was he influenced by this apprehension when he handed her in, that she had some difficulty in saving her own new writing-desk from being thrown out into the street. – At last, however, the door was closed upon the three females, and they set off at the sober pace in which the handsome, highly-fed four horses of a gentleman usually perform a journey of thirty miles: such was the distance of Northanger from Bath, to be now divided into two equal stages. Catherine's spirits revived as they drove from the door; for with Miss Tilney she felt no restraint; and, with the interest of a road entirely new to her, of an abbey before, and a curricle behind, she caught the last view of Bath without any regret, and met with every mile-stone before she expected it. The tediousness of a two hours' bait at Petty-France,[1] in which there was nothing to be done but to eat without being hungry, and loiter about without any thing to see, next followed – and her admiration of the style in which they travelled, of the fashionable chaise-and-four – postilions handsomely liveried, rising so regularly in their stirrups, and numerous out-riders properly mounted, sunk a little under this consequent inconvenience. Had their party been perfectly agreeable, the dealy would have been nothing; but General Tilney, though so charming a man, seemed always a check upon his children's spirits, and scarcely any thing was said but by himself; the observation of which, with his discontent at whatever the inn afforded, and his angry impatience at the waiters, made Catherine grow every moment more in awe of him, and appeared to lengthen the two hours into four. – At last, however, the order of release was given; and much was Catherine then surprized by the General's proposal of her taking his place in his son's curricle for the rest of the journey: – 'the day was fine, and he was anxious for her seeing as much of the country as possible.'

The remembrance of Mr. Allen's opinion, respecting young men's open carriages, made her blush at the mention of such a plan, and her first thought was to decline it; but her second was of greater deference for General Tilney's judgment; he could not propose any thing improper for her; and, in the course of a few minutes, she found herself with Henry in the curricle, as happy a being as ever existed. A very short trial convinced her that a curricle was the prettiest equipage in the world; the chaise-and-four wheeled off with some grandeur, to be sure, but it was a heavy and troublesome business, and she could not easily forget its having stopped two hours at Petty-France. Half the time would have been enough for the curricle, and so nimbly were the light horses disposed to move, that, had not the General chosen to have his own carriage lead the way, they could have passed it with ease in half a minute. But the merit of the curricle did not all belong to the horses; – Henry drove so well, – so quietly – without making any disturbance, without parading to her, or swearing at them; so different from the only gentleman-coachman whom it was in her power to compare him with! – And then his hat sat so well, and the innumerable capes of his great coat looked so becomingly important! – To be driven by him, next to being dancing with him, was certainly the greatest happiness in the world. In addition to every other delight, she had now that of listening to her own praise; of being thanked at least, on his sister's account, for her kindness in thus becoming her visitor; of hearing it ranked as real friendship, and described as creating real gratitude. His sister, he said, was uncomfortably circumstanced – she had no female companion – and, in the frequent absence of her father, was sometimes without any companion at all.

'But how can that be?' said Catherine, 'are not you with her?'

'Northanger is not more than half my home; I have an estab-lishment at my own house in Woodston, which is nearly twenty miles from my father's, and some of my time is necessarily spent there.'

'How sorry you must be for that!'

'I am always sorry to leave Eleanor.'

'Yes; but besides your affection for her, you must be so fond of the abbey! – After being used to such a home as the abbey, an ordinary parsonage-house must be very disagreeable.'

He smiled, and said, 'You have formed a very favourable idea of the abbey.'

'To be sure I have. Is not it a fine old place, just like what one reads about?'

'And are you prepared to encounter all the horrors that a building such as "what one reads about" may produce? – Have you a stout heart? – Nerves fit for sliding pannels and tapestry?'

'Oh! yes – I do not think I should be easily frightened, because there would be so many people in the house – and besides, it has never been uninhabited and left deserted for years, and then the family come back to it unawares, without giving any notice, as generally happens.'

'No, certainly. – We shall not have to explore our way into a hall dimly lighted by the expiring embers of a wood fire – nor be obliged to spread our beds on the floor of a room without windows, doors, or furniture. But you must be aware that when a young lady is (by whatever means) introduced into a dwelling of this kind, she is always lodged apart from the rest of the family. While they snugly repair to their own end of the house, she is formally conducted by Dorothy the ancient housekeeper[1] up a different staircase, and along many gloomy passages, into an apartment never used since some cousin or kin died in it about twenty years before. Can you stand such a ceremony as this? Will not your mind misgive you, when you find yourself in this gloomy chamber – too lofty and extensive for you, with only the feeble rays of a single lamp to take in its size – its walls hung with tapestry exhibiting figures as large as life, and the bed, of dark green stuff or purple velvet, presenting even a funereal appearance. Will not your heart sink within you?'

'Oh! but this will not happen to me, I am sure.'

'How fearfully will you examine the furniture of your apartment! – And what will you discern? – Not tables, toilettes, wardrobes, or drawers, but on one side perhaps the remains of a broken lute, on the other a ponderous chest which no efforts can open, and over the fire-place the portrait of some handsome warrior, whose features will so incomprehensibly strike you, that you will not be able to withdraw your eyes from it. Dorothy meanwhile, no less struck by your appearance, gazes on you in great agitation, and drops a few unintelligible hints. To raise your spirits, moreover, she gives you reason to suppose that the part of the abbey you inhabit is undoubtedly haunted, and informs you that you will not have a single domestic within call. With this parting cordial she curtseys off – you listen to the sound of her receding footsteps as long as the last echo can reach you – and when, with fainting spirits, you attempt to fasten your door, you discover, with increased alarm, that it has no lock.'

'Oh! Mr. Tilney, how frightful! – This is just like a book! – But it cannot really happen to me. I am sure your housekeeper is not really Dorothy. – Well, what then?'

'Nothing further to alarm perhaps may occur the first night. After surmounting your *unconquerable* horror of the bed, you will retire to rest, and get a few hour's unquiet slumber. But on the second, or at farthest the *third* night after your arrival, you will probably have a violent storm. Peals of thunder so loud as to seem to shake the edifice to its foundation will roll round the neighbouring mountains – and during the frightful gusts of wind which accompany it, you will probably think you discern (for your lamp is not extinguished) one part of the hanging more violently agitated than the rest. Unable of course to repress your curiosity in so favourable a moment for indulging it, you will instantly arise, and throwing your dressing-gown around you, proceed to examine this mystery. After a very short search, you will discover a division in the tapestry so artfully constructed as to defy the minutest inspection, and on opening it, a door will immediately appear – which door being only secured by m a s sy bars and a padlock, you will, after a few efforts, succeed in opening, – and, with your lamp in your hand, will pass through it into a small vaulted room.'

'No, indeed; I should be too much frightened to do any such thing.'

'What! not when Dorothy has given you to understand that there is a secret subterraneous communication between your apartment and the chapel of St. Anthony, scarcely two miles off – Could you shrink from so simple an adventure? No, no, you will proceed into this small vaulted room, and through this into several others, without perceiving any thing very remarkable in either. In one perhaps there may be a dagger, in another a few drops of blood, and in a third the remains of some instrument of torture; but there being nothing in all this out of the common way, and your lamp being nearly exhausted, you will return towards your own apartment. In repassing through the small vaulted room, however, your eyes will be attracted towards a large, old-fashioned cabinet of ebony and gold, which, though narrowly examining the furniture before, you had passed un-noticed. Impelled by an irresistible presentiment, you will eagerly advance to it, unlock its folding doors, and search into every drawer; – but for some time without discovering any thing of importance – perhaps nothing but a considerable hoard of diamonds. At last, however, by touching a secret spring, an inner compartment will open – a roll of paper appears: – you seize it – it contains many sheets of manuscript – you hasten with the precious treasure into your own chamber, but scarcely have you been able to decipher "Oh! thou – whomsoever thou mayst be, into whose hands these memoirs of the wretched Matilda may fall" – when your lamp suddenly expires in the socket, and leaves you in total darkness.'

'Oh! no, no – do not say so. Well, go on.'

But Henry was too much amused by the interest he had raised, to be able to carry it farther; he could no longer com-mand solemnity either of subject or voice, and was obliged to entreat her to use her own fancy in the perusal of Matilda's woes. Catherine, recollecting herself, grew ashamed of her eagerness, and began earnestly to assure him that her attention had been fixed without the smallest apprehension of really meeting with what he related. 'Miss Tilney, she was sure, would never put her into such a chamber as he had described! – She was not at all afraid.'

As they drew near the end of their journey, her impatience for a sight of the abbey – for some time suspended by his conversation on subjects very different – returned in full force, and every bend in the road was expected with solemn awe to afford a glimpse of its massy walls of grey stone, rising amidst a grove of ancient oaks, with the last beams of the sun playing in beautiful splendour on its high Gothic windows. But so low did the building stand, that she found herself passing through the great gates of the lodge into the very grounds of Northanger, without having discerned even an antique chimney.

She knew not that she had any right to be surprized, but there was a something in this mode of approach which she certainly had not expected. To pass between lodges of a modern appearance, to find herself with such ease in the very precincts of the abbey, and driven so rapidly along a smooth, level road of fine gravel, without obstacle, alarm or solemnity of any kind, struck her as odd and inconsistent. She was not long at leisure however for such considerations. A sudden scud of rain driving full in her face, made it impossible for her to observe any thing further, and fixed all her thoughts on the welfare of her new straw bonnet: – and she was actually under the Abbey walls, was springing, with Henry's assistance, from the carriage, was beneath the shelter of the old porch, and had even passed on to the hall, where her friend and the General were waiting to welcome her, without feeling one aweful foreboding of future misery to herself, or one moment's suspicion of any past scenes of horror being acted within the solemn edifice. The breeze had not seemed to waft the sighs of the murdered to her; it had wafted nothing worse than a thick mizzling rain; and having giving a good shake to her habit, she was ready to be shewn into the common drawing-room, and capable of considering where she was.

An abbey! – yes, it was delightful to be really in an abbey! – but she doubted, as she looked round the room, whether any thing within her observation, would have given her the consciousness. The furniture was in all the profusion and elegance of modern taste. The fire-place, where she had expected the ample width and ponderous carving of former times, was contracted to a Rumford,[1] with slabs of plain though handsome marble, and ornaments over it of the prettiest English china. The windows, to which she looked with peculiar dependence, from having heard the General talk of his preserving them in their Gothic form with reverential care, were yet less what her fancy had portrayed. To be sure, the pointed arch was preserved – the form of them was Gothic – they might be even casements – but every pane was so large, so clear, so light! To an imagination which had hoped for the smallest divisions, and the heaviest stone-work, for painted glass, dirt and cobwebs, the difference was very distressing.

The General, perceiving how her eye was employed, began to talk of the smallness of the room and simplicity of the furniture, where every thing being for daily use, pretended only to comfort, &c.; flattering himself however that there were some apartments in the Abbey not unworthy her notice – and was proceeding to mention the costly gilding of one in particular, when taking out his watch, he stopped short to pronounce it with surprize within twenty minutes of five! This seemed the word of separation, and Catherine found herself hurried away by Miss Tilney in such a manner as convinced her that the strictest punctuality to the family hours would be expected at Northanger.

Returning through the large and lofty hall, they ascended a broad staircase of shining oak, which, after many flights and many landing-places, brought them upon a long wide gallery. On one side it had a range of doors, and it was lighted on the other by windows which Catherine had only time to discover looked into a quadrangle, before Miss Tilney led the way into a chamber, and scarcely staying to hope she would find it comfortable, left her with an anxious entreaty that she would make as little alteration as possible in her dress.

CHAPTER VI

A MOMENT'S glance was enough to satisfy Catherine that her apartment was very unlike the one which Henry had endeavoured to alarm her by the description of. – It was by no means unreasonably large, and contained neither tapestry nor velvet. – The walls were papered, the floor was carpeted; the windows were neither less perfect, nor more dim than those of the drawing-room below; the furniture, though not of the latest fashion, was handsome and comfortable, and the air of the room altogether far from uncheerful. Her heart instantaneously at ease on this point, she resolved to lose no time in particular examination of any thing, as she greatly dreaded disobliging the General by any delay. Her habit therefore was thrown off with all possible haste, and she was preparing to unpin the linen package, which the chaise-seat had conveyed for her immediate accommodation, when her eye suddenly fell on a large high chest, standing back in a deep recess on one side of the fire-place. The sight of it made her start; and, forgetting every thing else, she stood gazing on it in motionless wonder, while these thoughts crossed her: –

'This is strange indeed! I did not expect such a sight as this! – An immense heavy chest! – What can it hold? – Why should it be placed here? – Pushed back too, as if meant to be out of sight! – I will look into it – cost me what it may, I will look into it – and directly too – by day-light. – If I stay till evening my candle may go out.' She advanced and examined it closely: it was of cedar, curiously inlaid with some darker wood, and raised, about a foot from the ground, on a carved stand of the same. The lock was silver, though tarnished from age; at each end were the imperfect remains of handles also of silver, broken perhaps prematurely by some strange violence; and, on the centre of the lid, was a mysterious cypher, in the same metal. Catherine bent over it intently, but without being able to distinguish any thing with certainty. She could not, in whatever direction she took it, believe the last letter to be a *T*; and yet that it should be any thing else in that house was a circumstance to raise no common degree of astonishment. If not originally their's, by what strange events could it have fallen into the Tilney family?

Her fearful curiosity was every moment growing greater; and seizing, with trembling hands, the hasp of the lock, she resolved at all hazards to satisfy herself at least as to its contents. With difficulty, for something seemed to resist her efforts, she raised the lid a few inches; but at that moment a sudden knocking at the door of the room made her, starting, quit her hold, and the lid closed with alarming violence. This ill-timed intruder was Miss Tilney's maid, sent by her mistress to be of use to Miss Morland; and though Catherine immediately dismissed her, it recalled her to the sense of what she ought to be doing, and forced her, in spite of her anxious desire to penetrate this mystery, to proceed in her dressing without further delay. Her progress was not quick, for her thoughts and her eyes were still bent on the object so well calculated to interest and alarm; and though she dared not waste a moment upon a second attempt, she could not remain many paces from the chest. At length, however, having slipped one arm into her gown, her toilette seemed so nearly finished, that the impatience of her curiosity might safely be indulged. One moment surely might be spared; and, so desperate should be the exertion of her strength, that, unless secured by supernatural means, the lid in one moment should be thrown back. With this spirit she sprang forward, and her confidence did not deceive her. Her resolute effort threw back the lid, and gave to her astonished eyes the view of a white cotton counterpane, properly folded, reposing at one end of the chest in undisputed possession!

She was gazing on it with the first blush of surprise, when Miss Tilney, anxious for her friend's being ready, entered the room, and to the rising shame of having harboured for some minutes an absurd expectation, was then added the shame of being caught in so idle a search. 'That is a curious old chest, is not it?' said Miss Tilney, as Catherine hastily closed it and turned away to the glass. 'It is impossible to say how many generations it has been here. How it came to be first put in this room I know not, but I have not had it moved, because I thought it might sometimes be of use in holding hats and bonnets. The worst of it is that its weight makes it difficult to open. In that corner, however, it is at least out of the way.'

Catherine had no leisure for speech, being at once blushing, tying her gown, and forming wise resolutions with the most violent dispatch. Miss Tilney gently hinted her fear of being late; and in half a minute they ran down stairs together, in an alarm not wholly unfounded, for General Tilney was pacing the drawing-room, his watch in his hand, and having, on the very instant of their entering, pulled the bell with violence, ordered 'Dinner to be on table *directly!*'

Catherine trembled at the emphasis with which he spoke, and sat pale and breathless, in a most humble mood, concerned for his children, and detesting old chests; and the General recovering his politeness as he looked at her, spent the rest of his time in scolding his daughter, for so foolishly hurrying her fair friend, who was absolutely out of breath from haste, when there was not the least occasion for hurry in the world: but Catherine could not at all get over the double distress of having involved her friend in a lecture and been a great simpleton herself, till they were happily seated at the dinner-table, when the General's complacent smiles, and a good appetite of her own, restored her to peace. The dining-parlour was a noble room, suitable in its dimensions to a much larger drawing-room than the one in common use, and fitted up in a style of luxury and expense which was almost lost on the unpractised eye of Catherine, who saw little more than its spaciousness and the number of their attendants. Of the former, she spoke aloud her admiration; and the General, with a very gracious countenance, acknowledged that it was by no means an ill-sized room; and further confessed, that, though as careless on such subjects as most people, he did look upon a tolerably large eating-room as one of the necessaries of life; he supposed, however, 'that she must have been used to much better sized apartments at Mr. Allen's?'

'No, indeed,' was Catherine's honest assurance; 'Mr. Allen's dining-parlour was not more than half as large:' and she had never seen so large a room as this in her life. The General's good-humour increased. – Why, as he *had* such rooms, he thought it would be simple not to make use of them; but, upon his honour, he believed there might be more comfort in rooms of only half their size. Mr. Allen's house, he was sure, must be exactly of the true size for rational happiness.

The evening passed without any further disturbance, and, in the occasional absence of General Tilney, with much positive cheerfulness. It was only in his presence that Catherine felt the smallest fatigue from her journey; and even then, even in moments of languor or restraint, a sense of general happiness preponderated, and she could think of her friends in Bath without one wish of being with them.

The night was stormy; the wind had been rising at intervals the whole afternoon; and by the time the party broke up, it blew and rained violently. Catherine, as she crossed the hall, listened to the tempest with sensations of awe; and, when she heard it rage round a corner of the ancient building and close with sudden fury a distant door, felt for the first time that she was really in an Abbey. – Yes, these were characteristic sounds; – they brought to her recollection a countless variety of dreadful situations and horrid scenes, which such buildings had witnessed, and such storms ushered in; and most heartily did she rejoice in the happier circumstances attending her entrance within walls so solemn! – *She* had nothing to dread from midnight assassins or drunken gallants. Henry had certainly been only in jest in what he had told her that morning. In a house so furnished, and so guarded, she could have nothing to explore or to suffer; and might go to her bedroom as securely as if it had been her own chamber at Fullerton. Thus wisely fortifying her mind, as she proceeded up stairs, she was enabled, especially on perceiving that Miss Tilney slept only two doors from her, to enter her room with a tolerably stout heart; and her spirits were immediately assisted by the cheerful blaze of a wood fire. 'How much better is this,' said she, as she walked to the fender – 'how much better to find a fire ready lit, than to have to wait shivering in the cold till all the family are in bed, as so many poor girls have been obliged to do, and then to have a faithful old servant frightening one by coming in with a faggot! How glad I am that Northanger is what it is! If it had been like some other places, I do not know that, in such a night as this, I could have answered for my courage: – but now, to be sure, there is nothing to alarm one.'

She looked round the room. The window curtains seemed in motion. It could be nothing but the violence of the wind penetrating through the divisions of the shutters; and she stept boldly forward, carelessly humming a tune, to assure herself of its being so, peeped courageously behind each curtain, saw nothing on either low window seat to scare her, and on placing a hand against the shutter, felt the strongest conviction of the wind's force. A glance at the old chest, as she turned away from this examination, was not without its use; she scorned the causeless fears of an idle fancy, and began with a most happy indifference to prepare herself for bed. 'She should take her time; she should not hurry herself; she did not care if she were the last person up in the house. But she would not make up her fire; *that* would seem cowardly, as if she wished for the protection of light after she were in bed.' The fire therefore died away, and Catherine, having spent the best part of an hour in her arrangements, was beginning to think of stepping into bed, when, on giving a parting glance round the room, she was struck by the appearance of a high, old-fashioned black cabinet, which, though in a situation conspicuous enough, had never caught her notice before. Henry's words, his description of the ebony cabinet which was to escape her observation at first, immediately rushed across her; and though there could be nothing really in it, there was something whimsical, it was certainly a very remarkable coincidence! She took her candle and looked closely at the cabinet. It was not absolutely ebony and gold; but it was Japan, black and yellow Japan of the handsomest kind; and as she held her candle, the yellow had very much the effect of gold. The key was in the door, and she had a strange fancy to look into it; not however with the smallest expectation of finding any thing, but it was so very odd, after what Henry had said. In short, she could not sleep till she had examined it. So, placing the candle with great caution on a chair, she seized the key with a very tremulous hand and tried to turn it; but it resisted her utmost strength. Alarmed, but not discouraged, she tried it another way; a bolt flew, and she believed herself successful; but how strangely mysterious! – the door was still immoveable. She paused a moment in breathless wonder. The wind roared down the chimney, the rain beat in torrents against the windows, and every thing seemed to speak the awfulness of her situation. To retire to bed, however, unsatisfied on such a point, would be vain, since sleep must be impossible with the consciousness of a cabinet so mysteriously closed in her immediate vicinity. Again therefore she applied herself to the key, and after moving it in every possible way for some instants with the determined celerity of hope's last effort, the door suddenly yielded to her hand: her heart leaped with exultation at such a victory, and having thrown open each folding door, the second being secured only by bolts of less wonderful construction than the lock, though in that her eye could not discern any thing unusual, a double range of small drawers appeared in view, with some larger drawers above and below them; and in the centre, a small door, closed also with a lock and key, secured in all probability a cavity of importance.

Catherine's heart beat quick, but her courage did not fail her. With a cheek flushed by hope, and an eye straining with curiosity, her fingers grasped the handle of a drawer and drew it forth. It was entirely empty. With less alarm and greater eagerness she seized a second, a third, a fourth; each was equally empty. Not one was left unsearched, and in not one was any thing found. Well read in the art of concealing a treasure, the possibility of false linings to the drawers did not escape her, and she felt round each with anxious acuteness in vain. The place in the middle alone remained now unexplored; and though she had 'never from the first had the smallest idea of finding any thing in any part of the cabinet, and was not in the least disappointed at her ill success thus far, it would be foolish not to examine it thoroughly while she was about it.' It was some time however before she could unfasten the door, the same difficulty occurring in the management of this inner lock as of the outer; but at length it did open; and not vain, as hitherto, was her search; her quick eyes directly fell on a roll of paper pushed back into the further part of the cavity, apparently for concealment, and her feelings at that moment were indescribable. Her heart fluttered, her knees trembled, and her cheeks grew pale. She seized, with an unsteady hand, the precious manuscript, for half a glance sufficed to ascertain written characters; and while she acknowledged with awful sensations this striking exemplification of what Henry had foretold, resolved instantly to peruse every line before she attempted to rest.

The dimness of the light her candle emitted made her turn to it with alarm; but there was no danger of its sudden extinction, it had yet some hours to burn; and that she might not have any greater difficulty in distinguishing the writing than what its ancient date might occasion, she hastily snuffed it. Alas! it was snuffed and extinguished in one. A lamp could not have expired with more awful effect. Catherine, for a few moments, was motionless with horror. It was done completely; not a remnant of light in the wick could give hope to the rekindling breath. Darkness impenetrable and immoveable filled the room. A violent gust of wind, rising with sudden fury, added fresh horror to the moment. Catherine trembled from head to foot. In the pause which succeeded, a sound like receding footsteps and the closing of a distant door struck on her affrighted ear. Human nature could support no more. A cold sweat stood on her forehead, the manuscript fell from her hand, and groping her way to the bed, she jumped hastily in, and sought some suspension of agony by creeping far underneath the clothes. To close her eyes in sleep that night, she felt must be entirely out of the question. With a curiosity so justly awakened, and feelings in every way so agitated, repose must be absolutely impossible. The storm too abroad so dreadful! – She had not been used to feel alarm from wind, but now every blast seemed fraught with awful intelligence. The manuscript so wonderfully found, so wonderfully accomplishing the morning's prediction, how was it to be accounted for? – What could it contain? – to whom could it relate? – by what means could it have been so long concealed? – and how singularly strange that it should fall to her lot to discover it! Till she had made herself mistress of its contents, however, she could have neither repose nor comfort; and with the sun's first rays she was determined to peruse it. But many were the tedious hours which must yet intervene. She shuddered, tossed about in her bed, and envied every quiet sleeper. The storm still raged, and various were the noises, more terrific even than the wind, which struck at intervals on her startled ear. The very curtains of her bed seemed at one moment in motion, and at another the lock of her door was agitated, as if by the attempt of somebody to enter. Hollow murmurs seemed to creep along the gallery, and more than once her blood was chilled by the sound of distant moans. Hour after hour passed away, and the wearied Catherine had heard three proclaimed by all the clocks in the house, before the tempest subsided, or she unknowingly fell fast asleep.

CHAPTER VII

THE housemaid's folding back her window-shutters at eight o'clock the next day, was the sound which first roused Catherine; and she opened her eyes, wondering that they could ever have been closed, on objects of cheerfulness; her fire was already burning, and a bright morning had succeeded the tempest of the night. Instantaneously with the consciousness of existence, returned her recollection of the manuscript; and springing from the bed in the very moment of the maid's going away, she eagerly collected every scattered sheet which had burst from the roll on its falling to the ground, and flew back to enjoy the luxury of their perusal on her pillow. She now plainly saw that she must not expect a manuscript of equal length with the generality of what she had shuddered over in books, for the roll, seeming to consist entirely of small disjointed sheets, was altogether but of trifling size, and much less than she had supposed it to be at first.

Her greedy eye glanced rapidly over a page. She started at its import. Could it be possible, or did not her senses play her false? – An inventory of linen, in coarse and modern characters, seemed all that was before her! If the evidence of sight might be trusted, she held a washing-bill in her hand. She seized another sheet, and saw the same articles with little variation; a third, a fourth, and a fifth presented nothing new. Shirts, stockings, cravats and waistcoats faced her in each. Two others, penned by the same hand, marked an expenditure scarcely more interesting, in letters, hair-powder,[1] shoe-string and breeches-ball.[2] And the larger sheet, which had inclosed the rest, seemed by its first cramp line, 'To poultice chesnut mare,' – a farrier's bill! Such was the collection of papers, (left perhaps, as she could then suppose, by the negligence of a servant in the place whence she had taken them,) which had filled her with expectation and alarm, and robbed her of half her night's rest! She felt humbled to the dust. Could not the adventure of the chest have taught her wisdom? A corner of it catching her eye as she lay, seemed to rise up in judgment against her. Nothing could now be clearer than the absurdity of her recent fancies. To suppose that a manuscript of many generations back could have remained undiscovered in a room such as that, so modern, so habitable! – or that she should be the first to possess the skill of unlocking a cabinet, the key of which was open to all!

How could she have so imposed on herself? – Heaven forbid that Henry Tilney should ever know her folly! And it was in a great measure his own doing, for had not the cabinet appeared so exactly to agree with his description of her advaentures, she should never have felt the smallest curiosity about it. This was the only comfort that occurred. Impatient to get rid of those hateful evidences of her folly, those detestable papers then scattered over the bed, she rose directly, and folding them up as nearly as possible in the same shape as before, returned them to the same spot within the cabinet, with a very hearty wish that no untoward accident might ever bring them forward again, to disgrace her even with herself.

Why the locks should have been so difficult to open however,

>mething remarkable, for she could now manage them
ct ease. In this there was surely something mysterious,
and she indulged in the flattering suggestion for half a minute,
till the possibility of the door's having been at first unlocked, and
of being herself its fastener, darted into her head, and cost her
another blush.

She got away as soon as she could from a room in which her
conduct produced such unpleasant reflections, and found her
way with all speed to the breakfast-parlour, as it had been
pointed out to her by Miss Tilney the evening before. Henry
was alone in it; and his immediate hope of her having been
undisturbed by the tempest, with an arch reference to the
character of the building they inhabited, was rather distressing.
For the world would she not have her weakness suspected; and
yet, unequal to an absolute falsehood, was constrained to acknowledge that the wind had kept her awake a little. 'But we have a
charming morning after it,' she added, desiring to get rid of the
subject; 'and storms and sleeplessness are nothing when they
are over. What beautiful hyacinths! – I have just learnt to love a
hyacinth.'

'And how might you learn? – By accident or argument?'

'Your sister taught me; I cannot tell how. Mrs. Allen used to
take pains, year after year, to make me like them; but I never
could, till I saw them the other day in Milsom-street; I am
naturally indifferent about flowers.'

'But now you love a hyacinth. So much the better. You have
gained a new source of enjoyment, and it is well to have as many
holds upon happiness as possible. Besides, a taste for flowers is
always desirable in your sex, as a means of getting you out of
doors, and tempting you to more frequent exercise than you
would otherwise take. And though the love of a hyacinth may be
rather domestic, who can tell, the sentiment once raised, but you
may in time come to love a rose?'

'But I do not want any such pursuit to get me out of doors.
The pleasure of walking and breathing fresh air is enough for
me, and in fine weather I am out more than half my time. –
Mamma says, I am never within.'

'At any rate, however, I am pleased that you have learnt to love a hyacinth. The mere habit of learning to love is the thing; and a teachableness of disposition in a young lady is a great blessing. – Has my sister a pleasant mode of instruction?'

Catherine was saved the embarrassment of attempting an answer, by the entrance of the General, whose smiling compliments announced a happy state of mind, but whose gentle hint of sympathetic early rising did not advance her composure.

The elegance of the breakfast set forced itself on Catherine's notice when they were seated at table; and, luckily, it had been the General's choice. He was enchanted by her approbation of his taste, confessed it to be neat and simple, thought it right to encourage the manufacture of his country; and for his part, to his uncritical palate, the tea was as well flavoured from the clay of Staffordshire, as from that of Dresden or Sève. But this was quite an old set, purchased two years ago. The manufacture was much improved since that time; he had seen some beautiful specimens when last in town, and had he not been perfectly without vanity of that kind, might have been tempted to order a new set. He trusted, however, that an opportunity might ere long occur of selecting one – though not for himself. Catherine was probably the only one of the party who did not understand him.

Shortly after breakfast Henry left them for Woodston, where business required and would keep him two or three days. They all attended in the hall to see him mount his horse, and immediately on re-entering the breakfast room, Catherine walked to a window in the hope of catching another glimpse of his figure. 'This is a somewhat heavy call upon your brother's fortitude,' observed the General to Eleanor. 'Woodston will make but a sombre appearance to-day.'

'Is it a pretty place?' asked Catherine.

'What say you, Eleanor? – speak your opinion, for ladies can best tell the taste of ladies in regard to places as well as men. I think it would be acknowledged by the most impartial eye to have many recommendations. The house stands among fine meadows facing the south-east, with an excellent kitchen-garden in the same aspect; the walls surrounding which I built and stocked myself about ten years ago, for the benefit of my son. It is a family living, Miss Morland; and the property in the place being chiefly my own, you may believe I take care that it shall not be a bad one. Did Henry's income depend solely on this living, he would not be ill provided for. Perhaps it may seem odd, that with only two younger children, I should think any profession necessary for him; and certainly there are moments when we could all wish him disengaged from every tie of business. But though I may not exactly make converts of you young ladies, I am sure your father, Miss Morland, would agree with me in thinking it expedient to give every young man some employment. The money is nothing, it is not an object, but employment is the thing. Even Frederick, my eldest son, you see, who will perhaps inherit as considerable a landed property as any private man in the county, has his profession.'

The imposing effect of this last argument was equal to his wishes. The silence of the lady proved it to be unanswerable.

Something had been said the evening before of her being shewn over the house, and he now offered himself as her conductor; and though Catherine had hoped to explore it accompanied only by his daughter, it was a proposal of too much happiness in itself, under any circumstances, not to be gladly accepted; for she had been already eighteen hours in the Abbey, and had seen only a few of its rooms. The netting-box, just leisurely drawn forth, was closed with joyful haste, and she was ready to attend him in a moment. 'And when they had gone over the house, he promised himself moreover the pleasure of accompanying her into the shrubberies and garden.' She curtsied her acquiescence. 'But perhaps it might be more agreeable to her to make those her first object. The weather was at present favourable, and at this time of year the uncertainty was very great of its continuing so. – Which would she prefer? He was equally at her service. – Which did his daughter think would most accord with her fair friend's wishes? – But he thought he could discern. – Yes, he certainly read in Miss Morland's eyes a judicious desire of making use of the present smiling weather. –

But when did she judge amiss? – The Abbey would be always safe and dry. – He yielded implicitly, and would fetch his hat and attend them in a moment.' He left the room, and Catherine, with a disappointed, anxious face, began to speak of her unwillingness that he should be taking them out of doors against his own inclination, under a mistaken idea of pleasing her; but she was stopt by Miss Tilney's saying, with a little confusion, 'I believe it will be wisest to take the morning while it is so fine; and do not be uneasy on my father's account, he always walks out at this time of day.'

Catherine did not exactly know how this was to be understood. Why was Miss Tilney embarrassed? Could there be any unwillingness on the General's side to shew her over the Abbey? The proposal was his own. And was not it odd that he should *always* take his walk so early? Neither her father nor Mr. Allen did so. It was certainly very provoking. She was all impatience to see the house, and had scarcely any curiosity about the grounds. If Henry had been with them indeed! – but now she should not know what was picturesque when she saw it. Such were her thoughts, but she kept them to herself, and put on her bonnet in patient discontent.

She was struck however, beyond her expectation, by the grandeur of the Abbey, as she saw it for the first time from the lawn. The whole building enclosed a large court; and two sides of the quadrangle, rich in Gothic ornaments, stood forward for admiration. The remainder was shut off by knolls of old trees, or luxuriant plantations, and the steep woody hills rising behind to give it shelter, were beautiful even in the leafless month of March. Catherine had seen nothing to compare with it; and her feelings of delight were so strong, that without waiting for any better authority, she boldly burst forth in wonder and praise. The General listened with assenting gratitude; and it seemed as if his own estimation of Northanger had waited unfixed till that hour.

The kitchen-garden was to be next admired, and he led the way to it across a small portion of the park.

The number of acres contained in this garden was such as

Catherine could not listen to without dismay, being more than double the extent of all Mr. Allen's, as well as her father's, including church-yard and orchard. The walls seemed countless in number, endless in length; a village of hot-houses seemed to arise among them, and a whole parish to be at work within the inclosure. The General was flattered by her looks of surprize, which told him almost as plainly, as he soon forced her to tell him in words, that she had never seen any gardens at all equal to them before; – and he then modestly owned that, 'without any ambition of that sort himself – without any solicitude about it, – he did believe them to be unrivalled in the kingdom. If he had a hobby-horse, it was *that*. He loved a garden. Though careless enough in most matters of eating, he loved good fruit – or if he did not, his friends and children did. There were great vexations however attending such a garden as his. The utmost care could not always secure the most valuable fruits. The pinery[1] had yielded only one hundred in the last year. Mr. Allen, he supposed, must feel these inconveniences as well as himself.'

'No, not at all. Mr. Allen did not care about the garden, and never went into it.'

With a triumphant smile of self-satisfaction, the General wished he could do the same, for he never entered his, without being vexed in some way or other, by its falling short of his plan.

'How were Mr. Allen's succession-houses[2] worked?' describing the nature of his own as they entered them.

'Mr. Allen had only one small hot-house, which Mrs. Allen had the use of for her plants in winter, and there was a fire in it now and then.'

'He is a happy man!' said the General, with a look of very happy contempt.

Having taken her into every division, and led her under every wall, till she was heartily weary of seeing and wondering, he suffered the girls at last to seize the advantage of an outer door, then expressing his wish to examine the effect of some recent alterations about the tea-house, proposed it as no unpleasant extension of their walk, if Miss Morland were not tired. 'But where are you going, Eleanor? – Why do you chuse that cold, damp path to it? Miss Morland will get wet. Our best way is across the park.'

'This is so favourite a walk of mine,' said Miss Tilney, 'that I always think it the best and nearest way. But perhaps it may be damp.'

It was a narrow winding path through a thick grove of old Scotch firs; and Catherine, struck by its gloomy aspect, and eager to enter it, could not, even by the General's disapprobation, be kept from stepping forward. He perceived her inclination, and having again urged the plea of health in vain, was too polite to make further opposition. He excused himself however from attending them: – 'The rays of the sun were not too cheerful for him, and he would meet them by another course.' He turned away; and Catherine was shocked to find how much her spirits were relieved by the separation. The shock however being less real than the relief, offered it no injury; and she began to talk with easy gaiety of the delightful melancholy which such a grove inspired.

'I am particularly fond of this spot,' said her companion, with a sigh. 'It was my mother's favourite walk.'

Catherine had never heard Mrs. Tilney mentioned in the family before, and the interest excited by this tender remembrance, shewed itself directly in her altered countenance, and in the attentive pause with which she waited for something more.

'I used to walk here so often with her!' added Eleanor; 'though I never loved it then, as I have loved it since. At that time indeed I used to wonder at her choice. But her memory endears it now.'

'And ought it not,' reflected Catherine, 'to endear it to her husband? Yet the General would not enter it.' Miss Tilney continuing silent, she ventured to say, 'Her death must have been a great affliction!'

'A great and increasing one,' replied the other, in a low voice. 'I was only thirteen when it happened; and though I felt my loss perhaps as strongly as one so young could feel it, I did not, I could not then know what a loss it was.' She stopped for a moment, and then added, with great firmness, 'I have no sister,

you know – and though Henry – though my brothers are very
affectionate, and Henry is a great deal here, which I am most
thankful for, it is impossible for me not to be often solitary.'

'To be sure you must miss him very much.'

'A mother would have been always present. A mother would
have been a constant friend; her influence would have been
beyond all other.'

'Was she a very charming woman? Was she handsome? Was
there any picture of her in the Abbey? And why had she been so
partial to that grove? Was it from dejection of spirits?' – were
questions now eagerly poured forth; – the first three received a
ready affirmative, the two others were passed by; and Catherine's
interest in the deceased Mrs. Tilney augmented with every
question, whether answered or not. Of her unhappiness in
marriage, she felt persuaded. The General certainly had been an
unkind husband. He did not love her walk: – could he therefore
have loved her? And besides, handsome as he was, there was a
something in the turn of his features which spoke his not having
behaved well to her.

'Her picture, I suppose,' blushing at the consummate art of
her own question, 'hangs in your father's room?'

'No; – it was intended for the drawing-room; but my father
was dissatisfied with the painting, and for some time it had no
place. Soon after her death I obtained it for my own, and hung it
in my bed-chamber – where I shall be happy to shew it you; – it
is very like.' – Here was another proof. A portrait – very like –
of a departed wife, not valued by the husband! – He must have
been dreadfully cruel to her!

Catherine attempted no longer to hide from herself the
nature of the feelings which, in spite of all his attentions, he had
previously excited; and what had been terror and dislike before,
was now absolute aversion. Yes, aversion! His cruelty to such a
charming woman made him odious to her. She had often read of
such characters; characters, which Mr. Allen had been used to
call unnatural and overdrawn; but here was proof positive of the
contrary.

She had just settled this point, when the end of the path

brought them directly upon the General; and in spite of all her virtuous indignation, she found herself again obliged to walk with him, listen to him, and even to smile when he smiled. Being no longer able however to receive pleasure from the surrounding objects, she soon began to walk with lassitude; the General perceived it, and with a concern for her health, which seemed to reproach her for her opinion of him, was most urgent for returning with his daughter to the house. He would follow them in a quarter of an hour. Again they parted – but Eleanor was called back in half a minute to receive a strict charge against taking her friend round the Abbey till his return. This second instance of his anxiety to delay what she so much wished for, struck Catherine as very remarkable.

CHAPTER VIII

An hour passed away before the General came in, spent, on the part of his young guest, in no very favourable consideration of his character. – 'This lengthened absence, these solitary rambles, did not speak a mind at ease, or a conscience void of reproach.' – At length he appeared; and, whatever might have been the gloom of his meditations, he could still smile with *them*. Miss Tilney, understanding in part her friend's curiosity to see the house, soon revived the subject; and her father being, contrary to Catherine's expectations, unprovided with any pretence for further delay, beyond that of stopping five minutes to order refreshments to be in the room by their return, was at last ready to escort them.

They set forward; and, with a grandeur of air, a dignified step, which caught the eye, but could not shake the doubts of the well-read Catherine, he led the way across the hall, through the common drawing-room and one useless anti-chamber,[1] into a room magnificent both in size and furniture – the real drawing-room, used only with company of consequence. – It was very noble – very grand – very charming! – was all that Catherine had to say, for her indiscriminating eye scarcely discerned the colour of the satin; and all minuteness of praise, all praise that had much meaning, was supplied by the General: the costliness or elegance of any room's fitting-up could be nothing to her; she cared for no furniture of a more modern date than the fifteenth century. When the General had satisfied his own curiosity, in a close examination of every well-known ornament, they proceeded into the library, an apartment, in its way, of equal magnificence, exhibiting a collection of books, on which an humble man might have looked with pride. - Catherine heard, admired, and wondered with more genuine feeling than before - gathered all that she could from this storehouse of knowledge, by running over the titles of half a shelf, and was ready to proceed. But suites of apartments did not spring up with her wishes. - Large as was the building, she had already visited the greatest part; though, on being told that, with the addition of the kitchen, the six or seven rooms she had now seen surrounded three sides of the court, she could scarcely believe it, or overcome the suspicion of there being many chambers secreted. It was some relief, however, that they were to return to the rooms in common use, by passing through a few of less importance, looking into the court, which, with occasional passages, not wholly unintricate, connected the different sides; - and she was further soothed in her progress, by being told, that she was treading what had once been a cloister, having traces of cells pointed out, and observing several doors, that were neither opened nor explained to her; - by finding herself successively in a billiard-room, and in the General's private apartment, without comprehending their connexion, or being able to turn aright when she left them; and lastly, by passing through a dark little room, owning Henry's authority, and strewed with his litter of books, guns and great coats.

From the dining-room of which, though already seen, and always to be seen at five o'clock, the General could not forego the pleasure of pacing out the length, for the more certain information of Miss Morland, as to what she neither doubted nor cared for, they proceeded by quick communication to the kitchen - the ancient kitchen of the convent, rich in the massy walls and smoke of former days, and in the stoves and hot closets of the present. The General's improving hand had not loitered here: every modern invention to facilitate the labour of the cooks, had been adopted within this, their spacious theatre; and, when the genius of others had failed, his own had often produced the perfection wanted. His endowments of this spot alone might at any time have placed him high among the benefactors of the convent.

With the walls of the kitchen ended all the antiquity of the Abbey; the fourth side of the quadrangle having, on account of its decaying state, been removed by the General's father, and the present erected in its place. All that was venerable ceased here. The new building was not only new, but declared itself to be so; intended only for offices, and enclosed behind by stable-yards, no uniformity of architecture had been thought necessary. Catherine could have raved at the hand which had swept away what must have been beyond the value of all the rest, for the purposes of mere domestic economy; and would willingly have been spared the mortification of a walk through scenes so fallen, had the General allowed it; but if he had a vanity, it was in the arrangement of his offices; and as he was convinced, that, to a mind like Miss Morland's, a view of the accommodations and comforts, by which the labours of her inferiors were softened, must always be gratifying, he should make no apology for leading her on. They took a slight survey of all; and Catherine was impressed, beyond her expectation, by their multiplicity and their convenience. The purposes for which a few shapeless pantries and a comfortless scullery were deemed sufficient at Fullerton, were here carried on in appropriate divisions, commodious and roomy. The number of servants continually appearing, did not strike her less than the number of their offices. Wherever they went, some pattened girl stopped to curtsey, or some footman in dishabille sneaked off. Yet this was an Abbey! – How inexpressibly different in these domestic arrangements from such as she had read about – from abbeys and castles, in which, though certainly larger than Northanger, all the dirty work of the house was to be done by two pair of female hands at the utmost. How they could get through it all, had often amazed Mrs. Allen; and, when Catherine saw what was necessary here, she began to be amazed herself.

They returned to the hall, that the chief stair-case might be ascended, and the beauty of its wood, and ornaments of rich carving might be pointed out: having gained the top, they turned in an opposite direction from the gallery in which her room lay, and shortly entered one on the same plan, but superior in length and breadth. She was here shewn successively into three large bed-chambers, with their dressing-rooms, most completely and handsomely fitted up; every thing that money and taste could do, to give comfort and elegance to apartments, had been bestowed on these; and, being furnished within the last five years, they were perfect in all that would be generally pleasing, and wanting in all that could give pleasure to Catherine. As they were surveying the last, the General, after slightly naming a few of the distinguished characters, by whom they had at times been honoured, turned with a smiling countenance to Catherine, and ventured to hope, that henceforward some of their earliest tenants might be 'our friends from Fullerton.' She felt the unexpected compliment, and deeply regretted the impossibility of thinking well of a man so kindly disposed towards herself, and so full of civility to all her family.

The gallery was terminated by folding doors, which Miss Tilney, advancing, had thrown open, and passed through, and seemed on the point of doing the same by the first door to the left, in another long reach of gallery, when the General, coming forwards, called her hastily, and, as Catherine thought, rather angrily back, demanding whither she were going? – And what was there more to be seen? – Had not Miss Morland already seen all that could be worth her notice? – And did she not suppose her friend might be glad of some refreshment after so much exercise? Miss Tilney drew back directly, and the heavy doors were closed upon the mortified Catherine, who, having seen, in a momentary glance beyond them, a narrower passage, more numerous openings, and symptoms of a winding stair-case, believed herself at last within the reach of something worth her notice; and felt, as she unwillingly paced back the gallery, that she would rather be allowed to examine that end of the house, than see all the finery of all the rest. – The General's evident desire of preventing such an examination was an additional stimulant. Something was certainly to be concealed; her fancy, though it had trespassed lately once or twice, could not mislead her here; and what that something was, a short sentence of Miss Tilney's, as they followed the General at some distance down stairs, seemed to point out: – 'I was going to take you into what was my mother's room – the room in which she died—' were all her words; but few as they were, they conveyed pages of intelligence to Catherine. It was no wonder that the General should shrink from the sight of such objects as that room must contain; a room in all probability never entered by him since the dreadful scene had passed, which released his suffering wife, and left him to the stings of conscience.

She ventured, when next alone with Eleanor, to express her wish of being permitted to see it, as well as all the rest of that side of the house; and Eleanor promised to attend her there, whenever they should have a convenient hour. Catherine understood her: – the General must be watched from home, before that room could be entered. 'It remains as it was, I suppose?' said she, in a tone of feeling.

'Yes, entirely.'

'And how long ago may it be that your mother died?'

'She has been dead these nine years.' And nine years, Catherine knew was a trifle of time, compared with what generally elapsed after the death of an injured wife, before her room was put to rights.

'You were with her, I suppose, to the last?'

'No,' said Miss Tilney, sighing; 'I was unfortunately from home. – Her illness was sudden and short; and, before I arrived it was all over.'

Catherine's blood ran cold with the horrid suggestions which naturally sprang from these words. Could it be possible? – Could Henry's father? – And yet how many were the examples to justify even the blackest suspicions! – And, when she saw him in the evening, while she worked with her friend, slowly pacing the drawing-room for an hour together in silent thoughtfulness, with downcast eyes and contracted brow, she felt secure from all possibility of wronging him. It was the air and attitude of a Montoni![1] – What could more plainly speak the gloomy workings of a mind not wholly dead to every sense of humanity, in its fearful review of past scenes of guilt? Unhappy man! – And the anxiousness of her spirits directed her eyes towards his figure so repeatedly, as to catch Miss Tilney's notice. 'My father,' she whispered, 'often walks about the room in this way; it is nothing unusual.'

'So much the worse!' thought Catherine; such ill-timed exercise was of a piece with the strange unseasonableness of his morning walks, and boded nothing good.

After an evening, the little variety and seeming length of which made her peculiarly sensible of Henry's importance among them, she was heartily glad to be dismissed; though it was a look from the General not designed for her observation which sent his daughter to the bell. When the butler would have lit his master's candle, however, he was forbidden. The latter was not going to retire. 'I have many pamphlets to finish,' said he to Catherine, 'before I can close my eyes; and perhaps may be poring over the affairs of the nation for hours after you are asleep. Can either of us be more meetly employed? *My* eyes will be blinding for the good of others; and *yours* preparing by rest for future mischief.'

But neither the business alleged, nor the magnificent compliment, could win Catherine from thinking, that some very different object must occasion so serious a delay of proper repose. To be kept up for hours, after the family were in bed, by stupid pamphlets, was not very likely. There must be some deeper cause: something was to be done which could be done only while the household slept; and the probability that Mrs. Tilney yet lived, shut up for causes unknown, and receiving from the pitiless hands of her husband a nightly supply of coarse food, was the conclusion which necessarily followed. Shocking as was the idea, it was at least better than a death unfairly hastened, as, in the natural course of things, she must ere long be released. The suddenness of her reputed illness; the absence of her daughter, and probably of her other children, at the time – all favoured the supposition of her imprisonment. – Its origin – jealousy perhaps, or wanton cruelty – was yet to be unravelled.

In revolving these matters, while she undressed, it suddenly struck her as not unlikely, that she might that morning have passed near the very spot of this unfortunate woman's confinement – might have been within a few paces of the cell in which she languished out her days; for what part of the Abbey could be more fitted for the purpose than that which yet bore the traces of monastic division? In the high-arched passage, paved with stone, which already she had trodden with peculiar awe, she well remembered the doors of which the General had given no account. To what might not those doors lead? In support of the plausibility of this conjecture, it further occurred to her, that the forbidden gallery, in which lay the apartments of the unfortunate Mrs. Tilney, must be, as certainly as her memory could guide her, exactly over this suspected range of cells, and the stair-case by the side of those apartments of which she had caught a transient glimpse, communicating by some secret means with those cells, might well have favoured the barbarous proceedings of her husband. Down that stair-case she had perhaps been conveyed in a state of well-prepared insensibility!

Catherine sometimes started at the boldness of her own surmises, and sometimes hoped or feared that she had gone too far; but they were supported by such appearances as made their dismissal impossible.

The side of the quadrangle, in which she supposed the guilty scene to be acting, being, according to her belief, just opposite her own, it struck her that, if judiciously watched, some rays of light from the General's lamp might glimmer through the lower windows, as he passed to the prison of his wife; and, twice before she stepped into bed, she stole gently from her room to the corresponding window in the gallery, to see if it appeared; but all abroad was dark, and it must yet be too early. The various ascending noises convinced her that the servants must still be up. Till midnight, she supposed it would be in vain to watch; but then, when the clock had struck twelve, and all was quiet, she would, if not quite appalled by darkness, steal out and look once more. The clock struck twelve – and Catherine had been half an hour asleep.

CHAPTER IX

THE next day afforded no opportunity for the proposed examination of the mysterious apartments. It was Sunday, and the whole time between morning and afternoon service was required by the General in exercise abroad or eating cold meat at home; and great as was Catherine's curiosity, her courage was not equal to a wish of exploring them after dinner, either by the fading light of the sky between six and seven o'clock, or by the yet more partial though stronger illumination of a treacherous lamp. The day was unmarked therefore by any thing to interest her imagination beyond the sight of a very elegant monument to the memory of Mrs. Tilney, which immediately fronted the family pew. By that her eye was instantly caught and long retained; and the perusal of the highly-strained epitaph, in which every virtue was ascribed to her by the inconsolable husband, who must have been in some way or other her destroyer, affected her even to tears.

That the General, having erected such a monument, should be able to face it, was not perhaps very strange, and yet that he could sit so boldly collected within its view, maintain so elevated an air, look so fearlessly around, nay, that he should even enter the church, seemed wonderful to Catherine. Not however that many instances of beings equally hardened in guilt might not be produced. She could remember dozens who had persevered in every possible vice, going on from crime to crime, murdering whomsoever they chose, without any feeling of humanity or remorse; till a violent death or a religious retirement closed their black career. The erection of the monument itself could not in the smallest degree affect her doubts of Mrs. Tilney's actual decease. Were she even to descend into the family vault where her ashes were supposed to slumber, were she to behold the coffin in which they were said to be enclosed – what could it avail in such a case? Catherine had read too much not to be perfectly aware of the ease with which a waxen figure might be introduced, and a supposititious funeral carried on.

The succeeding morning promised something better. The General's early walk, ill-timed as it was in every other view, was favourable here; and when she knew him to be out of the house, she directly proposed to Miss Tilney the accomplishment of her promise. Eleanor was ready to oblige her; and Catherine reminding her as they went of another promise, their first visit in consequence was to the portrait in her bed-chamber. It represented a very lovely woman, with a mild and pensive countenance, justifying, so far, the expectations of its new observer; but they were not in every respect answered, for Catherine had depended upon meeting with features, air, complexion that should be the very counterpart, the very image, if not of Henry's, of Eleanor's; – the only portraits of which she had been in the habit of thinking, bearing always an equal resemblance of mother and child. A face once taken was taken for generations. But here she was obliged to look and consider and study for a likeness. She contemplated it, however, in spite of this drawback, with much emotion; and, but for a yet stronger interest, would have left it unwillingly.

Her agitation as they entered the great gallery was too much for any endeavour at discourse; she could only look at her companion. Eleanor's countenance was dejected, yet sedate; and its composure spoke her enured to all the gloomy objects to which they were advancing. Again she passed through the folding-doors, again her hand was upon the important lock, and Catherine, hardly able to breathe, was turning to close the former with fearful caution, when the figure, the dreaded figure of the General himself at the further end of the gallery, stood before her! The name of 'Eleanor' at the same moment, in his loudest tone, resounded through the building, giving to his daughter the first intimation of his presence, and to Catherine terror upon terror. An attempt at concealment had been her first instinctive movement on perceiving him, yet she could scarcely hope to have escaped his eye; and when her friend, who with an apologizing look darted hastily by her, had joined and disappeared with him, she ran for safety to her own room, and, locking herself in, believed that she should never have courage to go down again. She remained there at least an hour, in the greatest agitation, deeply commiserating the state of her poor friend, and expecting a summons herself from the angry General to attend him in his own apartment. No summons however arrived; and at last, on seeing a carriage drive up to the Abbey, she was emboldened to descend and meet him under the protection of visitors. The breakfast-room was gay with company; and she was named to them by the General, as the friend of his daughter, in a complimentary style, which so well concealed his resentful ire, as to make her feel secure at least of life for the present. And Eleanor, with a command of countenance which did honour to her concern for his character, taking an early occasion of saying to her, 'My father only wanted me to answer a note,' she began to hope that she had either been unseen by the General, or that from some consideration of policy she should be allowed to suppose herself so. Upon this trust she dared still to remain in his presence, after the company left them, and nothing occurred to disturb it.

In the course of this morning's reflections, she came to a resolution of making her next attempt on the forbidden door alone. It would be much better in every respect that Eleanor should know nothing of the matter. To involve her in the danger of a second detection, to court her into an apartment which must wring her heart, could not be the office of a friend. The General's utmost anger could not be to herself what it might be to a daughter; and, besides, she thought the examination itself would be more satisfactory if made without any companion. It would be impossible to explain to Eleanor the suspicions, from which the other had, in all likelihood, been hitherto happily exempt; nor could she therefore, in *her* presence, search for those proofs of the General's cruelty, which however they might yet have escaped discovery, she felt confident of somewhere drawing forth, in the shape of some fragmented journal, continued to the last gasp. Of the way to the apartment she was now perfectly mistress; and as she wished to get it over before Henry's return, who was expected on the morrow, there was no time to be lost. The day was bright, her courage high; at four o'clock, the sun was now two hours above the horizon, and it would be only her retiring to dress half an hour earlier than usual.

It was done; and Catherine found herself alone in the gallery before the clocks had ceased to strike. It was no time for thought; she hurried on, slipped with the least possible noice through the folding doors, and without stopping to look or breathe, rushed forward to the one in question. The lock yielded to her hand, and, luckily, with no sullen sound that could alarm a human being. On tip-toe she entered; the room was before her; but it was some minutes before she could advance another step. She beheld what fixed her to the spot and agitated every feature. – She saw a large, well-proportioned apartment, an handsome dimity[1] bed, arranged as unoccupied with an housemaid's care, a bright Bath stove, mahogany wardrobes and neatly-painted chairs, on which the warm beams of a western sun gaily poured through two sash windows! Catherine had expected to have her feelings worked, and worked they were. Astonishment and doubt first seized them; and a shortly succeeding ray of common sense added some bitter emotions of shame. She could not be mistaken as to the room; but how grossly mistaken in every thing else! – in Miss Tilney's meaning, in her own calculation! This apartment, to which she had given a date so ancient, a position so awful, proved to be one end of what the General's father had built. There were two other doors in the chamber, leading probably into dressing-closets; but she had no inclination to open either. Would the veil in which Mrs. Tilney had lasted walked, or the volume in which she had last read, remain to tell what nothing else was allowed to whisper? No: whatever might have been the General's crimes, he had certainly too much wit to let them sue for detection. She was sick of exploring, and desired but to be safe in her own room, with her own heart only privy to its folly; and she was on the point of retreating as softly as she had entered, when the sound of footsteps, she could hardly tell where, made her pause and tremble. To be found there, even by a servant, would be unpleasant; but by the General, (and he seemed always at hand when least wanted,) much worse! – She listened – the sound had ceased; and resolving not to lose a moment, she passed through and closed the door. At that instant a door underneath was hastily opened; some one seemed with swift steps to ascend the stairs, by the head of which she had yet to pass before she could gain the gallery. She had no power to move. With a feeling of terror not very definable, she fixed her eyes on the staircase, and in a few moments it gave Henry to her view. 'Mr. Tilney!' she exclaimed in a voice of more than common astonishment. He looked astonished too. 'Good God!' she continued, not attending to his address, 'how came you here? – how came you up that staircase?'

'How came I up that staircase!' he replied, greatly surprized. 'Because it is my nearest way from the stable-yard to my own chamber; and why should I not come up it?'

Catherine recollected herself, blushed deeply, and could say no more. He seemed to be looking in her countenance for that explanation which her lips did not afford. She moved on towards the gallery. 'And may I not, in my turn,' said he, as he pushed back the folding doors, 'ask how *you* came here? – This passage is at least as extraordinary a road from the breakfast-parlour to your apartment, as that staircase can be from the stables to mine.'

'I have been,' said Catherine, looking down, 'to see your mother's room.'

'My mother's room! – Is there any thing extraordinary to be seen there?'

'No, nothing at all. – I thought you did not mean to come back till to-morrow.'

'I did not expect to be able to return sooner, when I went away; but three hours ago I had the pleasure of finding nothing to detain me. – You look pale. – I am afraid I alarmed you by running so fast up those stairs. Perhaps you did not know – you were not aware of their leading from the offices in common use?'

'No, I was not. – You have had a very fine day for your ride.'

'Very; – and does Eleanor leave you to find your way into all the rooms in the house by yourself?'

'Oh! no; she shewed me over the greatest part on Saturday – and we were coming here to these rooms – but only – (dropping her voice) – your father was with us.'

'And that prevented you;' said Henry, earnestly regarding her. – 'Have you looked into all the rooms in that passage?'

'No, I only wanted to see—Is not it very late? I must go and dress.'

'It is only a quarter past four, (shewing his watch) and you are not now in Bath. No theatre, no rooms to prepare for. Half an hour at Northanger must be enough.'

She could not contradict it, and therefore suffered herself to be detained, though her dread of further questions made her, for the first time in their acquaintance, wish to leave him. They walked slowly up the gallery. 'Have you had any letter from Bath since I saw you?'

'No, and I am very much surprized. Isabella promised so faithfully to write directly.'

'Promised so faithfully! – A faithful promise! – That puzzles me. – I have heard of a faithful performance. But a faithful promise – the fidelity of promising! It is a power little worth knowing however, since it can deceive and pain you. My mother's room is very commodious, is it not? Large and cheerful-looking, and the dressing closets so well disposed! It always strikes me as the most comfortable apartment in the house, and I rather wonder that Eleanor should not take it for her own. She sent you to look at it, I suppose?'

'No.'

'It has been your own doing entirely?' – Catherine said nothing – After a short silence, during which he had closely observed her, he added, 'As there is nothing in the room in itself to raise curiosity, this must have proceeded from a sentiment of respect for my mother's character, as described by Eleanor, which does honour to her memory. The world, I believe, never saw a better woman. But it is not often that virtue can boast an interest such as this. The domestic, unpretending merits of a person never known, do not often create that kind of fervent, venerating tenderness which would prompt a visit like yours. Eleanor, I suppose, has talked of her a great deal?'

'Yes, a great deal. That is – no, not much, but what she did say, was very interesting. Her dying so suddenly,' (slowly, and with hesitation it was spoken,) 'and you – none of you being at home – and your father, I thought – perhaps had not been very fond of her.'

'And from these circumstances,' he repled, (his quick eye fixed on her's,) 'you infer perhaps the probability of some negligence – some – (involuntarily she shook her head) – or it may be – of something still less pardonable.' She raised her eyes towards him more fully than she had ever done before. 'My mother's illness,' he continued, 'the seizure which ended in her death *was* sudden. The malady itself, one from which she had often suffered, a bilious fever – its cause therefore constitutional. On the third day, in short as soon as she could be prevailed on, a physician attended her, a very respectable man, and one in whom she had always placed great confidence. Upon his opinion of her danger, two others were called in the next day, and remained in almost constant attendance for four-and-twenty hours. On the fifth day she died. During the progress of her disorder, Frederick and I (*we* were both at home) saw her repeatedly; and from our own observation can bear witness to her having received every possible attention which could spring from the affection of those about her, or which her situation in life could command. Poor Eleanor *was* absent, and at such a distance as to return only to see her mother in her coffin.'

'But your father,' said Catherine, 'was *he* afflicted?'

'For a time, greatly so. You have erred in supposing him not attached to her. He loved her, I am persuaded, as well as it was possible for him to – We have not all, you know, the same tenderness of disposition – and I will not pretend to say that while she lived, she might not often have had much to bear, but though his temper injured her, his judgment never did. His value of her was sincere; and, if not permanently, he was truly afflicted by her death.'

'I am very glad of it,' said Catherine, 'it would have been very shocking!'—

'If I understand you rightly, you had formed a surmise of such horror as I have hardly words to—Dear Miss Morland, consider the dreadful nature of the suspicions you have entertained. What have you been judging from? Remember the country and the age in which we live. Remember that we are English, that we are Christians. Consult your own understanding, your own sense of the probable, your own observation of what is passing around you – Does our education prepare us for such atrocities? Do our laws connive at them? Could they be perpetrated without being known, in a country like this, where social and literary intercourse is on such a footing; where every man is surrounded by a neighbourhood of voluntary spies, and where roads and newspapers lay every thing open? Dearest Miss Morland, what ideas have you been admitting?'

They had reached the end of the gallery; and with tears of shame she ran off to her own room.

CHAPTER X

THE visions of romance were over. Catherine was completely awakened. Henry's address, short as it had been, had more thoroughly opened her eyes to the extravagance of her late fancies than all their several disappointments had done. Most grievously was she humbled. Most bitterly did she cry. It was not only with herself that she was sunk – but with Henry. Her folly, which now seemed even criminal, was all exposed to him, and he must despise her for ever. The liberty which her imagination had dared to take with the character of his father, could he ever forgive it? The absurdity of her curiosity and her fears, could they ever be forgotten? She hated herself more than she could express. He had – she thought he had, once or twice before this fatal morning, shewn something like affection for her. – But now – in short, she made herself as miserable as possible for about half an hour, went down when the clock struck five, with a broken heart, and could scarcely give intelligible answer to Eleanor's inquiry, if she was well. The formidable Henry soon followed her into the room, and the only difference in his behaviour to her, was that he paid her rather more attention than usual. Catherine had never wanted comfort more, and he looked as if he was aware of it.

The evening wore away with no abatement of this soothing politeness; and her spirits were gradually raised to a modest tranquillity. She did not learn either to forget or defend the past; but she learned to hope that it would never transpire farther, and that it might not cost her Henry's entire regard. Her thoughts being still chiefly fixed on what she had with such causeless terror felt and done, nothing could shortly be clearer, than that it had been all a voluntary, self-created delusion, each trifling circumstance receiving importance from an imagination resolved on alarm, and every thing forced to bend to one purpose by a mind which, before she entered the Abbey, had been craving to be frightened. She remembered with what feelings she had prepared for a knowledge of Northanger. She saw that the infatuation had been created, the mischief settled long before her quitting Bath, and it seemed as if the whole might be traced to the influence of that sort of reading which she had there indulged.

Charming as were all Mrs. Radcliffe's works, and charming even as were the works of all her imitators, it was not in them perhaps that human nature, at least in the midland counties of England, was to be looked for. Of the Alps and Pyrenees, with their pine forests and their vices, they might give a faithful delineation; and Italy, Switzerland, and the South of France, might be as fruitful in horrors as they were there represented. Catherine dared not doubt beyond her own country, and even of that, if hard pressed, would have yielded the northern and western extremities. But in the central part of England there was surely some security for the existence even of a wife not beloved, in the laws of the land, and the manners of the age. Murder was not tolerated, servants were not slaves, and neither poison nor sleeping potions to be procured, like rhubarb, from every druggist. Among the Alps and Pyrenees, perhaps, there were no mixed characters. There, such as were not as spotless as an angel, might have the dispositions of a fiend. But in England it was not so; among the English, she believed, in their hearts and habits, there was a general though unequal mixture of good and bad. Upon this conviction, she would not be surprized if even in Henry and Eleanor Tilney, some slight imperfection might hereafter appear; and upon this conviction she need not fear to acknowledge some actual specks in the character of their father, who, though cleared from the grossly injurious suspicions which she must ever blush to have entertained, she did believe, upon serious consideration, to be not perfectly amiable.

Her mind made up on these several points, and her resolution formed, of always judging and acting in future with the greatest good sense, she had nothing to do but to forgive herself and be happier than ever; and the lenient hand of time did much for her by insensible gradations in the course of another day. Henry's astonishing generosity and nobleness of conduct, in never alluding in the slightest way to what had passed, was of the greatest assistance to her; and sooner than she could have supposed it possible in the beginning of her distress, her spirits became absolutely comfortable, and capable, as heretofore, of continual improvement by any thing he said. There were still some subjects indeed, under which she believed they must always tremble; – the mention of a chest or a cabinet, for instance – and she did not love the sight of japan in any shape: but even *she* could allow, that an occasional memento of past folly, however painful, might not be without use.

The anxieties of common life began soon to succeed to the alarms of romance. Her desire of hearing from Isabella grew every day greater. She was quite impatient to know how the

Bath world went on, and how the Rooms were attended; and especially was she anxious to be assured of Isabella's having matched some fine netting-cotton, on which she had left her intent; and of her continuing on the best terms with James. Her only dependence for information of any kind was on Isabella. James had protested against writing to her till his return to Oxford; and Mrs. Allen had given her no hopes of a letter till she had got back to Fullerton. – But Isabella had promised and promised again; and when she promised a thing, she was so scrupulous in performing it! this made it so particularly strange!

For nine successive mornings, Catherine wondered over the repetition of a disappointment, which each morning became more severe: but, on the tenth, when she entered the breakfast-room, her first object was a letter, held out by Henry's willing hand. She thanked him as heartily as if he had written it himself. ''Tis only from James, however,' as she looked at the direction. She opened it; it was from Oxford; and to this purpose: –

'Dear Catherine,

Though, God knows, with little inclination for writing, I think it my duty to tell you, that every thing is at an end between Miss Thorpe and me. – I left her and Bath yesterday, never to see either again. I shall not enter into particulars, they would only pain you more. You will soon hear enough from another quarter to know where lies the blame; and I hope will acquit your brother of every thing but the folly of too easily thinking his affection returned. Thank God! I am undeceived in time! But it is a heavy blow! – After my father's consent had been so kindly given – but no more of this. She has made me miserable for ever! Let me soon hear from you, dear Catherine; you are my only friend; *your* love I do build upon. I wish your visit at Northanger may be over before Captain Tilney makes his engagement known, or you will be uncomfortably circum-stanced. – Poor Thorpe is in town: I dread the sight of him; his honest heart would feel so much. I have written to him and my father. Her duplicity hurts me more than all; till the very last, if I reasoned with her, she declared herself as much attached to me as ever, and laughed at my fears. I am ashamed to think how long I bore with it; but if ever man had reason to believe himself loved, I was that man. I cannot understand even now what she would be at, for there could be no need of my being played off to make her secure of Tilney. We parted at last by mutual consent – happy for me had we never met! I can never expect to know such another woman! Dearest Catherine, beware how you give your heart.

Believe me,' &c.

Catherine had not read three lines before her sudden change of countenance, and short exclamations of sorrowing wonder, declared her to be receiving unpleasant news; and Henry, earnestly watching her through the whole letter, saw plainly that it ended no better than it began. He was prevented, however, from even looking his surprize by his father's entrance. They went to breakfast directly; but Catherine could hardly eat any thing. Tears filled her eyes, and even ran down her cheeks as she sat. The letter was one moment in her hand, then in her lap, and then in her pocket; and she looked as if she knew not what she did. The General, between his cocoa and his newspaper, had luckily no leisure for noticing her; but to the other two her distress was equally visible. As soon as she dared leave the table she hurried away to her own room; but the house-maids were busy in it, and she was obliged to come down again. She turned into the drawing-room for privacy, but Henry and Eleanor had likewise retreated thither, and were at that moment deep in consultation about her. She drew back, trying to beg their pardon, but was, with gentle violence, forced to return; and the others withdrew, after Eleanor had affectionately expressed a wish of being of use or comfort to her.

After half an hour's free indulgence of grief and reflection, Catherine felt equal to encountering her friends; but whether she should make her distress known to them was another consideration. Perhaps, if particularly questioned, she might just give an idea – just distantly hint at it – but not more. To expose a friend, such a friend as Isabella had been to her – and then their own brother so closely concerned in it! – She believed she must wave the subject altogether. Henry and Eleanor were by themselves in the breakfast-room; and each, as she entered it, looked at her anxiously. Catherine took her place at the table, and, after a short silence, Eleanor said, 'No bad news from Fullerton, I hope? Mr. and Mrs Morland – your brothers and sisters – I hope they are none of them ill?'

'No, I thank you,' (sighing as she spoke,) 'they are all very well. My letter was from my brother at Oxford.'

Nothing further was said for a few minutes; and then speaking through her tears, she added, 'I do not think I shall ever wish for a letter again!'

'I am sorry,' said Henry, closing the book he had just opened; 'if I had suspected the letter of containing any thing unwelcome, I should have given it with very different feelings.'

'It contained something worse than any body could suppose! – Poor James is so unhappy! – You will soon know why.'

'To have so kind-hearted, so affectionate a sister,' replied Henry, warmly, 'must be a comfort to him under any distress.'

'I have one favour to beg,' said Catherine, shortly afterwards, in an agitated manner, 'that, if your brother should be coming here, you will give me notice of it, that I may go away.'

'Our brother! – Frederick!'

'Yes; I am sure I should be very sorry to leave you so soon, but something has happened that would make it very dreadful for me to be in the same house with Captain Tilney.'

Eleanor's work was suspended while she gazed with increasing astonishment; but Henry began to suspect the truth, and something, in which Miss Thorpe's name was included, passed his lips.

'How quick you are!' cried Catherine: 'you have guessed it, I declare! – And yet, when we talked about it in Bath, you little thought of its ending so. Isabella – no wonder *now* I have not heard from her – Isabella has deserted my brother, and is to marry your's! Could you have believed there had been such inconstancy and fickleness, and every thing that is bad in the world?'

'I hope, so far as concerns my brother, you are mis-informed.

I hope he has not had any material share in bringing on Mr. Morland's disappointment. His marrying Miss Thorpe is not probable. I think you must be deceived so far. I am very sorry for Mr. Morland – sorry that any one you love should be unhappy; but my surprize would be greater at Frederick's marrying her, than at any other part of the story.'

'It is very true, however; you shall read James's letter yourself. – Stay—there is one part—' recollecting with a blush the last line.

'Will you take the trouble of reading to us the passages which concern my brother?'

'No, read it yourself,' cried Catherine, whose second thoughts were clearer. 'I do not know what I was thinking of,' (blushing again that she had blushed before,) – 'James only means to give me good advice.'

He gladly received the letter; and, having read it through, with close attention, returned it saying, 'Well, if it is to be so, I can only say that I am sorry for it. Frederick will not be the first man who has chosen a wife with less sense than his family expected. I do not envy his situation, either as a lover or a son.'

Miss Tilney, at Catherine's invitation, now read the letter likewise; and, having expressed also her concern and surprize, began to inquire into Miss Thorpe's connexions and fortune.

'Her mother is a very good sort of woman,' was Catherine's answer.

'What was her father?'

'A lawyer, I believe. – They live at Putney.'

'Are they a wealthy family?'

'No, not very. I do not believe Isabella has any fortune at all: but that will not signify in your family. – Your father is so very liberal! He told me the other day, that he only valued money as it allowed him to promote the happiness of his children.' The brother and sister looked at each other. 'But,' said Eleanor, after a short pause, 'would it be to promote his happiness, to enable him to marry such a girl? – She must be an unprincipled one, or she could not have used your brother so. – And how strange an infatuation on Frederick's side! A girl who, before his eyes, is violating an engagement voluntarily entered into with another man! Is not it inconceivable, Henry? Frederick too, who always wore his heart so proudly! who found no woman good enough to be loved!'

'That is the most unpromising circumstance, the strongest presumption against him. When I think of his past declarations, I give him up. – Moreover, I have too good an opinion of Miss Thorpe's prudence, to suppose that she would part with one gentleman before the other was secured. It is all over with Frederick indeed! He is a deceased man – defunct in under-standing. Prepare for your sister-in-law, Eleanor, and such a sister-in-law as you must delight in! – Open, candid, artless, guileless, with affections strong but simple, forming no preten-sions, and knowing no disguise.'

'Such a sister-in-law, Henry, I should delight in,' said Eleanor, with a smile.

'But perhaps,' observed Catherine, 'though she has behaved so ill by our family, she may behave better by your's. Now she has really got the man she likes, she may be constant.'

'Indeed I am afraid she will,' replied Henry; 'I am afraid she will be very constant, unless a baronet should come in her way; that is Frederick's only chance. – I will get the Bath paper, and look over the arrivals.'

'You think it is all for ambition then? – And, upon my word, there are some things that seem very like it. I cannot forget, that, when she first knew what my father would do for them, she seemed quite disappointed that it was not more. I never was so deceived in any one's character in my life before.'

'Among all the great variety that you have known and studied.'

'My own disappointment and loss in her is very great; but, as for poor James, I suppose he will hardly ever recover it.'

'Your brother is certainly very much to be pitied at present; but we must not, in our concern for his sufferings, undervalue your's. You feel, I suppose, that, in losing Isabella, you lose half yourself: you feel a void in your heart which nothing else can occupy. Society is becoming irksome; and as for the amuse-ments in which you were wont to share at Bath, the very idea of them without her is abhorrent. You would not, for instance, now go to a ball for the world. You feel that you have no longer any friend to whom you can speak with unreserve; on whose regard you can place dependence; or whose counsel, in any difficulty, you could rely on. You feel all this?'

'No,' said Catherine, after a few moments' reflection, 'I do not – ought I? To say the truth, though I am hurt and grieved, that I cannot still love her, that I am never to hear from her, perhaps never to see her again, I do not feel so very, very much afflicted as one would have thought.'

'You feel, as you always do, what is most to the credit of human nature. – Such feelings ought to be investigated, that they may know themselves.'

Catherine, by some chance or other, found her spirits so very much relieved by this conversation, that she could not regret her being led on, though so unaccountably, to mention the circumstance which had produced it.

CHAPTER XI

From this time, the subject was frequently canvassed by the three young people; and Catherine found, with some surprize, that her two young friends were perfectly agreed in considering Isabella's want of consequence and fortune as likely to throw great difficulties in the way of her marrying their brother. Their persuasion that the General would, upon this ground alone, independent of the objection that might be raised against her character, oppose the connexion, turned her feelings moreover with some alarm towards herself. She was as insignificant, and perhaps as portionless as Isabella; and if the heir of the Tilney property had not grandeur and wealth enough in himself, at what point of interest were the demands of his younger brother to rest? The very painful reflections to which this thought led, could only be dispersed by a dependence on the effect of that particular partiality, which, as she was given to understand by his words as well as his actions, she had from the first been so fortunate as to excite in the General; and by a recollection of some most generous and disinterested sentiments on the subject of money, which she had more than once heard him utter, and which tempted her to think his disposition in such matters misunderstood by his children.

They were so fully convinced, however, that their brother would not have the courage to apply in person for his father's consent, and so repeatedly assured her that he had never in his life been less likely to come to Northanger than at the present time, that she suffered her mind to be at ease as to the necessity of any sudden removal of her own. But as it was not to be supposed that Captain Tilney, whenever he made his application, would give his father any just idea of Isabella's conduct, it occurred to her as highly expedient that Henry should lay the whole business before him as it really was, enabling the General by that means to form a cool and impartial opinion, and prepare his objections on a fairer ground than inequality of situations. She proposed it to him accordingly; but he did not catch at the measure so eagerly as she had expected. 'No,' said he, 'my father's hands need not be strengthened, and Frederick's confession of folly need not be forestalled. He must tell his own story.'

'But he will tell only half of it.'

'A quarter would be enough.'

A day or two passed away and brought no tidings of Captain Tilney. His brother and sister knew not what to think. Sometimes it appeared to them as if his silence would be the natural result of the suspected engagement, and at others that it was wholly incompatible with it. The General, meanwhile, though offended every morning by Frederick's remissness in writing, was free from any real anxiety about him; and had no more pressing solicitude than that of making Miss Morland's time at Northanger pass pleasantly. He often expressed his uneasiness on this head, feared the sameness of every day's society and employments would disgust her with the place, wished the Lady Frasers had been in the country, talked every now and then of having a large party to dinner, and once or twice began even to calculate the number of young dancing people in the neighbour-hood. But then it was such a dead time of year, no wild-fowl, no game, and the Lady Frasers were not in the country. And it all ended, at last, in his telling Henry one morning, that when he next went to Woodston, they would take him by surprize there some day or other, and eat their mutton with him. Henry was greatly honoured and very happy, and Catherine was quite delighted with the scheme. 'And when do you think, sir, I may look forward to this pleasure? – I must be at Woodston on Monday to attend the parish meeting,[1] and shall probably be obliged to stay two or three days.'

'Well, well, we will take our chance some one of those days. There is no need to fix. You are not to put yourself at all out of your way. Whatever you may happen to have in the house will be enough. I think I can answer for the young ladies making allowance for a bachelor's table. Let me see; Monday will be a busy day with you, we will not come on Monday; and Tuesday will be a busy one with me. I expect my surveyor from Brockham with his report in the morning; and afterwards I cannot in decency fail attending the club. I really could not face my acquaintance if I staid away now; for, as I am known to be in the country, it would be taken exceedingly amiss; and it is a rule with me, Miss Morland, never to give offence to any of my neighbours, if a small sacrifice of time and attention can prevent it. They are a set of very worthy men. They have half a buck from Northanger twice a year; and I dine with them whenever I can. Tuesday, therefore, we may say is out of the question. But on Wednesday, I think, Henry, you may expect us; and we shall be with you early, that we may have time to look about us. Two hours and three quarters will carry us to Woodston, I suppose; we shall be in the carriage by ten; so, about a quarter before one on Wednesday, you may look for us.'

A ball itself could not have been more welcome to Catherine than this little excursion, so strong was her desire to be acquaint-ed with Woodston; and her heart was still bounding with joy, when Henry, about an hour afterewards, came booted and great coated into the room where she and Eleanor were sitting, and said, 'I am come, young ladies, in a very moralizing strain, to observe that our pleasures in this world are always to be paid for, and that we often purchase them at a great disadvantage, giving ready-monied actual happiness for a draft on the future, that may not be honoured. Witness myself, at this present hour. Because I am to hope for the satisfaction of seeing you at Woodston on Wednesday, which bad weather, or twenty other causes may prevent, I must go away directly, two days before I intended it.'

'Go away!' said Catherine, with a very long face; 'and why?'

'Why! – How can you ask the question? – Because no time is to be lost in frightening my old housekeeper out of her wits, – because I must go and prepare a dinner for you to be sure.'

'Oh! not seriously!'

'Aye, and sadly too – for I had much rather stay.'

'But how can you think of such a thing, after what the General said? when he so particularly desired you not to give yourself any trouble, because *any thing* would do.'

Henry only smiled. 'I am sure it is quite unnecessary upon your sister's account and mine. You must know it to be so; and the General made such a point of your providing nothing extraordinary: – besides, if he had not said half so much as he did, he has always such an excellent dinner at home, that sitting down to a middling one for one day could not signify.'

'I wish I could reason like you, for his sake and my own. Good bye. As to-morrow is Sunday, Eleanor, I shall not return.'

He went; and, it being at any time a much simpler operation to Catherine to doubt her own judgment than Henry's, she was very soon obliged to give him credit for being right, however disagreeable to her his going. But the inexplicability of the General's conduct dwelt much on her thoughts. That he was very particular in his eating, she had, by her own unassisted observation, already discovered; but why he should say one thing so positively, and mean another all the while, was most unaccountable! How were people, at that rate, to be understood? Who but Henry could have been aware of what his father was at?

From Saturday to Wednesday, however, they were now to be without Henry. This was the sad finale of every reflection: – and Captain Tilney's letter would certainly come in his absence; and Wednesday she was very sure would be wet. The past, present, and future, were all equally in gloom. Her brother so unhappy, and her loss in Isabella so great; and Eleanor's spirits always affected by Henry's absence! What was there to interest or amuse her? She was tired of the woods and the shrubberies – always so smooth and so dry; and the Abbey in itself was no more to her now than any other house. The painful remembrance of the folly it had helped to nourish and perfect, was the only emotion which could spring from a consideration of the building. What a revolution in her ideas! she, who had so longed to be in an abbey! Now, there was nothing so charming to her imagination as the unpretending comfort of a well-connected Parsonage,[1] something like Fullerton, but better: Fullerton had its faults, but Woodston probably had none. – If Wednesday should ever come!

It did come, and exactly when it might be reasonably looked for. It came – it was fine – and Catherine trod on air. By ten o'clock, the chaise-and-four conveyed the trio from the Abbey; and, after an agreeable drive of almost twenty miles, they entered Woodston, a large and populous village, in a situation not unpleasant. Catherine was ashamed to say how pretty she thought it, as the General seemed to think an apology necessary for the flatness of the country, and the size of the village; but in her heart she preferred it to any place she had ever been at, and looked with great admiration at every neat house above the rank of a cottage, and at all the little chandler's shops which they passed. At the further end of the village, and tolerably disengaged from the rest of it, stood the Parsonage, a new-built substantial stone house, with its semi-circular sweep and green gates; and, as they drove up to the door, Henry, with the friends of his solitude, a large Newfoundland puppy and two or three terriers, was ready to receive and make much of them.

Catherine's mind was too full, as she entered the house, for her either to observe or to say a great deal; and, till called on by the General for her opinion of it, she had very little idea of the room in which she was sitting. Upon looking round it then, she perceived in a moment that it was the most comfortable room in the world; but she was too guarded to say so, and the coldness of her praise disappointed him.

'We are not calling it a good house,' said he. – 'We are not comparing it with Fullerton and Northanger – We are considering it as a mere Parsonage, small and confined, we allow, but decent perhaps, and habitable; and altogether not inferior to the generality; – or, in other words, I believe there are few country parsonages in England half so good. It may admit of improvement, however. Far be it from me to say otherwise; and any thing in reason – a bow thrown out, perhaps – though, between ourselves, if there is one thing more than another my aversion, it is a patched-on bow.'

Catherine did not hear enough of this speech to understand or be pained by it; and other subjects being studiously brought forward and supported by Henry, at the same time that a tray full of refreshments was introduced by his servant, the General was shortly restored to his complacency, and Catherine to all her usual ease of spirits.

The room in question was of a commodious, well-proportioned size, and handsomely fitted up as a dining parlour; and on their quitting it to walk round the grounds, she was shewn, first into a smaller apartment, belonging peculiarly to the master of the house, and made unusually tidy on the occasion; and afterwards into what was to be the drawing-room, with the appearance of which, though unfurnished, Catherine was delighted enough even to satisfy the General. It was a prettily-shaped room, the windows reaching to the ground, and the view from them pleasant, though only over green meadows; and she expressed her admiration at the moment with all the honest simplicity with which she felt it. 'Oh! why do not you fit up this room, Mr. Tilney? What a pity not to have it fitted up! It is the prettiest room I ever saw; – it is the prettiest room in the world!'

'I trust,' said the General, with a most satisfied smile, 'that it will very speedily be furnished: it waits only for a lady's taste!'

'Well, if it was my house, I should never sit any where else.

Oh! what a sweet little cottage there is among the trees – apple trees too! It is the prettiest cottage!' –

'You like it – you approve it as an object; – it is enough. Henry, remember that Robinson is spoken to about it. The cottage remains.'

Such a compliment recalled all Catherine's consciousness, and silenced her directly; and, though pointedly applied to by the General for her choice of the prevailing colour of the paper and hangings, nothing like an opinion on the subject could be drawn from her. The influence of fresh objects and fresh air, however, was of great use in dissipating these embarrassing associations; and, having reached the ornamental part of the premises, consisting of a walk round two sides of a meadow, on which Henry's genius had begun to act about half a year ago, she was sufficiently recovered to think it prettier than any pleasure-ground she had ever been in before, though there was not a shrub in it higher than the green bench in the corner.

A saunter into other meadows, and through part of the village, with a visit to the stables to examine some improvements, and a charming game of play with a litter of puppies just able to roll about, brought them to four o'clock, when Catherine scarcely thought it could be three. At four they were to dine, and at six to set off on their return. Never had any day passed so quickly!

She could not but observe that the abundance of the dinner did not seem to create the smallest astonishment in the General; nay, that he was even looking at the side-table for cold meat which was not there. His son and daughter's observations were of a different kind. They had seldom seen him eat so heartily at any table but his own; and never before known him so little disconcerted by the melted butter's being oiled.

At six o'clock, the General having taken his coffee, the carriage again received them; and so gratifying had been the tenor of his conduct throughout the whole visit, so well assured was her mind on the subject of his expectations, that, could she have felt equally confident of the wishes of his son, Catherine would have quitted Woodston with little anxiety as to the How or the When she might return to it.

CHAPTER XII

THE next morning brought the following very unexpected letter from Isabella: –

BATH, April —

My dearest Catherine,

I received your two kind letters with the greatest delight, and have a thousand apologies to make for not answering them sooner. I really am quite ashamed of my idleness; but in this horrid place one can find time for nothing. I have had my pen in my hand to begin a letter to you almost every day since you left Bath, but have always been prevented by some silly trifler or other. Pray write to me soon, and direct to my own home. Thank God! we leave this vile place to-morrow. Since you went away, I have had no pleasure in it - the dust is beyond any thing; and every body one cares for is gone. I believe if I could see you I should not mind the rest, for you are dearer to me than any body can conceive. I am quite uneasy about your dear brother, not having heard from him since he went to Oxford; and am fearful of some misunderstanding. Your kind offices will set all right: – he is the only man I ever did or could love, and I trust you will convince him of it. The spring fashions are partly down; and the hats the most frightful you can imagine. I hope you spend your time pleasantly, but am afraid you never think of me. I will not say all that I could of the family you are with, because I would not be ungenerous, or set you against those you esteem; but it is very difficult to know whom to trust, and young men never know their minds two days together. I rejoice to say, that the young man whom, of all others, I particularly abhor, has left Bath. You will know, from this description, I must mean Captain Tilney, who, as you may remember, was amazingly disposed to follow and tease me, before you went away. Afterwards he got worse, and became quite my shadow. Many girls might have been taken in, for never were such attentions; but I knew the fickle sex too well. He went away to his regiment two days ago, and I trust I shall never be plagued with him again. He is the greatest coxcomb I ever saw, and amazingly disagreeable. The last two days he was always by the side of Charlotte Davis: I pitied his taste, but took no notice of him. The last time we met was in Bath-street, and I turned directly into a shop that he might not speak to me; – I would not even look at him. He went into the Pump-room afterwards; but I would not have followed him for all the world. Such a contrast between him and your brother! – pray send me some news of the latter – I am quite unhappy about him, he seemed so uncomfortable when he went away, with a cold, or something that affected his spirits. I would write to him myself, but have mislaid his direction; and, as I hinted above, am afraid he took something in my conduct amiss. Pray explain every thing to his satisfaction; or, if he still harbours any doubt, a line from himself to me, or a call at Putney when next in town, might set all to rights. I have not been to the Rooms this age, nor to the Play, except going in last night with the Hodges's, for a frolic, at half-price: they teased me into it; and I was determined they should not say I shut myself up because Tilney was gone. We happened to sit by the Mitchells, and they pretended to be quite surprized to see me out. I knew their spite: – at one time they could not be civil to me, but now they are all friendship; but I am not such a fool as to be taken in by them. You know I have a pretty good spirit of my own. Anne Mitchell had tried to put on a turban like mine, as I wore it the week before at the Concert, but made wretched work of it – it happened to become my odd face I believe, at least Tilney told me so at the time, and said every eye was upon me; but he is the last man whose word I would take. I wear nothing but purple now: I know I look hideous in it, but no matter – it is your dear brother's favourite colour. Lose no time, my dearest, sweetest Catherine, in writing to him and to me,

Who ever am, &c.

Such a strain of shallow artifice could not impose even upon Catherine. Its inconsistencies, contradictions, and falsehood, struck her from the very first. She was ashamed of Isabella, and ashamed of having ever loved her. Her professions of attachment were now as disgusting as her excuses were empty, and her demands impudent. 'Write to James on her behalf! – No, James should never hear Isabella's name mentioned by her again.'

On Henry's arrival from Woodston, she made known to him and Eleanor their brother's safety, congratulating them with sincerity on it, and reading aloud the most material passages of her letter with strong indignation. When she had finished it, – 'So much for Isabella,' she cried, 'and for all our intimacy! She must think me an idiot, or she could not have written so; but perhaps this has served to make her character better known to me than mine is to her. I see what she has been about. She is a vain coquette, and her tricks have not answered. I do not believe she had ever any regard either for James or for me, and I wish I had never known her.'

'It will soon be as if you never had,' said Henry.

'There is but one thing that I cannot understand. I see that she has had designs on Captain Tilney, which have not succeeded; but I do not understand what Captain Tilney has been about all this time. Why should he pay her such attentions as to make her quarrel with my brother, and then fly off himself?'

'I have very little to say for Frederick's motives, such as I believe them to have been. He has his vanities as well as Miss Thorpe, and the chief difference is, that, having a stronger head, they have not yet injured himself. If the *effect* of his behaviour does not justify him with you, we had better not seek after the cause.'

'Then you do not suppose he ever really cared about her?'

'I am persuaded that he never did.'

'And only made believe to do so for mischief's sake?'

Henry bowed his assent.

'Well, then, I must say that I do not like him at all. Though it has turned out so well for us, I do not like him at all. As it happens, there is no great harm done, because I do not think Isabella has any heart to lose. But, suppose he had made her very much in love with him?'

'But we must first suppose Isabella to have had a heart to lose, – consequently to have been a very different creature; and, in that case, she would have met with very different treatment.'

'It is very right that you should stand by your brother.'

'And if you would stand by *your's*, you would not be much distressed by the disappointment of Miss Thorpe. But your mind is warped by an innate principle of general integrity, and therefore not accessible to the cool reasonings of family partiality, or a desire of revenge.'

Catherine was complimented out of further bitterness. Frederick could not be unpardonably guilty, while Henry made himself so agreeable. She resolved on not answering Isabella's letter; and tried to think no more of it.

CHAPTER XIII

Soon after this, the General found himself obliged to go to London for a week; and he left Northanger earnestly regretting that any necessity should rob him even for an hour of Miss Morland's company, and anxiously recommending the study of her comfort and amusement to his children as their chief object in his absence. His departure gave Catherine the first experimental conviction that a loss may be sometimes a gain. The happiness with which their time now passed, every employment voluntary, every laugh indulged, every meal a scene of ease and good-humour, walking where they liked and when they liked, their hours, pleasures and fatigues at their own command, made her thoroughly sensible of the restraint which the General's presence had imposed, and most thankfully feel their present release from it. Such ease and such delights made her love the place and the people more and more every day; and had it not been for a dread of its soon becoming expedient to leave the one, and an apprehension of not being equally beloved by the other, she would at each moment of each day have been perfectly happy; but she was now in the fourth week of her visit; before the General came home, the fourth week would be turned, and perhaps it might seem an intrusion if she staid much longer. This was a painful consideration whenever it occurred; and eager to get rid of such a weight on her mind, she very soon resolved to speak to Eleanor about it at once, propose going away, and be guided in her conduct by the manner in which her proposal might be taken.

Aware that if she gave herself much time, she might feel it difficult to bring forward so unpleasant a subject, she took the first opportunity of being suddenly alone with Eleanor, and of Eleanor's being in the middle of a speech about something very different, to start forth her obligation of going away very soon. Eleanor looked and declared herself much concerned. She had 'hoped for the pleasure of her company for a much longer time – had been misled (perhaps by her wishes) to suppose that a much longer visit had been promised – and could not but think that if Mr. and Mrs. Morland were aware of the pleasure it was to her to have her there, they would be too generous to hasten her return.' – Catherine explained. – 'Oh! as to *that*, papa and mamma were in no hurry at all. As long as she was happy, they would always be satisfied.'

'Then why, might she ask, in such a hurry herself to leave them?'

'Oh! because she had been there so long.'

'Nay, if you can use such a word, I can urge you no farther. If you think it long—'

'Oh! no, I do not indeed. For my own pleasure, I could stay with you as long again.' – And it was directly settled that, till she had, her leaving them was not even to be thought of. In having this cause of uneasiness so pleasantly removed, the force of the other was likewise weakened. The kindness, the earnestness of Eleanor's manner in pressing her to stay, and Henry's gratified look on being told that her stay was determined, were such sweet proofs of her importance with them, as left her only just so much solicitude as the human mind can never do comfortably without. She did – almost always – believe that Henry loved her, and quite always that his father and sister loved and even wished her to belong to them; and believing so far, her doubts and anxieties were merely sportive irritations.

Henry was not able to obey his father's injunction of remaining wholly at Northanger in attendance on the ladies, during his absence in London; the engagements of his curate at Woodston obliging him to leave them on Saturday for a couple of nights. His loss was not now what it had been while the General was at home; it lessened their gaiety, but did not ruin their comfort; and the two girls agreeing in occupation, and improving in intimacy, found themselves so well-sufficient for the time to themselves, that it was eleven o'clock, rather a late hour at the Abbey, before they quitted the supper-room on the day of Henry's departure. They had just reached the head of the stairs, when it seemed, as far as the thickness of the walls would allow them to judge, that a carriage was driving up to the door, and the next moment confirmed the idea by the loud noise of the house-bell. After the first perturbation of surprize had passed away, in a 'Good Heaven! what can be the matter?' it was quickly decided by Eleanor to be her eldest brother, whose arrival was often as sudden, if not quite so unseasonable, and accordingly she hurried down to welcome him.

Catherine walked on to her chamber, making up her mind as well as she could, to a further acquaintance with Captain Tilney, and comforting herself under the unpleasant impression his conduct had given her, and the persuasion of his being by far too fine a gentleman to approve of her, that at least they should not meet under such circumstances as would make their meeting materially painful. She trusted he would never speak of Miss Thorpe; and indeed, as he must by this time be ashamed of the part he had acted, there could be no danger of it; and as long as all mention of Bath scenes were avoided, she thought she could behave to him very civilly. In such considerations time passed away, and it was certainly in his favour that Eleanor should be so glad to see him, and have so much to say, for half an hour was almost gone since his arrival, and Eleanor did not come up.

At that moment Catherine thought she heard her step in the gallery, and listened for its continuance; but all was silent.

Scarcely, however, had she convicted her fancy of error, when the noise of something moving close to her door made her start; it seemed as if some one was touching the very doorway – and in another moment a slight motion of the lock proved that some hand must be on it. She trembled a little at the idea of any one's approaching so cautiously; but resolving not to be again overcome by trivial appearances of alarm, or misled by a raised imagination, she stepped quietly forward, and opened the door. Eleanor, and only Eleanor, stood there. Catherine's spirits however were tranquillized but for an instant, for Eleanor's cheeks were pale, and her manner greatly agitated. Though evidently intending to come in, it seemed an effort to enter the room, and a still greater to speak when there. Catherine, supposing some uneasiness on Captain Tilney's account, could only express her concern by silent attention; obliged her to be seated, rubbed her temples with lavender-water, and hung over her with affectionate solicitude. 'My dear Catherine, you must not – you must not indeed –' were Eleanor's first connected words. 'I am quite well. This kindness distracts me – I cannot bear it – I come to you on such an errand!'

'Errand! – to me!'

'How shall I tell you! – Oh! how shall I tell you!'

A new idea now darted into Catherine's mind, and turning as pale as her friend, she exclaimed, ' 'Tis a messenger from Woodston!'

'You are mistaken, indeed,' returned Eleanor, looking at her most compassionately – 'it is no one from Woodston. It is my father himself.' Her voice faltered, and her eyes were turned to the ground as she mentioned his name. His unlooked for return was enough in itself to make Catherine's heart sink, and for a few moments she hardly supposed there were any thing worse to be told. She said nothing; and Eleanor endeavouring to collect herself and speak with firmness, but with eyes still cast down, soon went on. 'You are too good, I am sure, to think the worse of me for the part I am obliged to perform. I am indeed a most unwilling messenger. After what has so lately passed, so lately been settled between us – how joyfully, how thankfully on my side! – as to your continuing here as I hoped for many, many weeks longer, how can I tell you that your kindness is not to be accepted – and that the happiness your company has hitherto given us is to be repaid by—but I must not trust myself with words. My dear Catherine, we are to part. My father has recollected an engagement that takes our whole family away on Monday. We are going to Lord Longtown's, near Hereford, for a fortnight. Explanation and apology are equally impossible. I cannot attempt either.'

'My dear Eleanor,' cried Catherine, suppressing her feelings as well as she could, 'do not be so distressed. A second engagement must give way to a first. I am very, very sorry we are to part – so soon, and so suddenly too; but I am not offended, indeed I am not. I can finish my visit here you know at any time; or I hope you will come to me. Can you, when you return from this lord's, come to Fullerton?'

'It will not be in my power, Catherine.'

'Come when you can, then.' –

Eleanor made no answer; and Catherine's thoughts recurring to something more directly interesting, she added, thinking aloud, 'Monday – so soon as Monday; – and you *all* go. Well, I am certain of—I shall be able to take leave however. I need not go till just before you do, you know. Do not be distressed, Eleanor, I can go on Monday very well. My father and mother's having no notice of it is of very little consequence. The General will send a servant with me, I dare say, half the way – and then I shall soon be at Salisbury, and then I am only nine miles from home.'

'Ah, Catherine! were it settled so, it would be somewhat less intolerable, though in such common attentions you would have received but half what you ought. But – how can I tell you? – To-morrow morning is fixed for your leaving us, and not even the hour is left to your choice; the very carriage is ordered, and will be here at seven o'clock, and no servant will be offered you.'

Catherine sat down, breathless and speechless. 'I could hardly believe my senses, when I heard it; – and no displeasure, no resentment that you can feel at this moment, however justly great, can be more than I myself—but I must not talk of what I felt. Oh! that I could suggest any thing in extenuation! Good God! what will your father and mother say! After courting you from the protection of real friends to this – almost double distance from your home, to have you driven out of the house, without the considerations even of decent civility! Dear, dear Catherine, in being the bearer of such a message, I seem guilty myself of all its insult; yet, I trust you will acquit me, for you must have been long enough in this house to see that I am but a nominal mistress of it, that my real power is nothing.'

'Have I offended the General?' said Catherine in a faltering voice.

'Alas! for my feelings as a daughter, all that I know, all that I answer for is, that you can have given him no just cause of offence. He certainly is greatly, very greatly discomposed; I have seldom seen him more so. His temper is not happy, and something has now occurred to ruffle it in an uncommon degree; some disappointment, some vexation, which just at this moment seems important; but which I can hardly suppose you to have any concern in, for how is it possible?'

It was with pain that Catherine could speak at all; and it was only for Eleanor's sake that she attempted it. 'I am sure,' said she, 'I am very sorry if I have offended him. It was the last thing I would willingly have done. But do not be unhappy, Eleanor. An engagement you know must be kept. I am only sorry it was not recollected sooner, that I might have written home. But it is of very little consequence.'

'I hope, I earnestly hope that to your real safety it will be of none; but to every thing else it is of the greatest consequence; to comfort, appearance, propriety, to your family, to the world. Were your friends, the Allens, still in Bath, you might go to them with comparative ease; a few hours would take you there; but a journey of seventy miles, to be taken post by you, at your age, alone, unattended!'

'Oh, the journey is nothing. Do not think about that. And if we are to part, a few hours sooner or later, you know, makes no difference. I can be ready by seven. Let me be called in time.'

Eleanor saw that she wished to be alone; and believing it better for each that they should avoid any further conversation, now left her with 'I shall see you in the morning.'

Catherine's swelling heart needed relief. In Eleanor's presence friendship and pride had equally restrained her tears, but no sooner was she gone than they burst forth in torrents. Turned from the house, and in such a way! – Without any reason that could justify, any apology that could atone for the abruptness, the rudeness, nay, the insolence of it. Henry at a distance – not able even to bid him farewell. Every hope, every expectation from him suspended, at least, and who could say how long? – Who could say when they might meet again? – And all this by such a man as General Tilney, so polite, so well-bred, and heretofore so particularly fond of her! It was as incomprehensible as it was mortifying and grievous. From what it could arise, and where it would end, were considerations of equal perplexity and alarm. The manner in which it was done so grossly uncivil; hurrying her away without any reference to her own convenience, or allowing her even the appearance of choice as to the time or mode of her travelling; of two days, the earliest fixed on, and of that almost the earliest hour, as if resolved to have her gone before he was stirring in the morning, that he might not be obliged even to see her. What could all this mean but an intentional affront? By some means or other she must have had the misfortune to offend him. Eleanor had wished to spare her from so painful a notion, but Catherine could not believe it possible that any injury or any misfortune could provoke such ill-will against a person not connected, or, at least, not supposed to be connected with it.

Heavily past the night. Sleep, or repose that deserved the name of sleep, was out of the question. That room, in which her disturbed imagination had tormented her on her first arrival, was again the scene of agitated spirits and unquiet slumbers. Yet how different now the source of her inquietude from what it had been then – how mournfully superior in reality and substance! Her anxiety had foundation in fact, her fears in probability; and with a mind so occupied in the contemplation of actual and natural evil, the solitude of her situation, the darkness of her chamber, the antiquity of the building were felt and considered without the smallest emotion; and though the wind was high, and often produced strange and sudden noises throughout the house, she heard it all as she lay awake, hour after hour, without curiosity or terror.

Soon after six Eleanor entered her room, eager to show attention or give assistance where it was possible; but very little remained to be done. Catherine had not loitered; she was almost dressed, and her packing almost finished. The possibility of some conciliatory message from the General occurred to her as his daughter appeared. What so natural, as that anger should pass away and repentance succeed it? and she only wanted to know how far, after what had passed, an apology might properly be received by her. But the knowledge would have been useless here, it was not called for; neither clemency nor dignity was put to the trial – Eleanor brought no message. Very little passed between them on meeting; each found her greatest safety in silence, and few and trivial were the sentences exchanged while they remained up stairs, Catherine in busy agitation completing her dress, and Eleanor with more good-will than experience intent upon filling the trunk. When every thing was done they left the room, Catherine lingering only half a minute behind her friend to throw a parting glance on every well-known cherished object, and went down to the breakfast-parlour, where breakfast was prepared. She tried to eat, as well to save herself from the pain of being urged, as to make her friend comfortable; but she had no appetite, and could not swallow many mouthfuls. The contrasts between this and her last breakfast in that room, gave her fresh misery, and strengthened her distaste for every thing before her. It was not four-and-twenty hours ago since they had met there to the same repast, but in circumstances how different! With what cheerful ease, what happy, though false security, had she then looked around her, enjoying every thing present, and fearing little in future, beyond Henry's going to Woodston for a day! Happy, happy breakfast! for Henry had been there, Henry had sat by her and helped her. These reflections were long indulged undisturbed by any address from her companion, who sat as deep in thought as herself; and the appearance of the carriage was the first thing to startle and recall them to the present moment. Catherine's colour rose at the sight of it; and the indignity with which she was treated striking at that instant on her mind with peculiar force, made her for a short time sensible only of resentment. Eleanor seemed now impelled into resolution and speech.

'You *must* write to me, Catherine,' she cried, 'you *must* let me hear from you as soon as possible. Till I know you to be safe at home, I shall not have an hour's comfort. For *one* letter, at all risks, all hazards, I must entreat. Let me have the satisfaction of knowing that you are safe at Fullerton, and have found your family well, and then, till I can ask for your correspondence as I ought to do, I will not expect more. Direct to me at Lord Long-town's, and, I must ask it, under cover to Alice.'

'No, Eleanor, if you are not allowed to receive a letter from me, I am sure I had better not write. There can be no doubt of my getting home safe.'

Eleanor only replied, 'I cannot wonder at your feelings. I will not importune you. I will trust to your own kindness of heart when I am at a distance from you.' But this, with the look of sorrow accompanying it, was enough to melt Catherine's pride in a moment, and she instantly said, 'Oh, Eleanor, I *will* write to you indeed.'

There was yet another point which Miss Tilney was anxious to settle, though somewhat embarrassed in speaking of. It had occurred to her, that after so long an absence from home, Catherine might not be provided with money enough for the expenses of her journey, and, upon suggesting it to her with most affection-ate offers of accommodation, it proved to be exactly the case. Catherine had never thought on the subject till that moment; but, upon examining her purse, was convinced that but for this kindness of her friend, she might have been turned from the house without even the means of getting home; and the distress in which she must have been thereby involved filling the minds of both, scarcely another word was said by either during the time of their remaining together. Short, however, was that time.

The carriage was soon announced to be ready; and Catherine, instantly rising, a long and affectionate embrace supplied the place of language in bidding each other adieu; and, as they entered the hall, unable to leave the house without some mention of one whose name had not yet been spoken by either, she paused a moment, and with quivering lips just made it intelligible that she left 'her kind remembrance for her absent friend.' But with this approach to his name ended all possibility of restraining her feelings; and, hiding her face as well as she could with her handkerchief, she darted across the hall, jumped into the chaise, and in a moment was driven from the door.

CHAPTER XIV

CATHERINE was too wretched to be fearful. The journey in itself had no terrors for her; and she began it without either dreading its length, or feeling its solitariness. Leaning back in one corner of the carriage, in a violent burst of tears, she was conveyed some miles beyond the walls of the Abbey before she raised her head; and the highest point of ground within the park was almost closed from her view before she was capable of turning her eyes towards it. Unfortunately, the road she now travelled was the same which only ten days ago she had so happily passed along in going to and from Woodston; and, for fourteen miles, every bitter feeling was rendered more severe by the review of objects on which she had first looked under impressions so different. Every mile, as it brought her nearer Woodston, added to her sufferings, and when within the distance of five, she passed the turning which led to it, and thought of Henry, so near, yet so unconscious, her grief and agitation were excessive.

The day which she had spent at that place had been one of the happiest of her life. It was there, it was on that day that the General had made use of such expressions with regard to Henry and herself, had so spoken and so looked as to give her the most positive conviction of his actually wishing their marriage. Yes, only ten days ago had he elated her by his pointed regard - had he even confused her by his too significant reference! And now – what had she done, or what had she omitted to do, to merit such a change?

The only offence against him of which she could accuse herself, had been such as was scarcely possible to reach his knowledge. Henry and her own heart only were privy to the shocking suspicions which she had so idly entertained; and equally safe did she believe her secret with each. Designedly, at least, Henry could not have betrayed her. If, indeed, by any strange mischance his father should have gained intelligence of what she had dared to think and look for, of her causeless fancies and injurious examinations, she could not wonder at any degree of his indignation. If aware of her having viewed him as a murderer, she could not wonder at his even turning her from his house. But a justification so full of torture to herself, she trusted would not be in his power.

Anxious as were all her conjectures on this point, it was not, however, the one on which she dwelt most. There was a thought yet nearer, a more prevailing, more impetuous concern. How Henry would think, and feel, and look, when he returned on the morrow to Northanger and heard of her being gone, was a question of force and interest to rise over every other, to be never ceasing, alternately irritating and soothing; it sometimes suggested the dread of his calm acquiescence, and at others was answered by the sweetest confidence in his regret and resentment. To the General, of course, he would not dare to speak; but to Eleanor – what might he not say to Eleanor about her?

In this unceasing recurrence of doubts and inquiries, on any one article of which her mind was incapable of more than momentary repose, the hours passed away, and her journey advanced much faster than she looked for. The pressing anxieties of thought, which prevented her from noticing any thing before her, when once beyond the neighbourhood of Woodston, saved her at the same time from watching her progress; and though no object on the road could engage a moment's attention, she found no stage of it tedious. From this, she was preserved too by another cause, by feeling no eagerness for her journey's conclusion; for to return in such a manner to Fullerton was almost to destroy the pleasure of a meeting with those she loved best, even after an absence such as her's – an eleven weeks absence. What had she to say that would not humble herself and pain her family; that would not increase her own grief by the confession of it, extend an useless resentment, and perhaps involve the innocent with the guilty in undistinguishing ill-will? She could never do justice to Henry and Eleanor's merit; she felt it too strongly for expression; and should a dislike be taken against them, should they be thought of unfavourably, on their father's account, it would cut her to the heart.

With these feelings, she rather dreaded than sought for the first view of that well-known spire which would announce her within twenty miles of home. Salisbury she had known to be her point on leaving Northanger; but after the first stage she had been indebted to the post-masters for the names of the places which were then to conduct her to it; so great had been her ignorance of her route. She met with nothing, however, to distress or frighten her. Her youth, civil manners and liberal pay, procured her all the attention that a traveller like herself could require; and stopping only to change horses, she travelled on for about eleven hours without accident or alarm, and between six and seven o'clock in the evening found herself entering Fullerton.

A heroine returning, at the close of her career, to her native village, in all the triumph of recovered reputation, and all the dignity of a countess, with a long train of noble relations in their several phaetons, and three waiting-maids in a travelling chaise-and-four, behind her, is an event on which the pen of the contriver may well delight to dwell; it gives credit to every conclusion, and the author must share in the glory she so liberally bestows. – But my affair is widely different; I bring back my heroine to her home in solitude and disgrace; and no sweet elation of spirits can lead me into minuteness. A heroine in a hack post-chaise, is such a blow upon sentiment, as no attempt at grandeur or pathos can withstand. Swiftly therefore shall her post-boy drive through the village, amid the gaze of Sunday groups, and speedy shall be her descent from it.

But, whatever might be the distress of Catherine's mind, as she thus advanced towards the Parsonage, and whatever the humiliation of her biographer in relating it, she was preparing enjoyment of no every-day nature for those to whom she went; first, in the appearance of her carriage – and secondly, in herself. The chaise of a traveller being a rare sight in Fullerton, the whole family were immediately at the window; and to have it stop at the sweep-gate was a pleasure to brighten every eye and occupy every fancy – a pleasure quite unlooked for by all but the two youngest children, a boy and girl of six and four years old, who expected a brother or sister in every carriage. Happy the glance that first distinguished Catherine! – Happy the voice that proclaimed the discovery! – But whether such happiness were the lawful property of George or Harriet could never be exactly understood.

Her father, mother, Sarah, George, and Harriet, all assembled at the door, to welcome her with affectionate eagerness, was a sight to awaken the best feelings of Catherine's heart; and in the embrace of each, as she stepped from the carriage, she found herself soothed beyond any thing that she had believed possible. So surrounded, so caressed, she was even happy! In the joyfulness of family love every thing for a short time was subdued, and the pleasure of seeing her, leaving them at first little leisure for calm curiosity, they were all seated round the tea-table, which Mrs. Morland had hurried for the comfort of the poor traveller, whose pale and jaded looks soon caught her notice, before any inquiry so direct as to demand a positive answer was addressed to her.

Reluctantly, and with much hesitation, did she then begin what might perhaps, at the end of half an hour, be termed by the courtesy of her hearers, an explanation; but scarcely, within that time, could they at all discover the cause, or collect the particulars of her sudden return. They were far from being an irritable race; far from any quickness in catching, or bitterness in resenting affronts: – but here, when the whole was unfolded, was an insult not to be overlooked, nor, for the first half hour, to be easily pardoned. Without suffering any romantic alarm, in the consideration of their daughter's long and lonely journey, Mr. and Mrs. Morland could not but feel that it might have been productive of much unpleasantness to her; that it was what they could never have voluntarily suffered; and that, in forcing her on such a measure, General Tilney had acted neither honourably nor feelingly – neither as a gentleman nor as a parent. Why he had done it, what could have provoked him to such a breach of hospitality, and so suddenly turned all his partial regard for their daughter into actual ill-will, was a matter which they were at least as far from divining as Catherine herself; but it did not oppress them by any means so long; and, after a due course of useless conjecture, that, 'it was a strange business, and that he must be a very strange man,' grew enough for all their indignation and wonder; though Sarah indeed still indulged in the sweets of incomprehensibility, exclaiming and conjecturing with youthful ardour. – 'My dear, you give yourself a great deal of needless trouble,' said her mother at last; 'depend upon it, it is something not at all worth understanding.'

'I can allow for his wishing Catherine away, when he recollected this engagement,' said Sarah, 'but why not do it civilly?'

'I am sorry for the young people,' returned Mrs. Morland; 'they must have a sad time of it; but as for any thing else, it is no matter now; Catherine is safe at home, and our comfort does not depend upon General Tilney.' Catherine sighed. 'Well,' continued her philosophic mother, 'I am glad I did not know of your journey at the time; but now it is all over perhaps there is no great harm done. It is always good for young people to be put upon exerting themselves; and you know, my dear Catherine, you always were a sad little shatter-brained creature; but now you must have been forced to have your wits about you, with so much changing of chaises and so forth; and I hope it will appear that you have not left any thing behind you in any of the pockets.'

Catherine hoped so too, and tried to feel an interest in her own amendment, but her spirits were quite worn down; and, to be silent and alone becoming soon her only wish, she readily agreed to her mother's next counsel of going early to bed. Her parents seeing nothing in her ill-looks and agitation but the natural consequence of mortified feelings, and of the unusual exertion and fatigue of such a journey, parted from her without any doubt of their being soon slept away; and though, when they all met the next morning, her recovery was not equal to their hopes, they were still perfectly unsuspicious of there being any deeper evil. They never once thought of her heart, which, for the parents of a young lady of seventeen, just returned from her first excursion from home, was odd enough!

As soon as breakfast was over, she sat down to fulfil her promise to Miss Tilney, whose trust in the effect of time and distance on her friend's disposition was already justified, for already did Catherine reproach herself with having parted from Eleanor coldly; with having never enough valued her merits or kindness; and never enough commiserated her for what she had been yesterday left to endure. The strength of these feelings, however, was far from assisting her pen; and never had it been harder for her to write than in addressing Eleanor Tilney. To compose a letter which might at once do justice to her sentiments and her situation, convey gratitude without servile regret, be guarded without coldness, and honest without resentment – a letter which Eleanor might not be pained by the perusal of – and, above all, which she might not blush herself, if Henry should chance to see, was an undertaking to frighten away all her powers of performance; and, after long thought and much perplexity, to be very brief was all that she could determine on with any confidence of safety. The money therefore which Eleanor had advanced was inclosed with little more than grateful thanks, and the thousand good wishes of a most affectionate heart.

'This has been a strange acquaintance,' observed Mrs. Morland, as the letter was finished; 'soon made and soon ended. – I am sorry it happens so, for Mrs. Allen thought them very pretty kind of young people; and you were sadly out of luck too in your Isabella. Ah! poor James! Well, we must live and learn;

and the next new friends you make I hope will be better worth keeping.'

Catherine coloured as she warmly answered, 'No friend can be better worth keeping than Eleanor.'

'If so, my dear, I dare say you will meet again some time or other; do not be uneasy. It is ten to one but you are thrown together again in the course of a few years; and then what a pleasure it will be!'

Mrs. Morland was not happy in her attempt at consolation. The hope of meeting again in the course of a few years could only put into Catherine's head what might happen within that time to make a meeting dreadful to her. She could never forget Henry Tilney, or think of him with less tenderness than she did at that moment; but he might forget her; and in that case to meet!—Her eyes filled with tears as she pictured her acquaintance so renewed; and her mother, perceiving her comfortable suggestions to have had no good effect, proposed, as another expedient for restoring her spirits, that they should call on Mrs. Allen.

The two houses were only a quarter of a mile apart; and, as they walked, Mrs. Morland quickly dispatched all that she felt on the score of James's disappointment. 'We are sorry for him,' said she; 'but otherwise there is no harm done in the match going off; for it could not be a desirable thing to have him engaged to a girl whom we had not the smallest acquaintance with, and who was so entirely without fortune; and now, after such behaviour, we cannot think at all well of her. Just at present it comes hard to poor James; but that will not last for ever; and I dare say he will be a discreeter man all his life, for the foolishness of his first choice.'

This was just such a summary view of the affair as Catherine could listen to; another sentence might have endangered her complaisance, and made her reply less rational; for soon were all her thinking powers swallowed up in the reflection of her own change of feelings and spirits since last she had trodden that well-known road. It was not three months ago since, wild with joyful expectation, she had there run backwards and forwards some ten times a-day, with an heart light, gay, and independent; looking forward to pleasures untasted and unalloyed, and free from the apprehension of evil as from the knowledge of it. Three months ago had seen her all this; and now, how altered a being did she return!

She was received by the Allens with all the kindness which her unlooked-for appearance, acting on a steady affection, would naturally call forth; and great was their surprize, and warm their displeasure, on hearing how she had been treated, – though Mrs. Morland's account of it was no inflated representation, no studied appeal to their passions. 'Catherine took us quite by surprize yesterday evening,' said she. 'She travelled all the way post by herself, and knew nothing of coming till Saturday night; for General Tilney, from some odd fancy or other, all of a sudden grew tired of having her there, and almost turned her out of the house. Very unfriendly, certainly; and he must be a very odd man; – but we are so glad to have her amongst us again! And it is a great comfort to find that she is not a poor helpless creature, but can shift very well for herself.'

Mr. Allen expressed himself on the occasion with the reasonable resentment of a sensible friend; and Mrs. Allen thought his expressions quite good enough to be immediately made use of again by herself. His wonder, his conjectures, and his explanations, became in succession her's, with the addition of this single remark – 'I really have not patience with the General' – to fill up every accidental pause. And, 'I really have not patience with the General,' was uttered twice after Mr. Allen left the room, without any relaxation of anger, or any material digression of thought. A more considerable degree of wandering attended the third repetition; and, after completing the fourth, she immediately added, 'Only think, my dear, of my having got that frightful great rent in my best Mechlin so charmingly mended, before I left Bath, that one can hardly see where it was. I must shew it you some day or other. Bath is a nice place, Catherine, after all. I assure you I did not above half like coming away. Mrs. Thorpe's being there was such a comfort to us, was not it? You know you and I were quite forlorn at first.'

'Yes, but *that* did not last long,' said Catherine, her eyes brightening at the recollection of what had first given spirit to her existence there.

'Very true: we soon met with Mrs. Thorpe, and then we wanted for nothing. My dear, do not you think these silk gloves wear very well? I put them on new the first time of our going to the Lower Rooms, you know, and I have worn them a great deal since. Do you remember that evening?'

'Do I! Oh! perfectly.'

'It was very agreeable, was not it? Mr. Tilney drank tea with us, and I always thought him a great addition, he is so very agreeable. I have a notion you danced with him, but am not quite sure. I remember I had my favourite gown on.'

Catherine could not answer; and, after a short trial of other subjects, Mrs. Allen again returned to – 'I really have not patience with the General! Such an agreeable, worthy man as he seemed to be! I do not suppose, Mrs. Morland, you ever saw a better-bred man in your life. His lodgings were taken the very day after he left them, Catherine. But no wonder; Milsom-street you know.' –

As they walked home again, Mrs. Morland endeavoured to impress on her daughter's mind the happiness of having such steady well-wishers as Mr. and Mrs. Allen, and the very little consideration which the neglect or unkindness of slight acquaintance like the Tilneys ought to have with her, while she could preserve the good opinion and affection of her earliest friends. There was a great deal of good sense in all this; but there are some situations of the human mind in which good sense has very little power; and Catherine's feelings contradicted almost every position her mother advanced. It was upon the behaviour of these very slight acquaintance that all her present happiness depended; and while Mrs. Morland was successfully confirming her own opinions by the justness of her own representations, Catherine was silently reflecting that *now* Henry must have arrived at Northanger; *now* he must have heard of her departure; and *now*, perhaps, they were all setting off for Hereford.

CHAPTER XV

CATHERINE'S disposition was not naturally sedentary, nor had her habits been ever very industrious; but whatever might hitherto have been her defects of that sort, her mother could not but perceive them now to be greatly increased. She could neither sit still, nor employ herself for ten minutes together, walking round the garden and orchard again and again, as if nothing but motion was voluntary; and it seemed as if she could even walk about the house rather than remain fixed for any time in the parlour. Her loss of spirits was a yet greater alteration. In her rambling and her idleness she might only be a caricature of herself; but in her silence and sadness she was the very reverse of all that she had been before.

For two days Mrs. Morland allowed it to pass even without a hint; but when a third night's rest had neither restored her cheerfulness, improved her in useful activity, nor given her a greater inclination for needle-work, she could no longer refrain from the gentle reproof of, 'My dear Catherine, I am afraid you are growing quite a fine lady. I do not know when poor Richard's cravats would be done, if he had no friend but you. Your head runs too much upon Bath; but there is a time for every thing – a time for balls and plays, and a time for work. You have had a long run of amusement, and now you must try to be useful.'

Catherine took up her work directly, saying, in a dejected voice, that 'her head did not run upon Bath—much.'

'Then you are fretting about General Tilney, and that is very simple of you: for ten to one whether you ever see him again. You should never fret about trifles.' After a short silence – 'I hope, my Catherine, you are not getting out of humour with home because it is not so grand as Northanger. That would be turning your visit into an evil indeed. Wherever you are you should always be contented, but especially at home, because there you must spend the most of your time. I did not quite like, at breakfast, to hear you talk so much about the French-bread at Northanger.'

'I am sure I do not care about the bread. It is all the same to me what I eat.'

'There is a very clever Essay in one of the books up stairs upon much such a subject, about young girls that have been spoilt for home by great acquaintance – "The Mirror,"[1] I think. I will look it out for you some day or other, because I am sure it will do you good.'

Catherine said no more, and, with an endeavour to do right, applied to her work; but, after a few minutes, sunk again, without knowing it herself, into languor and listlessness, moving herself in her chair, from the irritation of weariness, much oftener than she moved her needle. – Mrs. Morland watched the progress of this relapse; and seeing, in her daughter's absent and dissatisfied look, the full proof of that repining spirit to which she had now begun to attribute her want of cheerfulness, hastily left the room to fetch the book in question, anxious to lose no time in attacking so dreadful a malady. It was some time before she could find what she looked for; and other family matters occurring to detain her, a quarter of an hour had elapsed ere she returned down stairs with the volume from which so much was hoped. Her avocations above having shut out all noise but what she created herself, she knew not that a visitor had arrived within the last few minutes, till, on entering the room, the first object she beheld was a young man whom she had never seen before. With a look of much respect, he immediately rose, and being introduced to her by her conscious daughter as 'Mr. Henry Tilney,' with the embarrassment of real sensibility began to apologise for his appearance there, acknowledging that after what had passed he had little right to expect a welcome at Fullerton, and stating his impatience to be assured of Miss Morland's having reached her home in safety, as the cause of his intrusion. He did not address himself to an uncandid judge or a resentful heart. Far from comprehending him or his sister in their father's misconduct, Mrs. Morland had been always kindly disposed towards each, and instantly, pleased by his appearance, received him with the simple professions of unaffected benevolence; thanking him for such an attention to her daughter, assuring him that the friends of her children were always welcome there, and intreating him to say not another word of the past.

He was not ill inclined to obey this request, for, though his heart was greatly relieved by such unlooked-for mildness, it was not just at that moment in his power to say any thing to the purpose. Returning in silence to his seat, therefore, he remained for some minutes most civilly answering all Mrs. Morland's common remarks about the weather and roads. Catherine meanwhile, – the anxious, agitated, happy, feverish Catherine, – said not a word; but her glowing cheek and brightened eye made her mother trust that this good-natured visit would at least set her heart at ease for a time, and gladly therefore did she lay aside the first volume of the Mirror for a future hour.

Desirous of Mr. Morland's assistance, as well in giving encouragement, as in finding conversation for her guest, whose embarrassment on his father's account she earnestly pitied, Mrs. Morland had very early dispatched one of the children to summon him; but Mr. Morland was from home – and being thus without any support, at the end of a quarter of an hour she had nothing to say. After a couple of minutes unbroken silence, Henry, turning to Catherine for the first time since her mother's entrance, asked her, with sudden alacrity, if Mr. and Mrs. Allen were now at Fullerton? and on developing, from amidst all her perplexity of words in reply, the meaning, which one short syllable would have given, immediately expressed his intention of paying his respects to them, and, with a rising colour, asked her if she would have the goodness to shew him the way. 'You may see the house from this window, sir,' was information on Sarah's side, which produced only a bow of acknowledgment from the gentleman, and a silencing nod from her mother; for Mrs. Morland, thinking it probable, as a secondary considera-tion in his wish of waiting on their worthy neighbours, that he might have some explanation to give of his father's behaviour, which it must be more pleasant for him to communicate only to Catherine, would not on any account prevent her accompanying him. They began their walk, and Mrs. Morland was not entirely mistaken in his object in wishing it. Some explanation on his father's account he had to give; but his first purpose was to explain himself, and before they reached Mr. Allen's grounds he had done it so well, that Catherine did not think it could ever be repeated too often. She was assured of his affection; and that heart in return was solicited, which, perhaps, they pretty equally knew was already entirely his own; for, though Henry was now sincerely attached to her, though he felt and delighted in all the excellencies of her character and truly loved her society, I must confess that his affection originated in nothing better than gratitude, or, in other words, that a persuasion of her partiality for him had been the only cause of giving her a serious thought. It is a new circumstance in romance, I acknowledge, and dreadfully derogatory of an heroine's dignity; but if it be as new in common life, the credit of a wild imagination will at least be all my own.

A very short visit to Mrs. Allen, in which Henry talked at random, without sense or connection, and Catherine, wrapt in the contemplation of her own unutterable happiness, scarcely opened her lips, dismissed them to the extasies of another tête-à-tête; and before it was suffered to close, she was enabled to judge how far he was sanctioned by parental authority in his present application. On his return from Woodston, two days before, he had been met near the Abbey by his impatient father, hastily informed in angry terms of Miss Morland's departure, and ordered to think of her no more.

Such was the permission upon which he had now offered her his hand. The affrighted Catherine, amidst all the terrors of expectation, as she listened to this account, could not but rejoice in the kind caution with which Henry had saved her from the necessity of a conscientious rejection, by engaging her faith before he mentioned the subject; and as he proceeded to give the particulars, and explain the motives of his father's conduct, her feelings soon hardened into even a triumphant delight. The General had had nothing to accuse her of, nothing to lay to her charge, but her being the involuntary, unconscious object of a deception which his pride could not pardon, and which a better pride would have been ashamed to own. She was guilty only of being less rich than he had supposed her to be. Under a mistaken persuasion of her possessions and claims, he had courted her acquaintance in Bath, solicited her company at Northanger, and designed her for his daughter in law. On discovering his error, to turn her from the house seemed the best, though to his feelings an inadequate proof of his resentment towards herself, and his contempt of her family.

John Thorpe had first misled him. The General, perceiving his son one night at the theatre to be paying considerable attention to Miss Morland, had accidentally inquired of Thorpe, if he knew more of her than her name. Thorpe, most happy to be on speaking terms with a man of General Tilney's importance, had been joyfully and proudly communicative; – and being at that time not only in daily expectation of Morland's engaging Isabella, but likewise pretty well resolved upon marrying Catherine himself, his vanity induced him to represent the family as yet more wealthy than his vanity and avarice had made him believe them. With whomsoever he was, or was likely to be connected, his own consequence always required that theirs should be great, and as his intimacy with any acquaintance grew, so regularly grew their fortune. The expectations of his friend Morland, therefore, from the first over-rated, had ever since his introduction to Isabella, been gradually increasing; and by merely adding twice as much for the grandeur of the moment, by doubling what he chose to think the amount of Mr. Morland's preferment, trebling his private fortune, bestowing a rich aunt, and sinking half the children, he was able to represent the whole family to the General in a most respectable light. For Catherine, however, the peculiar object of the General's curiosity, and his own speculations, he had yet something more in reserve, and the ten or fifteen thousand pounds which her father could give her, would be a pretty addition to Mr. Allen's estate. Her intimacy there had made him seriously determine on her being handsomely legacied hereafter; and to speak of her therefore as the almost acknowledged future heiress of Fullerton naturally followed. Upon such intelligence the General had proceeded; for never had it occurred to him to doubt its authority. Thorpe's interest in the family, by his sister's approaching connection with one of its members, and his own views on another, (circumstances of which he boasted with almost equal openness,) seemed sufficient vouchers for his truth; and to these were added the absolute facts of the Allens being wealthy and childless, of Miss Morland's being under their care, and – as soon as his acquaintance allowed him to judge – of their treating her with parental kindness. His resolution was soon formed. Already had he discerned a liking towards Miss Morland in the countenance of his son; and thankful for Mr. Thorpe's communication, he almost instantly determined to spare no pains in weakening his boasted interest and ruining his dearest hopes. Catherine herself could not be more ignorant at the time of all this, than his own children. Henry and Eleanor, perceiving nothing in her situation likely to engage their father's particular respect, had seen with astonishment the suddenness, continuance and extent of his attention; and though latterly, from some hints which had accompanied an almost positive command to his son of doing every thing in his power to attach her, Henry was convinced of his father's believing it to be an advantageous connection, it was not till the late explanation at Northanger that they had the smallest idea of the false calculations which had hurried him on. That they were false, the General had learnt from the very person who had suggested them, from Thorpe himself, whom he had chanced to meet again in town, and who, under the influence of exactly opposite feelings, irritated by Catherine's refusal, and yet more by the failure of a very recent endeavour to accomplish a reconciliation between Morland and Isabella, convinced that they were separated for ever, and spurning a friendship which could be no longer serviceable, hastened to contradict all that he had said before to the advantage of the Morlands; – confessed himself to have been totally mistaken in his opinion of their circumstances and character, misled by the rhodomontade of his friend to believe his father a man of substance and credit, whereas the transactions of the two or three last weeks proved him to be neither; for after coming eagerly forward on the first overture of a marriage between the families, with the most liberal proposals, he had, on being brought to the point by the shrewdness of the relator, been constrained to acknowledge himself incapable of giving the young people even a decent support. They were, in fact, a necessitous family; numerous too almost beyond example; by no means respected in their own neighbourhood, as he had lately had particular opportunities of discovering; aiming at a style of life which their fortune could not warrant; seeking to better themselves by wealthy connexions; a forward, bragging, scheming race.

The terrified General pronounced the name of Allen with an inquiring look; and here too Thorpe had learnt his error. The Allens, he believed, had lived near them too long, and he knew the young man on whom the Fullerton estate must devolve. The General needed no more. Enraged with almost every body in the world but himself, he set out the next day for the Abbey, where his performances have been seen.

I leave it to my reader's sagacity to determine how much of all this it was possible for Henry to communicate at this time to Catherine, how much of it he could have learnt from his father, in what points his own conjectures might assist him, and what portion must yet remain to be told in a letter from James. I have united for their ease what they must divide for mine. Catherine, at any rate, heard enough to feel, that in suspecting General Tilney of either murdering or shutting up his wife, she had scarcely sinned against his character, or magnified his cruelty.

Henry, in having such things to relate of his father, was almost as pitiable as in their first avowal to himself. He blushed for the narrow-minded counsel which he was obliged to expose. The conversation between them at Northanger had been of the most unfriendly kind. Henry's indignation on hearing how Catherine had been treated, on comprehending his father's views, and being ordered to acquiesce in them, had been open and bold. The General, accustomed on every ordinary occasion to give the law in his family, prepared for no reluctance but of feeling, no opposing desire that should dare to clothe itself in words, could ill brook the opposition of his son, steady as the sanction of reason and the dictate of conscience could make it. But, in such a cause, his anger, though it must shock, could not intimidate Henry, who was sustained in his purpose by a conviction of its justice. He felt himself bound as much in honour as in affection to Miss Morland, and believing that heart to be his own which he had been directed to gain, no unworthy retraction of a tacit consent, no reversing decree of unjustifiable anger, could shake his fidelity, or influence the resolutions it prompted.

He steadily refused to accompany his father into Herefordshire, an engagement formed almost at the moment, to promote the dismissal of Catherine, and as steadily declared his intention of offering her his hand. The General was furious in his anger, and they parted in dreadful disagreement. Henry, in an agitation of mind which many solitary hours were required to compose, had returned almost instantly to Woodston; and, on the afternoon of the following day, had begun his journey to Fullerton.

CHAPTER XVI

Mr. and Mrs. Morland's surprize on being applied to by Mr. Tilney, for their consent to his marrying their daughter, was, for a few minutes, considerable; it having never entered their heads to suspect an attachment on either side; but as nothing, after all, could be more natural than Catherine's being beloved, they soon learnt to consider it with only the happy agitation of gratified pride, and, as far as they alone were concerned, had not a single objection to start. His pleasing manners and good sense were self-evident recommendations; and having never heard evil of him, it was not their way to suppose any evil could be told. Good-will supplying the place of experience, his character needed no attestation. 'Catherine would make a sad heedless young housekeeper to be sure,' was her mother's foreboding remark; but quick was the consolation of there being nothing like practice.

There was but one obstacle, in short, to be mentioned; but

till that one was removed, it must be impossible for them to sanction the engagement. Their tempers were mild, but their principles were steady, and while his parent so expressly forbad the connexion, they could not allow themselves to encourage it. That the General should come forward to solicit the alliance, or that he should even very heartily approve it, they were not refined enough to make any parading stipulation; but the decent appearance of consent must be yielded, and that once obtained – and their own hearts made them trust that it could not be very long denied – their willing approbation was instantly to follow. His *consent* was all that they wished for. They were no more inclined than entitled to demand his *money*. Of a very considerable fortune, his son was, by marriage settlements, eventually secure; his present income was an income of independence and comfort, and under every pecuniary view, it was a match beyond the claims of their daughter.

The young people could not be surprized at a decision like this. They felt and they deplored – but they could not resent it; and they parted, endeavouring to hope that such a change in the General, as each believed almost impossible, might speedily take place, to unite them again in the fullness of privileged affection. Henry returned to what was now his only home, to watch over his young plantations, and extend his improvements for her sake, to whose share in them he looked anxiously forward; and Catherine remained at Fullerton to cry. Whether the torments of absence were softened by a clandestine correspondence, let us not inquire. Mr. and Mrs. Morland never did – they had been too kind to exact any promise; and whenever Catherine received a letter, as, at that time, happened pretty often, they always looked another way.

The anxiety, which in this state of their attachment must be the portion of Henry and Catherine, and of all who loved either, as to its final event, can hardly extend, I fear, to the bosom of my readers, who will see in the tell-tale compression of the pages before them, that we are all hastening together to perfect felicity. The means by which their early marriage was effected can be the only doubt; what probable circumstance could work upon a temper like the General's? The circumstance which chiefly availed, was the marriage of his daughter with a man of fortune and consequence, which took place in the course of the summer – an accession of dignity that threw him into a fit of good-humour, from which he did not recover till after Eleanor had obtained his forgiveness of Henry, and his permission for him 'to be a fool if he liked it!'

The marriage of Eleanor Tilney, her removal from all the evils of such a home as Northanger had been made by Henry's banishment, to the home of her choice and the man of her choice, is an event which I expect to give general satisfaction among all her acquaintance. My own joy on the occasion is very sincere. I know no one more entitled, by unpretending merit, or better prepared by habitual suffering, to receive and enjoy felicity. Her partiality for this gentleman was not of recent origin; and he had been long withheld only by inferiority of situation from addressing her. His unexpected accession to title and fortune had removed all his difficulties; and never had the General loved his daughter so well in all her hours of companionship, utility, and patient endurance, as when he first hailed her, 'Your Ladyship!' Her husband was really deserving of her; independent of his peerage, his wealth, and his attachment, being to a precision the most charming young man in the world. Any further definition of his merits must be unnecessary; the most charming young man in the world is instantly before the imagination of us all. Concerning the one in question therefore I have only to add – (aware that the rules of composition forbid the introduction of a character not connected with my fable) – that this was the very gentleman whose negligent servant left behind him that collection of washing-bills, resulting from a long visit at Northanger, by which my heroine was involved in one of her most alarming adventures.

The influence of the Viscount and Viscountess in their brother's behalf was assisted by that right understanding of Mr. Morland's circumstances which, as soon as the General would allow himself to be informed, they were qualified to give. It taught him that he had been scarcely more misled by Thorpe's first boast of the family wealth, than by his subsequent malicious overthrow of it; that in no sense of the word were they necessitous or poor, and that Catherine would have three thousand pounds. This was so material an amendment of his late expectations, that it greatly contributed to smooth the descent of his pride; and by no means without its effect was the private intelligence, which he was at some pains to procure, that the Fullerton estate, being entirely at the disposal of its present proprietor, was consequently open to every greedy speculation.

On the strength of this, the General, soon after Eleanor's marriage, permitted his son to return to Northanger, and thence made him the bearer of his consent, very courteously worded in a page full of empty professions to Mr. Morland. The event which it authorized soon followed: Henry and Catherine were married, the bells rang and every body smiled; and, as this took place within a twelvemonth from the first day of their meeting, it will not appear, after all the dreadful delays occasioned by the General's cruelty, that they were essentially hurt by it. To begin perfect happiness at the respective ages of twenty-six and eighteen, is to do pretty well; and professing myself moreover convinced, that the General's unjust interference, so far from being really injurious to their felicity, was perhaps rather conducive to it, by improving their knowledge of each other, and adding strength to their attachment, I leave it to be settled by whomsoever it may concern, whether the tendency of this work be altogether to recommend parental tyranny, or reward filial disobedience.

LADY SUSAN

LETTER 1

Lady Susan Vernon to Mr. Vernon.

LANGFORD, December

My dear Brother

I can no longer refuse myself the pleasure of profitting by your kind invitation when we last parted, of spending some weeks with you at Churchill, and therefore if quite convenient to you and Mrs. Vernon to receive me at present, I shall hope within a few days to be introduced to a Sister whom I have so long desired to be acquainted with. My kind friends here are most affectionately urgent with me to prolong my stay, but their hospitable and chearful dispositions lead them too much into society for my present situation and state of mind; and I impatiently look forward to the hour when I shall be admitted into your delightful retirement. I long to be made known to your dear little Children, in whose hearts I shall be very eager to secure an interest. I shall soon have occasion for all my fortitude, as I am on the point of separation from my own daughter. The long illness of her dear Father prevented my paying her that attention which Duty and affection equally dictated, and I have but too much reason to fear that the Governess to whose care I consigned her, was unequal to the charge. I have therefore resolved on placing her at one of the best Private Schools in Town, where I shall have an opportunity of leaving her myself, in my way to you. I am determined you see, not to be denied admittance at Churchill. It would indeed give me most painful sensations to know that it were not in your power to receive me.

Yr most obliged and affec: Sister
S. Vernon.

LETTER 2

Lady Susan to Mrs. Johnson.

You were mistaken my dear Alicia, in supposing me fixed at this place for the rest of the winter. It greives me to say how greatly you were mistaken, for I have seldom spent three months more agreably than those which have just flown away. At present nothing goes smoothly. The Females of the Family are united against me. You foretold how it would be, when I first came to Langford; and Manwaring is so uncommonly pleasing that I was not without apprehensions myself. I remember saying to myself as I drove to the House, 'I like this Man; pray Heaven no harm come of it!' But I was determined to be discreet, to bear in mind my being only four months a widow, and to be as quiet as possible, – and I have been so; My dear Creature, I have admitted no one's attentions but Manwaring's, I have avoided all general flirtation whatever, I have distinguished no Creature besides of all the Numbers resorting hither, except Sir James Martin, on whom I bestowed a little notice in order to detach him from Miss Manwaring. But if the World could know my motive *there*, they would honour me. I have been called an unkind Mother, but it was the sacred impulse of maternal affection, it was the advantage of my Daughter that led me on; and if that Daughter were not the greatest simpleton on Earth, I might have been rewarded for my Exertions as I ought. – Sir James did make proposals to me for Frederica – but Frederica, who was born to be the torment of my life, chose to set herself so violently against the match, that I thought it better to lay aside the scheme for the present. I have more than once repented that I did not marry him myself, and were he but one degree less contemptibly weak I certainly should, but I must own myself rather romantic in that respect, and that Riches only, will not satisfy me. The event of all this is very provoking. Sir James is gone, Maria highly incensed, and Mrs. Manwaring insupportably jealous; so jealous in short, and so enraged against me, that in the fury of her temper I should not be surprised at her appealing to her Guardian if she had the liberty of addressing him – but there your Husband stands my friend, and the kindest, most amiable action of his Life was his throwing her off forever on her Marriage. Keep up his resentment therefore I charge you. We are now in a sad state; no house was ever more altered; the whole family are at war, and Manwaring scarcely dares speak to me. It is time for me to be gone; I have therefore determined on leaving them, and shall spend I hope a comfortable day with you in Town within this week. If I am as little in favour with Mr. Johnson as ever, you must come to me at No. 10 Wigmore Street – but I hope this may not be the case, for as Mr. Johnson with all his faults is a Man to whom that great word 'Respectable' is always given, and I am known to be so intimate with his wife, his slighting me has an awkward Look. I take Town in my way to that insupportable spot, a Country Village, for I am really going to Churchill. Forgive me my dear friend, it is my last resource. Were there another place in England open to me, I would prefer it. Charles Vernon is my aversion, and I am afraid of his wife. At Churchill however I must remain till I have something better in veiw. My young Lady accompanies me to Town, where I shall deposit her under the care of Miss Summers in Wigmore Street, till she becomes a little more reasonable. She will make good connections there, as the Girls are all of the best Families. The price is immense, and much beyond what I can ever attempt to pay.

Adeiu. I will send you a line, as soon as I arrive in Town. – Yours Ever,

S. Vernon.

LETTER 3

Mrs. Vernon to Lady De Courcy.

CHURCHILL.

My dear Mother

I am very sorry to tell you that it will not be in our power to keep our promise of spending the Christmas with you; and we are prevented that happiness by a circumstance which is not likely to make us any amends. Lady Susan in a letter to her Brother, has declared her intention of visiting us almost immediately – and as such a visit is in all probability an affair of convenience, it is impossible to conjecture it's length. I was by no means prepared for such an event, nor can I now account for her Ladyship's conduct. Langford appeared so exactly the place for her in every respect, as well from the elegant and expensive stile of Living there, as from her particular attachment to Mrs. Manwaring, that I was very far from expecting so speedy a distinction, tho' I always imagined from her increasing friendship for us since her Husband's death, that we should at some future period be obliged to receive her. Mr. Vernon I think was a great deal too kind to her, when he was in Staffordshire. Her behaviour to him, independent of her general Character, has been so inexcusably artful and ungenerous since our Marriage was first in agitation, that no one less amiable and mild than himself could have overlooked it at all; and tho' as his Brother's widow and in narrow circumstances it was proper to render her pecuniary assistance, I cannot help thinking his pressing invitation to her to visit us at Churchill perfectly unnecessary. Disposed however as he always is to think the best of every one, her display of Greif, and professions of regret, and general resolutions of prudence were sufficient to soften his heart, and make him really confide in her sincerity. But as for myself, I am still unconvinced; and plausibly as her Ladyship has now written, I cannot make up my mind, till I better understand her real meaning in coming to us. You may guess therefore my dear Madam, with what feelings I look forward to her arrival. She will have occasion for all those attractive Powers for which she is celebrated, to gain any share of my regard; and I shall certainly endeavour to guard myself against their influence, if not accompanied by something more substantial. She expresses a most eager desire of being acquainted with me, and makes very gracious mention of my children, but I am not quite weak enough to suppose a woman who has behaved with inattention if not unkindness to her own child, should be attached to any of mine. Miss Vernon is to be placed at a school in Town before her

Mother comes to us, which I am glad of, for her sake and my own. It must be to her advantage to be separated from her Mother: and a girl of sixteen who has received so wretched an education would not be a very desirable companion here. Reginald has long wished I know to see this captivating Lady Susan, and we shall depend on his joining our party soon. I am glad to hear that my Father continues so well, and am, with best Love &c.,

Cath. Vernon.

LETTER 4

Mr. De Courcy to Mrs. Vernon.

PARKLANDS.

My dear Sister

I congratulate you and Mr. Vernon on being about to receive into your family, the most accomplished Coquette in England. As a very distinguished Flirt, I have been always taught to consider her; but it has lately fallen in my way to hear some particulars of her conduct at Langford, which prove that she does not confine herself to that sort of honest flirtation which satisfies most people, but aspires to the more delicious gratification of making a whole family miserable. By her behaviour to Mr. Manwaring, she gave jealousy and wretchedness to his wife, and by her attentions to a young man previously attached to Mr. Manwaring's sister, deprived an amiable girl of her Lover. I learnt all this from a Mr. Smith now in this neighbourhood – (I have dined with him at Hurst and Wilford) – who is just come from Langford, where he was a fortnight in the house with her Ladyship, and who is therefore well qualified to make the communication.

What a Woman she must be! I long to see her, and shall certainly accept your kind invitation, that I may form some idea of those bewitching powers which can do so much – engaging at the same time and in the same house the affections of two Men who were neither of them at liberty to bestow them – and all this, without the charm of Youth. I am glad to find that Miss Vernon does not come with her Mother to Churchill, as she has not even Manners to recommend her, and according to Mr. Smith's account, is equally dull and proud. Where Pride and Stupidity unite, there can be no dissimulation worthy notice, and Miss Vernon shall be consigned to unrelenting contempt; but by all that I can gather, Lady Susan possesses a degree of captivating Deceit which must be pleasing to witness and detect. I shall be with you very soon, and am

your affec. Brother R. De Courcy.

LETTER 5

Lady Susan to Mrs. Johnson.

CHURCHILL.

I received your note my dear Alicia, just before I left Town, and rejoice to be assured that Mr. Johnson suspected nothing of your engagement the evening before; it is undoubtedly better to deceive him entirely; since he will be stubborn, he must be tricked. I arrived here in safety, and have no reason to complain of my reception from Mr. Vernon; but I confess myself not equally satisfied with the behaviour of his Lady. She is perfectly well bred indeed, and has the air of a woman of fashion, but her Manners are not such as can persuade me of her being pre-possessed in my favour. I wanted her to be delighted at seeing me – I was as amiable as possible on the occasion – but all in vain – she does not like me. To be sure, when we consider that I *did* take some pains to prevent my Brother-in-law's marrying her, this want of cordiality is not very surprising – and yet it shews an illiberal and vindictive spirit to resent a project which influenced me six years ago, and which never succeeded at last. I am sometimes half disposed to repent that I did not let Charles buy Vernon Castle when we were obliged to sell it, but it was a trying circumstance, especially as the sale took place exactly at the time of his marriage – and everybody ought to respect the delicacy of those feelings, which could not endure that my Husband's Dignity should be lessened by his younger brother's having possession of the Family Estate. Could Matters have been so arranged as to prevent the necessity of our leaving the Castle, could we have lived with Charles and kept him single, I should have been very far from persuading my husband to dispose of it elsewhere; but Charles was then on the point of marrying Miss De Courcy, and the event has justified me. Here are Children in abundance, and what benefit could have accrued to me from his purchasing Vernon? My having prevented it, may perhaps have given his wife an unfavourable impression – but where there is a disposition to dislike a motive will never be wanting; and as to money-matters, it has not with-held him from being very useful to me. I really have a regard for him, he is so easily imposed on!

The house is a good one, the Furniture fashionable, and everything announces plenty and elegance. Charles is very rich I am sure; when a Man has once got his name in a Banking House he rolls in money. But they do not know what to do with their fortune, keep very little company, and never go to Town but on business. We shall be as stupid as possible. I mean to win my Sister-in-law's heart through her Children; I know all their names already, and am going to attach myself with the greatest sensibility to one in particular, a young Frederic, whom I take on my lap and sigh over for his dear Uncle's sake.

Poor Manwaring! – I need not tell you how much I miss him – how perpetually he is in my Thoughts. I found a dismal letter from him on my arrival here, full of complaints of his wife and sister, and lamentations on the cruelty of his fate. I passed off the letter as his wife's, to the Vernons, and when I write to him, it must be under cover to you.

Yours Ever, S. V.

LETTER 6

Mrs. Vernon to Mr. De Courcy.

CHURCHILL.

Well my dear Reginald, I have seen this dangerous creature, and must give you some description of her, tho' I hope you will soon be able to form your own judgement. She is really excessively pretty. However you may chuse to question the allurements of a Lady no longer young, I must for my own part declare that I have seldom seen so lovely a Woman as Lady Susan. She is delicately fair, with fine grey eyes and dark eyelashes; and from her appearance one would not suppose her more than five and twenty, tho' she must in fact be ten years older. I was certainly not disposed to admire her, tho' always hearing she was beautiful; but I cannot help feeling that she possesses an uncommon union of Symmetry, Brilliancy and Grace. Her address to me was so gentle, frank and even affectionate, that if I had not known how much she has always disliked me for marrying Mr. Vernon, and that we had never met before, I should have imagined her an attached friend. One is apt I beleive to connect assurance of manner with coquetry, and to expect that an impudent address will necessarily attend an impudent mind; at least I was myself prepared for an improper degree of confidence in Lady Susan; but her Countenance is absolutely sweet, and her voice and manner winningly mild. I am sorry it is so, for what is this but Deceit? Unfortunately one knows her too well. She is clever and agreable, has all that knowledge of the world which makes conversation easy, and talks very well, with a happy command of Language, which is too often used I beleive to make Black appear White. She has already almost persuaded me of her being warmly attached to her daughter, tho' I have so long been convinced of the contrary. She speaks of her with so much tenderness and anxiety, lamenting so bitterly the neglect of her education, which she represents however as wholly unavoidable, that I am forced to recollect how many successive Springs her Ladyship spent in Town, while her daughter was left in Staffordshire to the care of servants or a Governess very little better, to prevent my beleiving whatever she says.

If her manners have so great an influence on my resentful heart, you may guess how much more strongly they operate on Mr. Vernon's generous temper. I wish I could be as well satisfied as he is, that it was really her choice to leave Langford for Churchill; and if she had not staid three months there before she discovered that her friends' manner of Living did not suit her situation or feelings, I might have beleived that concern for the loss of such a Husband as Mr. Vernon, to whom her own behaviour was far from unexceptionable, might for a time make her wish for retirement. But I cannot forget the length of her visit to the Manwarings, and when I reflect on the different mode of Life which she led with them, from that to which she must now submit, I can only suppose that the wish of establishing her reputation by following, tho' late, the path of propriety, occasioned her removal from a family where she must in reality have been particularly happy. Your friend Mr. Smith's story however cannot be quite true, as she corresponds regularly with Mrs. Manwaring; at any rate it must be exaggerated; it is scarcely possible that two men should be so grossly deceived by her at once.

Yrs &c. Cath. Vernon.

LETTER 7

Lady Susan to Mrs. Johnson.

CHURCHILL.

My dear Alicia

You are very good in taking notice of Frederica, and I am grateful for it as a mark of your friendship; but as I cannot have a doubt of the warmth of that friendship, I am far from exacting so heavy a sacrifice. She is a stupid girl, and has nothing to recommend her. I would not therefore on any account have you

encumber one moment of your precious time by sending her to
Edward Street, especially as every visit is so many hours de-
ducted from the grand affair of Education, which I really wish to
be attended to, while she remains with Miss Summers. I want
her to play and sing with some portion of Taste, and a good deal
of assurance, as she has *my* hand and arm, and a tolerable voice. *I*
was so much indulged in my infant years that I was never
obliged to attend to anything, and consequently am without
those accomplishments which are now necessary to finish a
pretty Woman. Not that I am an advocate for the prevailing
fashion of acquiring a perfect knowledge in all the Languages
Arts and Sciences; it is throwing time away; to be Mistress of
French, Italian, German, Music, Singing, Drawing &c. will
gain a Woman some applause, but will not add one Lover to her
list. Grace and Manner after all are of the greatest importance. I
do not mean therefore that Frederica's acquirements should be
more than superficial, and I flatter myself that she will not
remain long enough at school to understand anything thoroughly.
I hope to see her the wife of Sir James within a twelvemonth.
You know on what I ground my hope, and it is certainly a good
foundation, for School must be very humiliating to a girl of
Frederica's age; and by the bye, you had better not invite her
any more on that account, as I wish her to find her situation as
unpleasant as possible. I am sure of Sir James at any time, and
could make him renew his application by a Line. I shall trouble
you meanwhile to prevent his forming any other attachment
when he comes to Town; ask him to your House occasionally,
and talk to him about Frederica that he may not forget her.

Upon the whole I commend my own conduct in this affair
extremely, and regard it as a very happy mixture of circum-
spection and tenderness. Some Mothers would have insisted on
their daughter's accepting so great an offer on the first overture,
but I could not answer it to myself to force Frederica into a
marriage from which her heart revolted; and instead of adopting
so harsh a measure, merely propose to make it her own choice by
rendering her thoroughly uncomfortable till she does accept
him. But enough of this tiresome girl.

You may well wonder how I contrive to pass my time here – and for the first week, it was most insufferably dull. Now however, we begin to mend; our party is enlarged by Mrs. Vernon's brother, a handsome young Man, who promises me some amusement. There is something about him that rather interests me, a sort of sauciness, of familiarity which I shall teach him to correct. He is lively and seems clever, and when I have inspired him with greater respect for me than his sister's kind offices have implanted, he may be an agreable Flirt. There is exquisite pleasure in subduing an insolent spirit, in making a person predetermined to dislike, acknowledge one's superiority. I have disconcerted him already by my calm reserve; and it shall be my endeavour to humble the Pride of these self-important De Courcies still lower, to convince Mrs. Vernon that her sisterly cautions have been bestowed in vain, and to persuade Reginald that she has scandalously belied me. This project will serve at least to amuse me, and prevent my feeling so acutely this dreadful separation from You and all whom I love. Adeiu.

Yours Ever
S. Vernon.

LETTER 8

Mrs. Vernon to Lady De Courcy.

CHURCHILL.

My dear Mother

You must not expect Reginald back again for some time. He desires me to tell you that the present open weather induces him to accept Mr. Vernon's invitation to prolong his stay in Sussex that they may have some hunting together. He means to send for his Horses immediately, and it is impossible to say when you may see him in Kent. I will not disguise my sentiments on this change from you my dear Madam, tho' I think you had better not communicate them to my Father, whose excessive anxiety about Reginald would subject him to an alarm which might seriously affect his health and spirits. Lady Susan has certainly

contrived in the space of a fortnight to make my Brother like
her. In short, I am persuaded that his continuing here beyond
the time originally fixed for his return, is occasioned as much by a
degree of fascination towards her, as by the wish of hunting with
Mr. Vernon, and of course I cannot receive that pleasure from
the length of his visit which my Brother's company would
otherwise give me. I am indeed provoked at the artifice of this
unprincipled Woman. What stronger proof of her dangerous
abilities can be given, than this perversion of Reginald's Judgement, which when he entered the house was so decidedly against
her? In his last letter he actually gave me some particulars of her
behaviour at Langford, such as he received from a Gentleman
who knew her perfectly well, which if true must raise abhorrence
against her, and which Reginald himself was entirely disposed to
credit. His opinion of her I am sure, was as low as of any Woman
in England, and when he first came it was evident that he considered her as one entitled neither to Delicacy nor respect, and
that he felt she would be delighted with the attentions of any
Man inclined to flirt with her.

Her behaviour I confess has been calculated to do away such
an idea, I have not detected the smallest impropriety in it, –
nothing of vanity, of pretension, of Levity – and she is altogether
so attractive, that I should not wonder at his being delighted
with her, had he known nothing of her previous to this personal
acquaintance; but against reason, against conviction, to be so
well pleased with her as I am sure he is, does really astonish me.
His admiration was at first very strong, but no more than was
natural; and I did not wonder at his being struck by the gentleness and delicacy of her Manners; but when he has mentioned
her of late, it has been in terms of more extraordinary praise,
and yesterday he actually said, that he could not be surprised at
any effect produced on the heart of Man by such Loveliness and
such Abilities; and when I lamented in reply the badness of her
disposition, he observed that whatever might have been her
errors, they were to be imputed to her neglected Education and
early Marriage, and that she was altogether a wonderful Woman.

This tendency to excuse her conduct, or to forget it in the

warmth of admiration vexes me; and if I did not know that Reginald is too much at home at Churchill to need an invitation for lengthening his visit, I should regret Mr. Vernon's giving him any.

Lady Susan's intentions are of course those of absolute coquetry, or a desire of universal admiration. I cannot for a moment imagine that she has anything more serious in veiw, but it mortifies me to see a young Man of Reginald's sense duped by her at all. I am &c.

Cath. Vernon.

LETTER 9

Mrs. Johnson to Lady Susan.

EDWARD STREET.

My dearest Friend

I congratulate you on Mr. De Courcy's arrival, and advise you by all means to marry him; his Father's Estate is we know considerable, and I beleive certainly entailed.[1] Sir Reginald is very infirm, and not likely to stand in your way long. I hear the young Man well spoken of, and tho' no one can really deserve you my dearest Susan, Mr. De Courcy may be worth having. Manwaring will storm of course, but you may easily pacify him. Besides, the most scrupulous point of honour could not require you to wait for *his* emancipation. I have seen Sir James, – he came to Town for a few days last week, and called several times in Edward Street. I talked to him about you and your daughter, and he is so far from having forgotten you, that I am sure he would marry either of you with pleasure. I gave him hopes of Frederica's relenting, and told him a great deal of her improvements. I scolded him for making Love to Maria Manwaring; he protested that he had been only in joke, and we both laughed heartily at her disappointment, and in short were very agreable. He is as silly as ever. – Yours faithfully

Alicia.

LETTER 10

Lady Susan to Mrs. Johnson.

CHURCHILL.

I am much obliged to you my dear Friend, for your advice respecting Mr. De Courcy, which I know was given with the fullest conviction of it's expediency, tho' I am not quite determined on following it. I cannot easily resolve on anything so serious as Marriage, especially as I am not at present in want of money, and might perhaps till the old Gentleman's death, be very little benefited by the match. It is true that I am vain enough to beleive it within my reach. I have made him sensible of my power, and can now enjoy the pleasure of triumphing over a Mind prepared to dislike me, and prejudiced against all my past actions. His sister too, is I hope convinced how little the ungenerous representations of any one to the disadvantage of another will avail, when opposed to the immediate influence of Intellect and Manner. I see plainly that she is uneasy at my progress in the good opinion of her Brother, and conclude that nothing will be wanting on her part to counteract me; but having once made him doubt the justice of her opinion of me, I think I may defy her.

It has been delightful to me to watch his advances towards intimacy, especially to observe his altered manner in consequence of my repressing by the calm dignity of my deportment, his insolent approach to direct familiarity. My conduct has been equally guarded from the first, and I never behaved less like a Coquette in the whole course of my Life, tho' perhaps my desire of dominion was never more decided. I have subdued him entirely by sentiment and serious conversation, and made him I may venture to say at least *half* in Love with me, without the semblance of the most common-place flirtation. Mrs. Vernon's consciousness of deserving every sort of revenge that it can be in my power to inflict, for her ill-offices, could alone enable her to perceive that I am actuated by any design in behaviour so gentle and unpretending. Let her think and act as she chuses however; I have never yet found that the advice of a Sister could prevent a young Man's being in love if he chose it. We are advancing now towards some kind of confidence, and in short are likely to be engaged in a kind of platonic friendship. On *my* side, you may be sure of it's never being more, for if I were not already as much attached to another person as I can be to any one, I should make a point of not bestowing my affection on a Man who had dared to think so meanly of me.

Reginald has a good figure, and is not unworthy the praise you have heard given him, but is still greatly inferior to our friend at Langford. He is less polished, less insinuating than Manwaring, and is comparatively deficient in the power of saying those delightful things which put one in good humour with oneself and all the world. He is quite agreable enough however, to afford me amusement, and to make many of those hours pass very pleasantly which would be otherwise spent in endeavouring to overcome my sister-in-law's reserve, and listening to her Husband's insipid talk.

Your account of Sir James is most satisfactory, and I mean to give Miss Frederica a hint of my intentions very soon. – Yours &c.

S. Vernon.

LETTER 11

Mrs. Vernon to Lady De Courcy.

I really grow quite uneasy my dearest Mother about Reginald, from witnessing the very rapid increase of Lady Susan's influence. They are now on terms of the most particular friendship, frequently engaged in long conversations together, and she has contrived by the most artful coquetry to subdue his Judgement to her own purposes. It is impossible to see the intimacy between them, so very soon established, without some alarm, tho' I can hardly suppose that Lady Susan's veiws extend to marriage. I wish you could get Reginald home again, under any plausible pretence. He is not at all disposed to leave us, and I have given him as many hints of my Father's precarious state of health, as common decency will allow me to do in my own house. Her power over him must now be boundless, as she has entirely effaced all his former ill-opinion, and persuaded him not merely to forget, but to justify her conduct. Mr. Smith's account of her proceedings at Langford, where he accused her of having made Mr. Manwaring and a young Man engaged to Miss Manwaring distractedly in love with her, which Reginald firmly beleived when he came to Churchill, is now he is persuaded only a scandalous invention. He has told me so in a warmth of manner which spoke his regret at having ever beleived the contrary himself.

How sincerely do I greive that she ever entered this house! I always looked forward to her coming with uneasiness – but very far was it, from originating in anxiety for Reginald. I expected a most disagreable companion to myself, but could not imagine that my Brother would be in the smallest danger of being captivated by a Woman with whose principles he was so well acquainted, and whose character he so heartily despised. If you can get him away, it will be a good thing.

Yrs affec:ly
Cath. Vernon.

LETTER 12

Sir Reginald De Courcy to his Son.

PARKLANDS.

I know that young Men in general do not admit of any enquiry even from their nearest relations, into affairs of the heart; but I hope my dear Reginald that you will be superior to such as allow nothing for a Father's anxiety, and think themselves privileged to refuse him their confidence and slight his advice. You must be sensible that as an only son and the representative of an ancient Family, your conduct in Life is most interesting to your connections. In the very important concern of Marriage especially, there is everything at stake; your own happiness, that of your

Parents, and the credit of your name. I do not suppose that you would deliberately form an absolute engagement of that nature without acquainting your Mother and myself, or at least without being convinced that we should approve your choice; but I cannot help fearing that you may be drawn in by the Lady who has lately attached you, to a Marriage, which the whole of your Family, far and near, must highly reprobate.

Lady Susan's age is itself a material objection, but her want of character is one so much more serious, that the difference of even twelve years becomes in comparison of small account. Were you not blinded by a sort of fascination, it would be ridiculous in me to repeat the instances of great misconduct on her side, so very generally known. Her neglect of her husband, her encouragement of other Men, her extravagance and dissipation were so gross and notorious, that no one could be ignorant of them at the time, nor can now have forgotten them. To our Family, she has always been represented in softened colours by the benevolence of Mr. Charles Vernon; and yet in spite of his generous endeavours to excuse her, we know that she did, from the most selfish motives, take all possible pains to prevent his marrying Catherine.

My Years and increasing Infirmities make me very desirous my dear Reginald, of seeing you settled in the world. To the Fortune of your wife, the goodness of my own, will make me indifferent; but her family and character must be equally unexceptionable. When your choice is so fixed as that no objection can be made to either, I can promise you a ready and chearful consent; but it is my Duty to oppose a Match, which deep Art only could render probable, and must in the end make wretched.

It is possible that her behaviour may arise only from Vanity, or a wish of gaining the admiration of a Man whom she must imagine to be particularly prejudiced against her; but it is more likely that she should aim at something farther. She is poor, and may naturally seek an alliance which may be advantageous to herself. You know your own rights, and that it is out of my power to prevent your inheriting the family Estate. My Ability of distressing you during my Life, would be a species of revenge to which I should hardly stoop under any circumstances. I honestly tell you my Sentiments and Intentions. I do not wish to work on your Fears, but on your Sense and Affection. It would destroy every comfort of my Life, to know that you were married to Lady Susan Vernon. It would be the death of that honest Pride with which I have hitherto considered my son, I should blush to see him, to hear of him, to think of him.

I may perhaps do no good, but that of relieving my own mind, by this Letter; but I felt it my Duty to tell you that your partiality for Lady Susan is no secret to your friends, and to warn you against her. I should be glad to hear your reasons for disbeleiving Mr. Smith's intelligence; you had no doubt of it's authenticity a month ago.

If you can give me your assurance of having no design beyond enjoying the conversation of a clever woman for a short period, and of yeilding admiration only to her Beauty and Abilities without being blinded by them to her faults, you will restore me to happiness; but if you cannot do this, explain to me at least what has occasioned so great an alteration in your opinion of her.

I am &c.
Reginald De Courcy.

LETTER 13

Lady De Courcy to Mrs. Vernon.

PARKLANDS.

My dear Catherine,

Unluckily I was confined to my room when your last letter came, by a cold which affected my eyes so much as to prevent my reading it myself, so I could not refuse your Father when he offered to read it to me, by which means he became acquainted to my great vexation with all your fears about your Brother. I had intended to write to Reginald myself, as soon as my eyes would let me, to point out as well as I could the danger of an intimate acquaintance with so artful a woman as Lady Susan, to a young

Man of his age and high expectations. I meant moreover to have reminded him of our being quite alone now, and very much in need of him to keep up our spirits these long winter evenings. Whether it would have done any good, can never be settled now; but I am excessively vexed that Sir Reginald should know anything of a matter which we foresaw would make him so uneasy. He caught all your fears the moment he had read your Letter, and I am sure has not had the business out of his head since; he wrote by the same post to Reginald, a long letter full of it all, and particularly asking for an explanation of what he may have heard from Lady Susan to contradict the late shocking reports. His answer came this morning, which I shall enclose to you, as I think you will like to see it; I wish it was more satisfactory, but it seems written with such a determination to think well of Lady Susan, that his assurances as to Marriage &c., do not set my heart at ease. I say all I can however to satisfy your Father, and he is certainly less uneasy since Reginald's letter. How provoking it is my dear Catherine, that this unwelcome Guest of yours, should not only prevent our meeting this Christmas, but be the occasion of so much vexation and trouble. Kiss the dear Children for me. Your affec: Mother

C. De Courcy.

LETTER 14

Mr. De Courcy to Sir Reginald.

CHURCHILL.

My dear Sir

I have this moment received your Letter, which has given me more astonishment than I ever felt before. I am to thank my Sister I suppose, for having represented me in such a light as to injure me in your opinion, and give you all this alarm. I know not why she should chuse to make herself and her family uneasy by apprehending an Event, which no one but herself I can affirm, would ever have thought possible. To impute such a design to Lady Susan would be taking from her every claim to that excellent understanding which her bitterest Enemies have never denied her; and equally low must sink my pretensions to common sense, if I am suspected of matrimonial veiws in my behaviour to her. Our difference of age must be an insuperable objection, and I entreat you my dear Sir to quiet your mind, and no longer harbour a suspicion which cannot be more injurious to your own peace than to our Understandings.

I can have no veiw in remaining with Lady Susan than to enjoy for a short time (as you have yourself expressed it) the conversation of a Woman of high mental powers. If Mrs. Vernon would allow something to my affection for herself and her husband in the length of my visit, she would do more justice to us all; but my Sister is unhappily prejudiced beyond the hope of conviction against Lady Susan. From an attachment to her husband which in itself does honour to both, she cannot forgive those endeavours at preventing their union, which have been attributed to selfishness in Lady Susan. But in this case, as well as in many others, the World has most grossly injured that Lady, by supposing the worst, where the motives of her conduct have been doubtful.

Lady Susan had heard something so materially to the disadvantage of my Sister, as to persuade her that the happiness of Mr. Vernon, to whom she was always much attached, would be absolutely destroyed by the Marriage. And this circumstance while it explains the true motive of Lady Susan's conduct, and removes all the blame which has been so lavished on her, may also convince us how little the general report of any one ought to be credited, since no character however upright, can escape the malevolence of slander. If my Sister in the security of retirement, with as little opportunity as inclination to do Evil, could not avoid Censure, we must not rashly condemn those who living in the World and surrounded with temptation, should be accused of Errors which they are known to have the power of committing.

I blame myself severely for having so easily beleived the scandalous tales invented by Charles Smith to the prejudice of Lady Susan, as I am now convinced how greatly they have

traduced her. As to Mrs. Manwaring's jealousy, it was totally
his own invention; and his account of her attaching Miss Manwaring's Lover was scarcely better founded. Sir James Martin
had been drawn in by that young Lady to pay her some attention,
and as he is a Man of fortune, it was easy to see that *her* veiws
extended to Marriage. It is well known that Miss Manwaring is
absolutely on the catch for a husband, and no one therefore can
pity her, for losing by the superior attractions of another woman,
the chance of being able to make a worthy Man completely
miserable. Lady Susan was far from intending such a conquest,
and on finding how warmly Miss Manwaring resented her
Lover's defection, determined, in spite of Mr. and Mrs. Manwaring's most earnest entreaties, to leave the family. I have
reason to imagine that she did receive serious Proposals from
Sir James, but her removing from Langford immediately on the
discovery of his attachment, must acquit her on that article, with
every Mind of common candour.[1] You will, I am sure my dear
Sir, feel the truth of this reasoning, and will hereby learn to do
justice to the character of a very injured Woman.

I know that Lady Susan in coming to Churchill was governed
only by the most honourable and amiable intentions. Her
prudence and economy are exemplary, her regard for Mr.
Vernon equal even to *his* deserts, and her wish of obtaining my
sister's good opinion merits a better return than it has received.
As a Mother she is unexceptionable. Her solid affection for her
Child is shewn by placing her in hands, where her Education
will be properly attended to; but because she has not the blind
and weak partiality of most Mothers, she is accused of wanting
Maternal Tenderness. Every person of Sense however will
know how to value and commend her well directed affection,
and will join me in wishing that Frederica Vernon may prove
more worthy than she has yet done, of her Mother's tender
care.

I have now my dear Sir, written my real sentiments of Lady
Susan; you will know from this Letter, how highly I admire her
Abilities, and esteem her Character; but if you are not equally
convinced by my full and solemn assurance that your fears have

been most idly created, you will deeply mortify and distress me. — I am &c.

R. De Courcy.

LETTER 15

Mrs. Vernon to Lady De Courcy.

CHURCHILL.

My dear Mother

I return you Reginald's letter, and rejoice with all my heart that my Father is made easy by it. Tell him so, with my congratulations; but between ourselves, I must own it has only convinced *me* of my Brother's having no *present* intention of marrying Lady Susan – not that he is in no danger of doing so three months hence. He gives a very plausible account of her behaviour at Langford, I wish it may be true, but his intelligence must come from herself, and I am less disposed to beleive it, than to lament the degree of intimacy subsisting between them, implied by the discussion of such a subject.

I am sorry to have incurred his displeasure, but can expect nothing better while he is so very eager in Lady Susan's justification. He is very severe against me indeed, and yet I hope I have not been hasty in my judgement of her. Poor Woman! tho' I have reasons enough for my dislike, I can not help pitying her at present as she is in real distress, and with too much cause. She had this morning a letter from the Lady with whom she has placed her daughter, to request that Miss Vernon might be immediately removed, as she had been detected in an attempt to run away. Why, or whither she intended to go, does not appear; but as her situation seems to have been unexceptionable, it is a sad thing and of course highly afflicting to Lady Susan.

Frederica must be as much as sixteen, and ought to know better, but from what her Mother insinuates I am afraid she is a perverse girl. She has been sadly neglected however, and her Mother ought to remember it.

Mr. Vernon set off for Town as soon as she had determined

what should be done. He is if possible to prevail on Miss Summers to let Frederica continue with her, and if he cannot succeed, to bring her to Churchill for the present, till some other situation can be found for her. Her Ladyship is comforting herself meanwhile by strolling along the Shrubbery with Reginald, calling forth all his tender feelings I suppose on this distressing occasion. She has been talking a great deal about it to me, she talks vastly well, I am afraid of being ungenerous or I should say she talks *too* well to feel so very deeply. But I will not look for Faults. She may be Reginald's Wife. Heaven forbid it! – but why should I be quicker sighted than anybody else? Mr. Vernon declares that he never saw deeper distress than hers, on the receipt of the Letter – and is his Judgement inferior to mine?

She was very unwilling that Frederica should be allowed to come to Churchill, and justly enough, as it seems a sort of reward to Behaviour deserving very differently. But it was impossible to take her any where else, and she is not to remain here long.

'It will be absolutely necessary,' said she, 'as you my dear Sister must be sensible, to treat my daughter with some severity while she is here; – a most painful necessity, but I will endeavour to submit to it. I am afraid I have been often too indulgent, but my poor Frederica's temper could never bear opposition well. You must support and encourage me – You must urge the necessity of reproof, if you see me too lenient.'

All this sounds very reasonably. Reginald is so incensed against the poor silly Girl! Surely it is not to Lady Susan's credit that he should be so bitter against her daughter; his idea of her must be drawn from the Mother's description.

Well, whatever may be his fate, we have the comfort of knowing that we have done our utmost to save him. We must commit the event to an Higher Power. Yours Ever &c.

Cath. Vernon.

LETTER 16

Lady Susan to Mrs. Johnson.

CHURCHILL.

Never my dearest Alicia, was I so provoked in my life as by a Letter this morning from Miss Summers. That horrid girl of mine has been trying to run away. – I had not a notion of her being such a little Devil before; she seemed to have all the Vernon Milkiness; but on receiving the letter in which I declared my intentions about Sir James, she actually attempted to elope; at least, I cannot otherwise account for her doing it. She meant I suppose to go to the Clarkes in Staffordshire, for she has no other acquaintance. But she *shall* be punished, she *shall* have him. I have sent Charles to Town to make matters up if he can, for I do not by any means want her here. If Miss Summers will not keep her, you must find me out another school, unless we can get her married immediately. Miss S. writes word that she could not get the young Lady to assign any cause for her extraordinary conduct, which confirms me in my own private explanation of it.

Frederica is too shy I think, and too much in awe of me, to tell tales; but if the mildness of her Uncle *should* get anything from her, I am not afraid. I trust I shall be able to make my story as good as her's. If I am vain of anything, it is of my eloquence. Consideration and Esteem as surely follow command of Language, as Admiration waits on Beauty. And here I have opportunity enough for the exercise of my Talent, as the cheif of my time is spent in Conversation. Reginald is never easy unless we are by ourselves, and when the weather is tolerable, we pace the shrubbery for hours together. I like him on the whole very well, he is clever and has a good deal to say, but he is sometimes impertinent and troublesome. There is a sort of ridiculous delicacy about him which requires the fullest explanation of whatever he may have heard to my disadvantage, and is never satisfied till he thinks he has ascertained the beginning and end of everything.

This is *one* sort of Love – but I confess it does not particularly recommend itself to me. I infinitely prefer the tender and liberal spirit of Manwaring, which impressed with the deepest conviction of my merit, is satisfied that whatever I do must be right; and look with a degree of contempt on the inquisitive and doubting Fancies of that Heart which seems always debating on the reasonableness of it's Emotions. Manwaring is indeed beyond compare superior to Reginald – superior in everything but the power of being with me. Poor fellow! he is quite distracted by Jealousy, which I am not sorry for, as I know no better support of Love. He has been teizing me to allow of his coming into this country, and lodging somewhere near me *incog.* – but I forbid anything of the kind. Those women are inexcusable who forget what is due to themselves and the opinion of the World.

S. Vernon.

LETTER 17

Mrs. Vernon to Lady De Courcy.

CHURCHILL.

My dear Mother

Mr. Vernon returned on Thursday night, bringing his neice with him. Lady Susan had received a line from him by that day's post informing her that Miss Summers had absolutely refused to allow of Miss Vernon's continuance in her Academy. We were therefore prepared for her arrival, and expected them impatiently the whole evening. They came while we were at Tea, and I never saw any creature look so frightened in my life as Frederica when she entered the room.

Lady Susan who had been shedding tears before and shewing great agitation at the idea of the meeting, received her with perfect self-command, and without betraying the least tenderness of spirit. She hardly spoke to her, and on Frederica's bursting into tears as soon as we were seated, took her out of the room and did not return for some time; when she did, her eyes looked very red, and she was as much agitated as before. We saw no more of her daughter.

Poor Reginald was beyond measure concerned to see his fair friend in such distress, and watched her with so much tender solicitude that I, who occasionally caught her observing his countenance with exultation, was quite out of patience. This pathetic representation lasted the whole evening, and so ostentatious and artful a display had entirely convinced me that she did in fact feel nothing.

I am more angry with her than ever since I have seen her daughter. The poor girl looks so unhappy that my heart aches for her. Lady Susan is surely too severe, because Frederica does not seem to have the sort of temper to make severity necessary. She looks perfectly timid, dejected and penitent.

She is very pretty, tho' not so handsome as her Mother, nor at all like her. Her complexion is delicate, but neither so fair, nor so blooming as Lady Susan's – and she has quite the Vernon cast of countenance, the oval face and mild dark eyes, and there is peculiar sweetness in her look when she speaks either to her Uncle or me, for as we behave kindly to her, we have of course engaged her gratitude. Her Mother has insinuated that her temper is untractable, but I never saw a face less indicative of any evil disposition than her's; and from what I now see of the behaviour of each to the other, the invariable severity of Lady Susan, and the silent dejection of Frederica, I am led to beleive as heretofore that the former has no real Love for her daughter and has never done her justice, or treated her affectionately.

I have not yet been able to have any conversation with my neice; she is shy, and I think I can see that some pains are taken to prevent her being much with me. Nothing satisfactory transpires as to her reason for running away. Her kindhearted Uncle you may be sure, was too fearful of distressing her, to ask many questions as they travelled. I wish it had been possible for me to fetch her instead of him; I think I should have discovered the truth in the course of a Thirty mile Journey.

The small Pianoforté has been removed within these few

days at Lady Susan's request, into her Dressing room, and Frederica spends great part of the day there; *practising* it is called, but I seldom hear any noise when I pass that way. What she does with herself there I do not know, there are plenty of books in the room, but it is not every girl who has been running wild the first fifteen years of her life, that can or will read. Poor Creature! the prospect from her window is not very instructive, for that room overlooks the Lawn you know with the Shrubbery on one side, where she may see her Mother walking for an hour together, in earnest conversation with Reginald. A girl of Frederica's age must be childish indeed, if such things do not strike her. Is it not inexcusable to give such an example to a daughter? Yet Reginald still thinks Lady Susan the best of Mothers – still condemns Frederica as a worthless girl! He is convinced that her attempt to run away, proceeded from no justifiable cause, and had no provocation. I am sure I cannot say that it *had*, but while Miss Summers declares that Miss Vernon shewed no sign of Obstinacy or Perverseness during her whole stay in Wigmore Street till she was detected in this scheme, I cannot so readily credit what Lady Susan has made him and wants to make me beleive, that it was merely an impatience of restraint, and a desire of escaping from the tuition of Masters which brought on the plan of an elopement. Oh! Reginald, how is your Judgement enslaved! He scarcely dares even allow her to be handsome, and when I speak of her beauty, replies only that her eyes have no Brilliancy.

Sometimes he is sure that she is deficient in Understanding, and at others that her temper only is in fault. In short when a person is always to deceive, it is impossible to be consistent. Lady Susan finds it necessary for her own justification that Frederica should be to blame, and probably has sometimes judged it expedient to accuse her of ill-nature and sometimes to lament her want of sense. Reginald is only repeating after her Ladyship.

I am &c.
Cath. Vernon.

LETTER 18

From the same to the same.

My dear Madam

I am very glad to find that my description of Frederica Vernon has interested you, for I do beleive her truly deserving of our regard, and when I have communicated a notion that has recently struck me, your kind impression in her favour will I am sure be heightened. I cannot help fancying that she is growing partial to my brother, I so very often see her eyes fixed on his face with a remarkable expression of pensive admiration! He is certainly very handsome – and yet more – there is an openness in his manner that must be highly prepossessing, and I am sure she feels it so. Thoughtful and pensive in general her countenance always brightens with a smile when Reginald says anything amusing; and let the subject be ever so serious that he may be conversing on, I am much mistaken if a syllable of his uttering, escape her.

I want to make *him* sensible of all this, for we know the power of gratitude on such a heart as his; and could Frederica's artless affection detach him from her Mother, we might bless the day which brought her to Churchill. I think my dear Madam, you would not disapprove of her as a Daughter. She is extremely young to be sure, has had a wretched Education and a dreadful example of Levity in her Mother; but yet I can pronounce her disposition to be excellent, and her natural abilities very good.

Tho' totally without accomplishment, she is by no means so ignorant as one might expect to find her, being fond of books and spending the cheif of her time in reading. Her Mother leaves her more to herself now than she *did*, and I have her with me as much as possible, and have taken great pains to overcome her timidity. We are very good friends, and though she never opens her lips before her Mother, she talks enough when alone with me, to make it clear that if properly treated by Lady Susan she would always appear to much greater advantage. There cannot be a more gentle, affectionate heart, or more obliging manners, when acting without restraint. Her little Cousins are all very fond of her.

Yrs affec:ly
Cath. Vernon.

LETTER 19

Lady Susan to Mrs. Johnson.

CHURCHILL.

You will be eager I know to hear something farther of Frederica, and perhaps may think me negligent for not writing before. She arrived with her Uncle last Thursday fortnight, when of course I lost no time in demanding the reason of her behaviour, and soon found myself to have been perfectly right in attributing it to my own letter. The purport of it frightened her so thoroughly that with a mixture of true girlish perverseness and folly, without considering that she could not escape from my authority by running away from Wigmore Street, she resolved on getting out of the house, and proceeding directly by the stage to her friends the Clarkes, and had really got as far as the length of two streets in her journey, when she was fortunately miss'd, pursued, and overtaken.

Such was the first distinguished exploit of Miss Frederica Susanna Vernon, and if we consider that it was atchieved at the tender age of sixteen we shall have room for the most flattering prognostics of her future renown. I am excessively provoked however at the parade of propriety which prevented Miss Summers from keeping the girl; and it seems so extraordinary a peice of nicety, considering what are my daughter's family connections, that I can only suppose the Lady to be governed by the fear of never getting her money. Be that as it may however, Frederica is returned on my hands, and having now nothing else to employ her, is busy in pursueing the plan of Romance begun at Langford. She is actually falling in love with Reginald De Courcy. To disobey her Mother by refusing an unexceptionable offer is not enough; her affections must likewise be given without her Mother's approbation. I never saw a girl of her age, bid fairer to be the sport of Mankind. Her feelings are tolerably lively, and she is so charmingly artless in their display, as to afford the most reasonable hope of her being ridiculed and despised by every Man who sees her.

Artlessness will never do in Love matters, and that girl is born a simpleton who has it either by nature or affectation. I am not yet certain that Reginald sees what she is about; nor is it of much consequence; she is now an object of indifference to him, she would be one of contempt were he to understand her Emotions. Her beauty is much admired by the Vernons but it has no effect on *him*. She is in high favour with her Aunt altogether – because she is so little like myself of course. She is exactly the companion for Mrs. Vernon, who dearly loves to be first, and to have all the sense and all the wit of the Conversation to herself; Frederica will never eclipse her. When she first came, I was at some pains to prevent her seeing much of her Aunt, but I have since relaxed, as I beleive I may depend on her observing the rules I have laid down for their discourse.

But do not imagine that with all this Lenity, I have for a moment given up my plan of her marriage; No, I am unalterably fixed on that point, though I have not yet quite resolved on the manner of bringing it about. I should not chuse to have the business brought forward here, and canvassed by the wise heads of Mr. and Mrs. Vernon; and I cannot just now afford to go to Town. Miss Frederica therefore must wait a little.

Yours Ever
S. Vernon.

LETTER 20

Mrs Vernon to Lady De Courcy.

CHURCHILL.

We have a very unexpected Guest with us at present, my dear Mother. He arrived yesterday. I heard a carriage at the

door as I was sitting with my children while they dined, and
supposing I should be wanted left the Nursery soon afterwards
and was half way down stairs, when Frederica as pale as ashes
came running up, and rushed by me into her own room. I
instantly followed, and asked her what was the matter. 'Oh!'
cried she, 'he is come, Sir James is come – and what am I to do?'
This was no explanation; I begged her to tell me what she
meant. At that moment we were interrupted by a knock at the
door; it was Reginald, who came by Lady Susan's direction to
call Frederica down. 'It is Mr. De Courcy,' said she, colouring
violently, 'Mama has sent for me, and I must go.'

We all three went down together, and I saw my Brother
examining the terrified face of Frederica with surprise. In the
breakfast room we found Lady Susan and a young Man of
genteel appearance, whom she introduced to me by the name of
Sir James Martin, the very person, as you may remember,
whom it was said she had been at pains to detach from Miss
Manwaring. But the conquest it seems was not designed for
herself, or she has since transferred it to her daughter, for Sir
James is now desperately in love with Frederica, and with full
encouragement from Mama. The poor girl however I am sure
dislikes him; and tho' his person and address are very well, he
appears both to Mr. Vernon and me a very weak young Man.

Frederica looked so shy, so confused, when we entered the
room, that I felt for her exceedingly. Lady Susan behaved
with great attention to her Visitor, and yet I thought I could
perceive that she had no particular pleasure in seeing him. Sir
James talked a good deal, and made many civil excuses to me for
the liberty he had taken in coming to Churchill, mixing more
frequent laughter with his discourse than the subject required;
said many things over and over again, and told Lady Susan
three times that he had seen Mrs. Johnson a few Evenings before.
He now and then addressed Frederica, but more frequently her
Mother. The poor girl sat all this time without opening her
lips; her eyes cast down, and her colour varying every instant,
while Reginald observed all that passed, in perfect silence.

At length Lady Susan, weary I believe of her situation,

proposed walking, and we left the two Gentlemen together to put on our Pelisses.

As we went upstairs Lady Susan begged permission to attend me for a few moments in my Dressing room, as she was anxious to speak with me in private. I led her thither accordingly, and as soon as the door was closed she said, 'I was never more surprised in my life than by Sir James's arrival, and the suddenness of it requires some apology to *You* my dear Sister, tho' to *me* as a Mother, it is highly flattering. He is so warmly attached to my daughter that he could exist no longer without seeing her. Sir James is a young Man of an amiable disposition, and excellent character; a little too much of the *Rattle*[1] perhaps, but a year or two will rectify *that*, and he is in other respects so very eligible a Match for Frederica that I have always observed his attachment with the greatest pleasure, and am persuaded that you and my Brother will give the alliance your hearty approbation. I have never before mentioned the likelihood of it's taking place to any one, because I thought that while Frederica continued at school, it had better not be known to exist; but now, as I am convinced that Frederica is too old ever to submit to school confinement, and have therefore begun to consider her union with Sir James as not very distant, I had intended within a few days to acquaint yourself and Mr. Vernon with the whole business. I am sure my dear Sister, you will excuse my remaining silent on it so long, and agree with me that such circumstances, while they continue from any cause in suspense, cannot be too cautiously concealed. When you have the happiness of bestowing your sweet little Catherine some years hence on a Man, who in connection and character is alike unexceptionable, you will know what I feel now; tho' Thank Heaven! you cannot have all my reasons for rejoicing in such an Event. Catherine will be amply provided for, and not like my Frederica endebted to a fortunate Establishment for the comforts of Life.'

She concluded by demanding my congratulations. I gave them somewhat awkwardly I beleive; for in fact, the sudden disclosure of so important a matter took from me the power of speaking with any clearness. She thanked me however most affectionately for my kind concern in the welfare of herself and her daughter, and then said,

‘I am not apt to deal in professions, my dear Mrs. Vernon, and I never had the convenient talent of affecting sensations foreign to my heart; and therefore I trust you will beleive me when I declare that much as I had heard in your praise before I knew you, I had no idea that I should ever love you as I now do; and I must farther say that your friendship towards me is more particularly gratifying, because I have reason to beleive that some attempts were made to prejudice you against me. I only wish that They – whoever they are – to whom I am endebted for such kind intentions, could see the terms on which we now are together, and understand the real affection we feel for each other! But I will not detain you any longer. God bless you, for your goodness to me and my girl, and continue to you all your present happiness.’

What can one say of such a Woman, my dear Mother? – such earnestness, such solemnity of expression! and yet I cannot help suspecting the truth of everything she said.

As for Reginald, I beleive he does not know what to make of the matter. When Sir James first came, he appeared all astonishment and perplexity. The folly of the young Man, and the confusion of Frederica entirely engrossed him; and tho’ a little private discourse with Lady Susan has since had it’s effect, he is still hurt I am sure at her allowing of such a Man’s attentions to her daughter.

Sir James invited himself with great composure to remain here a few days; hoped we would not think it odd, was aware of it’s being very impertinent, but he took the liberty of a relation, and concluded by wishing with a laugh, that he might be really one soon. Even Lady Susan seemed a little disconcerted by this forwardness; – in her heart I am persuaded, she sincerely wishes him gone.

But something must be done for this poor Girl, if her feelings are such as both her Uncle and I beleive them to be. She must not be sacrificed to Policy or Ambition, she must not be even left to suffer from the dread of it. The Girl, whose heart can distinguish Reginald De Courcy, deserves, however he may slight her, a better fate than to be Sir James Martin's wife. As soon as I can get her alone, I will discover the real Truth, but she seems to wish to avoid me. I hope this does not proceed from anything wrong, and that I shall not find out I have thought too well of her. Her behaviour before Sir James certainly speaks the greatest consciousness[1] and Embarrassment; but I see nothing in it more like Encouragement.

Adieu my dear Madam,

Yrs &c.
Cath. Vernon.

LETTER 21

Miss Vernon to Mr. De Courcy.

Sir,

I hope you will excuse this liberty, I am forced upon it by the greatest distress, or I should be ashamed to trouble you. I am very miserable about Sir James Martin, and have no other way in the world of helping myself but by writing to you, for I am forbidden ever speaking to my Uncle or Aunt on the subject; and this being the case, I am afraid my applying to you will appear no better than equivocation, and as if I attended only to the letter and not the spirit of Mama's commands, but if *you* do not take my part, and persuade her to break it off, I shall be half-distracted, for I cannot bear him. No human Being but *you* could have any chance of prevailing with her. If you will therefore have the unspeakable great kindness of taking my part with her, and persuading her to send Sir James away, I shall be more obliged to you than it is possible for me to express. I always disliked him from the first, it is not a sudden fancy I assure you Sir, I always thought him silly and impertinent and disagreeable, and now he is grown worse than ever. I would rather work for my bread than marry him. I do not know how to apologise enough for this Letter, I know it is taking so great a liberty, I am aware how dreadfully angry it will make Mama, but I must run the risk. I am Sir, your most Humble Servant

F. S. V.

LETTER 22

Lady Susan to Mrs. Johnson.

This is insufferable! My dearest friend, I was never so enraged before, and must releive myself by writing to you, who I know will enter into all my feelings. Who should come on Tuesday but Sir James Martin? Guess my astonishment and vexation – for as you well know, I never wished him to be seen at Churchill. What a pity that you should not have known his intentions! Not content with coming, he actually invited himself to remain here a few days. I could have poisoned him; I made the best of it however, and told my story with great success to Mrs. Vernon who, whatever might be her real sentiments, said nothing in opposition to mine. I made a point also of Frederica's behaving civilly to Sir James, and gave her to understand that I was absolutely determined on her marrying him. She said something of her misery, but that was all. I have for some time been more particularly resolved on the Match, from seeing the rapid increase of her affection for Reginald, and from not feeling perfectly secure that a knowledge of *that* affection might not in the end awaken a return. Contemptible as a regard founded only on compassion, must make them both, in my eyes, I felt by no means assured that such might not be the consequence. It is true that Reginald had not in any degree grown cool towards me; but yet he had lately mentioned Frederica spontaneously and unnecessarily, and once had said something in praise of her person.

He was all astonishment at the appearance of my visitor; and at first observed Sir James with an attention which I was pleased to see not unmixed with jealousy; but unluckily it was impossible for me really to torment him, as Sir James tho' extremely gallant to me, very soon made the whole party understand that his heart was devoted to my daughter.

I had no great difficulty in convincing De Courcy when we were alone, that I was perfectly justified, all things considered, in desiring the match; and the whole business seemed most comfortably arranged. They could none of them help perceiving that Sir James was no Solonom, but I had positively forbidden Frederica's complaining to Charles Vernon or his wife, and they had therefore no pretence for Interference, though my impertinent Sister I beleive wanted only opportunity for doing so.

Everything however was going on calmly and quietly; and tho' I counted the hours of Sir James's stay, my mind was entirely satisfied with the posture of affairs. Guess then what I must feel at the sudden disturbance of all my schemes, and that too from a quarter, whence I had least reason to apprehend it. Reginald came this morning into my Dressing room, with a very unusual solemnity of countenance, and after some preface informed me in so many words, that he wished to reason with me on the Impropriety and Unkindness of allowing Sir James Martin to address my Daughter, contrary to *her* inclination. I was all amazement. When I found that he was not to be laughed out of his design, I calmly required an explanation, and begged to know by what he was impelled, and by whom commissioned to reprimand me. He then told me, mixing in his speech a few insolent compliments and illtimed expressions of Tenderness to which I listened with perfect indifference, that my daughter had acquainted him with some circumstances concerning herself, Sir James, and me, which gave him great uneasiness.

In short, I found that she had in the first place actually written to him, to request his interference, and that on receiving her Letter he had conversed with her on the subject of it, in order to understand the particulars and assure himself of her real wishes!

I have not a doubt but that the girl took this opportunity of making downright Love to him; I am convinced of it, from the manner in which he spoke of her. Much good, may such Love do him! I shall ever despise the Man who can be gratified by the Passion, which he never wished to inspire, nor solicited the avowal of. I shall always detest them both. He can have no true regard for me, or he would not have listened to her; And she, with her little rebellious heart and indelicate feelings to throw herself into the protection of a young Man with whom she had scarcely ever exchanged two words before. I am equally confounded at *her* Impudence and *his* Credulity. How dared he beleive what she told him in my disfavour! Ought he not to have felt assured that I must have unanswerable Motives for all that I had done! Where was his reliance on my Sense or Goodness then; where the resentment which true Love would have dictated against the person defaming me, that person, too, a Chit, a Child, without Talent or Education, whom he had been always taught to despise?

I was calm for some time, but the greatest degree of Forbearance may be overcome; and I hope I was afterwards sufficiently keen. He endeavoured, long endeavoured to soften my resentment, but that woman is a fool indeed who while insulted by accusation, can be worked on by compliments. At length he left me, as deeply provoked as myself, and he shewed his anger *more*. I was quite cool, but he gave way to the most violent indignation. I may therefore expect it will sooner subside; and perhaps his may be vanished for ever, while mine will be found still fresh and implacable.

He is now shut up in his apartment, whither I heard him go, on leaving mine. How unpleasant, one would think, must his reflections be! But some people's feelings are incomprehensible. I have not yet tranquillized myself enough to see Frederica. *She* shall not soon forget the occurrences of this day. She shall find that she has poured forth her tender Tale of Love in vain, and exposed herself forever to the contempt of the whole world, and the severest Resentment of her injured Mother.

Yrs affec:ly
S. Vernon.

LETTER 23

Mrs. Vernon to Lady De Courcy.

CHURCHILL.

Let me congratulate you, my dearest Mother. The affair which has given us so much anxiety is drawing to a happy conclusion. Our prospect is most delightful; and since matters have now taken so favourable a turn, I am quite sorry that I ever imparted my apprehensions to you; for the pleasure of learning that the danger is over, is perhaps dearly purchased by all that you have previously suffered.

I am so much agitated by Delight that I can scarcely hold a pen, but am determined to send you a few lines by James, that you may have some explanation of what must so greatly astonish you, as that Reginald should be returning to Parklands.

I was sitting about half an hour ago with Sir James in the Breakfast parlour, when my Brother called me out of the room. I instantly saw that something was the matter; his complexion raised, and he spoke with great emotion. You know his eager manner, my dear Madam, when his mind is interested.

'Catherine,' said he, 'I am going home today. I am sorry to leave you, but I must go. It is a great while since I have seen my Father and Mother. I am going to send James forward with my Hunters immediately, if you have any Letter therefore he can take it. I shall not be at home myself till Wednesday or Thursday, as I shall go through London, where I have business. But before I leave you,' he continued, speaking in a lower voice and with still greater energy, 'I must warn you of one thing. Do not let Frederica Vernon be made unhappy by that Martin. He wants to marry her – her Mother promotes the Match – but *she* cannot endure the idea of it. Be assured that I speak from the fullest conviction of the Truth of what I say. I *know* that Frederica is made wretched by Sir James' continuing here. She is a sweet girl, and deserves a better fate. Send him away immediately. *He* is only a fool – but what her Mother can mean, Heaven only knows! Good bye,' he added shaking my hand with earnestness – 'I do not know when you will see me again. But remember what I tell you of Frederica; you *must* make it your business to see justice done her. She is an amiable girl, and has a very superior Mind to what we have ever given her credit for.'

He then left me and ran upstairs. I would not try to stop him, for I knew what his feelings must be; the nature of mine as I listened to him, I need not attempt to describe. For a minute or two I remained in the same spot, over-powered by wonder – of a most agreeable sort indeed; yet it required some consideration to be tranquilly happy.

In about ten minutes after my return to the parlour, Lady Susan entered the room. I concluded of course that she and Reginald had been quarrelling, and looked with anxious curiosity for a confirmation of my beleif in her face. Mistress of Deceit however she appeared perfectly unconcerned, and after chatting on indifferent subjects for a short time, said to me, 'I find from Wilson that we are going to lose Mr. De Courcy. Is is true that he leaves Churchill this morning?' I replied that it was. 'He told us nothing of all this last night,' said she laughing, 'or even this morning at Breakfast. But perhaps he did not know it himself. Young Men are often hasty in their resolutions – and not more sudden in forming, than unsteady in keeping them. I should not be surprised if he were to change his mind at last, and not go.'

She soon afterwards left the room. I trust however my dear Mother, that we have no reason to fear an alteration of his present plan; things have gone too far. They must have quarrelled, and about Frederica too. Her calmness astonishes me. What delight will be yours in seeing him again, in seeing him still worthy your Esteem, still capable of forming your Happiness!

When I next write, I shall be able I hope to tell you that Sir James is gone, Lady Susan vanquished, and Frederica at peace. We have much to do, but it shall be done. I am all impatience to know how this astonishing change was effected. I finish as I began, with the warmest congratulations.

Yrs Ever,
Cath. Vernon.

LETTER 24

From the same to the same.

CHURCHILL.

Little did I imagine my dear Mother, when I sent off my last letter, that the delightful perturbation of spirits I was then in, would undergo so speedy, so melancholy a reverse! I never can sufficiently regret that I wrote to you at all. Yet who could have foreseen what has happened? My dear Mother, every hope which but two hours ago made me so happy, is vanished. The quarrel between Lady Susan and Reginald is made up, and we are all as we were before. One point only is gained; Sir James Martin is dismissed. What are we now to look forward to? I am indeed disappointed. Reginald was all but gone; his horse was ordered, and almost brought to the door! Who would not have felt safe?

For half an hour I was in momentary expectation of his departure. After I had sent off my Letter to you, I went to Mr. Vernon and sat with him in his room, talking over the whole matter. I then determined to look for Frederica, whom I had not seen since breakfast. I met her on the stairs and saw that she was crying.

'My dear Aunt,' said she, 'he is going, Mr. De Courcy is going, and it is all my fault. I am afraid you will be angry, but indeed I had no idea it would end so.'

'My Love,' replied I, 'do not think it necessary to apologize to me on that account. I shall feel myself under an obligation to anyone who is the means of sending my brother home; because, (recollecting myself) I know my Father wants very much to see him. But what is it that *you* have done to occasion all this?'

She blushed deeply as she answered, 'I was so unhappy about Sir James that I could not help – I have done something very wrong I know – but you have not an idea of the misery I have been in, and Mama had ordered me never to speak to you or my Uncle about it, – and –' 'You therefore spoke to my Brother, to engage *his* interference;' said I, wishing to save her the explanation. 'No – but I wrote to him. I did indeed. I got up this morning before it was light – I was two hours about it – and when my Letter was done, I thought I never should have courage to give it. After breakfast however, as I was going to my own room I met him in the passage, and then as I knew that everything must depend on that moment, I forced myself to give it. He was so good as to take it immediately; I dared not look at him – and ran away directly. I was in such a fright that I could hardly breathe. My dear Aunt, you do not know how miserable I have been.'

'Frederica,' said I, 'you ought to have told *me* all your distresses. You would have found in me a friend always ready to assist you. Do you think that your Uncle and I should not have espoused your cause as warmly as my Brother?'

'Indeed I did not doubt your goodness,' said she, colouring again, 'but I thought that Mr. De Courcy could do anything with my Mother; but I was mistaken; they have had a dreadful quarrel about it, and he is going. Mama will never forgive me, and I shall be worse off than ever.' 'No you shall not,' replied I. – 'In such a point as this, your Mother's prohibition ought not to have prevented your speaking to me on the subject. She has no right to make you unhappy, and she shall *not* do it. Your applying however to Reginald can be productive only of Good to all parties. I beleive it is best as it is. Depend upon it that you shall not be made unhappy any longer.'

At that moment, how great was my astonishment at seeing Reginald come out of Lady Susan's Dressing room. My heart misgave me instantly. His confusion on seeing me was very evident. Frederica immediately disappeared. 'Are you going?' said I. 'You will find Mr. Vernon in his own room.' 'No Catherine', replied he. 'I am *not* going. Will you let me speak to you a moment?'

We went into my room. 'I find,' continued he, his confusion increasing as he spoke, 'that I have been acting with my usual foolish impetuosity. I have entirely misunderstood Lady Susan, and was on the point of leaving the house under a false impression of her conduct. There has been some very great mistake – we have been all mistaken I fancy. Frederica does not know her Mother – Lady Susan means nothing but her Good – but Frederica will not make a friend of her. Lady Susan therefore does not always know what will make her daughter happy. Besides *I* could have no right to interfere – Miss Vernon was mistaken in applying to me. In short Catherine, everything has gone wrong – but it is now all happily settled. Lady Susan I beleive wishes to speak to you about it, if you are at leisure.'

'Certainly;' replied I, deeply sighing at the recital of so lame a story. I made no remarks however, for words would have been in vain. Reginald was glad to get away, and I went to Lady Susan; curious indeed to hear her account of it.

'Did not I tell you,' said she with a smile, 'that your Brother would not leave us after all?' 'You did indeed,' replied I very gravely, 'but I flattered myself that you would be mistaken.' 'I should not have hazarded such an opinion,' returned she, 'if it had not at that moment occurred to me, that his resolution of going might be occasioned by a Conversation in which we had been this morning engaged, and which had ended very much to his Dissatisfaction from our not rightly understanding each other's meaning. This idea struck me at the moment, and I instantly determined that an accidental dispute in which I might probably be as much to blame as himself, should not deprive you of your Brother. If you remember, I left the room almost immediately. I was resolved to lose no time in clearing up these mistakes as far as I could. The case was this. Frederica had set herself violently against marrying Sir James' – 'And can your Ladyship wonder that she should?' cried I with some warmth. 'Frederica has an excellent Understanding, and Sir James has none.' 'I am at least very far from regretting it, my dear Sister,' said she; 'on the contrary, I am grateful for so favourable a sign of my Daughter's sense. Sir James is certainly under par – (his boyish manners make him appear the worse) – and had Frederica possessed the penetration, the abilities, which I could have wished in my daughter, or had I even known her to possess so much as she does, I should not have been anxious for the match.' 'It is odd that you alone should be ignorant of your Daughter's sense.' 'Frederica never does justice to herself; her manners are shy and childish. She is besides afraid of me; she scarcely loves me. During her poor Father's life she was a spoilt child; the severity which it has since been necessary for me to shew, has entirely alienated her affection; neither has she any of that Brilliancy of Intellect, that Genius, or Vigour of Mind which will force itself forward.' 'Say rather that she has been unfortunate in her Education.' 'Heaven knows my dearest Mrs.

Vernon, how fully I am aware of *that*; but I would wish to forget every circumstance that might throw blame on the memory of one, whose name is sacred with me.'

Here she pretended to cry. I was out of patience with her. 'But what,' said I, 'was your Ladyship going to tell me about your disagreement with my Brother?' 'It originated in an action of my Daughter's, which equally marks her want of Judgement, and the unfortunate Dread of me I have been mentioning. She wrote to Mr. De Courcy.' 'I know she did. You had forbidden her speaking to Mr. Vernon or to me on the cause of her distress; what could she do therefore but apply to my Brother?' 'Good God!' – she exclaimed, 'what an opinion must you have of me! Can you possibly suppose that I was aware of her unhappiness? that it was my object to make my own child miserable, and that I had forbidden her speaking to you on the subject from a fear of your interrupting the Diabolical scheme? Do you think me destitute of every honest, every natural feeling? Am I capable of consigning *her* to everlasting Misery, whose welfare it is my first Earthly Duty to promote?' 'The idea is horrible. What then was your intention when you insisted on her silence?' 'Of what use my dear Sister, could be any application to you, however the affair might stand? Why should I subject you to entreaties, which I refused to attend to myself? Neither for your sake, for hers, nor for my own, could such a thing be desireable. Where my own resolution was taken, I could not wish for the inter-ference, however friendly, of another person. I was mistaken, it is true, but I beleived myself to be right.' 'But what was this mis-take, to which your Ladyship so often alludes? From whence arose so astonishing a misapprehension of your Daughter's feelings? Did not you know that she disliked Sir James?' 'I knew that he was not absolutely the Man she would have chosen. But I was persuaded that her objections to him did not arise from any perception of his Deficiency. You must not question me however my dear Sister, too minutely on this point' – con-tinued she, taking me affectionately by the hand. 'I honestly own that there is something to conceal. Frederica makes me very unhappy. Her applying to Mr. De Courcy hurt me particularly.'

'What is it that you mean to infer' said I, 'by this appearance of mystery? If you think your daughter at all attached to Reginald, her objecting to Sir James could not less deserve to be attended to, than if the cause of her objecting had been a consciousness of his folly. And why should your Ladyship at any rate quarrel with my brother for an interference which you must know, it was not in his nature to refuse, when urged in such a manner?'

'His disposition you know is warm, and he came to expostulate with me, his compassion all alive for this ill-used Girl, this Heroine in distress! We misunderstood each other. He beleived me more to blame than I really was; I considered his interference as less excusable than I now find it. I have a real regard for him, and was beyond expression mortified to find it as I thought so ill bestowed. We were both warm, and of course both to blame. His resolution of leaving Churchill is consistent with his general eagerness; when I understood his intention however, and at the same time began to think that we had perhaps been equally mistaken in each other's meaning, I resolved to have an explanation before it were too late. For any Member of your Family I must always feel a degree of affection, and I own it would have sensibly hurt me, if my acquaintance with Mr. De Courcy had ended so gloomily. I have now only to say farther, that as I am convinced of Frederica's having a reasonable dislike to Sir James, I shall instantly inform him that he must give up all hope of her. I reproach myself for having ever, tho' so innocently, made her unhappy on that score. She shall have all the retribution in my power to make; if she value her own happiness as much as I do, if she judge wisely and command herself as she ought, she may now be easy. Escuse me, my dearest Sister, for thus trespassing on your time, but I owed it to my own Character; and after this explanation I trust I am in no danger of sinking in your opinion.'

I could have said 'Not much indeed;' – but I left her almost in silence. It was the greatest stretch of Forbearance I could practise. I could not have stopped myself, had I begun. Her assurance, her Deceit – but I will not allow myself to dwell on them; they will strike you sufficiently. My heart sickens within me.

As soon as I was tolerably composed, I returned to the Parlour. Sir James's carriage was at the door, and he, merry as usual, soon afterwards took his leave. How easily does her Ladyship encourage, or dismiss a Lover!

In spite of this release, Frederica still looks unhappy, still fearful perhaps of her Mother's anger, and tho' dreading my Brother's departure jealous, it may be, of his staying. I see how closely she observes him and Lady Susan. Poor Girl, I have now no hope for her. There is not a chance of her affection being returned. He thinks very differently of her, from what he used to do, he does her some justice, but his reconciliation with her Mother precludes every dearer hope.

Prepare my dear Madam, for the worst. The probability of their marrying is surely heightened. He is more securely her's than ever. When that wretched Event takes place, Frederica must wholly belong to us.

I am thankful that my last Letter will precede this by so little, as every moment that you can be saved from feeling a Joy which leads only to disappointment is of consequence.

Yrs Ever,
Cath. Vernon.

LETTER 25

Lady Susan to Mrs. Johnson.

CHURCHILL.

I call on you dear Alicia, for congratulations. I am again myself; – gay and triumphant. When I wrote to you the other day, I was in truth in high irritation, and with ample cause. Nay, I know not whether I ought to be quite tranquil now, for I have had more trouble in restoring peace than I ever intended to submit to. This Reginald has a proud spirit of his own! – a spirit too, resulting from a fancied sense of superior Integrity which is peculiarly insolent. I shall not easily forgive him I assure you. He was actually on the point of leaving Churchill! I had scarcely concluded my last, when Wilson brought me word of it. I found therefore that something must be done, for I did not chuse to have my character at the mercy of a Man whose passions were so violent and resentful. It would have been trifling with my reputation, to allow of his departing with such an impression in my disfavour; in this light, condescension was necessary.

I sent Wilson to say that I desired to speak with him before he went. He came immediately. The angry emotions which had marked every feature when we last parted, were partially subdued. He seemed astonished at the summons, and looked as if half wishing and half fearing to be softened by what I might say.

If my Countenance expressed what I aimed at, it was composed and dignified – and yet with a degree of pensiveness which might convince him that I was not quite happy. 'I beg your pardon Sir, for the liberty I have taken in sending to you,' said I; 'but as I have just learnt your intention of leaving this place today, I feel it my duty to entreat that you will not on my account shorten your visit here, even an hour. I am perfectly aware that after what has passed between us, it would ill suit the feelings of either to remain longer in the same house. So very great, so total a change from the intimacy of Friendship, must render any future intercourse the severest punishment; and your resolution of quitting Churchill is undoubtedly in unison with our situation and with those lively feelings which I know you to possess. But at the same time, it is not for me to suffer such a sacrifice, as it must be, to leave Relations to whom you are so much attached and are so dear. My remaining here cannot give that pleasure to Mr. and Mrs. Vernon which your society must; and my visit has already perhaps been too long. My removal therefore, which must at any rate take place soon, may with perfect convenience be hastened; and I make it my particular request that I may not in any way be instrumental in separating a family so affectionately attached to each other. Where *I* go is of no consequence to anyone; of very little to myself; but *you* are of importance to all your connections.' Here I concluded, and I hope you will be satisfied with my speech. It's effect on Reginald justifies some portion of vanity, for it was no less favourable than instantaneous. Oh! how delightful it was, to watch the variations of his Countenance while I spoke, to see the struggle between returning Tenderness and the remains of Displeasure. There is something agreable in feelings so easily worked on. Not that I would envy him their possession, nor would for the world have such myself, but they are very convenient when one wishes to influence the passions of another. And yet this Reginald, whom a very few words from me softened at once into the utmost submission, and rendered more tractable, more attached, more devoted than ever, would have left me in the first angry swelling of his proud heart, without deigning to seek an explanation!

Humbled as he now is, I cannot forgive him such an instance of Pride; and am doubtful whether I ought not to punish him, by dismissing him at once after this our reconciliation, or by marrying and teizing him for ever. But these measures are each too violent to be adopted without some deliberation. At present my Thoughts are fluctuating between various schemes. I have many things to compass. I must punish Frederica, and pretty severely too, for her application to Reginald; I must punish him for receiving it so favourably, and for the rest of his conduct. I must torment my Sister-in-law for the insolent triumph of her Look and Manner since Sir James has been dismissed – for in reconciling Reginald to me, I was not able to save that ill-fated young Man – and I must make myself amends for the humiliations to which I have stooped within these few days. To effect all this I have various plans. I have also an idea of being soon in Town, and whatever may be my determination as to the rest, I shall probably put *that* project in execution – for London will be always the fairest field of action, however my veiws may be directed, and at any rate, I shall there be rewarded by your society and a little Dissipation for a ten weeks' penance at Churchill.

I beleive I owe it to my own Character, to complete the match between my daughter and Sir James, after having so long intended it. Let me know your opinion on this point. Flexibility of Mind, a Disposition easily biassed by others, is an attribute which you know I am not very desirous of obtaining; nor has Frederica any claim to the indulgence of her whims, at the expense of her Mother's inclination. Her idle Love for Reginald too; it is surely my duty to discourage such romantic nonsense. All things considered therefore, it seems encumbent on me to take her to Town, and marry her immediately to Sir James.

When my own will is effected, contrary to his, I shall have some credit in being on good terms with Reginald, which at present in fact I have not, for tho' he is still in my power, I have given up the very article by which our quarrel was produced, and at best, the honour of victory is doubtful.

Send me your opinion on all these matters, my dear Alicia, and let me know whether you can get Lodgings to suit me within a short distance of you.

Yr most attached
S. Vernon.

LETTER 26

Mrs. Johnson to Lady Susan.

EDWARD STREET.

I am gratified by your reference, and this is my advice; that you come to Town yourself without loss of time, but that you leave Frederica behind. It would surely be much more to the purpose to get yourself well established by marrying Mr. De Courcy, than to irritate him and the rest of his family, by making her marry Sir James. You should think more of yourself, and less of your Daughter. She is not of a disposition to do you credit in the World, and seems precisely in her proper place, at Churchill with the Vernons; but *you* are fitted for Society, and it is shameful to have you exiled from it. Leave Frederica therefore to punish herself for the plague she has given you, by indulging that romantic tender-heartedness which will always ensure her misery enough; and come yourself to Town, as soon as you can.

I have another reason for urging this.

Manwaring came to town last week, and has contrived, in spite of Mr. Johnson, to make opportunities of seeing me. He is absolutely miserable about you, and jealous to such a degree of

De Courcy, that it would be highly unadvisable for them to meet[1] at present; and yet if you do not allow him to see you here, I cannot answer for his not committing some great imprudence – such as going to Churchill for instance, which would be dreadful. Besides, if you take my advice, and resolve to marry De Courcy, it will be indispensably necessary for you to get Manwaring out of the way, and you only can have influence enough to send him back to his wife.

I have still another motive for your coming. Mr. Johnson leaves London next Tuesday. He is going for his health to Bath, where if the waters are favourable to his constitution and my wishes, he will be laid up with the gout many weeks. During his absence we shall be able to chuse our own society, and have true enjoyment. I would ask you to Edward Street but that he once forced from me a kind of promise never to invite you to my house. Nothing but my being in the utmost distress for Money, could have extorted it from me. I can get you however a very nice Drawingroom-apartment in Upper Seymour Street, and we may be always together, there or here, for I consider my promise to Mr. Johnson as comprehending only (at least in his absence) your not sleeping in the House.

Poor Manwaring gives me such histories of his wife's jealousy! – Silly Woman, to expect constancy from so charming a Man! But she was always silly; intolerably so, in marrying him at all. She, the Heiress of a large Fortune, he without a shilling! *One* title I know she might have had, besides Baronets. Her folly in forming the connection was so great, that tho' Mr Johnson was her Guardian and I do not in general share his feelings, I never can forgive her.

Adeiu,   Yours, Alicia.

LETTER 27

Mrs. Vernon to Lady De Courcy.

CHURCHILL.

This Letter my dear Mother, will be brought you by Reginald. His long visit is about to be concluded at last, but I fear the separation takes place too late to do us any good. *She* is going to Town, to see her particular friend, Mrs. Johnson. It was at first her intention that Frederica should accompany her for the benefit of Masters, but we over-ruled her there. Frederica was wretched in the idea of going, and I could not bear to have her at the mercy of her Mother. Not all the Masters in London could compensate for the ruin of her comfort. I should have feared too for her health, and for everything in short but her Principles; *there* I beleive she is not to be injured, even by her Mother, or all her Mother's friends; but with those friends (a very bad set I doubt not) she must have mixed, or have been left in total solitude, and I can hardly tell which would have been worse for her. If she is with her Mother moreover, she must alas! in all probability, be with Reginald – and that would be the greatest evil of all.

Here we shall in time be at peace. Our regular employments, our Books and conversation, with Exercise, the Children, and every domestic pleasure in my power to procure her, will, I trust, gradually overcome this youthful attachment. I should not have a doubt of it, were she slighted for any other woman in the world, than her own Mother.

How long Lady Susan will be in Town, or whether she returns here again, I know not. I could not be cordial in my invitation; but if she chuses to come, no want of cordiality on my part will keep her away.

I could not help asking Reginald if he intended being in Town this winter, as soon as I found that her Ladyship's steps would be bent thither; and tho' he professed himself quite undetermined, there was a something in his Look and voice as he spoke, which contradicted his words. I have done with Lamentation. I look upon the Event as so far decided, that I resign myself to it in despair. If he leaves you soon for London, everything will be concluded.

Yours affec:ly
Cath. Vernon.

LETTER 28

Mrs. Johnson to Lady Susan.

EDWARD STREET.

My dearest Friend,

I write in the greatest distress; the most unfortunate event has just taken place. Mr. Johnson has hit on the most effectual manner of plaguing us all. He had heard I imagine by some means or other, that you were soon to be in London, and immediately contrived to have such an attack of the Gout, as must at least delay his journey to Bath, if not wholly prevent it. I am persuaded the Gout is brought on, or kept off at pleasure; it was the same, when I wanted to join the Hamiltons to the Lakes; and three years ago when *I* had a fancy for Bath, nothing could induce him to have a Gouty symptom.

I have received yours, and have engaged the Lodgings in consequence. I am pleased to find that my Letter had so much effect on you, and that De Courcy is certainly your own. Let me hear from you as soon as you arrive, and in particular tell me what you mean to do with Manwaring. It is impossible to say when I shall be able to see you. My confinement must be great. It is such an abominable trick, to be ill here, instead of at Bath, that I can scarcely command myself at all. At Bath, his old Aunts would have nursed him, but here it all falls upon me – and he bears pain with such patience that I have not the common excuse for losing my temper.

Yrs Ever,
Alicia.

LETTER 29

Lady Susan to Mrs. Johnson.

UPPER SEYMOUR STREET.

My dear Alicia

There needed not this last fit of the Gout to make me detest Mr Johnson; but now the extent of my aversion is not to be estimated. To have you confined, a Nurse in his apartment! My dear Alicia, of what a mistake were you guilty in marrying a Man of his age! – just old enough to be formal, ungovernable and to have the Gout – too old to be agreable, and too young to die.

I arrived last night about five, and had scarcely swallowed my dinner when Manwaring made his appearance. I will not dissemble what real pleasure his sight afforded me, nor how strongly I felt the contrast between his person and manners, and those of Reginald, to the infinite disadvantage of the latter. For an hour or two, I was even stagger'd in my resolution of marrying him – and though this was too idle and nonsensical an idea to remain long on my mind, I do not feel very eager for the conclusion of my Marriage, or look forward with much impatience to the time when Reginald according to our agreement is to be in Town. I shall probably put off his arrival, under some pretence or other. He must not come till Manwaring is gone.

I am still doubtful at times, as to Marriage. If the old Man would die, I might not hesitate; but a state of dependance on the caprice of Sir Reginald, will not suit the freedom of my spirit; and if I resolve to wait for that event, I shall have excuse enough at present, in having been scarcely ten months a Widow.

I have not given Manwaring any hint of my intention – or allowed him to consider my acquaintance with Reginald as more than the commonest flirtation; and he is tolerably appeased. Adeiu till we meet. I am enchanted with my Lodgings.

Yrs Ever,
S. Vernon.

LETTER 30

Lady Susan to Mr. De Courcy.

UPPER SEYMOUR STREET.

I have received your Letter; and tho' I do not attempt to conceal that I am gratified by your impatience for the hour of meeting, I yet feel myself under the necessity of delaying that hour beyond the time originally fixed. Do not think me unkind for such an exercise of my power, or accuse me of Instability, without first hearing my reasons. In the course of my journey from Churchill, I had ample leisure for reflection on the present state of our affairs, and every reveiw has served to convince me that they require a delicacy and cautiousness of conduct, to which we have hitherto been too little attentive. We have been hurried on by our feelings to a degree of Precipitance which ill accords with the claims of our Friends, or the opinion of the World. We have been unguarded in forming this hasty Engagement; but we must not complete the imprudence by ratifying it, while there is so much reason to fear the Connection would be opposed by those Friends on whom you depend.

It is not for us to blame any expectation on your Father's side of your marrying to advantage; where possessions are so extensive as those of your Family, the wish of increasing them, if not strictly reasonable, is too common to excite surprise or resentment. He has a right to require a woman of fortune in his daughter-in-law, and I am sometimes quarreling with myself for suffering you to form a connection so imprudent. But the influence of reason is often acknowledged too late by those who feel like me.

I have now been but a few months a widow; and however little endebted to my Husband's memory for any happiness derived from him during an Union of some years, I cannot forget that the indelicacy of so early a second marriage, must subject me to the censure of the World, and incur what would be still more insupportable, the displeasure of Mr. Vernon. I might perhaps harden myself in time against the injustice of general reproach; but the loss of *his* valued Esteem, I am as you well know, ill fitted to endure; and when to this, may be added the consciousness of having injured you with your Family, how am I to support myself. With feelings so poignant as mine, the conviction of having divided the son from his Parents, would make me, even with *you*, the most miserable of Beings.

It will surely therefore be advisable to delay our Union, to delay it till appearances are more promising, till affairs have taken a more favourable turn. To assist us in such a resolution, I feel that absence will be necessary. We must not meet. Cruel as this sentence may appear, the necessity of pronouncing it, which can alone reconcile it to myself, will be evident to you when you have considered our situation in the light in which I have found myself imperiously obliged to place it. You may be, you must be well assured that nothing but the strongest conviction of Duty, could induce me to wound my own feelings by urging a lengthened separation; and of Insensibility to yours, you will hardly suspect me. Again therefore I say that we ought not, we must not yet meet. By a removal for some Months from each other, we shall tranquillize the sisterly fears of Mrs. Vernon, who, accustomed herself to the enjoyment of riches, considers Fortune as necessary every where, and whose Sensibilities are not of a nature to comprehend ours.

Let me hear from you soon, very soon. Tell me that you submit to my Arguments, and do not reproach me for using such. I cannot bear reproaches. My spirits are not so high as to need being repressed. I must endeavour to seek amusement abroad, and fortunately many of my Friends are in town – among them, the Manwarings. You know how sincerely I regard both Husband and wife.

I am ever, Faithfully Yours
S. Vernon.

LETTER 31

Lady Susan to Mrs. Johnson.

UPPER SEYMOUR STREET.

My dear Friend,

That tormenting creature Reginald is here. My Letter, which was intended to keep him longer in the Country, has hastened him to Town. Much as I wish him away however, I cannot help being pleased with such a proof of attachment. He is devoted to me, heart and soul. He will carry this note himself, which is to serve as an Introduction to you, with whom he longs to be acquainted. Allow him to spend the Evening with you, that I may be in no danger of his returning here. I have told him that I am not quite well, and must be alone – and should he call again there might be confusion, for it is impossible to be sure of servants. Keep him therefore I entreat you in Edward Street. You will not find him a heavy companion, and I allow you to flirt with him as much as you like. At the same time do not forget my real interest; say all that you can to convince him that I shall be quite wretched if he remain here; you know my reasons – Propriety and so forth. I would urge them more myself, but that I am impatient to be rid of him, as Manwaring comes within half an hour. Adeiu.

S. V.

LETTER 32

Mrs. Johnson to Lady Susan.

EDWARD STREET.

My dear Creature,

I am in agonies, and know not what to do, nor what *you* can do. Mr. De Courcy arrived, just when he should not. Mrs. Manwaring had that instant entered the House, and forced herself into her Guardian's presence, tho' I did not know a

syllable of it till afterwards, for I was out when both she and
Reginald came, or I would have sent him away at all events; but
she was shut up with Mr. Johnson, while *he* waited in the Drawing
room for me. She arrived yesterday in pursuit of her Husband;
but perhaps you know this already from himself. She came to
this house to entreat my Husband's interference, and before I
could be aware of it, everything that you could wish to be concealed, was known to him; and unluckily she had wormed out of
Manwaring's servant that he had visited you every day since
your being in Town, and had just watched him to your door
herself! What could I do? Facts are such horrid things! All is by
this time known to De Courcy, who is now alone with Mr.
Johnson. Do not accuse me; indeed, it was impossible to prevent
it. Mr. Jonhson has for some time suspected De Courcy of
intending to marry you, and would speak with him alone, as
soon as he knew him to be in the House.

That detestable Mrs. Manwaring, who for your comfort, has
fretted herself thinner and uglier than ever, is still here, and they
have been all closeted together. What can be done? If Manwaring is now with you, he had better be gone. At any rate I
hope he will plague his wife more than ever. With anxious
wishes,

Yrs faithfully
Alicia.

LETTER 33

Lady Susan to Mrs. Johnson.

UPPER SEYMOUR STREET.

This Eclaircissement is rather provoking. How unlucky that
you should have been from home! I thought myself sure of you
at seven. I am undismayed however. Do not torment yourself
with fears on my account. Depend upon it, I can make my own
story good with Reginald. Manwaring is just gone; he brought
me the news of his wife's arrival. Silly Woman! what does she

expect by such Manœuvres? Yet, I wish she had staid quietly at Langford.

Reginald will be a little enraged at first, but by Tomorrow's Dinner, everything will be well again.

Adeiu.

S. V.

LETTER 34

Mr. De Courcy to Lady Susan.

HOTEL.

I write only to bid you Farewell. The spell is removed. I see you as you are. Since we parted yesterday, I have received from indisputable authority, such an history of you as must bring the most mortifying conviction of the Imposition I have been under, and the absolute necessity of an immediate and eternal separation from you. You cannot doubt to what I allude; Langford – Langford – that word will be sufficient. I received my information in Mr. Johnson's house, from Mrs. Manwaring herself.

You know how I have loved you, you can intimately judge of my present feelings; but I am not so weak as to find indulgence in describing them to a woman who will glory in having excited their anguish, but whose affection they have never been able to gain.

R. De Courcy.

LETTER 35

Lady Susan to Mr. De Courcy.

UPPER SEYMOUR STREET.

I will not attempt to describe my astonishment on reading the note, this moment received from you. I am bewilder'd in my endeavours to form some rational conjecture of what Mrs. Manwaring can have told you, to occasion so extraordinary a change in your sentiments. Have I not explained everything to you with respect to myself which could bear a doubtful meaning, and which the ill-nature of the World had interpreted to my

Discredit? What can you *now* have heard to stagger your Esteem for me? Have I ever had a concealment from you? Reginald, you agitate me beyond expression. I cannot suppose that the old story of Mrs. Manwaring's jealousy can be revived again, or at least, be *listened* to again. Come to me immediately, and explain what is at present absolutely incomprehensible. Believe me, the single word of *Langford* is not of such potent intelligence, as to supersede the necessity of more. If we *are* to part, it will at least be handsome to take your personal Leave. But I have little heart to jest; in truth, I am serious enough – for to be sunk, tho' but an hour, in your opinion, is an humiliation to which I know not how to submit. I shall count every moment till your arrival.

S. V.

LETTER 36

Mr. De Courcy to Lady Susan.

HOTEL.

Why would you write to me? Why do you require particulars? But since it must be so, I am obliged to declare that all the accounts of your misconduct during the life and since the death of Mr. Vernon which had reached me in common with the World in general, and gained my entire beleif before I saw you, but which you by the exertion of your perverted Abilities had made me resolve to disallow, have been unanswerably proved to me. Nay, more, I am assured that a connection, of which I had never before entertained a thought, has for some time existed, and still continues to exist between you and the Man, whose family you robbed of it's Peace, in return for the hospitality with which you were received into it! That you have corresponded with him ever since your leaving Langford – not with his wife – but with him – and he now visits you every day. Can you, dare you deny it? and all this at the time when I was an encouraged, an accepted Lover! From what have I not escaped! I have only to be grateful. Far from me be all complaint, and every sigh of regret. My own Folly has endangered me, my Preservation I owe to the kindness, the Integrity of another. But the unfortunate Mrs. Manwaring, whose agonies while she related the past, seemed to threaten her reason – how is *she* to be consoled?

After such a discovery as this, you will scarcely affect farther wonder at my meaning in bidding you Adeiu. My Understanding is at length restored, and teaches me no less to abhor the Artifices which had subdued me, than to despise myself for the weakness, on which their strength was founded.

R. De Courcy.

LETTER 37

Lady Susan to Mr. De Courcy.

UPPER SEYMOUR STREET.

I am satisfied – and will trouble you no more when these few Lines are dismissed. The Engagement which you were eager to form a fortnight ago, is no longer compatible with your veiws, and I rejoice to find that the prudent advice of your Parents has not been given in vain. Your restoration to Peace will, I doubt not, speedily follow this act of filial Obedience, and I flatter myself with the hope of surviving *my* share in this disappointment.

S. V.

LETTER 38

Mrs. Johnson to Lady Susan.

EDWARD STREET.

I am greived, tho' I cannot be astonished at your rupture with Mr. De Courcy; he had just informed Mr. Johnson of it by letter. He leaves London he says to-day. Be assured that I partake in all your feelings, and do not be angry if I say that our intercourse even by Letter must soon be given up. It makes me miserable – but Mr. Johnson vows that if I persist in the connection, he will settle in the country for the rest of his life – and you know it is impossible to submit to such an extremity while any other alternative remains.

You have heard of course that the Manwarings are to part; I am afraid Mrs. M. will come home to us again. But she is still so fond of her Husband and frets so much about him that perhaps she may not live long.

Miss Manwaring is just come to Town to be with her Aunt, and they say, that she declares she will have Sir James Martin before she leaves London again. If I were you, I would certainly get him myself. I had almost forgot to give you my opinion of De Courcy, I am really delighted with him, he is full as handsome I think as Manwaring, and with such an open, goodhumoured Countenance that one cannot help loving him at first sight. Mr. Johnson and he are the greatest friends in the World. Adeiu, my dearest Susan. I wish matters did not go so perversely. That unlucky visit to Langford! But I dare say you did all for the best, and there is no defying Destiny.

Yr sincerely attached
Alicia.

LETTER 39

Lady Susan to Mrs. Johnson.

UPPER SEYMOUR STREET.

My dear Alicia

I yeild to the necessity which parts us. Under such circumstances you could not act otherwise. Our friendship cannot be impaired by it; and in happier times, when your situation is as independant as mine, it will unite us again in the same Intimacy as ever. For this I shall impatiently wait; and meanwhile can safely assure you that I never was more at ease, or better satisfied with myself and everything about me, than at the present hour. Your Husband I abhor – Reginald I despise – and I am secure of never seeing either again. Have I not reason to rejoice? Manwaring is more devoted to me than ever; and were he at liberty, I doubt if I could resist even Matrimony offered by *him*. This Event, if his wife live with you, it may be in your power to hasten. The violence of her feelings, which must wear her out, may be easily kept in irritation. I rely on your friendship for this. I am now satisfied that I never could have brought myself to marry Reginald; and am equally determined that Frederica never *shall*. To-morrow I shall fetch her from Churchill, and let Maria Manwaring tremble for the consequence. Frederica shall be Sir James's wife before she quits my house. *She* may whimper, and the Vernons may storm; I regard them not. I am tired of submitting my will to the Caprices of others – of resigning my own Judgement in deference to those, to whom I owe no Duty, and for whom I feel no respect. I have given up too much – have been too easily worked on; but Frederica shall now find the difference.

Adeiu, dearest of Friends. May the next Gouty Attack be more favourable. And may you always regard me as unalterably yours

S. Vernon.

LETTER 40

Lady De Courcy to Mrs. Vernon.

PARKLANDS.

My dear Catherine

I have charming news for you, and if I had not sent off my Letter this morning, you might have been spared the vexation of knowing of Reginald's being gone to Town, for he is returned, Reginald is returned, not to ask our consent to his marrying Lady Susan, but to tell us that they are parted forever! He has been only an hour in the House, and I have not been able to learn particulars, for he is so very low, that I have not the heart to ask questions; but I hope we shall soon know all. This is the most joyful hour he has ever given us, since the day of his birth.

Nothing is wanting but to have you here, and it is our particular wish and entreaty that you would come to us as soon as you can. You have owed us a visit many long weeks. I hope nothing will make it inconvenient to Mr. Vernon, and pray bring all my Grand Children, and your dear Neice is included of course; I long to see her. It has been a sad heavy winter hitherto, without Reginald, and seeing nobody from Churchill; I never found the season so dreary before, but this happy meeting will make us young again. Frederica runs much in my thoughts, and when Reginald has recovered his usual good spirits, (as I trust he soon will) we will try to rob him of his heart once more, and I am full of hopes of seeing their hands joined at no great distance.

Yr affec: Mother
C. De Courcy.

LETTER 41

Mrs. Vernon to Lady De Courcy.

CHURCHILL.

My dear Madam

Your Letter has surprised me beyond measure. Can it be true that they are really separated – and for ever? I should be overjoyed if I dared depend on it, but after all that I have seen, how can one be secure? And Reginald really with you! My surprise is the greater, because on Wednesday, the very day of his coming to Parklands, we had a most unexpected and unwelcome visit from Lady Susan, looking all chearfulness and good humour, and seeming more as if she were to marry him when she got back to Town, than as if parted from him for ever. She staid nearly two hours, was as affectionate and agreable as ever, and not a syllable, not a hint was dropped of any Disagreement or coolness between them. I asked her whether she had seen my Brother since his arrival in Town – not as you may suppose with any doubt of the fact – but merely to see how she looked. She immediately answered without any embarrassment that he had been kind enough to call on her on Monday, but she beleived he had already returned home – which I was very far from crediting.

Your kind invitation is accepted by us with pleasure, and on Thursday next, we and our little ones will be with you. Pray Heaven! Reginald may not be in Town again by that time!

I wish we could bring dear Frederica too, but I am sorry to add that her Mother's errand hither was to fetch her away; and miserable as it made the poor Girl, it was impossible to detain her. I was thoroughly unwilling to let her go, and so was her Uncle; and all that could be urged, we *did* urge. But Lady Susan declared that as she was now about to fix herself in Town for several Months, she could not be easy if her Daughter were not with her, for Masters, &c. Her Manner, to be sure, was very kind and proper – and Mr. Vernon beleives that Frederica will now be treated with affection. I wish I could think so too!

The poor girl's heart was almost broke at taking leave of us. I charged her to write to me very often, and to remember that if she were in any distress, we should be always her friends. I took care to see her alone, that I might say all this, and I hope made her a little more comfortable. But I shall not be easy till I can go to Town and judge of her situation myself.

I wish there were a better prospect than now appears, of the Match, which the conclusion of your Letter declares your expectation of. At present it is not very likely.

Yrs &c.
Cath. Vernon.

CONCLUSION

This Correspondence, by a meeting between some of the Parties and a separation between the others, could not, to the great detriment of the Post office Revenue, be continued longer. Very little assistance to the State could be derived from the Epistolary Intercourse of Mrs. Vernon and her neice, for the former soon perceived by the stile of Frederica's Letters, that they were written under her Mother's inspection, and therefore deferring all particular enquiry till she could make it personally in Town, ceased writing minutely or often.

Having learnt enough in the meanwhile from her open-hearted Brother, of what had passed between him and Lady Susan to sink the latter lower than ever in her opinion, she was proportionably more anxious to get Frederica removed from such a Mother, and placed under her own care; and tho' with little hope of success, was resolved to leave nothing unattempted that might offer a chance of obtaining her Sister-in-law's consent to it. Her anxiety on the subject made her press for an early visit to London; and Mr. Vernon who, as it must have already appeared, lived only to do whatever he was desired, soon found some accomodating Business to call him thither. With a heart full of the Matter, Mrs. Vernon waited on Lady Susan, shortly after her arrival in Town; and she was met with such an easy and chearful affection as made her almost turn from her with horror. No remembrance of Reginald, no consciousness of Guilt, gave one look of embarrassment. She was in excellent spirits, and seemed eager to shew at once, by every possible attention to her Brother and Sister, her sense of their kindness, and her pleasure in their society.

Frederica was no more altered than Lady Susan; the same restrained Manners, the same timid Look in the presence of her Mother as heretofore, assured her Aunt of her situation's being uncomfortable, and confirmed her in the plan of altering it. No unkindness however on the part of Lady Susan appeared. Persecution on the subject of Sir James was entirely at an end – his name merely mentioned to say that he was not in London; and in all her conversation she was solicitous only for the welfare and improvement of her Daughter, acknowledging in terms of grateful delight that Frederica was now growing every day more and more what a Parent could desire.

Mrs. Vernon surprised and incredulous, knew not what to suspect, and without any change in her own veiws, only feared greater difficulty in accomplishing them. The first hope of anything better was derived from Lady Susan's asking her whether she thought Frederica looked quite as well as she had done at Churchill, as she must confess herself to have sometimes an anxious doubt of London's perfectly agreeing with her.

Mrs. Vernon encouraging the doubt, directly proposed her Neice's returning with them into the country. Lady Susan was unable to express her sense of such kindness; yet knew not from a variety of reasons how to part with her Daughter; and as, though her own plans were not yet wholly fixed, she trusted it would ere long be in her power to take Frederica into the country herself, concluded by declining entirely to profit by such unexampled attention. Mrs. Vernon however persevered in the offer of it, and though Lady Susan continued to resist, her resistance in the course of a few days seemed somewhat less formidable.

The lucky alarm of an Influenza, decided what might not have been decided quite so soon. Lady Susan's maternal fears were then too much awakened for her to think of anything but Frederica's removal from the risk of infection. Above all Disorders in the World, she most dreaded the influenza for her daughter's constitution. Frederica returned to Churchill with her Uncle and Aunt, and three weeks afterwards Lady Susan announced her being married to Sir James Martin.

Mrs. Vernon was then convinced of what she had only suspected before, that she might have spared herself all the trouble of urging a removal, which Lady Susan had doubtless resolved on from the first. Frederica's visit was nominally for six weeks; but her Mother, though inviting her to return in one or two affectionate Letters, was very ready to oblige the whole Party by consenting to a prolongation of her stay, and in the course of two months ceased to write of her absence, and in the course of two more, to write to her at all.

Frederica was therefore fixed in the family of her Uncle and Aunt, till such time as Reginald De Courcy could be talked, flattered and finessed[1] into an affection for her – which, allowing leisure for the conquest of his attachment to her Mother, for his abjuring all future attachments and detesting the Sex, might be reasonably looked for in the course of a Twelvemonth. Three Months might have done it in general, but Reginald's feelings were no less lasting than lively.

Whether Lady Susan was, or was not happy in her second Choice – I do not see how it can ever be ascertained – for who would take her assurance of it, on either side of the question? The World must judge from Probability. She had nothing against her, but her Husband, and her Conscience.

Sir James may seem to have drawn an harder Lot than mere Folly merited. I leave him therefore to all the Pity that anybody can give him. For myself, I confess that *I* can pity only Miss Manwaring, who coming to Town and putting herself to an expence in Cloathes, which impoverished her for two years, on purpose to secure him, was defrauded of her due by a Woman ten years older than herself.

FINIS

THE WATSONS

THE first winter assembly in the Town of D.[1] in Surry was to be held on Tuesday October the 13th, and it was generally expected to be a very good one; a long list of Country Families was confidently run over as sure of attending, and sanguine hopes were entertained that the Osbornes themselves would be there. – The Edwardes' invitation to the Watsons followed of course. The Edward's were people of fortune who lived in the Town and kept their coach; the Watsons inhabited a village about three miles distant, were poor and had no close carriage; and ever since there had been Balls in the place, the former were accustomed to invite the Latter to dress dine and sleep at their House, on every monthly return throughout the winter. – On the present occasion, as only two of Mr. W.'s children were at home, and one was always necessary as companion to himself, for he was sickly and had lost his wife, one only could profit by the kindness of their friends; Miss Emma Watson who was very recently returned to her family from the care of an Aunt who had brought her up, was to make her first public appearance in the Neighbourhood; and her eldest sister, whose delight in a Ball was not lessened by a ten years Enjoyment, had some merit in chearfully undertaking to drive her and all her finery in the old chair[2] to D. on the important morning. – As they splashed along the dirty Lane Miss Watson thus instructed and cautioned her inexperienced sister. – 'I dare say it will be a very good Ball, and among so many officers, you will hardly want partners. You will find Mrs. Edwards' maid very willing to help you, and I would advise you to ask Mary Edwards's opinion if you are at all at a loss for she has a very good Taste. – If Mr. E. does not lose his money at cards, you will stay as late as you can wish for; if he does, he will hurry you home perhaps – but you are sure of some comfortable soup. – I hope you will be in good looks –. I should not be surprised if you were to be thought one of the prettiest girls in the room, there is a great deal in Novelty. Perhaps Tom Musgrave may take notice of you – but I would advise you by all means not to give him any encouragement. He generally pays attention to every new girl, but he is a great flirt and never means anything serious.' 'I think I have heard you speak of him before,' said Emma. 'Who is he?' 'A young Man of very good fortune, quite independant, and remarkably agreable, an universal favourite wherever he goes. Most of the girls hereabouts are in love with him, or have been. I believe I am the only one among them that have escaped with a whole heart, and yet I was the first he paid attention to, when he came into this Country, six years ago; and very great attention indeed did he pay me. Some people say that he has never seemed to like any girl so well since, tho' he is always behaving in a particular way to one or another.' –

'And how came *your* heart to be the only cold one?' – said Emma smiling. 'There was a reason for that' – replied Miss W. changing colour. – 'I have not been very well used Emma among them, I hope you will have better luck.' – 'Dear Sister, I beg your pardon, if I have unthinkingly given you pain.' – 'When first we knew Tom Musgrave,' continued Miss W. without seeming to hear her, 'I was very much attached to a young Man of the name of Purvis a particular friend of Robert's, who used to be with us a great deal. Every body thought it would have been a Match.' A sigh accompanied these words, which Emma respected in silence – but her sister after a short pause went on – 'You will naturally ask why it did not take place, and why he is married to another Woman, while I am still single. – But you must ask him – not me – you must ask Penelope. – Yes Emma, Penelope was at the bottom of it all. – She thinks everything fair for a Husband; I trusted her, she set him against me, with a view of gaining him herself, and it ended in his discontinuing his visits and soon after marrying somebody else. – Penelope makes light of her conduct, but *I* think such Treachery very bad.

It has been the ruin of my happiness. I shall never love any Man as I loved Purvis. I do not think Tom Musgrave should be named with him in the same day.' – 'You quite shock me by what you say of Penelope' – said Emma. 'Could a sister do such a thing? – Rivalry, Treachery between sisters! – I shall be afraid of being acquainted with her – but I hope it was not so. Appearances were against her' – 'You do not know Penelope. – There is nothing she would not do to get married – she would as good as tell you so herself. – Do not trust her with any secrets of your own, take warning by me, do not trust her; she has her good qualities, but she has no Faith, no Honour, no Scruples, if she can promote her own advantage. – I wish with all my heart she was well married. I declare I had rather have her well-married than myself.' – 'Than yourself! – Yes I can suppose so. A heart, wounded like yours can have little inclination for Matrimony.' – 'Not much indeed – but you know we must marry. – I could do very well single for my own part – A little Company, and a pleasant Ball now and then, would be enough for me, if one could be young for ever, but my Father cannot provide for us, and it is very bad to grow old and be poor and laughed at. – I have lost Purvis, it is true but very few people marry their first Loves. I should not refuse a man because he was not Purvis –. Not that I can ever quite forgive Penelope.' – Emma shook her head in acquiescence. – 'Penelope however has had her Troubles' – continued Miss W. – 'she was sadly disappointed in Tom Musgrave, who afterwards transferred his attentions from me to her, and whom she was very fond of; but he never means anything serious, and when he had trifled with her long enough, he began to slight her for Margaret, and poor Penelope was very wretched –. And since then, she has been trying to make some match at Chichester; she wont tell us with whom, but I beleive it is a rich old Dr. Harding, Uncle to the friend she goes to see; – and she has taken a vast deal of trouble about him and given up a great deal of Time to no purpose as yet. – When she went away the other day she said it should be the last time. – I suppose you did not know what her particular Business was at Chichester – nor guess at the object that could take her away, from Stanton

just as you were coming home after so many years absence.' –
'No indeed, I had not the smallest suspicion of it. I considered
her engagement to Mrs. Shaw just at that time as very unfortunate for me. I had hoped to find all my sisters at home; to
be able to make an immediate friend of each.' – 'I suspect the
Dr. to have an attack of the Asthma, – and that she was hurried
away on that account – the Shaws are quite on her side. – At
least I believe so – but she tells me nothing. She professes to
keep her own counsel; she says, and truly enough, that "too
many Cooks spoil the Broth".' – 'I am sorry for her anxieties,'
said Emma, – 'but I do not like her plans or her opinions. I
shall be afraid of her. – She must have too masculine and bold a
temper. – To be so bent on Marriage – to pursue a Man merely
for the sake of situation – is a sort of thing that shocks me; I
cannot understand it. Poverty is a great Evil, but to a woman of
Education and feeling it ought not, it cannot be the greatest. – I
would rather be Teacher at a school (and I can think of nothing
worse) than marry a Man I did not like.' – 'I would rather do
any thing than be Teacher at a school' – said her sister. '*I* have
been at school, Emma, and know what a Life they lead; *you*
never have. – I should not like marrying a disagreable Man any
more than yourself, – but I do not think there *are* many very
disagreable Men; – I think I could like any good humoured
Man with a comfortable Income. – I suppose my Aunt brought
you up to be rather refined.' 'Indeed I do not know. – My conduct
must tell you how I have been brought up. I am no judge of it
myself. I cannot compare my Aunt's method with any other
persons, because I know no other.' – 'But I can see in a great
many things that you are very refined. I have observed it ever
since you came home, and I am afraid it will not be for your
happiness. Penelope will laugh at you very much.' '*That* will
not be for my happiness I am sure. – If my opinions are wrong, I
must correct them – if they are above my situation, I must
endeavour to conceal them. – But I doubt whether Ridicule, –
Has Penelope much wit?' – 'Yes – she has great spirits, and never
cares what she says.' – 'Margaret is more gentle I imagine?' –
'Yes – especially in company; she is all gentleness and mildness

when anybody is by. – But she is a little fretful and perverse among ourselves. – Poor creature! she is possessed with the notion of Tom Musgrave's being more seriously in love with her, than he ever was with any body else, and is always expecting him to come to the point. This is the second time within this twelvemonth that she has gone to spend a month with Robert and Jane on purpose to egg him on, by her absence – but I am sure she is mistaken, and that he will no more follow her to Croydon now than he did last March. – He will never marry unless he can marry somebody very great; Miss Osborne perhaps, or something in that stile. – ' 'Your account of this Tom Musgrave, Elizabeth, gives me very little inclination for his acquaintance.' 'You are afraid of him, I do not wonder at you.' – 'No indeed – I dislike and despise him.' – 'Dislike and Despise Tom Musgrave! No, *that* you never can. I defy you not to be delighted with him if he takes notice of you. – I hope he will dance with you – and I dare say he will, unless the Osbornes come with a large party, and then he will not speak to any body else. – ' 'He seems to have most engaging manners!' – said Emma. – 'Well, we shall see how irresistable Mr. Tom Musgrave and I find each other. – I suppose I shall know him as soon as I enter the Ball-room; he *must* carry some of his Charm in his face.' – 'You will not find him in the Ballroom I can tell you, You will go early that Mrs. Edwards may get a good place by the fire, and he never comes till late; and if the Osbornes are coming, he will wait in the Passage, and come in with them. – I should like to look in upon you Emma. If it was but a good day with my Father, I would wrap myself up, and James should drive me over, as soon as I had made Tea for him; and I should be with you by the time the Dancing began.' 'What! would you come late at night in this Chair?' – 'To be sure I would. – There, I said you were very refined; – and *that's* an instance of it.' – Emma for a moment made no answer – at last she said – 'I wish Elizabeth, you had not made a point of my going to this Ball, I wish you were going instead of me. Your pleasure would be greater than mine. I am a stranger here, and know nobody but the Edwardses; my Enjoyment therefore must be very doubtful.

Yours among all your acquaintance would be certain. – It is not
too late to change. Very little apology could be requisite to the
Edwardes, who must be more glad of your company than of
mine, and I should most readily return to my Father; and should
not be at all afraid to drive this quiet old Creature, home. Your
Cloathes I would undertake to find means of sending to you.' –
'My dearest Emma' cried Elizabeth warmly – 'do you think I
would do such a thing? – Not for the Universe – but I shall
never forget your goodnature in proposing it. You must have a
sweet temper indeed; – I never met with any thing like it! –
And would you really give up the Ball, that I might be able to go
to it! – Beleive me Emma, I am not so selfish as that comes to.
No, tho' I am nine years older than you are, I would not be
the means of keeping you from being seen. – You are very
pretty, and it would be very hard that you should not have as
fair a chance as we have all had, to make your fortune. – No
Emma, whoever stays at home this winter, it shan't be you. I
am sure I should never have forgiven the person who kept me
from a Ball at nineteen.' Emma expressed her gratitude, and for a
few minutes they jogged on in silence. – Elizabeth first spoke. –
'You will take notice who Mary Edwards dances with.' – 'I will
remember her partners if I can – but you know they will be all
strangers to me.' 'Only observe whether she dances with
Captain Hunter, more than once; I have my fears in that quarter.
Not that her Father or Mother like officers, but if she does you
know, it is all over with poor Sam. – And I have promised to
write him word who she dances with.' 'Is Sam attached to Miss
Edwardes?' – 'Did not you know *that*?' – 'How should I know
it? How should I know in Shropshire, what is passing of that
nature in Surry? – It is not likely that circumstances of such
delicacy should make any part of the scanty communication
which passed between you and me for the last fourteen years.'
'I wonder I never mentioned it when I wrote. Since you have
been at home, I have been so busy with my poor Father and our
great wash that I have had no leisure to tell you anything – but
indeed I concluded you knew it all. – He has been very much in
love with her these two years, and it is a great disappointment to

him that he cannot always get away to our Balls – but Mr. Curtis won't often spare him, and just now it is a sickly time at Guilford – ' 'Do you suppose Miss Edwardes inclined to like him?' 'I am afraid not: You know she is an only Child, and will have at least ten thousand pounds.' – 'But still she may like our Brother.' 'Oh! no –. The Edwardes look much higher. Her Father and Mother would never consent to it. Sam is only a Surgeon you know. – Sometimes I think she does like him. But Mary Edwardes is rather prim and reserved; I do not always know what she would be at.' – 'Unless Sam feels on sure grounds with the Lady herself, It seems a pity to me that he should be encouraged to think of her at all.' – 'A young Man must think of somebody,' said Elizabeth – 'and why should not he be as lucky as Robert, who has got a good wife and six thousand pounds?' 'We must not all expect to be individually lucky' replied Emma. 'The Luck of one member of a Family is Luck to all. – ' 'Mine is all to come I am sure' – said Elizabeth giving another sigh to the remembrance of Purvis. – 'I have been unlucky enough, and I cannot say much for you, as my Aunt married again so foolishly. – Well – you will have a good Ball I dare say. The next turning will bring us to the Turnpike. You may see the Church Tower over the hedge, and the White Hart is close by it. – I shall long to know what you think of Tom Musgrave.' Such were the last audible sounds of Miss Watson's voice, before they passed thro' the Turnpike gate and entered on the pitching of the Town – the jumbling and noise of which made farther Conversation most thoroughly undesirable. – The old Mare trotted heavily on, wanting no direction of the reins to take the right Turning, and making only one Blunder, in proposing to stop at the Milleners, before she drew up towards Mr. Edward's door. – Mr. E. lived in the best house in the Street, and the best in the place, if Mr. Tomlinson the Banker might be indulged in calling his newly erected House at the end of the Town with a Shrubbery and sweep[1] in the Country. – Mr. E.'s House was higher than most of its neighbours with two windows on each side the door, the windows guarded by posts and chain, the door approached by a flight of stone steps. – 'Here we are' –

said Elizabeth – as the Carriage ceased moving – 'safely arrived; – and by the Market Clock, we have been only five and thirty minutes coming. – which *I* think is doing pretty well, tho' it would be nothing for Penelope. – Is not it a nice Town? – The Edwards' have a noble house you see, and they live quite in stile. The door will be opened by a Man in Livery with a powder'd head, I can tell you.'

Emma had seen the Edwardses only one morning at Stanton, they were therefore all but Strangers to her, and tho' her spirits were by no means insensible to the expected joys of the Evening, she felt a little uncomfortable in the thought of all that was to precede them. Her conversation with Elizabeth too giving her some very unpleasant feelings, with respect to her own family, had made her more open to disagreable impressions from any other cause, and increased her sense of the awkwardness of rushing into Intimacy on so slight an acquaintance. – There was nothing in the manners of Mrs. or Miss Edwardes to give immediate change to these Ideas; – the Mother tho' a very freindly woman, had a reserved air, and a great deal of formal Civility – and the daughter, a genteel looking girl of twenty-two, with her hair in papers, seemed very naturally to have caught something of the stile of the Mother who had brought her up. – Emma was soon left to know what they could be, by Elizabeth's being obliged to hurry away – and some very, very languid remarks on the probable Brilliancy of the Ball, were all that broke at intervals a silence of half an hour before they were joined by the Master of the house. – Mr. Edwards had a much easier, and more communicative air than the Ladies of the Family; he was fresh from the Street, and he came ready to tell what ever might interest. – After a cordial reception of Emma, he turned to his daughter with 'Well Mary, I bring you good news. – The Osbornes will certainly be at the Ball tonight. – Horses for two Carriages are ordered from the White Hart, to be at Osborne Castle by nine. –' 'I am glad of it' – observed Mrs. E., 'because their coming gives a credit to our Assemblies. The Osbornes being known to have been at the first Ball, will dispose a great many people to attend the second. – It is more than they deserve, for in fact they add nothing to the pleasure of the Evening, they come so late, and go so early; – but Great People have always their charm.' – Mr. Edwards proceeded to relate every other little article of news which his morning's lounge had supplied him with, and they chatted with greater briskness, till Mrs. E.'s moment for dressing arrived, and the young Ladies were carefully recommended to lose no time. – Emma was shewn to a very comfortable apartment, and as soon as Mrs. E.'s civilities could leave her to herself, the happy occupation, the first Bliss of a Ball began. – The girls, dressing in some measure together, grew unavoidably better acquainted; Emma found in Miss E. – the shew of good sense, a modest unpretending mind, and a great wish of obliging – and when they returned to the parlour where Mrs. E. was sitting respectably attired in one of the two Sattin gowns which went thro' the winter, and a new cap from the Milliners, they entered it with much easier feelings and more natural smiles than they had taken away. – Their dress was now to be examined; Mrs. Edwards acknowledged herself too old-fashioned to approve of every modern extravagance however sanctioned – and tho' complacently veiwing her daughter's good looks, would give but a qualified admiration; and Mr. E. not less satisfied with Mary, paid some Compliments of good humoured Gallantry to Emma at her expence. – The discussion led to more intimate remarks, and Miss Edwardes gently asked Emma if she were not often reckoned very like her youngest brother. – Emma thought she could perceive a faint blush accompany the question, and there seemed something still more suspicious in the manner in which Mr. E. took up the subject. – 'You are paying Miss Emma no great compliment I think Mary,' said he hastily –. 'Mr. Sam Watson is a very good sort of young Man, and I dare say a very clever Surgeon, but his complexion has been rather too much exposed to all weathers, to make a likeness to him very flattering.' Mary apologized in some confusion. 'She had not thought a strong Likeness at all incompatible with very different degrees of Beauty. – There might be resemblance in Countenance; and the complexion, and even the features be very unlike.' – 'I know nothing of my Brother's Beauty,' said Emma, 'for I have not seen him since he was seven years old – but my father reckons us alike.' 'Mr. Watson!' – cried Mr. Edwardes, 'Well, you astonish me. – There is not the least likeness in the world; Your brother's eyes are grey, yours are brown, He has a long face, and a wide mouth. – My dear, do *you* perceive the least resemblance?' – 'Not the least. – Miss Emma Watson puts me very much in mind of her eldest Sister, and sometimes I see a look of Miss Penelope – and once or twice there has been a glance of Mr. Robert – but I cannot perceive any likeness to Mr. Samuel.' 'I see the likeness between her and Miss Watson,' replied Mr. E. – 'very strongly – but I am not sensible of the others. – I do not much think she is like any of the Family *but* Miss Watson; but I am very sure there is no resemblance between her and Sam.' –

This matter was settled, and they went to Dinner. – 'Your Father, Miss Emma, is one of my oldest friends' – said Mr. Edwardes, as he helped her to wine, when they were drawn round the fire to enjoy their Desert, – 'We must drink to his better health. – It is a great concern to me I assure you that he should be such an Invalid. – I know nobody who likes a game of cards in a social way, better than he does; and very few people that play a fairer rubber. – It is a thousand pities that he should be so deprived of the pleasure. For now we have a quiet little Whist club that meets three times a week at the White Hart, and if he could but have his health, how much he would enjoy it.' 'I dare say he would Sir – and I wish with all my heart he were equal to it.' 'Your Club would be better fitted for an Invalid,' said Mrs. E. 'if you did not keep it up so late.' – This was an old greivance. – 'So late, my dear, what are you talking of;' cried the Husband with sturdy pleasantry –. 'We are always at home before Midnight. They would laugh at Osborne Castle to hear you call *that* late; they are but just rising from dinner at midnight.' – 'That is nothing to the purpose.' – retorted the Lady calmly. 'The Osbornes are to be no rule for us. You had better meet every night, and break up two hours sooner.' So far, the subject was very often carried; – but Mr. and

Mrs. Edwards were so wise as never to pass that point; and Mr. Edwards now turned to something else. – He had lived long enough in the Idleness of a Town to become a little of a Gossip, and having some curiosity to know more of the Circumstances of his young Guest than had yet reached him, he began with, 'I think Miss Emma, I remember your Aunt very well about thirty years ago; I am pretty sure I danced with her in the old rooms at Bath, the year before I married –. She was a very fine woman then – but like other people I suppose she is grown somewhat older since that time. – I hope she is likely to be happy in her second choice.'

'I hope so, I beleive so, Sir' – said Emma in some agitation. – 'Mr. Turner had not been dead a great while I think?' 'About two years Sir.' 'I forget what her name is now?' – 'O'brien.' 'Irish! Ah! I remember – and she is gone to settle in Ireland. – I do not wonder that you should not wish to go with her into *that* Country Miss Emma – but it must be a great deprivation to her, poor Lady! – After bringing you up like a Child of her own.' – 'I was not so ungrateful Sir,' said Emma warmly, 'as to wish to be any where but with her. – It did not suit them, it did not suit Captain O'brien that I should be of the party.' – 'Captain!' – repeated Mrs. E. 'the Gentleman is in the army then?' 'Yes Ma'am.' – 'Aye – there is nothing like your officers for captivating the Ladies, Young or Old. – There is no resisting a Cockade my dear.' – 'I hope there is.' – said Mrs. E. gravely, with a quick glance at her daughter; – and Emma had just recovered from her own perturbation in time to see a blush on Miss E.'s cheek, and in remembering what Elizabeth had said of Captain Hunter, to wonder and waver between his influence and her brother's. –

'Elderly Ladies should be careful how they make a second choice.' observed Mr. Edwardes. – 'Carefulness – Discretion – should not be confined to Elderly Ladies, or to a second choice' added his wife. 'It is quite as necessary to young Ladies in their first.' – 'Rather more so, my dear' – replied he, 'because young Ladies are likely to feel the effects of it longer. When an old Lady plays the fool, it is not in the course of nature that she should suffer from it many years.' Emma drew her hand across her eyes – and Mrs. Edwards on perceiving it, changed the subject to one of less anxiety to all. –

With nothing to do but to expect the hour of setting off, the afternoon was long to the two young Ladies; and tho' Miss Edwards was rather discomposed at the very early hour which her mother always fixed for going, that early hour itself was watched for with some eagerness. – The entrance of the Tea things at seven o'clock was some relief – and luckily Mr. and Mrs. Edwards always drank a dish extraordinary, and ate an additional muffin when they were going to sit up late, which lengthened the ceremony almost to the wished for moment. At a little before eight, the Tomlinsons carriage was heard to go by, which was the constant signal for Mrs. Edwards to order hers to the door; and in a very few minutes, the party were transported from the quiet warmth of a snug parlour, to the bustle, noise and draughts of air of the broad Entrance-passage of an Inn. – Mrs. Edwards carefully guarding her own dress, while she attended with yet greater Solicitude to the proper security of her young Charges' Shoulders and Throats, led the way up the wide staircase, while no sound of a Ball but the first Scrape of one violin, blessed the ears of her followers, and Miss Edwards on hazarding the anxious enquiry of whether there were many people come yet was told by the Waiter as she knew she should, that 'Mr. Tomlinson's family were in the room.' In passing along a short gallery to the Assembly-room, brilliant in lights before them, they were accosted by a young Man in a morning dress and Boots, who was standing in the doorway of a Bedchamber, apparently on purpose to see them go by. – 'Ah! Mrs. E. – how do you do? – How do you do Miss E.?' – he cried, with an easy air; – 'You are determined to be in good time I see, as usual. – The Candles are but this moment lit' – 'I like to get a good seat by the fire you know, Mr. Musgrave.' replied Mrs. E. 'I am this moment going to dress,' said he – 'I am waiting for my stupid fellow. – We shall have a famous Ball, The Osbornes are certainly coming; you may depend upon *that* for I was with Lord Osborne this morning –'

The party passed on – Mrs. E's sattin gown swept along the clean floor of the Ball-room, to the fireplace at the upper end, where one party only were formally seated, while three or four Officers were lounging together, passing in and out from the adjoining card-room. – A very stiff meeting between these near neighbours ensued – and as soon as they were all duely placed again, Emma in the low whisper which became the solemn scene, said to Miss Edwardes, 'The gentleman we passed in the passage, was Mr. Musgrave, then? – He is reckoned remarkably agreable I understand. –' Miss E. answered hesitatingly – 'Yes – he is very much liked by many people. – But *we* are not very intimate.' – 'He is rich, is not he?' – 'He has about 8 or 900£ a year[1] I beleive. – He came into possession of it, when he was very young, and my Father and Mother think it has given him rather an unsettled turn. – He is no favourite with them.' – The cold and empty appearance of the Room and the demure air of the small cluster of Females at one end of it began soon to give way; the inspiriting sound of other Carriages was heard, and continual accessions of portly Chaperons, and strings of smartly-dressed girls were received, with now and then a fresh gentleman straggler, who if not enough in Love to station himself near any fair Creature seemed glad to escape into the Card-room. – Among the increasing numbers of Military Men, one now made his way to Miss Edwards, with an air of Empressément, which decidedly said to her Companion 'I am Captain Hunter.' – and Emma, who could not but watch her at such a moment, saw her looking rather distressed, but by no means displeased, and heard an engagement formed for the two first dances, which made her think her Brother Sam's a hopeless case. –

Emma in the meanwhile was not unobserved, or unadmired herself. – A new face and a very pretty one, could not be slighted – her name was whispered from one party to another, and no sooner had the signal been given, by the Orchestra's striking up a favourite air, which seemed to call the young Men to their duty, and people the centre of the room, than she found herself engaged to dance with a Brother officer, introduced by Captain

Hunter. – Emma Watson was not more than of the middle height – well made and plump, with an air of healthy vigour. – Her skin was very brown, but clear, smooth and glowing –; which with a lively Eye, a sweet smile, and an open Countenance, gave beauty to attract, and expression to make that beauty improve on acquaintance. – Having no reason to be dissatisfied with her partner, the Evening began very pleasantly to her; and her feelings perfectly coincided with the reiterated observation of others, that it was an excellent Ball. – The two first dances were not quite over, when the returning sound of Carriages after a long interruption, called general notice, and 'the Osbornes are coming, the Osbornes are coming' – was repeated round the room. – After some minutes of extraordinary bustle without, and watchful curiosity within, the important Party, preceded by the attentive Master of the Inn to open a door which was never shut, made their appearance. They consisted of Lady Osborne, her son Lord Osborne, her daughter Miss Osborne; Miss Carr, her daughter's friend, Mr. Howard formerly Tutor to Lord Osborne, now Clergyman of the Parish in which the Castle stood, Mrs. Blake, a widow-sister who lived with him, her son a fine boy of ten years old, and Mr. Tom Musgrave; who probably imprisoned within his own room, had been listening in bitter impatience to the sound of the Music, for the last half hour. In their progress up the room, they paused almost immediately behind Emma, to receive the Compliments of some acquaintance, and she heard Lady Osborne observe that they had made a point of coming early for the gratification of Mrs. Blake's little boy, who was uncommonly fond of dancing. – Emma looked at them all as they passed – but chiefly and with most interest on Tom Musgrave, who was certainly a genteel, good looking young man. – Of the females, Lady Osborne had by much the finest person; – tho' nearly fifty, she was very handsome, and had all the Dignity of Rank. –

Lord Osborne was a very fine young man; but there was an air of Coldness, of Carelessness, even of Awkwardness about him, which seemed to speak him out of his Element in a Ball room. He came in fact only because it was judged expedient for him to please the Borough – he was not fond of Women's company, and he never danced. – Mr. Howard was an agreeable-looking Man, a little more than Thirty. –

At the conclusion of the two Dances, Emma found herself, she knew not how, seated amongst the Osborne set; and she was immediately struck with the fine Countenance and animated gestures of the little boy, as he was standing before his Mother, wondering when they should begin. – 'You will not be surprised at Charles's impatience,' said Mrs. Blake, a lively pleasant-looking little Woman of five- or six- and thirty, to a Lady who was standing near her, 'when you know what a partner he is to have. Miss Osborne has been so very kind as to promise to dance the two first dances with him.' – 'Oh! yes – we have been engaged this week,' cried the boy, 'and we are to dance down every couple.' – On the other side of Emma, Miss Osborne, Miss Carr, and a party of young Men were standing engaged in very lively consultation – and soon afterwards she saw the smartest officer of the sett, walking off to the Orchestra to order the dance, while Miss Osborne passing before her, to her little expecting Partner hastily said – 'Charles, I beg your pardon for not keeping my engagement, but I am going to dance these two dances with Colonel Beresford. I know you will excuse me, and I will certainly dance with you after Tea.' And without staying for an answer, she turned again to Miss Carr, and in another minute was led by Colonel Beresford to begin the set. If the poor little boy's face had in it's happiness been interesting[1] to Emma, it was infinitely more so under this sudden reverse; – he stood the picture of disappointment, with crimson'd cheeks, quivering lips, and eyes bent on the floor. His mother, stifling her own mortification, tried to sooth his, with the prospect of Miss Osborne's second promise; – but tho' he contrived to utter with an effort of Boyish Bravery 'Oh! I do not mind it' – it was very evident by the unceasing agitation of his features that he minded it as much as ever. – Emma did not think, or reflect; – she felt and acted –. 'I shall be very happy to dance with you Sir, if you like it.' said she, holding out her hand with the most unaffected good humour. – The Boy in one moment restored to all his first delight – looked joyfully at his Mother and stepping forwards with an honest and simple Thank you Maam was instantly ready to attend his new acquaintance. – The Thankfulness of Mrs. Blake was more diffuse; – with a look, most expressive of unexpected pleasure, and lively Gratitude, she turned to her neighbour with repeated and fervent acknowledgements of so great and condescending a kindness to her boy. – Emma with perfect truth could assure her that she could not be giving greater pleasure than she felt herself – and Charles being provided with his gloves and charged to keep them on, they joined the Set which was now rapidly forming, with nearly equal complacency. – It was a Partnership which could not be noticed without surprise. It gained her a broad stare from Miss Osborne and Miss Carr as they pased her in the dance. 'Upon my word Charles you are in luck,' (said the former as she turned him) 'you have got a better partner than me' – to which the happy Charles answered 'Yes.' – Tom Musgrave who was dancing with Miss Carr, gave her many inquisitive glances; and after a time Lord Osborne himself came under pretence of talking to Charles, stood to look at his partner. – Tho' rather distressed by such observation, Emma could not repent what she had done, so happy had it made both the boy and his Mother; the latter of whom was continually making opportunities of addressing her with the warmest civility. – Her little partner she found, tho' bent cheifly on dancing, was not unwilling to speak, when her questions or remarks gave him anything to say; and she learnt, by a sort of inevitable enquiry that he had two brothers and a sister, that they and their Mama all lived with his Uncle at Wickstead, that his Uncle taught him Latin, that he was very fond of riding, and had a horse of his own given him by Lord Osborne; and that he had been out once already with Lord Osborne's Hounds. – At the end of these Dances Emma found they were to drink tea; – Miss E. gave her a caution to be at hand, in a manner which convinced her of Mrs. E.'s holding it very important to have them both close to her when she moved into the Tearoom; and Emma was accordingly on the alert to gain her proper station. It was always the pleasure of the company to have a little bustle and croud when they thus adjourned for refreshment; – the Tearoom was a small room within the Cardroom, and in passing thro' the latter, where the passage was straightened by Tables, Mrs. E. and her party were for a few moments hemmed in. It happened close by Lady Osborne's Cassino Table; Mr. Howard who belonged to it spoke to his Nephew; and Emma on perceiving herself the object of attention both to Lady O. and him, had just turned away her eyes in time, to avoid seeming to hear her young companion delightedly whisper aloud 'Oh! Uncle, do look at my partner. She is so pretty!' As they were immediately in motion again however Charles was hurried off without being able to receive his Uncle's suffrage. – On entering the Tearoom, in which two long Tables were prepared, Lord Osborne was to be seen quite alone at the end of one, as if retreating as far as he could from the Ball, to enjoy his own thoughts, and gape without restraint. – Charles instantly pointed him out to Emma – 'There's Lord Osborne – Let you and I go and sit by him.' – 'No, no,' said Emma laughing 'you must sit with my friends.'

Charles was now free enough to hazard a few questions in his turn. 'What o'clock was it?' – 'Eleven.' – 'Eleven! – And I am not at all sleepy. Mama said I should be asleep before ten. – Do you think Miss Osborne will keep her word with me, when Tea is over?' 'Oh! yes. – I suppose so.' – tho' she felt that she had no better reason to give than that Miss Osborne had *not* kept it before. – 'When shall you come to Osborne Castle?' – 'Never, probably. – I am not acquainted with the family.' 'But you may come to Wickstead and see Mama, and she can take you to the Castle. – There is a monstrous curious stuff'd Fox there, and a Badger – anybody would think they were alive. It is a pity you should not see them.' –

On rising from Tea, there was again a scramble for the pleasure of being first out of the room, which happened to be increased by one or two of the card parties having just broken up and the players being disposed to move exactly the different way. Among these was Mr. Howard – his sister leaning on his arm – and no sooner were they within reach of Emma, than Mrs. B. calling her notice by a friendly touch, said 'Your goodness to Charles, my dear Miss Watson, brings all his family upon you. Give me leave to introduce my Brother – Mr. H.' Emma curtsied, the gentleman bowed – made a hasty request for the honour of her hand in the next two dances, to which as hasty an affirmative was given, and they were immediately impelled in opposite directions. – Emma was very well pleased with the circumstance; – there was a quietly-chearful, gentlemanlike air in Mr. H. which suited her – and in a few minutes afterwards, the value of her Engagement increased, when as she was sitting in the Cardroom somewhat screened by a door, she heard Lord Osborne, who was lounging on a vacant Table near her, call Tom Musgrave towards him and say, 'Why do not you dance with that beautiful Emma Watson? – I want you to dance with her – and I will come and stand by you.' – 'I was determining on it this very moment my Lord, I'll be introduced and dance with her directly.' – 'Aye do – and if you find she does not want much Talking to, you may introduce me by and bye.' – 'Very well my Lord –. If she is like her Sisters, she will only want to be listened to. – I will go this moment. I shall find her in the Tea room. That stiff old Mrs. E. has never done tea.' – Away he went – Lord Osborne after him – and Emma lost no time in hurrying from her corner, exactly the other way, forgetting in her haste that she left Mrs. Edwardes behind. – 'We had quite lost you' – said Mrs. E. – who followed her with Mary, in less than five minutes. – 'If you prefer this room to the other, there is no reason why you should not be here, but we had better all be together.' Emma was saved the Trouble of apologizing, by their being joined at the moment by Tom Musgrave, who requesting Mrs. E. aloud to do him the honour of presenting him to Miss Emma Watson, left that good Lady without any choice in the business, but that of testifying by the coldness of her manner that she did it unwillingly. The honour of dancing with her, was solicited without loss of time – and Emma, however she might like to be thought a beautiful girl by Lord or Commoner, was so little disposed to favour Tom Musgrave himself, that she had considerable satisfaction in avowing her prior Engagement. – He was evidently surprised and discomposed. – The stile of her last partner had probably led him to beleive her not overpowered with applications. – 'My little friend Charles Blake,' he cried, 'must not expect to engross you the whole evening. We can never suffer this – It is against the rules of the Assembly – and I am sure it will never be patronised by our good friend here Mrs. E.; She is by much too nice a judge of Decorum to give her license to such a dangerous Particularity.' – 'I am not going to dance with Master Blake Sir.' The Gentleman a little disconcerted, could only hope he might be more fortunate another time – and seeming unwilling to leave her, tho' his friend Lord Osborne was waiting in the Doorway for the result, as Emma with some amusement perceived – he began to make civil enquiries after her family. – 'How comes it, that we have not the pleasure of seeing your Sisters here this Evening? – Our Assemblies have been used to be so well treated by them, that we do not know how to take this neglect.' – 'My eldest Sister is the only one at home – and she could not leave my Father' – 'Miss Watson the only one at home! – You astonish me! – It seems but the day before yesterday that I saw them all three in this Town. But I am afraid I have been a very sad neighbour of late. I hear dreadful complaints of my negligence wherever I go, and I confess it is a shameful length of time since I was at Stanton. – But I shall *now* endeavour to make myself amends for the past.' – Emma's calm curtsey in reply must have struck him as very unlike the encouraging warmth he had been used to receive from her Sisters, and gave him probably the novel sensation of doubting his own influence, and of wishing for more attention than she bestowed. The dancing now recommenced; Miss Carr being impatient to *call*, everybody was required to stand up – and Tom Musgrave's curiosity was appeased, on seeing Mr. Howard come forward and claim Emma's hand – 'That will do as well for me' – was Lord Osborne's remark, when his friend carried him the news – and he was continually at Howard's Elbow during the two dances. – The frequency of his appearance there, was the only unpleasant part of her engagement, the only objection she could make to Mr.

Howard. – In himself, she thought him as agreable as he looked; tho' chatting on the commonest topics he had a sensible, unaffected, way of expressing himself, which made them all worth hearing, and she only regretted that he had not been able to make his pupil's Manners as unexceptionable as his own. – The two dances seemed very short, and she had her partner's authority for considering them so. – At their conclusion the Osbornes and their Train were all on the move. 'We are off at last,' said his Lordship to Tom – 'How much longer do *you* stay in this Heavenly place? – till Sunrise?' – 'No faith! my Lord, I have had quite enough of it. I assure you – I shall not shew myself here again when I have had the honour of attending Lady Osborne to her Carriage. I shall retreat in as much secrecy as possible to the most remote corner of the House, where I shall order a Barrel of Oysters, and be famously snug.' 'Let us see you soon at the Castle; and bring me word how she looks by daylight.' – Emma and Mrs. Blake parted as old acquaintance, and Charles shook her by the hand and wished her 'goodbye' at least a dozen times. From Miss Osborne and Miss Carr she received something like a jerking curtsey as they passed her; even Lady Osborne gave her a look of complacency – and his Lordship actually came back after the others were out of the room, to 'beg her pardon', and look in the window seat behind her for the gloves which were visibly compressed in his hand. –

As Tom Musgrave was seen no more, we may suppose his plan to have succeeded, and imagine him mortifying with his Barrel of Oysters, in dreary solitude – or gladly assisting the Landlady in her Bar to make fresh Negus[1] for the happy Dancers above. Emma could not help missing the party, by whom she had been, tho' in some respects unpleasantly, distinguished, and the two Dances which followed and concluded the Ball, were rather flat, in comparison with the others. – Mr. E. having play'd with good luck, they were some of the last in the room – 'Here we are, back again I declare' – said Emma sorrowfully, as she walked into the Dining room, where the Table was prepared, and the neat Upper maid was lighting the Candles – 'My dear

Miss Edwards – how soon it is at an end! – I wish it could all come over again! –' A great deal of kind pleasure was expressed in her having enjoyed the Evening so much – and Mr. Edwards was as warm as herself, in praise of the fullness, brilliancy and Spirit of the Meeting, tho' as he had been fixed the whole time at the same Table in the same Room, with only one change of chairs, it might have seemed a matter scarcely perceived. – But he had won four rubbers out of five, and everything went well. His daughter felt the advantage of this gratified state of mind, in the course of the remarks and retrospections which now ensued, over the welcome soup. – 'How came you not to dance with either of the Mr. Tomlinsons, Mary?' – said her Mother. 'I was always engaged when they asked me.' 'I thought you were to have stood up with Mr. James, the last two dances; Mrs. Tomlinson told me he was gone to ask you – and I had heard you say two minutes before that you were *not* engaged.' – 'Yes – but – there was a mistake – I had misunderstood – I did not know I was engaged. – I thought it had been for the two Dances after, if we staid so long – but Captain Hunter assured me it was for those very Two. –'

'So, you ended with Captain Hunter Mary, did you?' said her Father. 'And who did you begin with?' 'Captain Hunter.' was repeated, in a very humble tone – 'Hum! – That is being constant however. But who else did you dance with?' 'Mr. Norton, and Mr. Styles.' 'And who are they?' 'Mr. Norton is a Cousin of Captain Hunter's.' – 'And who is Mr. Styles?' 'One of his particular friends.' – 'All in the same Regiment' added Mrs. E. – 'Mary was surrounded by Red coats the whole Evening. I should have been better pleased to see her dancing with some of our old Neighbours I confess. –' 'Yes, yes, we must not neglect our old Neighbours –. But if these soldiers are quicker than other people in a Ball room, what are young Ladies to do?' 'I think there is no occasion for their engaging themselves so many Dances beforehand, Mr. Edwards.' – 'No – perhaps not – but I remember my dear when you and I did the same.' – Mrs. E. said no more, and Mary breathed again. – A great deal of goodhumoured pleasantry followed – and Emma went to bed in charming Spirits, her head full of Osbornes, Blakes and Howards. –

The next morning brought a great many visitors. It was the way of the place always to call on Mrs. E. on the morning after a Ball, and this neighbourly inclination was increased in the present instance by a general spirit of curiosity on Emma's account, as Everybody wanted to look again at the girl who had been admired the night before by Lord Osborne. –

Many were the eyes, and various the degrees of approbation with which she was examined. Some saw no fault, and some no Beauty –. With some her brown skin was the annihilation of every grace, and others could never be persuaded that she were half so handsome as Elizabeth Watson had been ten years ago. – The morning passed quietly away in discussing the merits of the Ball with all this succession of Company – and Emma was at once astonished by finding it Two o'clock, and considering that she had heard nothing of her Father's Chair. After this discovery she had walked twice to the window to examine the Street, and was on the point of asking leave to ring the bell and make enquiries, when the light sound of a Carriage driving up to the door set her heart at ease. She stepd again to the window – but instead of the convenient but very un-smart Family Equipage perceived a neat Curricle.[1] – Mr. Musgrave was shortly afterwards announced; – and Mrs. Edwards put on her very stiffest look at the sound. – Not at all dismayed however by her chilling air, he paid his Compliments to each of the Ladies with no unbecoming Ease, and continuing to address Emma, presented her a note, which he had the honour of bringing from her Sister; But to which he must observe that a verbal postscript from himself would be requisite. –'

The note, which Emma was beginning to read rather *before* Mrs. Edwards had entreated her to use no ceremony, contained a few lines from Elizabeth importing that their Father in consequence of being unusually well had taken the sudden resolution of attending the Visitation that day, and that as his Road lay quite wide from R., it was impossible for her to come home till the following morning, unless the Edwardses would send her which was hardly to be expected, or she could meet with any chance conveyance, or did not mind walking so far. – She had scarcely run her eye thro' the whole, before she found herself obliged to listen to Tom Musgrave's farther account. 'I received that note from the fair hands of Miss Watson only ten minutes ago,' said he – 'I met her in the village of Stanton, whither my good Stars prompted me to turn my Horses heads – she was at that moment in quest of a person to employ on the Errand, and I was fortunate enough to convince her that she could not find a more willing or speedy Messenger than myself –. Remember, I say nothing of my Disinterestedness. – My reward is to be the indulgence of conveying you to Stanton in my Curricle. – Tho' they are not written down, I bring your Sister's Orders for the same. – ' Emma felt distressed; she did not like the proposal – she did not wish to be on terms of intimacy with the Proposer – and yet fearful of encroaching on the Edwardes', as well as wishing to go home herself, she was at a loss how entirely to decline what he offered – Mrs. E. continued silent, either not understanding the case, or waiting to see how the young Lady's inclination lay. Emma thanked him – but professed herself very unwilling to give him so much trouble. 'The Trouble was of course, Honour, Pleasure, Delight. What had he or his Horses to do?' – Still she hesitated. 'She beleived she must beg leave to decline his assistance – she was rather afraid of the sort of carriage –. The distance was not beyond a walk. – ' Mrs. E. was silent no longer. She enquired into the particulars – and then said 'We shall be extremely happy Miss Emma, if you can give us the pleasure of your company till tomorrow – but if you can not conveniently do so, our Carriage is quite at your Service, and Mary will be pleased with the opportunity of seeing your Sister.' – This was precisely what Emma had longed for; and she accepted the offer most thankfully; acknowledging that as Elizabeth was entirely alone, it was her wish to return home to dinner. – The plan was warmly opposed by their Visitor. 'I cannot suffer it indeed. I must not be deprived of the happiness of escorting you. I assure you there is not a possibility of fear with my Horses. You might guide them yourself. *Your Sisters* all know

how quiet they are; They have none of them the smallest scruple
in trusting themselves with me, even on a Race Course. - Beleive
me' - added he lowering his voice - ' *You* are quite safe, the danger
is only *mine*.' - Emma was not more disposed to oblige him for
all this. - 'And as to Mrs. Edwardes' carriage being used the day
after a Ball, it is a thing quite out of rule I assure you - never
heard of before - the old Coachman will look as black as his
Horses -. Won't he Miss Edwards?' - No notice was taken. The
Ladies were silently firm, and the gentleman found himself
obliged to submit.

    'What a famous Ball we had last night!' - he cried, after a
short pause. 'How long did you keep it up, after the Osbornes
and I went away?' - 'We had two dances more.' - 'It is making
it too much of a fatigue I think, to stay so late. - I suppose your
Set was not a very full one.' - 'Yes, quite as full as ever, except
the Osbornes. There seemed no vacancy anywhere - and everybody danced with uncommon spirit to the very last.' - Emma
said this - tho' against her conscience. - 'Indeed! perhaps I
might have looked in upon you again, if I had been aware of as
much; - for I am rather fond of dancing than not. - Miss Osborne
is a charming girl, is not she?' 'I do not think her handsome.'
replied Emma, to whom all this was cheifly addressed. 'Perhaps
she is not critically handsome,[1] but her Manners are delightful.
And Fanny Carr is a most interesting little creature. You can
imagine nothing more *naive* or *piquante*; and What do you thing
of[2] *Lord Osborne* Miss Watson?' 'That he would be handsome,
even tho' he were *not* a Lord - and perhaps - better bred;
More desirous of pleasing, and shewing himself pleased in a
right place. -' 'Upon my word, you are severe upon my friend! -
I assure you Lord Osborne is a very good fellow. -' 'I do not
dispute his virtues - but I do not like his careless air. -' 'If it
were not a breach of confidence,' replied Tom with an important look, 'perhaps I might be able to win a more favourable
opinion of poor Osborne. -' Emma gave him no Encouragement,
and he was obliged to keep his friend's secret. - He was also
obliged to put an end to his visit - for Mrs. Edwards having
ordered her Carriage, there was no time to be lost on Emma's

side in preparing for it. – Miss Edwards accompanied her home, but as it was Dinner hour at Stanton, staid with them only a few minutes, – 'Now my dear Emma, said Miss W., as soon as they were alone, you must talk to me all the rest of the day, without stopping, or I shall not be satisfied. But first of all Nanny shall bring in the dinner. Poor thing! – You will not dine as you did yesterday, for we have nothing but some fried beef. – How nice Mary Edwards looks in her new pelisse! – And now tell me how you like them all, and what I am to say to Sam. I have begun my letter, Jack Stokes is to call for it tomorrow, for his Uncle is going within a mile of Guilford the next day. –' Nanny brought in the dinner; – 'We will wait upon ourselves,' continued Elizabeth 'and then we shall lose no time. – And so, you would not come home with Tom Musgrave?' – 'No. You had said so much against him that I could not wish either for the obligation, or the Intimacy which the use of his Carriage must have created –. I should not even have liked the appearance of it. –' 'You did very right; tho' I wonder at your forbearance, and I do not think I could have done it myself. – He seemed so eager to fetch you, that I could not say no, tho' it rather went against me to be throwing you together, so well as I knew his Tricks; – but I did long to see you, and it was a clever way of getting you home; Besides it won't do to be too nice. – Nobody could have thought of the Edwards' letting you have their Coach, – after the Horses being out so late. – But what am I to say to Sam?' – 'If you are guided by me, you will not encourage him to think of Miss Edwards. – The Father is decidedly against him, the Mother shews him no favour, and I doubt his having any interest with Mary. She danced twice with Captain Hunter, and I think shews him in general as much Encouragement as is consistent with her disposition, and the circumstances she is placed in. – She once mentioned Sam, and certainly with a little confusion – but that was perhaps merely oweing to the consciousness of his liking her, which may very probably have come to her knowledge.' – 'Oh! dear Yes – she has heard enough of that from us all. Poor Sam! – He is out of luck as well as other people. – For the life of me Emma, I cannot help feeling for those that are cross'd in

Love. – Well – now begin, and give me an account of everything
as it happened. –' Emma obeyed her – and Elizabeth listened
with very little interruption till she heard of Mr. H. as a partner.
– 'Dance with Mr. H. – Good Heavens! You don't say so!
Why – he is quite one of the great and Grand ones; – Did not
you find him very high?' 'His manners are of a kind to give *me*
much more Ease and confidence than Tom Musgrave's.' 'Well –
go on. I should have been frightened out of my wits, to have had
anything to do with the Osborne's set.' – Emma concluded her
narration. – 'And so, you really did not dance with Tom
M. at all? – But you must have liked him, you must have been
struck with him altogether.' – 'I do *not* like him, Elizabeth –. I
allow his person and air to be good – and that his manners to a
certain point – his address[1] rather – is pleasing. – But I see
nothing else to admire in him. – On the contrary, he seems very
vain, very conceited, absurdly anxious for Distinction, and
absolutely contemptible in some of the measures he takes for
becoming so. – There is a ridiculousness about him that enter-
tains me – but his company gives me no other agreable Emotion.'
'My dearest Emma! – You are like nobody else in the World. –
It is well Margaret is not by. – You do not offend *me*, tho' I
hardly know how to beleive you. But Margaret would never
forgive such words.' 'I wish Margaret could have heard him
profess his ignorance of her being out of the Country; he declared it seemed only two days since he had seen her. –' 'Aye –
that is just like him. And yet this is the Man, she *will* fancy so
desperately in love with her. – He is no favourite of mine, as you
well know, Emma; – but you must think him agreable. Can
you lay your hand on your heart, and say you do not?' – 'Indeed
I can, Both Hands; and spread to their widest extent.' – 'I
should like to know the Man you *do* think agreable.' 'His name is
Howard.' 'Howard! Dear me. I cannot think of *him*, but as
playing cards with Lady Osborne, and looking proud. – I must
own however that it *is* a releif to me, to find you can speak as you
do, of Tom Musgrave; my heart did misgive me that you would
like him too well. You talked so stoutly beforehand, that I was
sadly afraid your Brag would be punished. – I only hope it will

last; – and that he will not come on to pay you much attention; it is a hard thing for a woman to stand against the flattering ways of a Man, when he is bent upon pleasing her. –' As their quietly-sociable little meal concluded, Miss Watson could not help observing how comfortably it had passed. 'It is so delightful to me,' said she, 'to have Things going on in peace and good-humour. Nobody can tell how much I hate quarrelling. Now, tho' we have had nothing but fried beef, how good it has all seemed. – I wish everybody were as easily satisfied as you – but poor Margaret is very snappish, and Penelope owns she had rather have Quarrelling going on, than nothing at all.' – Mr. Watson returned in the Evening, not the worse for the exertion of the day, and consequently pleased with what he had done, and glad to talk of it, over his own Fireside. –

Emma had not foreseen any interest to herself in the oc-currences of a Visitation – but when she heard Mr. Howard spoken of as the Preacher, and as having given them an excellent Sermon, she could not help listening with a quicker Ear. – 'I do not know when I have heard a Discourse more to my mind' – continued Mr. W. 'or one better delivered. – He reads extremely well, with great propriety and in a very impressive manner; and at the same time without any Theatrical grimace or violence. – I own, I do not like much action in the pulpit – I do not like the studied air and artificial inflexions of voice, which your very popular and most admired Preachers generally have. – A simple delivery is much better calculated to inspire Devotion, and shews a much better Taste. – Mr. H. read like a scholar and a gentleman.' – 'And what had you for dinner Sir?' – said his eldest Daughter. – He related the Dishes and told what he had ate himself. 'Upon the whole,' he added, 'I have had a very comfortable day; my old friends were quite surprised to see me amongst them – and I must say that everybody paid me great attention, and seemed to feel for me as an Invalid. – They would make me sit near the fire, and as the partridges were pretty high, Dr. Richards would have them sent away to the other end of the Table, that they might not offend Mr. Watson – which I thought very kind of him. – But what pleased me as much as anything

was Mr. Howard's attention; – There is a pretty steep flight of
steps up to the room we dine in – which do not quite agree with
my gouty foot – and Mr. Howard walked by me from the bottom
to the top, and would make me take his arm. – It struck me as
very becoming in so young a Man, but I am sure I had no claim
to expect it; for I never saw him before in my Life. – By the bye,
he enquired after one of my Daughters, but I do not know which.
I suppose you know among yourselves.' –

*

On the third day after the Ball, as Nanny at five minutes
before three, was beginning to bustle into the parlour with the
Tray and the Knife-case, she was suddenly called to the front
door, by the sound of as smart a rap as the end of a riding-whip
could give – and tho' charged by Miss W. to let nobody in,
returned in half a minute, with a look of awkward dismay, to
hold the parlour door open for Lord Osborne and Tom Musgrave. – The surprise of the young Ladies may be imagined. No
visitors would have been welcome at such a moment; but such
visitors as these – such a one as Lord Osborne at least, a noble-
man and a stranger, was really distressing. – He looked a little
embarrassed himself, – as, on being introduced by his easy,
voluble friend, he muttered something of doing himself the
honour of waiting on Mr. Watson. – Tho' Emma could not
but take the compliment of the visit to herself, she was very far
from enjoying it. She felt all the inconsistency of such an acquaintance with the very humble stile in which they were
obliged to live; and having in her Aunt's family been used to
many of the Elegancies of Life, was fully sensible of all that
must be open to the ridicule of Richer people in her present
home. – Of the pain of such feelings, Elizabeth knew very
little; – her simpler Mind, or juster reason saved her from such
mortification – and tho' shrinking under a general sense of
Inferiority, she felt no particular Shame. – Mr. Watson, as the
Gentlemen had already heard from Nanny, was not well enough
to be down stairs; – With much concern they took their seats –
Lord Osborne near Emma, and the convenient Mr. Musgrave in

high spirits at his own importance, on the other side of the fireplace with Elizabeth. – *He* was at no loss for words; – but when Lord Osborne had hoped that Emma had not caught cold at the Ball, he had nothing more to say for some time, and could only gratify his Eye by occasional glances at his fair neighbour. – Emma was not inclined to give herself much trouble for his Entertainment – and after hard labour of mind, he produced the remark of it's being a very fine day, and followed it up with the question of, 'Have you been walking this morning?' 'No, my Lord. We thought it too dirty.' 'You should wear half-boots.' – After another pause, 'Nothing sets off a neat ankle more than a half-boot; nankin galoshed with black looks very well. – Do not you like Half-boots?' 'Yes – but unless they are so stout as to injure their beauty, they are not fit for Country walking.' – 'Ladies should ride in dirty weather. – Do you ride?' 'No my Lord.' 'I wonder every Lady does not. – A woman never looks better than on horseback. –' 'But every woman may not have the inclination, or the means.' 'If they knew how much it became them, they would all have the inclination, and I fancy Miss Watson – when once they had the inclination, the means would soon follow.' – 'Your Lordship thinks we always have our own way. – *That* is a point on which Ladies and Gentlemen have long disagreed – But without pretending to decide it, I may say that there are some circumstances which even *Women* cannot controul. – Female Economy will do a great deal my Lord, but it cannot turn a small income into a large one.' – Lord Osborne was silenced. Her manner had been neither sententious nor sarcastic, but there was a something in it's mild seriousness, as well as in the words themselves which made his Lordship think; – and when he addressed her again, it was with a degree of considerate propriety, totally unlike the half-awkward, half-fearless stile of his former remarks. – It was a new thing with him to wish to please a woman; it was the first time that he had ever felt what was due to a woman, in Emma's situation. – But as he wanted neither Sense nor a good disposition, he did not feel it without effect. – 'You have not been long in this Country I understand,' said he in the tone of a Gentleman. 'I hope you are pleased with it.' – He was rewarded by a gracious answer, and a more liberal full veiw of her face than she had yet bestowed. Unused to exert himself, and happy in contemplating her, he then sat in silence for some minutes longer, while Tom Musgrave was chattering to Elizabeth, till they were interrupted by Nanny's approach, who half opening the door and putting in her head, said 'Please Ma'am, Master wants to know why he be'nt to have his dinner.' – The Gentlemen, who had hitherto disregarded every symptom, however positive, of the nearness of that Meal, now jumped up with apologies, while Elizabeth called briskly after Nanny 'to tell Betty to take up the Fowls.' – 'I am sorry it happens so' – she added, turning good-humouredly towards Musgrave – 'but you know what early hours we keep. –' Tom had nothing to say for himself, he knew it very well, and such honest simplicity, such shameless Truth rather bewildered him. – Lord Osborne's parting Compliments took some time, his inclination for speech seeming to increase with the shortness of the term for indulgence. – He recommended Exercise in defiance of dirt – spoke again in praise of Half-boots – begged that his Sister might be allow'd to send Emma the name of her Shoemaker – and concluded with saying, 'My Hounds will be hunting this Country next week – I beleive they will throw off at Stanton Wood on Wednesday at 9 o'clock. – I mention this, in hopes of your being drawn out to see what's going on. – If the morning's tolerable, pray do us the honour of giving us your good wishes in person. –'

The Sisters looked on each other with astonishment, when their Visitors had withdrawn. 'Here's an unaccountable Honour!' cried Elizabeth at last. 'Who would have thought of Lord Osborne's coming to Stanton. – He is very handsome – but Tom Musgrave looks all to nothing, the smartest and most fashionable Man of the two. I am glad he did not say anything to me; I would not have had to talk to such a great Man for the world. Tom was very agreable, was not he? – But did you hear him ask where Miss Penelope and Miss Margaret were, when he first came in? – It put me out of patience. – I am glad Nanny had not laid the Cloth however, it would have looked so awkward; –

just the Tray did not signify. –' To say that Emma was not flattered by Lord Osborne's visit, would be to assert a very unlikely thing, and describe a very odd young Lady; but the gratification was by no means unalloyed; His coming was a sort of notice which might please her vanity, but did not suit her pride, and she would rather have known that he wished the visit without presuming to make it, than have seen him at Stanton. – Among other unsatisfactory feelings it once occurred to her to wonder why Mr. Howard had not taken the same privilege of coming, and accompanied his Lordship – but she was willing to suppose that he had either known nothing about it, or had declined any share in a measure which carried quite as much Impertinence in it's form as Goodbreeding. – Mr. W. was very far from being delighted, when he heard what had passed; – a little peevish under immediate pain, and ill disposed to be pleased, he only replied – 'Phoo! Phoo! – What occasion could there be for Lord O.'s coming. I have lived here fourteen years without being noticed by any of the family. It is some foolery of that idle fellow T. Musgrave. I cannot return the visit. – *I* would not if I could.' And when T. Musgrave was met with again, he was commissioned with a message of excuse to Osborne Castle, on the too-sufficient plea of Mr. Watson's infirm state of health. –

A week or ten days rolled quietly away after this visit, before any new bustle arose to interrupt even for half a day, the tranquil and affectionate intercourse of the two Sisters, whose mutual regard was increasing with the intimate knowledge of each other which such intercourse produced. – The first circumstance to break in on this serenity, was the receipt of a letter from Croydon to announce the speedy return of Margaret, and a visit of two or three days from Mr. and Mrs. Robert Watson, who undertook to bring her home and wished to see their Sister Emma. – It was an expectation to fill the thoughts of the Sisters at Stanton, and to busy the hours of one of them at least – for as Jane had been a woman of fortune, the preparations for her entertainment were considerable, and as Elizabeth had at all times more good will than method in her guidance of the house, she could make no change without a Bustle. – An absence of fourteen years had made all her Brothers and Sisters Strangers to Emma, but in her expectation of Margaret there was more than the awkwardness of such an alienation; she had heard things which made her dread her return; and the day which brought the party to Stanton seemed to her the probable conclusion of almost all that had been comfortable in the house. – Robert Watson was an Attorney at Croydon, in a good way of Business; very well satisfied with himself for the same, and for having married the only daughter of the Attorney to whom he had been Clerk, with a fortune of six thousand pounds. – Mrs. Robert was not less pleased with herself for having had that six thousand pounds, and for being now in possession of a very smart house in Croydon, where she gave genteel parties, and wore fine cloathes. – In her person there was nothing remarkable; her manners were pert and conceited. – Margaret was not without beauty; she had a slight, pretty figure, and rather wanted Countenance than good features; – but the sharp and anxious expression of her face made her beauty in general little felt. – On meeting her long-absent Sister, as on every occasion of shew, her manner was all affection and her voice all gentleness; continual smiles and a very slow articulation being her constant resource when determined on pleasing. –

She was now so 'delighted to see dear, dear Emma' that she could hardly speak a word in a minute. – 'I am sure we shall be great friends' – she observed, with much sentiment, as they were sitting together. – Emma scarcely knew how to answer such a proposition – and the manner in which it was spoken, she could not attempt to equal. Mrs. R. W. eyed her with much familiar curiosity and Triumphant Compassion; – the loss of the Aunt's fortune was uppermost in her mind, at the moment of meeting; – and she could not but feel how much better it was to be the daughter of a gentleman of property in Croydon, than the neice of an old woman who threw herself away on an Irish Captain. – Robert was carelessly kind, as became a prosperous Man and a brother; more intent on settling with the Post-Boy, inveighing against the Exorbitant advance in Posting, and pondering over a doubtful halfcrown, than on welcoming a

Sister, who was no longer likely to have any property for him to get the direction of. – 'Your road through the village is infamous, Elizabeth;' said he, 'worse than ever it was. By Heaven! I would endite[1] it if I lived near you. Who is Surveyor now?' – There was a little neice at Croydon, to be fondly enquired after by the kind-hearted Elizabeth, who regretted very much her not being of the party. – 'You are very good' – replied her Mother – 'and I assure you it went very hard with Augusta to have us come away without her. I was forced to say we were only going to Church and promise to come back for her directly. – But you know it would not do, to bring her without her maid, and I am as particular as ever in having her properly attended to.' 'Sweet little Darling!' – cried Margaret – 'It quite broke my heart to leave her. –' 'Then why was you in such a hurry to run away from her?' cried Mrs. R. – 'You are a sad shabby girl. – I have been quarrelling with you all the way we came, have not I? – Such a visit as this, I never heard of! – You know how glad we are to have any of you with us – if it be for months together. – And I am sorry, (with a witty smile) we have not been able to make Croydon agreable this autumn.' – 'My dearest Jane – do not overpower me with your Raillery. – You know what inducements I had to bring me home, – spare me, I entreat you –. I am no match for your arch sallies. –' 'Well, I only beg you will not set your Neighbours against the place. – Perhaps Emma may be tempted to go back with us, and stay till Christmas, if you don't put in your word.' – Emma was greatly obliged. 'I assure you we have very good society at Croydon. – I do not much attend the Balls, they are rather too mixed, – but our parties are very select and good. – I had seven Tables last week in my Drawingroom. Are you fond of the Country? How do you like Stanton?' – 'Very much' – replied Emma, who thought a comprehensive answer, most to the purpose. – She saw that her Sister-in-law despised her immediately. – Mrs. R. W. was indeed wondering what sort of a home Emma could possibly have been used to in Shropshire, and setting it down as certain that the Aunt could never have had six thousand pounds. – 'How charming Emma is! –' whispered Margaret to Mrs. Robert in her most languishing tone. – Emma was quite distress'd by such behaviour; – and she did not like it better when she heard Margaret five minutes afterwards say to Elizabeth in a sharp quick accent, totally unlike the first – 'Have you heard from Pen. since she went to Chichester? – I had a letter the other day. – I don't find she is likely to make anything of it. I fancy she'll come back "Miss Penelope" as she went. –'

Such, she feared would be Margaret's common voice, when the novelty of her own appearance were over; the tone of artificial Sensibility was not recommended by the idea. – The Ladies were invited upstairs to prepare for dinner. 'I hope you will find things tolerably comfortable Jane' – said Elizabeth as she opened the door of the spare bed-chamber. – 'My good creature,' replied Jane, 'use no ceremony with me, I intreat you. I am one of those who always take things as they find them. I hope I can put up with a small apartment for two or three nights, without making a peice of work. I always wish to be treated quite "en famille" when I come to see you – and now I do hope you have not been getting a great dinner for us. – Remember we never eat suppers.' – 'I suppose,' said Margaret rather quickly to Emma, 'you and I are to be together; Elizabeth always takes care to have a room to herself.' – 'No – Elizabeth gives me half her's.' – 'Oh!' - (in a soften'd voice, and rather mortified to find she was not ill used) 'I am sorry I am not to have the pleasure of your company – especially as it makes me nervous to be much alone.'

Emma was the first of the females in the parlour again; on entering it she found her brother alone. – 'So Emma,' said he, 'you are quite the Stranger at home. It must seem odd enough to you to be here. – A pretty peice of work your Aunt Turner has made of it! – By Heaven! A woman should never be trusted with money. I always said she ought to have settled something on you, as soon as her Husband died.' 'But that would have been trusting *me* with money,' replied Emma, 'and *I* am a woman too. –' 'It might have been secured to your future use, without your having any power over it now. – What a blow it must have been upon you! – To find yourself, instead of heiress of 8 or

9000 £, sent back a weight upon your family, without a sixpence. – I hope the old woman will smart for it.' 'Do not speak disrespectfully of her – She was very good to me; and if she has made an imprudent choice, she will suffer more from it herself, than I can possibly do.' 'I do not mean to distress you, but you know every body must think her an old fool. – I thought Turner had been reckoned an extraordinary sensible, clever man. – How the Devil came he to make such a will?' – 'My Uncle's sense is not at all impeached in my opinion, by his attachment to my Aunt. She had been an excellent wife to him. The most Liberal and enlightened Minds are always the most confiding. – The event has been unfortunate, but my Uncle's memory is if possible endeared to me by such a proof of tender respect for my Aunt.' – 'That's odd sort of Talking! – He might have provided decently for his widow, without leaving every thing that he had to dispose of, or any part of it at her mercy.' – 'My Aunt may have erred' – said Emma warmly – 'she *has* erred – but my Uncle's conduct was faultless. I was her own Neice, and he left to herself the power and the pleasure of providing for me.' – 'But unluckily she has left the pleasure of providing for you, to your Father, and without the power. – That's the long and the short of the business. After keeping you at a distance from your family for such a length of time as must do away all natural affection among us and breeding you up (I suppose) in a superior stile, you are returned upon their hands without a sixpence.' 'You know,' replied Emma struggling with her tears, 'my Uncle's melancholy state of health. – He was a greater Invalid than my father. He could not leave home.' 'I do not mean to make you cry.' – said Robert rather softened – and after a short silence, by way of changing the subject, he added – 'I am just come from my Father's room, he seems very indifferent. It will be a sad break-up when he dies. Pity, you can none of you get married! – You must come to Croydon as well as the rest, and see what you can do there. – I beleive if Margaret had had a thousand or fifteen hundred pounds, there was a young man who would have thought of her.' Emma was glad when they were joined by the others; it was better to look at her Sister-in-law's finery than listen to Robert, who had equally irritated and greived her. – Mrs. Robert exactly as smart as she had been at her own party, came in with apologies for her dress – 'I would not make you wait,' said she, 'so I put on the first thing I met with. – I am afraid I am a sad figure. – My dear Mr. W. – (to her husband) you have not put any fresh powder in your hair.' – 'No – I do not intend it. – I think there is powder enough in my hair for my wife and sisters. –' 'Indeed you ought to make some alteration in your dress before dinner when you are out visitting, tho' you do not at home.' 'Nonsense.' – 'It is very odd you should not like to do what other gentlemen do. Mr. Marshall and Mr. Hemmings change their dress every day of their Lives before dinner. And what was the use of my putting up your last new Coat, if you are never to wear it.' – 'Do be satisfied with being fine yourself, and leave your husband alone.' – To put an end to this altercation, and soften the evident vexation of her sister-in-law, Emma (tho' in no Spirits to make such nonsense easy) began to admire her gown. – It produced immediate complacency. – 'Do you like it?' – said she. – 'I am very happy. – It has been excessively admired; – but sometimes I think the pattern too large. – I shall wear one tomorrow that I think you will prefer to this. – Have you seen the one I gave Margaret?' –

Dinner came, and except when Mrs. R. looked at her husband's head, she continued gay and flippant, chiding Elizabeth for the profusion on the Table, and absolutely protesting against the entrance of the roast Turkey – which formed the only exception to 'You see your dinner'. – 'I do beg and entreat that no Turkey may be seen today. I am really frightened out of my wits with the number of dishes we have already. Let us have no Turkey I beseech you.' – 'My dear,' replied Elizabeth 'the Turkey is roasted, and it may just as well come in, as stay in the Kitchen. Besides if it is cut, I am in hopes my Father may be tempted to eat a bit, for it is rather a favourite dish.' 'You may have it in my dear, but I assure you I shan't touch it.' –

Mr. Watson had not been well enough to join the party at dinner, but was prevailed on to come down and drink tea with them. – 'I wish we may be able to have a game of cards tonight,' said Elizabeth to Mrs. R. after seeing her father comfortably seated in his arm chair. – 'Not on my account my dear, I beg. You know I am no card player. I think a snug chat infinitely better. I always say cards are very well sometimes, to break a formal circle, but one never wants them among friends.' 'I was thinking of it's being something to amuse my father,' answered Elizabeth – 'if it was not disagreable to you. He says his head won't bear Whist – but perhaps if we make a round game he may be tempted to sit down with us.' – 'By all means my dear Creature. I am quite at your service. Only do not oblige me to chuse the game, that's all. *Speculation*[1] is the only round game at Croydon now, but I can play anything. – When there is only one or two of you at home, you must be quite at a loss to amuse him – why do not you get him to play at Cribbage? – Margaret and I have played at Cribbage, most nights that we have not been engaged.' – A sound like a distant Carriage was at this moment caught; everybody listened; it became more decided; it certainly drew nearer. – It was an unusual sound in Stanton at any time of the day, for the Village was on no very public road, and contained no gentleman's family but the Rector's. – The wheels rapidly approached; – in two minutes the general expectation was answered; they stopped beyond a doubt at the garden gate of the Parsonage. 'Who could it be? – it was certainly a postchaise. – Penelope was the only creature to be thought of. She might perhaps have met with some unexpected opportunity of returning.' – A pause of suspense ensued. – Steps were distinguished, first along the paved Footway which led under the windows of the house to the front door, and then within the passage. They were the steps of a Man. It could not be Penelope. It must be Samuel. – The door opened, and displayed Tom Musgrave in the wrap of a Travellor. – He had been in London and was now on his way home, and he had come half a mile out of his road merely to call for ten minutes at Stanton. He loved to take people by surprise, with sudden visits at extraordinary seasons; and in the present instance had had the additional motive of being able to tell the Miss Watsons, whom he depended on finding sitting quietly employed after tea, that he was

going home to an 8 o'clock dinner. – As it happened however, he
did not give more surprise than he received, when instead of
being shewn into the usual little sitting room, the door of the
best parlour a foot larger each way than the other was thrown
open, and he beheld a circle of smart people whom he could not
immediately recognise arranged with all the honours of visiting
round the fire, and Miss Watson sitting at the best Pembroke
Table,[1] with the best Tea things before her. He stood for a few
seconds, in silent amazement. – 'Musgrave!' – ejaculated Margaret in a tender voice. – He recollected himself, and came forward, delighted to find such a circle of Friends, and blessing his
good fortune for the unlooked-for Indulgence. – He shook
hands with Robert, bowed and smiled to the Ladies, and did
everything very prettily; but as to any particularity of address
or Emotion towards Margaret, Emma who closely observed him,
perceived nothing that did not justify Elizabeth's opinions tho'
Margaret's modest smiles imported that she meant to take the
visit to herself. – He was persuaded without much difficulty to
throw off his greatcoat, and drink tea with them. 'For whether
he dined at 8 or 9, as he observed, was a matter of very little
consequence.' – and without seeming to seek, he did not turn
away from the chair close to Margaret which she was assiduous
in providing him. – She had thus secured him from her Sisters –
but it was not immediately in her power to preserve him from her
Brother's claims, for as he came avowedly from London, and had
left it only four hours ago, the last current report as to public
news, and the general opinion of the day must be understood,
before Robert could let his attention be yeilded to the less
national, and important demands of the Women. – At last however he was at liberty to hear Margaret's soft address, as she
spoke her fears of his having had a most terrible, cold, dark
dreadful Journey. – 'Indeed you should not have set out so
late. –' 'I could not be earlier,' he replied. 'I was detained chatting at the Bedford,[2] by a friend. – All hours are alike to me. –
How long have you been in the Country Miss Margaret?' –
'We came only this morning. – My kind Brother and Sister
brought me home this very morning. – 'Tis singular is not it?'

'You were gone a great while, were not you? a fortnight I sup-pose?' – '*You* may call a fortnight a great while Mr. Musgrave,' said Mrs. Robert smartly – 'but *we* think a month very little. I assure you we bring her home at the end of a month, much against our will.' 'A month! have you really been gone a month! 'tis amazing how Time flies. –' 'You may imagine,' said Margaret in a sort of Whisper, what are my Sensations in finding myself once more at Stanton. You know what a sad visitor I make. – And I was so excessively impatient to see Emma; – I dreaded the meeting, and at the same time longed for it. – Do you not comprehend the sort of feeling?' – 'Not at all,' cried he aloud. 'I could never dread a meeting with Miss Emma Watson, – or any of her Sisters.' It was lucky that he added that finish. – 'Were you speaking to me?' – said Emma, who had caught her own name. – 'Not absolutely' – he answered – 'but I was thinking of you, – as many at a greater distance are probably doing at this moment. – Fine open weather Miss Emma! – Charming season for Hunting.' 'Emma is delightful, is not she?' – whispered Margaret. 'I have found her more than answer my warmest hopes. – Did you ever see anything more perfectly beautiful? – I think even *you* must be a convert to a brown complexion.' – He hesitated; Margaret was fair herself, and he did not par-ticularly want to compliment her; but Miss Osborne and Miss Carr were likewise fair, and his devotion to them carried the day. 'Your Sister's complexion,' said he at last, 'is as fine as a dark complexion can be, but I still profess my preference of a white skin. You have seen Miss Osborne? – she is my model for a truly feminine complexion, and she is very fair.' – 'Is she fairer than me?' – Tom made no reply. – 'Upon my Honour Ladies,' said he, giving a glance over his own person, 'I am highly endebted to your Condescension for admitting me, in such Dishabille into your Drawing room. I really did not consider how unfit I was to be here or I hope I should have kept my distance. Lady Osborne would tell me that I were growing as careless as her son, if she saw me in this condition.' – The Ladies were not wanting in civil returns; and Robert Watson stealing a veiw of his own head in an opposite glass, – said with

equal civility, 'You cannot be more in dishabille than myself. –
We got here so late, that I had not time even to put a little fresh
powder in my hair.' – Emma could not help entering into what
she supposed her Sister-in-law's feelings at that moment. –
When the Tea-things were removed, Tom began to talk of his
Carriage – but the old Card Table being set out, and the fish[1]
and counters with a tolerably clean pack brought forward from
the beaufit[2] by Miss Watson, the general voice was so urgent
with him to join their party, that he agreed to allow himself
another quarter of an hour. Even Emma was pleased that he
would stay, for she was beginning to feel that a family party
might be the worst of all parties; and the others were delighted. –
'What's your Game?' – cried he, as they stood round the
Table. – 'Speculation I beleive,' said Elizabeth – 'My Sister
recommends it, and I fancy we all like it. I know *you* do, Tom.' –
'It is the only round game played at Croydon now,' said Mrs.
Robert – 'we never think of any other. I am glad it is a favourite
with you.' – 'Oh! me!' cried Tom. 'Whatever you decide on,
will be a favourite with *me*. – I have had some pleasant hours at
Speculation in my time – but I have not been in the way of it
now for a long while. – Vingt-un is the game at Osborne Castle; I
have played nothing but Vingt-un of late. You would be astonished to hear the noise we make there. – The fine old, lofty Drawing-
room rings again. Lady Osborne sometimes declares she cannot
hear herself speak. – Lord Osborne enjoys it famously – he makes
the best Dealer without exception that I ever beheld – such
quickness and spirit! he lets nobody dream over their cards – I
wish you could see him overdraw himself on both his own
cards - it is worth anything in the World!' – 'Dear me!' – cried
Margaret 'why should not we play at vingt un? – I think it is a
much better game than Speculation. I cannot say I am very
fond of Speculation.' Mrs. Robert offered not another word in
support of the game. – She was quite vanquished, and the
fashions of Osborne-Castle carried it over the fashions of Croydon. – 'Do you see much of the Parsonage family at the Castle,
Mr. Musgrave? –' said Emma, as they were taking their seats. –
'Oh! yes – they are almost always there. Mrs. Blake is a nice

little good-humoured Woman, she and I are sworn friends; and Howard's a very gentlemanlike good sort of fellow! – You are not forgotten I assure you by any of the party. I fancy you must have a little cheek-glowing now and then Miss Emma. Were you not rather warm last Saturday about 9 or 10 o'clock in the Evening –? I will tell you how it was. – I see you are dieing to know. – Says Howard to Lord Osborne –' At this interesting moment he was called on by the others, to regulate the game and determine some disputable point; and his attention was so totally engaged in the business and afterwards by the course of the game as never to revert to what he had been saying before; – and Emma, tho' suffering a good deal from Curiosity, dared not remind him. – He proved a very useful addition to their Table; without him, it would have been a party of such very near relations as could have felt little Interest, and perhaps maintained little complaisance, but his presence gave variety and secured good manners. – He was in fact excellently qualified to shine at a round Game; and few situations made him appear to greater advantage. He played with spirit, and had a great deal to say and tho' with no wit himself, could sometimes make use of the wit of an absent friend; and had a lively way of retailing a commonplace, or saying a mere nothing, that had great effect at a Card Table. The ways, and good Jokes of Osborne Castle were now added to his ordinary means of Entertainment; he repeated the smart sayings of one Lady, detailed the oversights of another, and indulged them even with a copy of Lord Osborne's stile of overdrawing himself on both cards. – The Clock struck nine, while he was thus agreably occupied; and when Nanny came in with her Master's Bason of Gruel, he had the pleasure of observing to Mr. Watson that he should leave him at supper, while he went home to dinner himself. – The Carriage was ordered to the door – and no entreaties for his staying longer could now avail, – for he well knew, that if he staid he must sit down to supper in less than ten minutes – which to a Man whose heart had been long fixed on calling his next meal a Dinner, was quite insupportable. – On finding him determined to go, Margaret began to wink and nod at Elizabeth to ask him to dinner for the following day; and Elizabeth at last not able to resist hints, which her own hospitable, social temper more than half seconded, gave the invitation. 'Would he give Robert the meeting, they should be very happy.' 'With the greatest pleasure' – was his first reply. In a moment afterwards – 'That is if I can possibly get here in time – but I shoot with Lord Osborne, and therefore must not engage – You will not think of me unless you see me.' – And so, he departed, delighted with the uncertainty in which he had left it. –

*

Margaret in the joy of her heart under circumstances which she chose to consider as peculiarly propitious, would willingly have made a confidante of Emma when they were alone for a short time the next morning; and had proceeded so far as to say – 'The young man who was here last night my dear Emma and returns today, is more interesting to me, than perhaps you may be aware –' but Emma pretending to understand nothing extraordinary in the words, made some very inapplicable reply, and jumping up, ran away from a subject which was odious to her feelings. –

As Margaret would not allow a doubt to be repeated of Musgrave's coming to dinner, preparations were made for his Entertainment much exceeding what had been deemed necessary the day before; and taking the office of superintendance intirely from her sister, she was half the morning in the Kitchen herself directing and scolding. – After a great deal of indifferent Cooking, and anxious Suspense however they were obliged to sit down without their Guest. – T. Musgrave never came, and Margaret was at no pains to conceal her vexation under the disappointment, or repress the peevishness of her Temper –. The Peace of the party for the remainder of that day, and the whole of the next, which comprised the length of Robert and Jane's visit, was continually invaded by her fretful displeasure, and querulous attacks. – Elizabeth was the usual object of both. Margaret had just respect enough for her Brother and Sister's opinion, to behave properly by *them*, but Elizabeth and the maids could never do anything right – and Emma, whom she seemed no longer to think about, found the continuance of the gentle voice beyond her calculation short. Eager to be as little among them as possible, Emma was delighted with the alternative of sitting above, with her father, and warmly entreated to be his constant Companion each Evening – and as Elizabeth loved company of any kind too well, not to prefer being below, at all risks, as she had rather talk of Croydon to Jane, with every interruption of Margaret's perverseness, than sit with only her father, who frequently could not endure Talking at all, the affair was so settled, as soon as she could be persuaded to beleive it no sacrifice on her Sister's part. – To Emma, the exchange was most acceptable, and delightful. Her father, if ill, required little more than gentleness and silence; and, being a Man of Sense and Education, was if able to converse, a welcome companion. –

In *his* chamber, Emma was at peace from the dreadful mortifications of unequal Society, and family Discord – from the immediate endurance of Hard-hearted prosperity, low-minded Conceit, and wrong-headed folly, engrafted on an untoward Disposition. – She still suffered from them in the Contemplation of their existence; in memory and in prospect, but for the moment, she ceased to be tortured by their effects. – She was at leisure, she could read and think, – tho' her situation was hardly such as to make reflection very soothing. The Evils arising from the loss of her Uncle, were neither trifling, nor likely to lessen; and when Thought had been freely indulged, in contrasting the past and the present, the employment of mind, the dissipation of unpleasant ideas which only reading could produce, made her thankfully turn to a book. – The change in her home society, and stile of Life in consequence of the death of one friend and the imprudence of another had indeed been striking. – From being the first object of Hope and Solicitude of an Uncle who had formed her mind with the care of a Parent, and of Tenderness to an Aunt whose amiable temper had delighted to give her every indulgence, from being the Life and Spirit of a House, where all had been comfort and Elegance, and the expected Heiress of an easy Independance, she was become

of importance to no one, a burden on those, whose affection she
could not expect, an addition in an House, already overstocked,
surrounded by inferior minds with little chance of domestic
comfort, and as little hope of future support. – It was well for
her that she was naturally chearful; – for the Change had been
such as might have plunged weak spirits in Despondence. –

She was very much pressed by Robert and Jane to return
with them to Croydon, and had some difficulty in getting a
refusal accepted; as they thought too highly of their own kindness and situation, to suppose the offer could appear in a less
advantageous light to anybody else. – Elizabeth gave them her
interest, tho' evidently against her own, in privately urging
Emma to go – 'You do not know what you refuse Emma' – said
she – 'nor what you have to bear at home. – I would advise you
by all means to accept the invitation, there is always something
lively going on at Croydon, you will be in company almost every
day, and Robert and Jane will be very kind to you. – As for me, I
shall be no worse off without you, than I have been used to be;
but poor Margaret's disagreable ways are new to *you*, and they
would vex you more than you think for, if you stay at home. –'
Emma was of course un-influenced, except to greater esteem for
Elizabeth, by such representations – and the Visitors departed
without her. –

SANDITON

CHAPTER I

A GENTLEMAN and Lady travelling from Tunbridge towards that part of the Sussex Coast which lies between Hastings and E. Bourne, being induced by Business to quit the high road, and attempt a very rough Lane, were overturned in toiling up its long ascent half rock, half sand. – The accident happened just beyond the only Gentleman's House near the Lane – a House, which their Driver on being first required to take that direction, had conceived to be necessarily their object, and had with most unwilling Looks been constrained to pass by –. He had grumbled and shaken his shoulders so much indeed, and pitied and cut his Horses so sharply, that he might have been open to the suspicion of overturning them on purpose (especially as the Carriage was not his Masters own) if the road had not indisputably become considerably worse than before, as soon as the premises of the said House were left behind – expressing with a most intelligent portentous countenance that beyond it no wheels but cart wheels could safely proceed. The severity of the fall was broken by their slow pace and the narrowness of the Lane, and the Gentleman having scrambled out and helped out his companion, they niether of them at first felt more than shaken and bruised. But the Gentleman had in the course of the extrication sprained his foot – and soon becoming sensible of it, was obliged in a few moments to cut short, both his remonstrance to the Driver and his congratulations to his wife and himself – and sit down on the bank, unable to stand. – 'There is something wrong here,' said he – putting his hand to his ancle – 'But never mind, my Dear – (looking up at her with a smile) – It could not

have happened, you know, in a better place. – Good out of
Evil –. The very thing perhaps to be wished for. We shall soon
get releif. – *There*, I fancy lies my cure' – pointing to the neat-
looking end of a Cottage, which was seen romantically situated
among wood on a high Eminence at some little Distance – 'Does
not *that* promise to be the very place?' – His wife fervently
hoped it was – but stood, terrified and anxious, neither able to do
or suggest anything – and receiving her first real comfort from
the sight of several persons now coming to their assistance. The
accident had been discerned from a Hayfield adjoining the
House they had passed – and the persons who approached,
were a well-looking Hale, Gentlemanlike Man, of middle age,
the Proprietor of the Place, who happened to be among his Hay-
makers at the time, and three or four of the ablest of them
summoned to attend their Master – to say nothing of all the rest
of the field, Men, Women and Children – not very far off. – Mr.
Heywood, such was the name of the said Proprietor, advanced
with a very civil salutation – much concern for the accident –
some surprise at any body's attempting that road in a Carriage –
and ready offers of assistance. His courtesies were received with
Good-breeding and gratitude and while one or two of the Men
lent their help to the Driver in getting the Carriage upright
again, the Travellor said – 'You are extremely obliging Sir, and
I take you at your word. – The injury to my Leg is I dare say
very trifling, but it is always best in these cases to have a surgeon's
opinion without loss of time; and as the road does not seem at
present in a favourable state for my getting up to his house
myself, I will thank you to send off one of these good People for
the Surgeon.' 'The Surgeon Sir!' – replied Mr. Heywood – 'I
am afraid you will find no surgeon at hand here, but I dare say
we shall do very well without him.' – 'Nay Sir, if *he* is not in the
way, his Partner will do just as well – or rather better –. I would
rather see his Partner indeed – I would prefer the attendance of
his Partner. – One of these good people can be with him in
three minutes I am sure. I need not ask whether I see the
House; (looking towards the Cottage) for excepting your own,
we have passed none in this place, which can be the Abode of a

Gentleman.' – Mr. H. looked very much astonished – and
replied – 'What Sir! are you expecting to find a Surgeon in that
Cottage? – We have neither Surgeon nor Partner in the Parish I
assure you.' – 'Excuse me Sir' – replied the other. 'I am sorry to
have the appearance of contradicting you – but though from the
extent of the Parish or some other cause you may not be aware of
the fact; – Stay – Can I be mistaken in the place? – Am I not in
Willingden? – Is not this Willingden?' 'Yes Sir, this is certainly
Willingden.' 'Then Sir, I can bring proof of your having a
Surgeon in the Parish – whether you may know it or not. Here
Sir – (taking out his Pocket book –) if you will do me the favour
of casting your eye over these advertisements, which I cut out
myself from the Morning Post and the Kentish Gazette,[1] only
yesterday morning in London – I think you will be convinced
that I am not speaking at random. You will find it an advertisement Sir, of the dissolution of a Partnership in the Medical
Line – in your own Parish – extensive Business – undeniable
Character – respectable references – wishing to form a separate
Establishment – You will find it at full length Sir' – offering him
the two little oblong extracts. – 'Sir' – said Mr. Heywood with a
good humoured smile – 'if you were to shew me all the Newspapers that are printed in one week throughout the Kingdom,
you would not persuade me of there being a Surgeon in Willingden, – for having lived here ever since I was born, Man and Boy
fifty-seven years, I think I must have *known* of such a person, at
least I may venture to say that he has not *much Business* – To be
sure, if Gentlemen were to be often attempting this Lane in
Post-chaises, it might not be a bad speculation for a Surgeon to
get a House at the top of the Hill. – But as to that Cottage, I
can assure you Sir that it is in fact – (inspite of its spruce air at
this distance –) as indifferent a double Tenement as any in the
Parish, and that my Shepherd lives at one end, and three old
women at the other.' He took the peices of paper as he spoke –
and having looked them over, added – 'I beleive I can explain it
Sir. – Your mistake is in the place. – There are two Willingdens
in this Country – and your advertisements refer to the other –
which is Great Willingden, or Willingden Abbots, and lies

seven miles off, on the other side of Battel – quite down in the
Weald. And *we* Sir – ' (speaking rather proudly) 'are not in the
Weald.' – 'Not *down* in the Weald I am sure Sir,' replied the
Traveller, pleasantly. 'It took us half an hour to climb your
Hill. – Well Sir – I dare say it is as you say, and I have made an
abominably stupid Blunder. – All done in a moment; – the
advertisements did not catch my eye till the last half hour of our
being in Town; – when everything was in the hurry and confusion which always attend a short stay there – One is never
able to complete anything in the way of Business you know till
the Carriage is at the door – and accordingly satisfying myself
with a breif enquiry, and finding we were actually to pass within
a mile or two of a *Willingden*, I sought no farther ... My Dear –'
(to his wife) 'I am very sorry to have brought you into this
Scrape. But do not be alarmed about my Leg. It gives me no
pain while I am quiet, – and as soon as these good people have
succeeded in setting the Carriage to rights and turning the
Horses round, the best thing we can do will be to measure back
our steps into the Turnpike road and proceed to Hailsham, and
so Home, without attempting anything farther. – Two hours
take us home, from Hailsham – And when once at home, we
have our remedy at hand you know. – A little of our own Bracing
Sea Air will soon set me on my feet again. – Depend upon it my
Dear, it is exactly a case for the Sea. Saline air and immersion[1]
will be the very thing. – My sensations tell me so already.' – In a
most friendly manner Mr. Heywood here interposed, entreating
them not to think of proceeding till the ancle had been examined,
and some refreshment taken, and very cordially pressing them to
make use of his House for both purposes. – 'We are always well
stocked,' said he, 'with all the common remedies for Sprains
and Bruises – and I will answer for the pleasure it will give my
Wife and daughters to be of service to you and this Lady in every
way in their power.' – A twinge or two, in trying to move his
foot disposed the Travellor to think rather more as he had done
at first of the benefit of immediate assistance – and consulting
his wife in the few words of 'Well my Dear, I beleive it will be
better for us.' – turned again to Mr. H – and said – 'Before we

accept your Hospitality Sir, – and in order to do away with any unfavourable impression which the sort of wild goose-chace you find me in, may have given rise to – allow me to tell you who we are. My name is Parker. – Mr. Parker of Sanditon; this Lady, my wife Mrs. Parker. – We are on our road home from London; – *My* name perhaps – tho' I am by no means the first of my Family, holding Landed Property in the Parish of Sanditon, may be unknown at this distance from the Coast – but Sanditon itself – everybody has heard of Sanditon, – the favourite – for a young and rising Bathing-place, certainly the favourite spot of all that are to be found along the coast of Sussex; – the most favoured by Nature, and promising to be the most chosen by Man.' – 'Yes – I have heard of Sanditon.' replied Mr. H. – 'Every five years, one hears of some new place or other starting up by the Sea, and growing the fashion. – How they can half of them be filled, is the wonder! *Where* People can be found with Money or Time to go to them! – Bad things for a Country; – sure to raise the price of Provisions and make the poor good for nothing – as I dare say you find, Sir.' 'Not at all Sir, not at all' – cried Mr. Parker eagerly. 'Quite the contrary I assure you. – A common idea – but a mistaken one. It may apply to your large, overgrown Places, like Brighton, or Worthing, or East Bourne – but *not* to a small Village like Sanditon, precluded by its size from experiencing any of the evils of Civilization, while the growth of the place, the Buildings, the Nursery Grounds, the demand for every thing, and the sure resort of the very best Company, those regular, steady, private Families of thorough Gentility and Character, who are a blessing everywhere, excite the industry of the Poor and diffuse comfort and improvement among them of every sort. – No Sir, I assure you, Sanditon is not a place—' 'I do not mean to take exceptions to *any* place in particular Sir,' answered Mr. H. – 'I only think our Coast is too full of them altogether – But had we not better try to get you' – 'Our Coast too full' – repeated Mr. P. – 'On that point perhaps we may not totally disagree; – at least there are *enough*. Our Coast is abundant enough; it demands no more. – Every body's Taste and every body's finances may be suited –

And those good people who are trying to add to the number, are
in my opinion excessively absurd, and must soon find themselves
the Dupes of their own fallacious Calculations. – Such a place as
Sanditon Sir, I may say was wanted, was called for. – Nature
had marked it out – had spoken in most intelligible Characters –
The finest, purest Sea Breeze on the Coast – acknowledged to be
so – Excellent Bathing – fine hard Sand – Deep Water ten yards
from the Shore – no Mud – no Weeds – no slimey rocks – Never
was there a place more palpably designed by Nature for the
resort of the Invalid – the very Spot which Thousands seemed in
need of. – The most desirable distance from London! One
complete, measured mile nearer than East Bourne. Only conceive
Sir, the advantage of saving a whole Mile, in a long Journey.
But Brinshore Sir, which I dare say you have in your eye – the
attempts of two or three speculating People about Brinshore,
this last Year, to raise that paltry Hamlet, lying, as it does
between a stagnant marsh, a bleak Moor and the constant
effluvia of a ridge of putrifying sea weed, can end in nothing
but their own Disappointment. What in the name of Common
Sense is to *recommend* Brinshore? – A most insalubrious Air –
Roads proverbially detestable – Water Brackish beyond example,
impossible to get a good dish of Tea within three miles of the
place – and as for the Soil – it is so cold and ungrateful that it
can hardly be made to yeild a Cabbage. – Depend upon it Sir,
that this is a faithful Description of Brinshore – not in the
smallest degree exaggerated – and if you have heard it differently
spoken of –' 'Sir I never heard it spoken of in my Life before,'
said Mr. Heywood. 'I did not know there was such a place in
the World.' 'You did not! – There my Dear – (turning with
exultation to his Wife) – you see how it is. So much for the
Celebrity of Brinshore! – This Gentleman did not know there
was such a place in the World. – Why, in truth Sir, I fancy we
may apply to Brinshore, that line of the Poet Cowper[1] in his
description of the religious Cottager, as opposed to Voltaire –
"*She*, never heard of half a mile from home."' – 'With all my
Heart Sir - Apply any Verses you like to it – But I want to see
something applied to your Leg – and I am sure by your Lady's

countenance that she is quite of my opinion and thinks it a pity
to lose any more time – And here come my Girls to speak for
themselves and their Mother. (two or three genteel looking
young Women followed by as many Maid servants, were now
seen issueing from the House) – I began to wonder the Bustle
should not have reached *them*. – A thing of this kind soon makes
a Stir in a lonely place like ours. – Now Sir, let us see how you
can be best conveyed into the House.' – The young Ladies
approached and said every thing that was proper to recommend
their Father's offers; and in an unaffected manner calculated to
make the Strangers easy – And as Mrs. P. – was exceedingly
anxious for relief – and her Husband by this time, not much less
disposed for it – a very few civil scruples were enough – especially
as the Carriage being now set up, was discovered to have received such Injury on the fallen side as to be unfit for present
use. – Mr. Parker was therefore carried into the House, and his
Carriage wheeled off to a vacant Barn.—

CHAPTER II

THE acquaintance, thus oddly begun, was neither short nor
unimportant. For a whole fortnight the Travellors were fixed at
Willingden; Mr. P.'s sprain proving too serious for him to move
sooner. – He had fallen into very good hands. The Heywoods
were a thoroughly respectable family, and every possible attention was paid in the kindest and most unpretending manner, to
both Husband and wife. *He* was waited on and nursed, and *she*
cheered and comforted with unremitting kindness – and as every
office of Hospitality and friendliness was received as it ought –
as there was not more good will on one side than Gratitude on
the other – nor any deficiency of generally pleasant manners on
either, they grew to like each other in the course of that fortnight, exceedingly well. – Mr. Parker's Character and History
were soon unfolded. All that he understood of himself, he readily
told, for he was very openhearted; – and where he might be

himself in the dark, his conversation was still giving information, to such of the Heywoods as could observe. – By such he was perceived to be an Enthusiast; – on the subject of Sanditon, a complete Enthusiast. – Sanditon, – the success of Sanditon as a small, fashionable Bathing Place was the object, for which he seemed to live. A very few years ago, and it had been a quiet Village of no pretensions; but some natural advantages in its position and some accidental circumstances having suggested to himself, and the other principal Land Holder, the probability of its becoming a profitable Speculation, they had engaged in it, and planned and built, and praised and puffed, and raised it to a Something of young Renown – and Mr. Parker could now think of very little besides. – The Facts, which in more direct communication, he laid before them were that he was about five and thirty – had been married, – very happily married seven years – and had four sweet Children at home; – that he was of a respectable Family, and easy though not large fortune; – no Profession – succeeding as eldest son to the Property which two or three Generations had been holding and accumulating before him; – that he had two Brothers and two Sisters – all single and all independant – the eldest of the two former indeed, by collateral Inheritance, quite as well provided for as himself. – His object in quitting the high road, to hunt for an advertising Surgeon, was also plainly stated; – it had not proceeded from any intention of spraining his ancle or doing himself any other Injury for the good of such Surgeon – nor (as Mr. H. had been apt to suppose) from any design of entering into Partnership with him –; it was merely in consequence of a wish to establish some medical Man at Sanditon, which the nature of the Advertisement induced him to expect to accomplish in Willingden. – He was convinced that the advantage of a medical Man at hand would very materially promote the rise and prosperity of the Place – would in fact tend to bring a prodigious influx; – nothing else was wanting. He had *strong* reason to beleive that *one* family had been deterred last year from trying Sanditon on that account – and probably very many more – and his own Sisters who were sad Invalids, and whom he was very anxious to get to Sanditon this Summer, could hardly be expected to hazard themselves in a place where they could not have immediate medical advice. – Upon the whole, Mr. P. was evidently an amiable, family-man, fond of Wife, Children, Brothers and Sisters – and generally kind-hearted; – Liberal, gentleman-like, easy to please; – of a sanguine turn of mind, with more Imagination than Judgement. And Mrs. P. was as evidently a gentle, amiable, sweet tempered Woman, the properest wife in the World for a Man of strong Understanding, but not of capacity to supply the cooler reflection which her own Husband sometimes needed, and so entirely waiting to be guided on every occasion, that whether he were risking his Fortune or spraining his Ancle, she remained equally useless. – Sanditon was a second Wife and four Children to him – hardly less Dear – and certainly more engrossing. – He could talk of it for ever. – It had indeed the highest claims; – not only those of Birthplace, Property, and Home, – it was his Mine, his Lottery, his Speculation and his Hobby Horse; his Occupation his Hope and his Futurity. – He was extremely desirous of drawing his good friends at Willingden thither; and his endeavours in the cause, were as grateful and disinterested, as they were warm. – He wanted to secure the promise of a visit – to get as many of the Family as his own house would contain, to follow him to Sanditon as soon as possible – and healthy as they all undeniably were – foresaw that every one of them would be benefited by the sea. – He held it indeed as certain, that no person could be really well, no person, (however upheld for the present by fortuitous aids of exercise and spirits in a semblance of Health) could be really in a state of secure and permanent Health without spending at least six weeks by the Sea every year. – The Sea air and Sea Bathing together were nearly infallible, one or the other of them being a match for every Disorder, of the Stomach, the Lungs or the Blood; They were anti-spasmodic,[1] anti-pulmonary, anti-sceptic, anti-bilious and anti-rheumatic. Nobody could catch cold by the Sea, Nobody wanted Appetite by the Sea, Nobody wanted Spirits, Nobody wanted Strength. – They were healing, softing, relaxing – fortifying and bracing – seem-

ingly just as was wanted – sometimes one, sometimes the other. –
If the Sea breeze failed, the Sea-Bath was the certain corrective;
– and where Bathing disagreed, the Sea Breeze alone was evidently
designed by Nature for the cure. – His eloquence however
could not prevail. Mr. and Mrs. H. never left home. Marrying
early and having a very numerous Family, their movements had
been long limitted to one small circle; and they were older in
Habits than in Age. – Excepting two Journeys to London in the
year, to receive his Dividends, Mr. H. went no farther than his
feet or his well-tried old Horse could carry him, and Mrs.
Heywood's Adventurings were only now and then to visit her
Neighbours, in the old Coach which had been new when they
married and fresh lined on their eldest Son's coming of age ten
years ago. – They had very pretty Property – enough, had their
family been of reasonable Limits to have allowed them a very
gentlemanlike share of Luxuries and Change – enough for them
to have indulged in a new Carriage and better roads, an occasional month at Tunbridge Wells, and symptoms of the
Gout and a Winter at Bath; – but the maintenance, Education
and fitting out of fourteen Children demanded a very quiet,
settled, careful course of Life – and obliged them to be stationary
and healthy at Willingden. What Prudence had at first enjoined,
was now rendered pleasant by Habit. They never left home, and
they had a gratification in saying so. – But very far from wishing
their Children to do the same, they were glad to promote *their*
getting out into the World, as much as possible. *They* staid at
home, that their Children *might* get out; – and while making
that home extremely comfortable, welcomed every change from
it which could give useful connections or respectable acquaintance to Sons or Daughters. When Mr. and Mrs. Parker therefore ceased from soliciting a family-visit, and bounded their
veiws to carrying back one Daughter with them, no difficulties
were started. It was general pleasure and consent. – Their
invitation was to Miss Charlotte Heywood, a very pleasing
young woman of two and twenty, the eldest of the Daughters at
home, and the one, who under her Mother's directions had been
particularly useful and obliging to them; who had attended

them most, and knew them best. – Charlotte was to go, – with
excellent health, to bathe and be better if she could – to receive
every possible pleasure which Sanditon could be made to
supply by the gratitude of those she went with – and to buy new
Parasols, new Gloves, and new Broches, for her sisters and herself
at the Library, which Mr. P. was anxiously wishing to support. –
All that Mr. Heywood himself could be persuaded to promise
was, that he would send everyone to Sanditon, who asked his
advice, and that nothing should ever induce him (as far as the
future could be answered for) to spend even five shillings at
Brinshore.—

CHAPTER III

Every Neighbourhood should have a great Lady. – The great
Lady of Sanditon, was Lady Denham; and in their Journey
from Willingden to the Coast, Mr. Parker gave Charlotte a more
detailed account of her, than had been called for before. – She
had been necessarily often mentioned at Willingden, – for being
his Colleague in Speculation, Sanditon itself could not be talked
of long, without the introduction of Lady Denham and that she
was a very rich old Lady, who had buried two Husbands, who
knew the value of Money, was very much looked up to and had a
poor Cousin living with her, were facts already well known, but
some further particulars of her history and her Character served
to lighten the tediousness of a long Hill, or a heavy bit of road,
and to give the visiting Young Lady a suitable Knowledge of the
Person with whom she might now expect to be daily associating.
– Lady D. had been a rich Miss Brereton, born to Wealth but
not to Education. Her first Husband had been a Mr. Hollis, a man
of considerable Property in the Country, of which a large share
of the Parish of Sanditon, with Manor and Mansion House
made a part. He had been an elderly Man when she married
him; – her own age about thirty. – Her motives for such a Match
could be little understood at the distance of forty years, but she
had so well nursed and pleased Mr. Hollis, that at his death he

left her everything – all his Estates, and all at her Disposal.
After a widowhood of some years, she had been induced to
marry again. The late Sir Harry Denham, of Denham Park in
the Neighbourhood of Sanditon had succeeded in removing her
and her large Income to his own Domains, but he could not
succeed in the veiws of permanently enriching his family, which
were attributed to him. She had been too wary to put anything out
of her own Power – and when on Sir Harry's Decease she returned
again to her own House at Sanditon, she was said to have made
this boast to a friend 'that though she had *got* nothing but her
Title from the Family, still she had *given* nothing for it.' – For
the Title, it was to be supposed that she had married – and Mr.
P. acknowledged there being just such a degree of value for it
apparent now, as to give her conduct that natural explanation.
'There is at times,' said he – 'a little self-importance – but it is
not offensive; – and there are moments, there are points, when
her Love of Money is carried greatly too far. But she is a good-
natured Woman, a very goodnatured Woman, – a very obliging,
friendly Neighbour; a chearful, independant, valuable character.
– and her faults may be entirely imputed to her want of Education. She has good natural Sense, but quite uncultivated. – She
has a fine active mind, as well as a fine healthy frame for a
Woman of seventy, and enters into the improvement of Sanditon
with a spirit truly admirable – though now and then, a Littleness
will appear. She cannot look forward quite as I would have her –
and takes alarm at a trifling present expence, without considering
what returns it *will* make her in a year or two. That is – we think
differently, we now and then, see things *differently*, Miss H. –
Those who tell their own Story you know must be listened to
with Caution. – When you see us in contact, you will judge for
yourself.' – Lady D. was indeed a great Lady beyond the common wants of Society – for she had many Thousands a year to
bequeath, and three distinct sets of People to be courted by; her
own relations, who might very reasonably wish for her Original
Thirty Thousand Pounds among them, the legal Heirs of Mr.
Hollis, who must hope to be more endebted to *her* sense of
Justice than he had allowed them to be to *his*, and those Members

of the Denham Family, whom her second Husband had hoped
to make a good Bargain for. – By all of these, or by Branches of
them, she had no doubt been long, and still continued to be,
well attacked; – and of these divisions, Mr. P. did not hesitate to
say that Mr. Hollis' Kindred were the *least* in favour and Sir
Harry Denham's the *most*. – The former he beleived, had done
themselves irremediable harm by expressions of very unwise
and unjustifiable resentment at the time of Mr. Hollis's death; –
the Latter, to the advantage of being the remnant of a Connection which she certainly valued, joined those of having been
known to her from their Childhood, and of being always at hand
to preserve their interest by reasonable attention. Sir Edward,
the present Baronet, nephew to Sir Harry, resided constantly at
Denham Park; and Mr. P. had little doubt, that he and his
Sister Miss D. who lived with him, would be principally
remembered in her Will. He sincerely hoped it. – Miss Denham
had a very small provision – and her Brother was a poor Man for
his rank in Society. 'He is a warm friend to Sanditon' – said Mr.
Parker – 'and his hand would be as liberal as his heart, had he
the Power. – He would be a noble Coadjutor! – As it is, he does
what he can – and is running up a tasteful little Cottage Ornèe,[1]
on a strip of Waste Ground Lady D. has granted him, which I
have no doubt we shall have many a Candidate for, before the
end even of *this* Season.' Till within the last twelvemonth, Mr.
P. had considered Sir Edward as standing without a rival, as
having the fairest chance of succeeding to the greater part of all
that she had to give – but there was now another person's claims
to be taken into the account, those of the young female relation,
whom Lady D. had been induced to receive into her Family.
After having always protested against any such Addition, and
long and often enjoyed the repeated defeats she had given to
every attempt of her relations to introduce this young Lady, or
that young Lady as a Companion at Sanditon House, she had
brought back with her from London last Michaelmas a Miss
Brereton, who bid fair by her Merits to vie in favour with Sir
Edward, and to secure for herself and her family that share of the
accumulated Property which they had certainly the best right to

inherit. – Mr. Parker spoke warmly of Clara Brereton, and the interest of his story increased very much with the introduction of such a Character. Charlotte listened with more than amusement now; – it was solicitude and Enjoyment, as she heard her described to be lovely, amiable, gentle, unassuming, conducting herself uniformly with great good sense, and evidently gaining by her innate worth, on the affections of her Patroness. – Beauty, Sweetness, Poverty and Dependance, do not want the imagination of a Man to operate upon. With due exceptions – Woman feels for Woman very promptly and compassionately. He gave the particulars which had led to Clara's admission at Sanditon, as no bad exemplification of that mixture of Character, that union of Littleness with Kindness with Good Sence with even Liberality which he saw in Lady D. – After having avoided London for many years, principally on account of these very Cousins, who were continually writing, inviting and tormenting her, and whom she was determined to keep at a distance, she had been obliged to go there last Michaelmas with the certainty of being detained at least a fortnight. – She had gone to an Hotel – living by her own account as prudently as possible, to defy the reputed expensiveness of such a home, and at the end of three Days calling for her Bill, that she might judge of her state. – Its amount was such as determined her on staying not another hour in the House, and she was preparing in all the anger and perturbation which a beleif of very gross imposition *there*, and an ignorance of where to go for better usage, to leave the Hotel at all hazards, when the Cousins, the politic and lucky Cousins, who seemed always to have a spy on her, introduced themselves at this important moment, and learning her situation, persuaded her to accept such a home for the rest of her stay as their humbler house in a very inferior part of London, could offer. – She went; was delighted with her welcome and the hospitality and attention she received from every body – found her good Cousins the B.s beyond her expectation worthy people – and finally was impelled by a personal knowledge of their narrow Income and pecuniary difficulties, to invite one of the girls of the family to pass the Winter with her. The invitation was to *one*, for six months – with the probability of another being then to take her place; – but in *selecting* the one, Lady D. had shewn the good part of her Character – for passing by the actual *daughters* of the House, she had chosen Clara, a Neice—, more helpless and more pitiable of course than any – a dependant on Poverty – an additional Burthen on an encumbered Circle – and one, who had been so low in every worldly veiw, as with all her natural endowments and powers, to have been preparing for a situation little better than a Nursery Maid. - Clara had returned with her - and by her good sence and merit had now, to all appearance secured a very strong hold in Lady D.'s regard. The six months had long been over – and not a syllable was breathed of any change, or exchange. – She was a general favourite; – the influence of her steady conduct and mild, gentle Temper was felt by everybody. The prejudices which had met her at first in some quarters, were all dissipated. She was felt to be worthy of Trust – to be the very companion who would guide and soften Lady D. – who would enlarge her mind and open her hand. – She was as thoroughly amiable as she was lovely – and since having had the advantage of their Sanditon Breezes, that Loveliness was complete.

CHAPTER IV

'AND whose very snug-looking Place is this?' – said Charlotte, as in a sheltered Dip within two miles of the Sea, they passed close by a moderate-sized house, well fenced and planted, and rich in the Garden, Orchard and Meadows which are the best embellishments of such a Dwelling. 'It seems to have as many comforts about it as Willingden.' – 'Ah' - said Mr. P. – 'This is my old House – the house of my Forefathers – the house where I and all my Brothers and Sisters were born and bred – and where my own three eldest Children were born – where Mrs. P. and I lived till within the last two years – till our new House was finished. – I am glad you are pleased with it. - It is an honest old Place – and Hillier keeps it in very good order. I have given it up

you know to the Man who occupies the cheif of my Land. *He*
gets a better House by it – and I, a rather better situation! – one
other Hill brings us to Sanditon – modern Sanditon – a beautiful
Spot. – Our Ancestors, you know always built in a hole. – Here
were we, pent down in this little contracted Nook, without Air
or Veiw, only one mile and three quarters from the noblest
expanse of Ocean between the South foreland and the Land's
end, and without the smallest advantage from it. You will not
think I have made a bad exchange, when we reach Trafalgar
House – which by the bye, I almost wish I had not named
Trafalgar – for Waterloo is more the thing now. However,
Waterloo is in reserve – and if we have encouragement enough
this year for a little Crescent to be ventured on – (as I trust we
shall) then, we shall be able to call it Waterloo Crescent – and
the name joined to the form of the Building, which always
takes, will give us the command of Lodgers—. In a good Season
we should have more applications than we could attend to.' –
'It was always a very comfortable House' – said Mrs. Parker –
looking at it through the back window with something like the
fondness of regret. – 'And such a nice Garden – such an excellent
Garden.' 'Yes, my Love, but *that* we may be said to carry with
us. – *It* supplies us, as before, with all the fruit and vegetables
we want; and we have in fact all the comfort of an excellent
Kitchen Garden, without the constant Eyesore of its formalities;
or the yearly nuisance of its decaying vegetation. – Who can
endure a Cabbage Bed in October?' 'Oh! dear – yes – We are
quite as well off for Gardenstuff as ever we were – for if it is
forgot to be brought at any time, we can always buy what we
want at Sanditon-House. – The Gardiner there, is glad enough
to supply us—. But it was a nice place for the Children to run
about in. So Shady in Summer!' 'My dear, we shall have shade
enough on the Hill and more than enough in the course of a very
few years; – The Growth of my Plantations is a general astonishment. In the mean while we have the Canvas Awning, which
gives us the most complete comfort within doors – and you can
get a Parasol at Whitby's for little Mary at any time, or a large
Bonnet at Jebb's – and as for the Boys, I must say I would

rather *them* run about in the Sunshine than not. I am sure we
agree my dear, in wishing our Boys to be as hardy as possible.' –
'Yes indeed, I am sure we do – and I will get Mary a little
Parasol, which will make her as proud as can be. How Grave she
will walk about with it, and fancy herself quite a little Woman. –
Oh! I have not the smallest doubt of our being a great deal
better off where we are now. If we any of us want to bathe, we
have not a quarter of a mile to go. – But you know, (still looking
back) one loves to look at an old friend, at a place where one has
been happy. – The Hilliers did not seem to feel the Storms last
Winter at all. – I remember seeing Mrs. Hillier after one of
those dreadful Nights, when *we* had been literally rocked in our
bed, and she did not seem at all aware of the Wind being anything more than common.' 'Yes, yes – that's likely enough. *We*
have all the Grandeur of the Storm, with less real danger,
because the Wind meeting with nothing to oppose or confine it
around our House, simply rages and passes on – while down in
this Gutter – nothing is known of the state of the Air, below the
Tops of the Trees – and the Inhabitants may be taken totally
unawares, by one of those dreadful Currents which do more
mischief in a Valley, when they *do* arise than an open Country
ever experiences in the heaviest Gale. – But my dear Love – as to
Gardenstuff; – you were saying that any accidental omission is
supplied in a moment by Lady D.'s Gardiner – but it occurs to
me that we ought to go elsewhere upon such occasions – and
that old Stringer and his son have a higher claim. I encouraged
him to set up – and am afraid he does not do very well – that is,
there has not been time enough yet. – He *will* do very well beyond a doubt – but at first it is Uphill work; and therefore we
must give him what Help we can – and when any Vegetables or
fruit happen to be wanted – and it will not be amiss to have
them often wanted, to have something or other forgotten most
days; – Just to have a nominal supply you know, that poor old
Andrew may not lose his daily Job – but in fact to buy the
cheif of our consumption of the Stringers. – ' 'Very well my
Love, that can be easily done – and Cook will be satisfied –
which will be a great comfort, for she is always complaining of

old Andrew now, and says he never brings her what she wants. – There – now the old House is quite left behind. – What is it, your Brother Sidney says about it's being a Hospital?' 'Oh! my dear Mary, merely a Joke of his. He pretends to advise me to make a Hospital of it. He pretends to laugh at my Improvements. Sidney says any thing you know. He has always said what he chose of and to us, all. Most Families have such a member among them I believe Miss Heywood. – There is a someone in most families privileged by superior abilities or spirits to say anything. – In ours, it is Sidney; who is a very clever Young Man, – and with great powers of pleasing. – He lives too much in the World to be settled; that is his only fault. – He is here and there and every where. I wish we may get him to Sanditon. I should like to have you acquainted with him. – And it would be a fine thing for the Place! – Such a young Man as Sidney, with his neat equipage and fashionable air, – You and I Mary, know what effect it might have: Many a respectable Family, many a careful Mother, many a pretty Daughter, might it secure us, to the prejudice of E. Bourne and Hastings.' – They were now approaching the Church and real village of Sanditon, which stood at the foot of the Hill they were afterwards to ascend – a Hill, whose side was covered with the Woods and enclosures of Sanditon House and whose Height ended in an open Down where the new Buildings might soon be looked for. A branch only, of the Valley, winding more obliquely towards the Sea, gave a passage to an inconsiderable Stream, and formed at its mouth, a third Habitable Division, in a small cluster of Fisherman's Houses. – The Village contained little more than Cottages, but the Spirit of the day had been caught, as Mr. P. observed with delight to Charlotte, and two or three of the best of them were smartened up with a white Curtain and 'Lodgings to let' –, and farther on, in the little Green Court of an old Farm House, two Females in elegant white were actually to be seen with their books and camp stools – and in turning the corner of the Baker's shop, the sound of a Harp might be heard through the upper Casement. – Such sights and sounds were highly Blissful to Mr. P. – Not that he had any personal concern in the success of the Village itself; for considering it as too remote from the Beach, he had done nothing there – but it was a most valuable proof of the increasing fashion of the place altogether. If the *Village* could attract, the Hill might be nearly full. – He anticipated an amazing Season. – At the same time last year, (late in July) there had not been a single Lodger in the Village! – nor did he remember any during the whole Summer, excepting one family of children who came from London for sea air after the hooping Cough, and whose Mother would not let them be nearer the shore for fear of their tumbling in. – 'Civilization, Civilization indeed!' – cried Mr. P., delighted –. 'Look my dear Mary – Look at William Heeley's windows. – Blue Shoes, and nankin Boots! – Who would have expected such a sight at a Shoemaker's in old Sanditon! – This is new within the Month. There was no blue Shoe when we passed this way a month ago. – Glorious indeed! – Well, I think I *have* done something in my Day. – Now, for our Hill, our health-breathing Hill. – '

In ascending, they passed the Lodge-Gates of Sanditon House, and saw the top of the House itself among its Groves. It was the last Building of former Days in that line of the Parish. A little higher up, the Modern began; and in crossing the Down, a Prospect House, a Bellevue Cottage, and a Denham Place were to be looked at by Charlotte with the calmness of amused Curiosity, and by Mr. P. with the eager eye which hoped to see scarcely any empty houses. – More Bills at the Window than he had calculated on; – and a smaller shew of company on the Hill – Fewer Carriages, fewer Walkers. He had fancied it just the time of day for them to be all returning from their Airings to dinner – But the Sands and the Terrace always attracted some—. and the Tide must be flowing – about half-Tide now. – He longed to be on the Sands, the Cliffs, at his own House, and everywhere out of his House at once. His Spirits rose with the very sight of the Sea and he could almost feel his Ancle getting stronger already. – Trafalgar House, on the most elevated spot on the Down was a light elegant Building, standing in a small Lawn with a very young plantation round it, about an hundred yards from the brow of a steep, but not very lofty Cliff – and the nearest to it, of every Building, excepting one short row of smart-looking Houses, called the Terrace, with a broad walk in front, aspiring to be the Mall of the Place. In this row were the best Milliner's shop and the Library – a little detached from it, the Hotel and Billiard Room – Here began the Descent to the Beach, and to the Bathing Machines – and this was therefore the favourite spot for Beauty and Fashion. – At Trafalgar House, rising at a little distance behind the Terrace, the Travellers were safely set down, and all was happiness and Joy between Papa and Mama and their Children; while Charlotte having received possession of her apartment, found amusement enough in standing at her ample Venetian window,[1] and looking over the miscellaneous foreground of unfinished Buildings, waving Linen, and tops of Houses, to the Sea, dancing and sparkling in Sunshine and Freshness. –

CHAPTER V

WHEN they met before dinner, Mr. P. was looking over Letters. – 'Not a Line from Sidney!' – said he. – 'He is an idle fellow. – I sent him an account of my accident from Willingden, and thought he would have vouchsafed me an Answer. – But perhaps it implies that he is coming himself. – I trust it may. – But here is a Letter from one of my Sisters. *They* never fail me. – Women are the only Correspondents to be depended on. – Now Mary, (smiling at his Wife) – before I open it, what shall we guess as to the state of health of those it comes from – or rather what would Sidney say if he were here? – Sidney is a saucy fellow, Miss H. – And you must know, he will have it there is a good deal of Imagination in my two Sisters' complaints – but it really is not so – or very little – They have wretched health, as you have heard us say frequently, and are subject to a variety of very serious Disorders. – Indeed, I do not beleive they know what a day's health is; – and at the same time, they are such excellent useful Women and have so much energy of Character that, where any Good is to be done, they force themselves on exertions which to those who do not thoroughly know them, have an extraordinary appearance. - But there is really no affectation about them. They have only weaker constitutions and stronger minds than are often met with, either separate or together. – And our Youngest Brother – who lives with them, and who is not much above twenty, I am sorry to say, is almost as great an Invalid as themselves. – He is so delicate that he can engage in no Profession. – Sidney laughs at him – but it really is no Joke – though Sidney often makes me laugh at them all inspite of myself. – Now, if he were here, I know he would be offering odds, that either Susan Diana or Arthur would appear by this letter to have been at the point of death within the last month.' – Having run his eye over the Letter, he shook his head and began – : 'No chance of seeing them at Sanditon I am sorry to say. – A very indifferent account of them indeed. Seriously, a *very* indifferent account. – Mary, you will be quite sorry to hear how ill they have been and are. – Miss H., if you will give me leave, I will read Diana's Letter aloud. – I like to have my friends acquainted with each other – and I am afraid this is the only sort of acquaintance I shall have the means of accomplishing between you. – And I can have no scruple on Diana's account – for her Letters shew her exactly as she is, the most active, friendly, warmhearted Being in existence, and therefore must give a good impression.' He read. – 'My dear Tom, We were all much greived at your accident, and if you had not described yourself as fallen into such very good hands, I should have been with you at all hazards the day after the receipt of your Letter, though it found me suffering under a more severe attack than usual of my old greivance, Spasmodic Bile and hardly able to crawl from my Bed to the Sofa. – But how were you treated? – Send me more Particulars in your next. – If indeed a simple Sprain, as you denominate it, nothing would have been so judicious as Friction, Friction by the hand alone, supposing it could be applied *instantly*. – Two years ago I happened to be calling on Mrs. Sheldon when her Coachman sprained his foot as he was cleaning the Carriage and could hardly limp into the

House – but by the immediate use of Friction alone steadily persevered in, (and I rubbed his Ancle with my own hand for six Hours without Intermission) – he was well in three days. – Many Thanks my dear Tom, for the kindness with respect to us, which had so large a share in bringing on your accident – But pray never run into Peril again, in looking for an Apothecary on our account, for had you the most experienced Man in his Line settled at Sanditon, it would be no recommendation to us. We have entirely done with the whole Medical Tribe. We have consulted Physician after Physician in vain, till we are quite convinced that they can do nothing for us and that we must trust to our own knowledge of our own wretched Constitutions for any releif. – But if you think it advisable for the interest of the *Place*, to get a Medical Man there, I will undertake the commission with pleasure, and have no doubt of succeeding. – I could soon put the necessary Irons in the fire. – As for getting to Sanditon myself, it is quite an Impossibility. I greive to say that I dare not attempt it, but my feelings tell me too plainly that in my present state, the Sea air would probably be the death of me. – And neither of my dear Companions will leave me, or I would promote their going down to you for a fortnight. But in truth, I doubt whether Susan's nerves would be equal to the effort. She has been suffering much from the Headache and Six Leaches a day for ten days together releived her so little that we thought it right to change our measures – and being convinced on examination that much of the Evil lay in her Gum, I persuaded her to attack the disorder there. She has accordingly had three Teeth drawn, and is decidedly better, but her Nerves are a good deal deranged. She can only speak in a whisper – and fainted away twice this morning on poor Arthur's trying to suppress a cough. He, I am happy to say is tolerably well – tho' more languid than I like – and I fear for his Liver. – I have heard nothing of Sidney since your being together in Town, but conclude his scheme to the I. of Wight has not taken place, or we should have seen him in his way. – Most sincerely do we wish you a good Season at Sanditon, and though we cannot contribute to your Beau Monde in person, we are doing our utmost to send

you Company worth having; and think we may safely reckon on
securing you two large Families, one a rich West Indian[1] from
Surry, the other, a most respectable Girls Boarding School, or
Academy, from Camberwell.[2] – I will not tell you how many
People I have employed in the business – Wheel within wheel. –
But Success more than repays. – Yours most affectionately – &c'
'Well' – said Mr. P. – as he finished. 'Though I dare say Sidney
might find something extremely entertaining in this Letter and
make us laugh for half an hour together I declare *I* by myself,
can see nothing in it but what is either very pitiable or very
creditable. – With all their sufferings, you perceive how much
they are occupied in promoting the Good of others! – So anxious
for Sanditon! Two large Families – One, for Prospect House
probably, the other, for No. 2. Denham Place – or the end house
of the Terrace, – and extra Beds at the Hotel. – I told you my
Sisters were excellent Women, Miss H.' 'And I am sure they
must be very extraordinary ones.' – said Charlotte. 'I am
astonished at the chearful style of the Letter, considering the
state in which both Sisters appear to be. – Three Teeth drawn at
once! – frightful! – Your Sister Diana seems almost as ill as
possible, but those three Teeth of your Sister Susan's, are more
distressing than all the rest. – ' 'Oh! – they are so used to the
operation – to every operation – and have such Fortitude! – '
'Your Sisters know what they are about, I dare say, but their
Measures seem to touch on Extremes. – I feel that in any illness,
I should be so anxious for Professional advice, so very little
venturesome for myself, or any body I loved! – But then, *we*
have been so healthy a family, that I can be no Judge of what the
habit of self-doctoring may do. – ' 'Why to own the truth,' said
Mrs. P. – 'I *do* think the Miss Parkers carry it too far sometimes – and so do you my Love, you know. – You often think
they would be better, if they would leave themselves more
alone – and especially Arthur. I know you think it a great pity
they should give *him* such a turn for being ill. – ' 'Well, well –
my dear Mary – I grant you, it *is* unfortunate for poor Arthur,
that, at his time of Life he should be encouraged to give way to
Indisposition. It *is* bad; – it *is* bad that he should be fancying

himself too sickly for any Profession – and sit down at one and
twenty, on the interest of his own little Fortune, without any
idea of attempting to improve it, or of engaging in any occupation that may be of use to himself or others. – But let us talk of
pleasanter things. – These two large Families are just what we
wanted – But – here is something at hand, pleasanter still –
Morgan, with his "Dinner on Table." ' –

CHAPTER VI

THE Party were very soon moving after Dinner. Mr. P. could
not be satisfied without an early visit to the Library, and the
Library Subscription book, and Charlotte was glad to see as
much, and as quickly as possible, where all was new. They were
out in the very quietest part of a Watering-place Day, when the
important Business of Dinner or of sitting after Dinner was going
on in almost every inhabited Lodging; – here and there a solitary
Elderly Man might be seen, who was forced to move early and
walk for health – but in general, it was a thorough pause of
Company, it was Emptiness and Tranquillity on the Terrace, the
Cliffs, and the Sands. – The Shops were deserted – the Straw
Hats and pendant Lace seemed left to their fate both within the
House and without, and Mrs. Whitby at the Library was sitting
in her inner room, reading one of her own Novels, for want of
Employment. The List of Subscribers was but commonplace.
The Lady Denham, Miss Brereton, Mr. and Mrs. P. – Sir
Edward Denham and Miss Denham, whose names might be
said to lead off the Season, were followed by nothing better
than – Mrs. Mathews – Miss Mathews, Miss E. Mathews, Miss
H. Mathews. – Dr. and Mrs. Brown – Mr. Richard Pratt. –
Lieut. Smith R.N. Capt. Little, – Limehouse. – Mrs. Jane
Fisher. Miss Fisher. Miss Scroggs. – Rev. Mr. Hanking. Mr.
Beard – Solicitor, Grays Inn. – Mrs. Davis, and Miss Merry-
weather. – Mr. P. could not but feel that the List was not only

without Distinction, but less numerous than he had hoped. It was but July however, and August and September were the Months; – And besides, the promised large Families from Surry and Camberwell, were an ever-ready consolation. – Mrs. Whitby came forward without delay from her Literary recess, delighted to see Mr. Parker again, whose manners recommended him to every body, and they were fully occupied in their various Civilities and Communications, while Charlotte having added her name to the List as the first offering to the success of the Season, was busy in some immediate purchases for the further good of Every body, as soon as Miss Whitby could be hurried down from her Toilette, with all her glossy Curls and smart Trinkets to wait on her. – The Library of course, afforded every thing; all the useless things in the World that could not be done without, and among so many pretty Temptations, and with so much good will for Mr. P. to encourage Expenditure, Charlotte began to feel that she must check herself – or rather she reflected that at two and Twenty there could be no excuse for her doing otherwise – and that it would not do for her to be spending all her Money the very first Evening. She took up a Book; it happened to be a volume of *Camilla*. She had not *Camilla's* Youth,[1] and had no intention of having her Distress, – so, she turned from the Drawers of rings and Broches repressed farther solicitation and paid for what she bought. – For her particular gratification, they were then to take a Turn on the Cliff – but as they quitted the Library they were met by two Ladies whose arrival made an alteration necessary, Lady Denham and Miss Brereton. – They had been to Trafalgar House, and been directed thence to the Library, and though Lady D. was a great deal too active to regard the walk of a mile as any thing requiring rest, and talked of going home again directly, the Parkers knew that to be pressed into their House, and obliged to take her Tea with them, would suit her best, – and therefore the stroll on the Cliff gave way to an immediate return home. – 'No, no,' said her Ladyship – 'I will not have you hurry your Tea on my account. – I know you like your Tea late. – My early hours are not to put my Neighbours to inconvenience. No, no, Miss Clara and I will get back to our own Tea. – We came out with no other Thought. – We wanted just to see you and make sure of your being really come –, but we get back to our own Tea.' – She went on however towards Trafalgar House and took possession of the Drawing room very quietly – without seeming to hear a word of Mrs. P.'s orders to the Servant as they entered, to bring Tea directly. Charlotte was fully consoled for the loss of her walk, by finding herself in company with those, whom the conversation of the morning had given her a great curiosity to see. She observed them well. – Lady D. was of middle height, stout, upright and alert in her motions, with a shrewd eye, and self-satisfied air – but not an unagreable Countenance – and tho' her manner was rather downright and abrupt as of a person who valued herself on being free-spoken, there was a good humour and cordiality about her – a civility and readiness to be acquainted with Charlotte herself, and a heartiness of welcome towards her old friends, which was inspiring the Good will, she seemed to feel; – And as for Miss Brereton, her appearance so completely justified Mr. P.'s praise that Charlotte thought she had never beheld a more lovely, or more Interesting young Woman. – Elegantly tall, regularly handsome, with great delicacy of complexion and soft Blue eyes, a sweetly modest and yet naturally graceful Address, Charlotte could see in her only the most perfect representation of whatever Heroine might be most beautiful and bewitching, in all the numerous volumes they had left behind them on Mrs. Whitby's shelves. – Perhaps it might be partly oweing to her having just issued from a Circulating Library – but she could not separate the idea of a complete Heroine from Clara Brereton. Her situation with Lady Denham so very much in favour of it! – She seemed placed with her on purpose to be ill-used. Such Poverty and Dependance joined to such Beauty and Merit, seemed to leave no choice in the business. – These feelings were not the result of any spirit of Romance in Charlotte herself. No, she was a very sober-minded young Lady, sufficiently well-read in Novels to supply her Imagination with amusement, but not at all unreasonably influenced by them; and while she pleased herself the first five minutes with fancying the Persecutions which *ought* to be the Lot of the interesting Clara, especially in the form of the most barbarous conduct on Lady Denham's side, she found no reluctance to admit from subsequent observation, that they appeared to be on very comfortable Terms. – She could see nothing worse in Lady Denham, than the sort of oldfashioned formality of always calling her *Miss Clara* – nor anything objectionable in the degree of observance and attention which Clara paid. – On one side it seemed protecting kindness, on the other grateful and affectionate respect. – The Conversation turned entirely upon Sanditon, its present number of Visitants and the Chances of a good Season. It was evident that Lady D. had more anxiety, more fears of loss, than her Coadjutor. She wanted to have the Place fill faster, and seemed to have many harassing apprehensions of the Lodgings being in some instances underlet. – Miss Diana Parker's two large Families were not forgotten. 'Very good, very good,' said her Ladyship. – 'A West Indy Family and a school. That sounds well. That will bring Money.' – 'No people spend more freely, I beleive, than W. Indians.' observed Mr. Parker. – 'Aye – so I have heard – and because they have full Purses, fancy themselves equal, may be, to your old Country Families. But then, they who scatter their Money so freely, never think of whether they may not be doing mischeif by raising the price of Things – And I have heard that's very much the case with your West-injines – and if they come among us to raise the price of our necessaries of Life, we shall not much thank them Mr. Parker.' – 'My dear Madam, They can only raise the price of consumeable Articles, by such an extraordinary Demand for them and such a diffusion of Money among us, as must do us more Good than harm. – Our Butchers and Bakers and Traders in general cannot get rich without bringing Prosperity to *us*. – If *they* do not gain, our rents must be insecure – and in proportion to their profit must be ours eventually in the increased value of our Houses.' 'Oh! – well. – But I should not like to have Butcher's meat raised, though – and I shall keep it down as long as I can. – Aye – that young Lady smiles I see; – I dare say she thinks me an odd sort of a

Creature, – but *she* will come to care about such matters herself
in time. Yes, Yes, my Dear, depend upon it, you will be thinking
of the price of Butcher's meat in time – though you may not
happen to have quite such a Servants Hall full to feed, as I have. –
And I do beleive *those* are best off, that have fewest Servants. –
I am not a Woman of Parade, as all the World knows, and if it
was not for what I owe to poor Mr. Hollis's memory, I should
never keep up Sanditon House as I do; – it is not for my own
pleasure. – Well Mr Parker – and the other is a Boarding
school, a French Boarding School, is it? – No harm in that. –
They'll stay their six weeks. – And out of such a number, who
knows but some may be consumptive and want Asses milk –
and I have two Milch asses at this present time. – But perhaps
the little Misses may hurt the Furniture. – I hope they will
have a good sharp Governess to look after them. – ' Poor Mr.
Parker got no more credit from Lady D. than he had from his
Sisters, for the Object which had taken him to Willingden.
'Lord! my dear Sir,' she cried, 'how could you think of such a
thing? I am very sorry you met with your accident, but upon
my word you deserved it. – Going after a Doctor! – Why, what
should we do with a Doctor here? It would be only encouraging
our Servants and the Poor to fancy themselves ill, if there was a
Doctor at hand. – Oh! pray, let us have none of the Tribe at
Sanditon. We go on very well as we are. There is the Sea and the
Downs and my Milch-Asses – and I have told Mrs. Whitby
that if any body enquires for a Chamber-Horse,[1] they may be
supplied at a fair rate – (poor Mr. Hollis's Chamber-Horse, as
good as new) – and what can People want for more? – Here
have I lived seventy good years in the world and never took
Physic above twice – and never saw the face of a Doctor in all
my Life, on my *own* account. – And I verily beleive if my poor
dear Sir Harry had never seen one neither, he would have been
alive now. – Ten fees, one after another, did the Man take who
sent *him* out of the World. – I beseech you Mr. Parker, no
Doctors here.' – The Tea things were brought in. – 'Oh! my
dear Mrs. Parker – you should not indeed – why would you do
so? I was just upon the point of wishing you good Evening. But

since you are so very neighbourly, I beleive Miss Clara and I must stay.'—

CHAPTER VII

THE popularity of the Parkers brought them some visitors the very next morning; – amongst them, Sir Edward Denham and his Sister, who having been at Sanditon H— drove on to pay their Compliments; and the duty of Letter-writing being accomplished, Charlotte was settled with Mrs. P. – in the Drawing room in time to see them all. – The Denhams were the only ones to excite particular attention. Charlotte was glad to complete her knowledge of the family by an introduction to them, and found them, the better half at least – (for while single, the *Gentleman* may sometimes be thought the better half, of the pair) – not unworthy notice. – Miss D. was a fine young woman, but cold and reserved, giving the idea of one who felt her consequence with Pride and her Poverty with Discontent, and who was immediately gnawed by the want of an handsomer Equipage than the simple Gig in which they travelled, and which their Groom was leading about still in her sight. – Sir Edward was much her superior in air and manner; – certainly handsome, but yet more to be remarked for his very good address and wish of paying attention and giving pleasure. – He came into the room remarkably well, talked much – and very much to Charlotte, by whom he chanced to be placed – and she soon perceived that he had a fine Countenance, a most pleasing gentleness of voice, and a great deal of Conversation. She liked him. – Sober-minded as she was, she thought him agreable, and did not quarrel with the suspicion of his finding her equally so, which *would* arise from his evidently disregarding his Sisters'[1] motion to go, and persisting in his station and his discourse. – I make no apologies for my Heroine's vanity. – If there are young Ladies in the World at her time of Life, more dull of Fancy and more careless of pleasing, I know them not, and never wish to know them. – At last, from the low French windows of the Drawing room which commanded the road and all the Paths across the Down, Charlotte and Sir Edward as they sat, could not but observe Lady D. and Miss B. walking by – and there was instantly a slight change in Sir Edward's countenance – with an anxious glance after them as they proceeded – followed by an early proposal to his Sister – not merely for moving, but for walking on together to the Terrace – which altogether gave an hasty turn to Charlotte's fancy, cured her of her halfhour's fever, and placed her in a more capable state of judging, when Sir Edward was gone, of *how* agreable he had actually been. – 'Perhaps there was a good deal in his Air and Address; And his Title did him no harm.' She was very soon in his company again. The first object of the Parkers, when their House was cleared of morning visitors was to get out themselves; – the Terrace was the attraction to all; – Every body who walked, must begin with the Terrace, and there, seated on one of the two Green Benches by the Gravel walk, they found the united Denham Party; – but though united in the Gross, very distinctly divided again – the two superior Ladies being at one end of the bench, and Sir Edward and Miss B. at the other. – Charlotte's first glance told her that Sir Edward's air was that of a Lover. – There could be no doubt of his Devotion to Clara. – How Clara received it, was less obvious – but she was inclined to think not very favourably; for tho' sitting thus apart with him (which probably she might not have been able to prevent) her air was calm and grave. – That the young Lady at the other end of the Bench was doing Penance, was indubitable. The difference in Miss Denham's countenance, the change from Miss Denham sitting in cold Grandeur in Mrs. Parker's Drawing-room to be kept from silence by the efforts of others, to Miss D. at Lady D.'s Elbow, listening and talking with smiling attention or solicitous eagerness, was very striking – and very amusing – or very melancholy, just as Satire or Morality might prevail. – Miss Denham's Character was pretty well decided with Charlotte. Sir Edward's required longer Observation. He surprised her by quitting Clara immediately on their all joining and agreeing to walk, and by addressing his attentions entirely to herself. –

Stationing himself close by her, he seemed to mean to detach her as much as possible from the rest of the Party and to give her the whole of his Conversation. He began, in a tone of great Taste and Feeling, to talk of the Sea and the Sea shore – and ran with Energy through all the usual Phrases employed in praise of their Sublimity, and descriptive of the *undescribable* Emotions they excite in the Mind of Sensibility. – The terrific Grandeur of the Ocean in a Storm, its glassy surface in a calm, its Gulls and its Samphire, and the deep fathoms of its Abysses, its quick vicissitudes, its direful Deceptions, its Mariners tempting it in Sunshine and overwhelmed by the sudden Tempest, All were eagerly and fluently touched; – rather commonplace perhaps – but doing very well from the Lips of a handsome Sir Edward, – and she could not but think him a Man of Feeling – till he began to stagger her by the number of his Quotations, and the bewilderment of some of his sentences. – 'Do you remember,' said he, 'Scotts' beautiful Lines on the Sea? – Oh! what a description they convey! – They are never out of my Thoughts when I walk here. – That Man who can read them unmoved must have the nerves of an Assassin! – Heaven defend me from meeting such a Man un-armed.' – 'What description do you mean?' – said Charlotte. 'I remember none at this moment, of the Sea, in either of Scotts' Poems.'[1] – 'Do not you indeed? – Nor can I exactly recall the beginning at this moment – But – you cannot have forgotten his description of Woman. –

"Oh! Woman in our Hours of Ease –"

Delicious! Delicious! – Had he written nothing more, he would have been Immortal. And then again, that unequalled, unrivalled address to Parental affection—

"Some feelings are to Mortals given
With less of Earth in them than Heaven" &c

But while we are on the subject of Poetry, what think you Miss H. of Burns Lines to his Mary? – Oh! there is Pathos to madden one! – If ever there was a Man who *felt*, it was Burns. – Montgomery has all the Fire of Poetry, Wordsworth has the true soul of it – Campbell[1] in his pleasures of Hope has touched the extreme of our Sensations – "Like Angel's visits, few and far between." Can you conceive any thing more subduing, more melting, more fraught with the deep Sublime than that Line? – But Burns – I confess my sence of his Pre-eminence Miss H. – If Scott *has* a fault, it is the want of Passion. – Tender, Elegant, Descriptive – but *Tame*. – The Man who cannot do justice to the attributes of Woman is my contempt. – Sometimes indeed a flash of feeling seems to irradiate him – as in the Lines we were speaking of – "Oh! Woman in our hours of Ease" – . But Burns is always on fire. – His Soul was the Altar in which lovely Woman sat enshrined, his Spirit truly breathed the immortal Incence which is her Due. – ' 'I have read several of Burns' Poems with great delight,' said Charlotte as soon as she had time to speak, 'but I am not poetic enough to separate a Man's Poetry entirely from his Character; – and poor Burns's known Irregularities, greatly interrupt my enjoyment of his Lines. – I have difficulty in depending on the *Truth* of his Feelings as a Lover. I have not faith in the *sincerity* of the affections of a Man of his Description. He felt and he wrote and he forgot.' 'Oh! no no' – exclaimed Sir Edward in an extasy. 'He was all ardour and Truth! – His Genius and his Susceptibilities might lead him into some Aberrations – But who is perfect? – It were Hypercriticism, it were Pseudo-philosophy to expect from the soul of high toned Genius, the grovellings of a common mind. – The Coruscations of Talent, elicited by impassioned feeling in the breast of Man, are perhaps incompatible with some of the prosaic Decencies of Life; – nor can you, loveliest Miss Heywood (speaking with an air of deep sentiment) – nor can any Woman be a fair Judge of what a Man may be propelled to say, write or do, by the sovereign impulses of illimitable Ardour.' This was very fine; – but if Charlotte understood it at all, not very moral – and being moreover by no means pleased with his extraordinary stile of compliment, she gravely answered 'I really know nothing of the matter. – This is a charming day. The Wind I fancy must be Southerly.' 'Happy, happy Wind, to engage Miss Heywood's Thoughts! – ' She began to think him downright silly. – His

chusing to walk with her, she had learnt to understand. It was
done to pique Miss Brereton. She had read it, in an anxious
glance or two on his side – but why he should talk so much
Nonsense, unless he could do no better, was un-intelligible. –
He seemed very sentimental, very full of some Feelings or other,
and very much addicted to all the newest-fashioned hard words –
had not a very clear Brain she presumed, and talked a good deal
by rote. – The Future might explain him further – but when
there was a proposition for going into the Library she felt that
she had had quite enough of Sir Edward for one morning, and
very gladly accepted Lady D.'s invitation of remaining on the
Terrace with her. – The others all left them, Sir Edward with
looks of very gallant despair in tearing himself away, and they
united their agreableness – that is, Lady Denham like a true
great Lady, talked and talked only of her own concerns, and
Charlotte listened – amused in considering the contrast between
her two companions. – Certainly, there was no strain of doubtful
Sentiment, nor any phrase of difficult interpretation in Lady
D's discourse. Taking hold of Charlotte's arm with the ease of
one who felt that any notice from her was an Honour, and
communicative, from the influence of the same conscious
Importance or a natural love of talking, she immediately said in
a tone of great satisfaction – and with a look of arch sagacity –
'Miss Esther wants me to invite her and her Brother to spend a
week with me at Sanditon House, as I did last Summer – but
I shan't. – She has been trying to get round me every way, with
her praise of this, and her praise of that; but I saw what she was
about. – I saw through it all. – I am not very easily taken-in my
Dear.' Charlotte could think of nothing more harmless to be
said, than the simple enquiry of – 'Sir Edward and Miss Denham?' – 'Yes, my Dear. *My young Folks*, as I call them sometimes, for I take them very much by the hand. I had them with
me last Summer about this time, for a week; from Monday to
Monday; and very delighted and thankful they were. – For they
are very good young People my Dear. I would not have you
think that I *only* notice them, for poor dear Sir Harry's sake.
No, no; they are very deserving themselves, or trust me, they

would not be so much in *my* Company. – I am not the Woman to help any body blindfold. – I always take care to know what I am about and who I have to deal with, before I stir a finger. – I do not think I was ever over-reached in my Life; and That is a good deal for a Woman to say that has been married twice. – Poor dear Sir Harry (between ourselves) thought at first to have got more. – But (with a bit of a sigh) He is gone, and we must not find fault with the Dead. Nobody could live happier together than us – and he was a very honourable Man, quite the Gentleman of ancient Family. – And when he died, I gave Sir Edward his Gold Watch. –' She said this with a look at her Companion which implied its right to produce a great Impression – and seeing no rapturous astonishment in Charlotte's countenance, added quickly – 'He did not bequeath it to his Nephew, my dear – It was no bequest. It was not in the Will. He only told me, and *that* but once, that he should wish his Nephew to have his Watch; but it need not have been binding, if I had not chose it. –' 'Very kind indeed! very Handsome;' – said Charlotte, absolutely forced to affect admiration. – 'Yes, my dear – and it is not the *only* kind thing I have done by him. – I have been a very liberal friend to Sir Edward. And poor young Man, he needs it bad enough; – For though I am *only* the *Dowager* my Dear, and he is the *Heir*, things do not stand between us in the way they commonly do between those two parties. – Not a shilling do I receive from the Denham Estate. Sir Edward has no Payments to make *me*. He don't stand uppermost, beleive me. – It is *I* that help *him*.' 'Indeed! – He is a very fine young Man; – particularly Elegant in his Address.' – This was said cheifly for the sake of saying something – but Charlotte directly saw that it was laying her open to suspicion by Lady D.'s giving a shrewd glance at her and replying – 'Yes, yes, he is very well to look at – and it is to be hoped that some Lady of large fortune will think so – for Sir Edward *must* marry for Money. – He and I often talk that matter over. – A handsome young fellow like him, will go smirking and smiling about and paying girls compliments but he knows he *must* marry for Money. – And Sir Edward is a very steady young Man in the main, and has got very good notions.' 'Sir Edward

Denham,' said Charlotte, 'with such personal Advantages may be almost sure of getting a Woman of fortune, if he chuses it.' – This glorious sentiment seemed quite to remove suspicion. 'Aye my Dear – That's very sensibly said' cried Lady D – 'And if we could but get a young Heiress to S.! But Heiresses are monstrous scarce! I do not think we have had an Heiress here, or even a Co –[1] since Sanditon has been a public place. Families come after Families, but as far as I can learn, it is not one in an hundred of them that have any real Property, Landed or Funded. – An Income perhaps, but no Property. Clergymen may be, or Lawyers from Town, or Half pay officers, or Widows with only a jointure. And what good can such people do anybody? – except just as they take our empty Houses – and (between ourselves) I think they are great fools for not staying at home. Now, if we could get a young Heiress to be sent here for her health – (and if she was ordered to drink asses milk I could supply her) – and as soon as she got well, have her fall in love with Sir Edward!' – 'That would be very fortunate indeed.' 'And Miss Esther must marry somebody of fortune too – She must get a rich Husband. Ah! young Ladies that have no Money are very much to be pitied! – But' – after a short pause – 'if Miss Esther thinks to talk me into inviting them to come and stay at Sanditon House, she will find herself mistaken. – Matters are altered with me since last Summer you know –. I have Miss Clara with me now, which makes a great difference.' She spoke this so seriously that Charlotte instantly saw in it the evidence of real penetration and prepared for some fuller remarks – but it was followed only by – 'I have no fancy for having my House as full as an Hotel. I should not chuse to have my two Housemaids Time taken up all the morning, in dusting out Bed rooms. – They have Miss Clara's room to put to rights as well as my own every day. – If they had hard Places, they would want Higher Wages. –' For objections of this Nature, Charlotte was not prepared, and she found it so impossible even to affect simpathy, that she could say nothing. – Lady D. soon added, with great glee – 'And besides all this my Dear, am I to be filling my House to the prejudice of Sanditon? – If People want to be by the Sea, why dont they take

Lodgings? – Here are a great many empty Houses – three on this very Terrace; no fewer than three Lodging Papers staring us in the face at this very moment, Numbers 3, 4 and 8. 8, the Corner House may be too large for them, but either of the two others are nice little snug Houses, very fit for a young Gentleman and his sister – And so, my dear, the next time Miss Esther begins talking about the dampness of Denham Park, and the Good Bathing always does her, I shall advise them to come and take one of these Lodgings for a fortnight. – Don't you think that will be very fair? – Charity begins at home you know.' – Charlotte's feelings were divided between amusement and indignation – but indignation had the larger and the increasing share. – She kept her Countenance and she kept a civil Silence. She could not carry her forbearance farther; but without attempting to listen longer, and only conscious that Lady D. was still talking on in the same way, allowed her Thoughts to form themselves into such a Meditation as this. – 'She is thoroughly mean. I had not expected any thing so bad. – Mr. P. spoke too mildly of her. – His Judgement is evidently not to be trusted. – His own Goodnature misleads him. He is too kind hearted to see clearly. – I must judge for myself. – And their very *connection* prejudices him. – He has persuaded her to engage in the same Speculation – and because their object in that Line is the same, he fancies she feels like him in others. – But she is very, very mean. – I can see no Good in her. – Poor Miss Brereton! – And she makes every body mean about her. – This poor Sir Edward and his Sister, – how far Nature meant them to be respectable I cannot tell, – but they are *obliged* to be Mean in their Servility to her. – And I am Mean too, in giving her my attention, with the appearance of coinciding with her. – Thus it is, when Rich People are Sordid.' –

CHAPTER VIII

THE two Ladies continued walking together till rejoined by the others, who as they issued from the Library were followed by a

young Whitby running off with five volumes under his arm to
Sir Edward's Gig - and Sir Edward approaching Charlotte,
said 'You may perceive what has been our Occupation. My
Sister wanted my Counsel in the selection of some books. -
We have many leisure hours, and read a great deal. - I am no
indiscriminate Novel-Reader. The mere Trash of the common
Circulating Library, I hold in the highest contempt. You will
never hear me advocating those puerile Emanations which detail
nothing but discordant Principles incapable of Amalgamation,
or those vapid tissues of ordinary Occurrences from which no
useful Deductions can be drawn. - In vain may we put them
into a literary Alembic; - we distil nothing which can add to
Science. - You understand me I am sure?' 'I am not quite certain that I do. - But if you will describe the sort of Novels which
you *do* approve, I dare say it will give me a clearer idea.' 'Most
willingly, Fair Questioner. - The Novels which I approve are
such as display Human Nature with Grandeur - such as shew
her in the Sublimities of intense Feeling - such as exhibit the
progress of strong Passion from the first Germ of incipient
Susceptibility to the utmost Energies of Reason half-dethroned, -
where we see the strong spark of Woman's Captivations elicit
such Fire in the Soul of Man as leads him - (though at the risk
of some Aberration from the strict line of Primitive Obligations) -
hazard all, dare all, atcheive all, to obtain her. - Such are the
Works which I peruse with delight, and I hope I may say, with
Amelioration. They hold forth the most splendid Portraitures of
high Conceptions, Unbounded Veiws, illimitable Ardour,
indomptible Decision - and even when the Event is mainly
anti-prosperous to the high-toned Machinations of the prime
Character, the potent, pervading Hero of the Story, it leaves us
full of Generous Emotions for him; - our Hearts are paralized -.
T'were Pseudo-Philosophy to assert that we do not feel more
enwraped by the brilliancy of his Career, than by the tranquil
and morbid Virtues of any opposing Character. Our approbation of the Latter is but Eleemosynary.[1] - These are the Novels
which enlarge the primitive Capabilities of the Heart, and which
it cannot impugn the Sense or be any Dereliction of the character,

of the most anti-puerile Man, to be conversant with.' – 'If I
understand you aright' – said Charlotte – 'our taste in Novels is
not at all the same.' And here they were obliged to part – Miss
D. being too much tired of them all, to stay any longer. – The
truth was that Sir Edward whom circumstances had confined
very much to one spot had read more sentimental Novels than
agreed with him. His fancy had been early caught by all the
impassioned, and most exceptionable parts of Richardsons; and
such Authors as have since appeared to tread in Richardson's
steps, so far as Man's determined pursuit of Woman in defiance
of every opposition of feeling and convenience is concerned, had
since occupied the greater part of his literary hours, and formed
his Character. – With a perversity of Judgement, which must be
attributed to his not having by Nature a very strong head, the
Graces, the Spirit, the Sagacity, and the Perseverance, of the
Villain of the Story outweighed all his absurdities and all his
Atrocities with Sir Edward. With him, such Conduct was
Genius, Fire and Feeling. – It interested and inflamed him; and
he was always more anxious for its Success and mourned over
its Discomfitures with more Tenderness than could ever have
been contemplated by the Authors. – Though he owed many of
his ideas to this sort of reading, it were unjust to say that he
read nothing else, or that his Language were not formed on a
more general Knowledge of modern Literature. – He read all
the Essays, Letters, Tours and Criticisms of the day – and with
the same ill-luck which made him derive only false Principles
from Lessons of Morality, and incentives to Vice from the
History of its Overthrow, he gathered only hard words and
involved sentences from the style of our most approved
Writers. –

Sir Edward's great object in life was to be seductive. – With
such personal advantages as he knew himself to possess, and such
Talents as he did also give himself credit for, he regarded it as
his Duty. – He felt that he was formed to be a dangerous Man –
quite in the line of the Lovelaces.[1] – The very name of Sir
Edward he thought, carried some degree of fascination with it. –
To be generally gallant and assiduous about the fair, to make

fine speeches to every pretty Girl, was but the inferior part of the Character he had to play. – Miss Heywood, or any other young Woman with any pretensions to Beauty, he was entitled (according to his own veiws of Society) to approach with high Compliments and Rhapsody on the slightest acquaintance; but it was Clara alone on whom he had serious designs; it was Clara whom he meant to seduce. – Her seduction was quite determined on. Her Situation in every way called for it. She was his rival in Lady D.'s favour, she was young, lovely and dependant. – He had very early seen the necessity of the case, and had now been long trying with cautious assiduity to make an impression on her heart, and to undermine her Principles. – Clara saw through him, and had not the least intention of being seduced – but she bore with him patiently enough to confirm the sort of attachment which her personal Charms had raised. – A greater degree of discouragement indeed would not have affected Sir Edward –. He was armed against the highest pitch of Disdain or Aversion. – If she could not be won by affection, he must carry her off. He knew his Business. – Already had he had many Musings on the Subject. If he *were* constrained so to act, he must naturally wish to strike out something new, to exceed those who had gone before him – and he felt a strong curiosity to ascertain whether the Neighbourhood of Tombuctoo[1] might not afford some solitary House adapted for Clara's reception; – but the Expence alas! of Measures in that masterly style was ill-suited to his Purse, and Prudence obliged him to prefer the quietest sort of ruin and disgrace for the object of his Affections, to the more renowned. –

CHAPTER IX

ONE day, soon after Charlotte's arrival at Sanditon, she had the pleasure of seeing just as she ascended from the Sands to the Terrace, a Gentleman's Carriage with Post Horses standing at the door of the Hotel, as very lately arrived, and by the quantity of Luggage taking off, bringing, it might be hoped, some respectable family determined on a long residence. – Delighted to have such good news for Mr. and Mrs. P., who had both gone home some time before, she proceeded for Trafalgar House with as much alacrity as could remain, after having been contending for the last two hours with a very fine wind blowing directly on shore; but she had not reached the little Lawn, when she saw a Lady walking nimbly behind her at no great distance; and convinced that it could be no acquaintance of her own, she resolved to hurry on and get into the House if possible before her. But the Stranger's pace did not allow this to be accomplished; – Charlotte was on the steps and had rung, but the door was not opened, when the other crossed the Lawn; – and when the Servant appeared, they were just equally ready for entering the House. – The ease of the Lady, her 'How do you do Morgan? – ' and Morgan's Looks on seeing her, were a moment's astonishment – but another moment brought Mr. P. into the Hall to welcome the Sister he had seen from the Drawing room, and she was soon introduced to Miss Diana Parker. There was a great deal of surprise but still more pleasure in seeing her. – Nothing could be kinder than her reception from both Husband and Wife. 'How did she come? and with whom? – And they were so glad to find her equal to the Journey! – And that she was to belong to *them*, was a thing of course.' Miss Diana P. was about four and thirty, of middling height and slender; – delicate looking rather than sickly; with an agreable face, and a very animated eye; – her manners resembling her Brother's in their ease and frankness, though with more decision and less mildness in her Tone. She began an account of herself without delay. – Thanking them for their Invitation, but '*that* was quite out of the question, for they were all three come, and meant to get into Lodgings and make some stay.' – 'All three come! – What! – Susan and Arthur! – Susan able to come too! – This was better and better.' 'Yes – we are actually all come. Quite unavoidable – Nothing else to be done. – You shall hear all about it. – But my dear Mary, send for the Children; – I long to see them.' – 'And how has Susan born the Journey? – and how is Arthur? – and why do not we see him here with you?' – 'Susan has born it

wonderfully. She had not a wink of sleep either the night before
we set out, or last night at Chichester, and as this is not so common with her as with *me*, I have had a thousand fears for her –
but she had kept up wonderfully. – had no Hysterics of consequence till we came within sight of poor old Sanditon – and the
attack was not very violent – nearly over by the time we reached
your Hotel – so that we got her out of the Carriage extremely
well, with only Mr. Woodcock's assistance – and when I left her
she was directing the Disposal of the Luggage, and helping old
Sam uncord the Trunks. – She desired her best Love, with a
thousand regrets at being so poor a Creature that she could not
come with me. And as for poor Arthur, he would not have been
unwilling himself, but there is so much Wind that I did not
think he could safely venture, – for I am *sure* there is Lumbago
hanging about him – and so I helped him on with his great
Coat and sent him off to the Terrace, to take us Lodgings. –
Miss Heywood must have seen our Carriage standing at the
Hotel. – I knew Miss Heywood the moment I saw her before me
on the Down. – My dear Tom I am so glad to see you walk so
well. Let me feel your Ancle. – That's right; all right and clean.
The play of your Sinews a *very* little affected: – barely percep-
tible. – Well – now for the explanation of my being here. – I
told you in my Letter, of the two considerable Families, I was
hoping to secure for you – the West Indians, and the Seminary. –'
Here Mr. P. drew his Chair still nearer to his Sister, and took
her hand again most affectionately as he answered 'Yes, Yes; –
How active and how kind you have been!' – 'The West-indians,'
she continued, 'whom I look upon as the *most* desirable of the
two – as the Best of the Good – prove to be a Mrs. Griffiths and
her family. I know them only through others. – You must have
heard me mention Miss Capper, the particular friend of *my*
very particular friend Fanny Noyce; – now, Miss Capper is
extremely intimate with a Mrs. Darling, who is on terms of
constant correspondence with Mrs. Griffiths herself. – Only a
short chain, you see, between us, and not a Link wanting. Mrs.
G. meant to go to the Sea, for her Young People's benefit – had
fixed on the coast of Sussex, but was undecided as to the where,

wanted something Private, and wrote to ask the opinion of her friend Mrs. Darling. – Miss Capper happened to be staying with Mrs. D. when Mrs. G.'s Letter arrived, and was consulted on the question; *she* wrote the same day to Fanny Noyce and mentioned it to her – and Fanny all alive for *us*, instantly took up her pen and forwarded the circumstance to me – except as to *Names* – which have but lately transpired. – There was but *one* thing for *me* to do. – I answered Fanny's Letter by the same Post and pressed for the recommendation of Sanditon. Fanny had feared your having no house large enough to receive such a Family. – But I seem to be spinning out my story to an endless length. – You see how it was all managed. I had the pleasure of hearing soon afterwards by the same simple link of connection that Sanditon *had been* recommended by Mrs. Darling, and that the West-indians were very much disposed to go thither. – This was the state of the case when I wrote to you; – but two days ago; – yes, the day before yesterday – I heard again from Fanny Noyce, saying that *she* had heard from Miss Capper, who by a Letter from Mrs. Darling understood that Mrs. G. – has expressed herself in a letter to Mrs. D. more doubtingly on the subject of Sanditon. – Am I clear? I would be anything rather than not clear.' – 'Oh! perfectly, perfectly. Well?' – 'The reason of this hesitation, was her having no connections in the place, and no means of ascertaining that she should have good accomodations on arriving there; – and she was particularly careful and scrupulous on all those matters more on account of a certain Miss Lambe a young Lady (probably a Neice) under her care, than on her own account or her Daughters. – Miss Lambe has an immense fortune – richer than all the rest – and very delicate health. – One sees clearly enough by all this, the *sort* of Woman Mrs. G. must be – as helpless and indolent, as Wealth and a Hot Climate are apt to make us. But we are not all born to equal energy. – What was to be done? – I had a few moments indecision; – Whether to offer to write to *you*, – or to Mrs. Whitby to secure them a House? – but neither pleased me. – I hate to employ others, when I am equal to act myself – and my conscience told me that this was an occasion which called for me.

Here was a family of helpless Invalides whom I might essentially serve. – I sounded Susan – the same Thought had occurred to her. – Arthur made no difficulties – our plan was arranged immediately, we were off yesterday morning at six –, left Chichester at the same hour today – and here we are. – ' 'Excellent! – Excellent! –' cried Mr. Parker. – 'Diana, you are unequalled in serving your friends and doing Good to all the World. – I know nobody like you. – Mary, my Love, is not she a wonderful Creature? – Well – and now, what House do you design to engage for them? – What is the size of their family? – ' 'I do not at all know' – replied his Sister – 'have not the least idea; – never heard any particulars; – but I am very sure that the largest house at Sanditon cannot be *too* large. They are more likely to want a second. – I shall take only one however, and that, but for a week certain. – Miss Heywood, I astonish you. – You hardly know what to make of me. – I see by your Looks, that you are not used to such quick measures.' – The words 'Unaccountable Officiousness! – Activity run mad!' – had just passed through Charlotte's mind – but a civil answer was easy. 'I dare say I do look surprised,' said she – 'because these are very great exertions, and I know what Invalides both you and your Sister are.' 'Invalides indeed. – I trust there are not three People in England who have so sad a right to that appellation! – But my dear Miss Heywood, we are sent into this World to be as extensively useful as possible, and where some degree of Strength of Mind is given, it is not a feeble body which will excuse us – or incline us to excuse ourselves. – The World is pretty much divided between the Weak of Mind and the Strong – between those who can act and those who can not, and it is the bounden Duty of the Capable to let no opportunity of being useful escape them. – My Sister's Complaints and mine are happily not often of a Nature, to threaten Existence *immediately* – and as long as we *can* exert ourselves to be of use of others, I am convinced that the Body is the better, for the refreshment the Mind receives in doing its Duty. – While I have been travelling, with this object in veiw, I have been perfectly well.' – The entrance of the Children ended this little panegyric on her own Disposition – and after having noticed

and caressed them all, – she prepared to go. – 'Cannot you dine
with us? – Is not it possible to prevail on you to dine with us?'
was then the cry; and *that* being absolutely negatived, it was
'And when shall we see you again? and how can we be of use to
you?' – and Mr. P. warmly offered his assistance in taking the
house for Mrs. G. – 'I will come to you the moment I have
dined,' said he, 'and we will go about together.' – But this was
immediately declined. – 'No, my dear Tom, upon no account in
the World, shall you stir a step on any business of mine. – Your
Ancle wants rest. I see by the position of your foot, that you have
used it too much already. – No, I shall go about my House-
taking directly. Our Dinner is not ordered till six – and by that
time I hope to have completed it. It is now only half past four. –
As to seeing *me* again today – I cannot answer for it; the others
will be at the Hotel all the Evening, and delighted to see you at
any time, but as soon as I get back I shall hear what Arthur has
done about our own Lodgings, and probably the moment
Dinner is over, shall be out again on business relative to them,
for we hope to get into some Lodgings or other and be settled
after breakfast tomorrow. – I have not much confidence in poor
Arthur's skill for Lodging-taking, but he seemed to like the
commission. – ' 'I think you are doing too much,' said Mr. P.
'You will knock yourself up. You should not move again after
Dinner.' 'No, indeed you should not,' cried his wife, 'for Dinner
is such a mere *name* with you all, that it can do you no good. – I
know what your appetites are. – ' 'My appetite is very much
mended I assure you lately. I have been taking some Bitters of
my own decocting, which have done wonders. Susan never
eats I grant you – and just at present *I* shall want nothing; I
never eat for about a week after a Journey – but as for Arthur,
he is only too much disposed for Food. We are often obliged to
check him.' – 'But you have not told me any thing of the *other*
Family coming to Sanditon,' said Mr. P. as he walked with her to
the door of the House – 'the Camberwell Seminary; have we a
good chance of *them*?' 'Oh! Certain – quite certain. – I had
forgotten them for the moment, but I had a letter three days
ago from my friend Mrs. Charles Dupuis which assured me of

Camberwell. Camberwell will be here to a certainty, and very soon. – *That* good Woman (I do not know her name) not being so wealthy and independant as Mrs. G. – can travel and chuse for herself. – I will tell you how I got at *her*. Mrs. Charles Dupuis lives almost next door to a Lady, who has a relation lately settled at Clapham, who actually attends the Seminary and gives lessons on Eloquence and Belles Lettres to some of the Girls. – I got that Man a Hare from one of Sidney's friends – and he recommended Sanditon; – Without *my* appearing however – Mrs. Charles Dupuis managed it all. –'

CHAPTER X

IT was not a week, since Miss Diana Parker had been told by her feelings, that the Sea Air would probably in her present state, be the death of her, and now she was at Sanditon, intending to make some Stay, and without appearing to have the slightest recollection of having written or felt any such thing. – It was impossible for Charlotte not to suspect a good deal of fancy in such an extraordinary state of health. – Disorders and Recoveries so very much out of the common way, seemed more like the amusement of eager Minds in want of employment than of actual afflictions and releif. The Parkers, were no doubt a family of Imagination and quick feelings – and while the eldest Brother found vent for his superfluity of sensation as a Projector,[1] the Sisters were perhaps driven to dissipate theirs in the invention of odd complaints. – The *whole* of their menta vivacity was evidently not so employed; Part was laid out in a Zeal for being useful. – It should seem that they must either be very busy for the Good of others, or else extremely ill themselves. Some natural delicacy of Constitution in fact, with an unfortunate turn for Medecine, especially quack Medecine, had given them an early tendency at various times, to various Disorders; – the rest of their sufferings was from Fancy, the love of Distinction and the love of the Wonderful. – They had Charitable hearts

and many amiable feelings – but a spirit of restless activity, and
the glory of doing more than anybody else, had their share in
every exertion of Benevolence – and there was Vanity in all they
did, as well as in all they endured. – Mr. and Mrs. P. spent a
great part of the Evening at the Hotel; but Charlotte had only
two or three veiws of Miss Diana posting over the Down after
a House for this Lady whom she had never seen, and who had
never employed her. She was not made acquainted with the
others till the following day, when, being removed into Lodgings
and all the party continuing quite well, their Brother and Sister
and herself were entreated to drink tea with them. – They were
in one of the Terrace Houses – and she found them arranged for
the Evening in a small neat Drawing room, with a beautiful
veiw of the Sea if they had chosen it, – but though it had been a
very fair English Summer-day, – not only was there no open
window, but the Sopha and the Table, and the Establishment in
genera. was all at the other end of the room by a brisk fire. –
Miss P. whom, remembering the three Teeth drawn in one
day, Charlotte approached with a peculiar degree of respectful
Compassion, was not very unlike her Sister in person or manner –
tho' more thin and worn by Illness and Medecine, more
relaxed in air, and more subdued in voice. She talked however,
the whole Evening as incessantly as Diana – and excepting that
she sat with salts in her hand, took Drops two or three times
from one, out of the several Phials already at home on the Mantel-
peice, – and made a great many odd faces and contortions,
Charlotte could perceive no symptoms of illness which she, in
the boldness of her own good health, would not have undertaken to cure, by putting out the fire, opening the Window, and
disposing of the Drops and the salts by means of one or the
other. She had had considerable curiosity to see Mr. Arthur
Parker; and having fancied him a very puny, delicate-looking
young Man, the smallest very materially of not a robust Family,
was astonished to find him quite as tall as his Brother and a great
deal Stouter – Broad made and Lusty – and with no other look
of an Invalide, than a sodden complexion. – Diana was evidently
the cheif of the family; principal Mover and Actor; – she had

been on her Feet the whole Morning, on Mrs. G.'s business or their own, and was still the most alert of the three. – Susan had only superintended their final removal from the Hotel, bringing two heavy Boxes herself, and Arthur had found the air so cold that he had merely walked from one House to the other as nimbly as he could, – and boasted much of sitting by the fire till he had cooked up a very good one. – Diana, whose exercise had been too domestic to admit of calculation, but who, by her own account, had not once sat down during the space of seven hours, confessed herself a little tired. She had been too successful however for much fatigue; for not only had she by walking and talking down a thousand difficulties at last secured a proper House at eight guineas per week for Mrs. G. – ; she had also opened so many Treaties with Cooks, Housemaids, Washer-women and Bathing Women, that Mrs. G. would have little more to do on her arrival, than to wave her hand and collect them around her for choice. – Her concluding effort in the cause, had been a few polite lines of Information to Mrs. G. herself – time not allowing for the circuitous train of intelligence which had been hitherto kept up, – and she was now regaling in the delight of opening the first Trenches of an acquaintance with such a powerful discharge of unexpected Obligation. Mr. and Mrs. P. – and Charlotte had seen two Post chaises crossing the Down to the Hotel as they were setting off, – a joyful sight – and full of speculation. – The Miss P.s – and Arthur had also seen something; – they could distinguish from their window that there *was* an arrival at the Hotel, but not its amount. Their Visitors answered for two Hack-Chaises. – Could it be the Camberwell Seminary? – No – No. – Had there been a third carriage, perhaps it might; but it was very generally agreed that two Hack chaises could never contain a Seminary. – Mr. P. was confident of another new Family. – When they were all finally seated, after some removals to look at the Sea and the Hotel, Charlotte's place was by Arthur, who was sitting next to the Fire with a degree of Enjoyment which gave a good deal of merit to his civility in wishing her to take his Chair. – There was nothing dubious in her manner of declining it, and he sat down again with much satisfaction. She drew back her Chair to have all the advantage of his Person as a screen, and was very thankful for every inch of Back and Shoulders beyond her pre-conceived idea. Arthur was heavy in Eye as well as figure, but by no means indisposed to talk; – and while the other four were cheifly engaged together, he evidently felt it no penance to have a fine young Woman next to him, requiring in common Politeness some attention – as his Brother who felt the decided want of some motive for action, some Powerful object of animation for him, observed with considerable pleasure. – Such was the influence of Youth and Bloom that he began even to make a sort of apology for having a Fire. 'We should not have one at home,' said he, 'but the Sea air is always damp. I am not afraid of any thing so much as Damp. – ' 'I am so fortunate,' said C. 'as never to know whether the air is damp or dry. It has always some property that is wholesome and invigorating to me, –' '*I* like the Air too, as well as any body can;' replied Arthur, 'I am very fond of standing at an open Window when there is no Wind – but unluckily a Damp air does not like *me*. – It gives me the Rheumatism. – You are not rheumatic I suppose? – ' 'Not at all.' 'That's a great blessing. – But perhaps you are nervous.' 'No – I beleive not. I have no idea that I am.' – '*I* am very nervous. – To say the truth Nerves are the worst part of my Complaints in *my* opinion. My Sisters think me Bilious, but I doubt it. – ' 'You are quite in the right, to doubt it as long as you possibly can, I am sure. – ' 'If I were Bilious,' he continued, 'you know Wine would disagree with me, but it always does me good. – The more Wine I drink (in Moderation) the better I am. – I am always best of an Evening. – If you had seen me to day before Dinner, you would have thought me a very poor Creature. – ' Charlotte could beleive it—. She kept her countenance however, and said – 'As far as I can understand what nervous complaints are, I have a great idea of the efficacy of air and exercise for them: – daily, regular Exercise; – and I should recommend rather more of it to *you* than I suspect you are in the habit of taking.' – 'Oh! I am very fond of exercise myself' – he replied – 'and mean to walk a great deal while I am here, if the Weather is temperate. I shall be out every

morning before breakfast – and take several turns upon the
Terrace, and you will often see me at Trafalgar House.' – 'But
you do not call a walk to Trafalgar House much exercise? – ' 'Not,
as to mere distance, but the Hill is so steep! – Walking up that
Hill, in the middle of the day, would throw me into such a
Perspiration! – You would see me all in a Bath[1] by the time I
got there! – I am very subject to Perspiration, and there cannot
be a surer sign of Nervousness. – ' They were now advancing so
deep in Physics, that Charlotte veiwed the entrance of the Servant
with the Tea things, as a very fortunate Interruption. – It produced a great and immediate change. The young Man's attentions were instantly lost. He took his own Cocoa from the
Tray, – which seemed provided with almost as many Teapots
&c as there were persons in company, Miss P. drinking one sort
of Herb-Tea and Miss Diana another, and turning completely
to the Fire, sat coddling and cooking it to his own satisfaction
and toasting some Slices of Bread, brought up ready-prepared
in the Toast rack – and till it was all done, she heard nothing of
his voice but the murmuring of a few broken sentences of self-
approbation and success. – When his Toils were over however,
he moved back his Chair into as gallant a Line as ever, and proved
that he had not been working only for himself, by his earnest
invitation to her to take both Cocoa and Toast. – She was already helped to Tea – which surprised him – so totally self-
engrossed had he been. – 'I thought I should have been in
time,' said he, 'but cocoa takes a great deal of Boiling.' – 'I am
much obliged to you,' replied Charlotte – 'but I *prefer* Tea.'
'Then I will help myself,' said he. – 'A large Dish of rather
weak Cocoa every evening, agrees with me better than any
thing.' – It struck her however, as he poured out this rather
weak Cocoa, that it came forth in a very fine, dark coloured
stream – and at the same moment, his Sisters both crying out –
'Oh! Arthur, you get your Cocoa stronger and stronger every
Evening'—, with Arthur's somewhat conscious reply of '*Tis*
rather stronger than it should be tonight' – convinced her that
Arthur was by no means so fond of being starved as they could
desire, or as he felt proper himself. – He was certainly very

happy to turn the conversation on dry Toast, and hear no more
of his sisters. – 'I hope you will eat some of this Toast,' said he,
'I reckon myself a very good Toaster; I never burn my Toasts –
I never put them too near the Fire at first – and yet, you see,
there is not a Corner but what is well browned. – I hope you like
dry Toast.' – 'With a reasonable quantity of Butter spread over
it, very much' – said Charlotte – 'but not otherwise. – ' 'No
more do I' – said he exceedingly pleased – 'We think quite
alike there. – So far from dry Toast being wholesome, *I* think it
a very bad thing for the Stomach. Without a little butter to
soften it, it hurts the Coats of the Stomach. I am sure it does. – I
will have the pleasure of spreading some for you directly – and
afterwards I will spread some for myself. – Very bad indeed for
the Coats of the Stomach – but there is no convincing *some*
people. – It irritates and acts like a nutmeg grater. – ' He could
not get command of the Butter however, without a struggle;
His Sisters accusing him of eating a great deal too much, and
declaring he was not to be trusted; – and he maintaining that he
only eat enough to secure the Coats of his Stomach; – and besides, he only wanted it now for Miss Heywood. – Such a plea
must prevail, he got the butter and spread away for her with an
accuracy of Judgement which at least delighted himself; but
when her Toast was done, and he took his own in hand, Charlotte
could hardly contain herself as she saw him watching his sisters,
while he scrupulously scraped off almost as much butter as he
put on, and then seize an odd moment for adding a great dab
just before it went into his Mouth. – Certainly, Mr. Arthur P.'s
enjoyments in Invalidism were very different from his sisters –
by no means so spiritualized. – A good deal of Earthy Dross
hung about him. Charlotte could not but suspect him of adopting
that line of Life, principally for the indulgence of an indolent
Temper – and to be determined on having no Disorders but
such as called for warm rooms ..nd good Nourishment. – In
one particular however, she soon found that he had caught
something from *them*. – 'What!' said he – 'Do you venture
upon two dishes of strong Green Tea in one Evening? – What
Nerves you must have! – How I envy you. – Now, if *I* were to

swallow only one such dish – what do you think it's effect would
be upon me? – ' 'Keep you awake perhaps all night' – replied
Charlotte, meaning to overthrow his attempts at Surprise, by
the Grandeur of her own Conceptions. – 'Oh! if that were
all!' – he exclaimed. – 'No – it acts on me like Poison and would
entirely take away the use of my right side, before I had swallowed
it five minutes. – It sounds almost incredible – but it has happened
to me so often that I cannot doubt it. – The use of my right
Side is entirely taken away for several hours!' 'It sounds rather
odd to be sure' – answered Charlotte coolly – ' but I dare say it
would be proved to be the simplest thing in the World, by those
who have studied right sides and Green Tea scientifically and
thoroughly understand all the possibilities of their action on
each other.' – Soon after Tea, a Letter was brought to Miss
D. P. from the Hotel. – 'From Mrs. Charles Dupuis' – said
she. – 'some private hand.' – And having read a few lines,
exclaimed aloud 'Well, this is very extraordinary! very extraordinary indeed! – That both should have the same name. –
Two Mrs. Griffiths! – This is a Letter of recommendation and
introduction to me, of the Lady from Camberwell – and *her*
name happens to be Griffiths too. – ' A few lines more however,
and the colour rushed into her Cheeks, and with much Perturbation she added – 'The oddest thing that ever was! – a Miss
Lambe too! – a young Westindian of large Fortune. – But it
cannot be the same. – Impossible that it should be the same.' –
She read the Letter aloud for comfort. – It was merely to 'introduce the Bearer, Mrs. G. – from Camberwell, and the three
young Ladies under her care, to Miss D. P.'s notice. – Mrs. G. –
being a stranger at Sanditon, was anxious for a respectable
Introduction – and Mrs. C. Dupuis therefore, at the instance of
the intermediate friend, provided her with this Letter, knowing
that she could not do her dear Diana a greater kindness than by
giving her the means of being useful. – Mrs. G.'s cheif solicitude
would be for the accomodation and comfort of one of the young
Ladies under her care, a Miss Lambe, a young W. Indian of
large Fortune, in delicate health.' – 'It was very strange! – very
remarkable! – very extraordinary' but they were all agreed in

determining it to be *impossible* that there should not be two Families; such a totally distinct set of people as were concerned in the reports of each made that matter quite certain. There *must* be two Families. – Impossible to be otherwise. 'Impossible' and 'Impossible', was repeated over and over again with great fervour. – An accidental resemblance of Names and circumstances, however striking at first, involved nothing really incredible – and so it was settled. – Miss Diana herself derived an immediate advantage to counterbalance her Perplexity. She must put her shawl over her shoulders, and be running about again. Tired as she was, she must instantly repair to the Hotel, to investigate the truth and offer her services. –

CHAPTER XI

It would not do. – Not all that the whole Parker race could say among themselves, could produce a happier catastrophée than that the Family from Surry and the Family from Camberwell were one and the same. – The rich Westindians, and the young Ladies Seminary had all entered Sanditon in those two Hack chaises. The Mrs. G. who in her friend Mrs. Darling's hands, had wavered as to coming and been unequal to the Journey, was the very same Mrs. G. whose plans were at the same period (under another representation) perfectly decided, and who was without fears or difficulties. – All that had the appearance of Incongruity in the reports of the two, might very fairly be placed to the account of the Vanity, the Ignorance, or the blunders of the many engaged in the cause by the vigilance and caution of Miss Diana P. – *Her* intimate friends must be officious like herself, and the subject had supplied Letters and Extracts and Messages enough to make everything appear what it was not. Miss D. probably felt a little awkward on being first obliged to admit her mistake. A long Journey from Hampshire taken for nothing – a Brother disappointed – an expensive House on her hands for a week, must have been some of her immediate re-

flections – and much worse than all the rest, must have been the
sort of sensation of being less clear-sighted and infallible than
she had beleived herself. – No part of it however seemed to
trouble her long. There were so many to share in the shame and
the blame, that probably when she had divided out their proper
portions to Mrs. Darling, Miss Capper, Fanny Noyce, Mrs. C.
Dupuis and Mrs. C. D.'s Neighbour, there might be a mere
trifle of reproach remaining for herself. – At any rate, she was
seen all the following morning walking about after Lodgings
with Mrs. G. – as alert as ever. – Mrs. G. was a very well-be-
haved, genteel kind of Woman, who supported herselt by receiving such great girls and young Ladies, as wanted either
Masters for finishing their Education, or a home for beginning
their Displays – She had several more under her care than the
three who were now come to Sanditon, but the others all happened to be absent. – Of these three, and indeed of all, Miss
Lambe was beyond comparison the most important and precious,
as she paid in proportion to her fortune. – She was about seventeen, half Mulatto, chilly and tender,[1] had a maid of her own,
was to have the best room in the Lodgings, and was always of the
first consequence in every plan of Mrs. G. – The other Girls,
two Miss Beauforts were just such young Ladies as may be met
with, in at least one family out of three, throughout the Kingdom;
they had tolerable complexions, shewey figures, an upright
decided carriage and an assured Look; – they were very accomplished and very Ignorant, their time being divided between
such pursuits as might attract admiration, and those Labours
and Expedients of dexterous Ingenuity, by which they could
dress in a stile much beyond what they *ought* to have afforded;
they were some of the first in every change of fashion – and the
object of all, was to captivate some Man of much better fortune
than their own. – Mrs. G. had preferred a small, retired place,
like Sanditon, on Miss Lambe's account – and the Miss B.s –,
though naturally preferring any thing to Smallness and Retirement, yet having in the course of the Spring been involved in the
inevitable expense of six new Dresses each for a three days visit,
were constrained to be satisfied with Sanditon also, till their

circumstances were retrieved. There, with the hire of a Harp for one, and the purchase of some Drawing paper for the other and all the finery they could already command, they meant to be very economical, very elegant and very secluded; with the hope on Miss Beaufort's side, of praise and celebrity from all who walked within the sound of her Instrument, and on Miss Letitia's, of curiosity and rapture in all who came near her while she sketched – and to Both, the consolation of meaning to be the most stylish Girls in the Place. – The particular introduction of Mrs. G. to Miss Diana Parker, secured them immediately an acquaintance with the Trafalgar House-family, and with the Denhams; – and the Miss Beauforts were soon satisfied with 'the Circle in which they moved in Sanditon' to use a proper phrase, for every body must now 'move in a Circle', – to the prevalence of which rototory Motion, is perhaps to be attributed the Giddiness and false steps of many. – Lady Denham had other motives for calling on Mrs. G. besides attention to the Parkers. – In Miss Lambe, here was the very young Lady, sickly and rich, whom she had been asking for; and she made the acquaintance for Sir Edward's sake, and the sake of her Milch asses. How it might answer with regard to the Baronet, remained to be proved, but as to the Animals, she soon found that all her calculations of Profit would be vain. Mrs. G. would not allow Miss L. to have the smallest sympton of a Decline, or any complaint which Asses milk could possibly relieve. 'Miss L. was under the constant care of an exprienced Physician; – and his Prescriptions must be their rule' – and except in favour of some Tonic Pills, which a Cousin of her own had a Property in, Mrs. G. did never deviate from the strict Medecinal page. – The corner house of the Terrace was the one in which Miss D. P. had the pleasure of settling her new friends, and considering that it commanded in front the favourite Lounge of all the Visitors at Sanditon, and on one side, whatever might be going on at the Hotel, there could not have been a more favourable spot for the seclusions of the Miss Beauforts. And accordingly, long before they had suited themselves with an Instrument, or with Drawing paper, they had, by the frequency of their appearance at the low Windows upstairs, in order to close the blinds, or open the Blinds, to arrange a flower pot on the Balcony, or look at nothing through a Telescope, attracted many an eye upwards, and made many a Gazer gaze again. – A little Novelty has a great effect in so small a place; the Miss Beauforts, who would have been nothing at Brighton, could not move here without notice; – and even Mr. Arthur Parker, though little disposed for supernumerary exertion, always quitted the Terrace, in his way to his Brothers by this corner House, for the sake of a glimpse of the Miss Bs –, though it was half a quarter of a mile round about, and added two steps to the ascent of the Hill.

CHAPTER XII

CHARLOTTE had been ten days at Sanditon without seeing Sanditon House, every attempt at calling on Lady D. having been defeated by meeting with her beforehand. But now it was to be more resolutely undertaken, at a more early hour, that nothing might be neglected of attention to Lady D. or amusement to Charlotte. – 'And if you should find a favourable opening my Love,' said Mr. P. (who did not mean to go with them) – 'I think you had better mention the poor Mullins's situation, and sound her Ladyship as to a Subscription for them. I am not fond of charitable subscriptions in a place of this kind – It is a sort of tax upon all that come – Yet as their distress is very great and I almost promised the poor Woman yesterday to get something done for her, I beleive we must set a subscription on foot – and therefore the sooner the better, – and Lady Denham's name at the head of the List will be a very necessary beginning. – You will not dislike speaking to her about it, Mary?' – 'I will do whatever you wish me,' replied his Wife – 'but you would do it so much better yourself. I shall not know what to say.' – 'My dear Mary,' cried he, 'it is impossible you can be really at a loss. Nothing can be more simple. You have only to state the present afflicted situation of the family, their earnest application to me, and my being willing to promote a little subscription for their releif, provided it meet with her approbation. – . 'The easiest thing in the World' – cried Miss Diana Parker who happened to be calling on them at the moment—. 'All said and done, in less time than you have been talking of it now. – And while you are on the subject of subscriptions Mary, I will thank you to mention a very melancholy case to Lady D. which has been represented to me in the most affecting terms. – There is a poor Woman in Worcestershire, whom some friends of mine are exceedingly interested about, and I have undertaken to collect whatever I can for her. If you would mention the circumstance to Lady Denham! – Lady Denham *can* give, if she is properly attacked – and I look upon her to be the sort of Person who, when once she is prevailed on to undraw her Purse, would as readily give ten guineas as five. – And therefore, if you find her in a Giving mood, you might as well speak in favour of another Charity which I and a few more, have very much at heart · the establishment of a Charitable Repository at Burton on Trent. – And then, – there is the family of the poor Man who was hung last assizes at York, tho' we really *have* raised the sum we wanted for putting them all out, yet if you *can* get a Guinea from her on their behalf, it may as well be done. – ' 'My dear Diana!' exclaimed Mrs. P. – 'I could no more mention these things to Lady D. – than I could fly.' – 'Where's the difficulty? – I wish I could go with you myself – but in five minutes I must be at Mrs. G. – to encourage Miss Lambe in taking her first Dip. She is so frightened, poor Thing, that I promised to come and keep up her Spirits, and go in the Machine with her if she wished it – and as soon as that is over, I must hurry home, for Susan is to have Leaches at one o'clock – which will be a three hours business, – therefore I really have not a moment to spare – besides that (between ourselves) I ought to be in bed myself at this present time, for I am hardly able to stand – and when the Leaches have done, I dare say we shall both go to our rooms for the rest of the day.' – 'I am sorry to hear it, indeed; but if this is the case I hope Arthur will come to us.' – 'If Arthur takes my advice, he will go to bed too, for if he stays up by himself, he will certainly eat and drink more than he ought; – but you see Mary, how impossible it is for me to go with you to Lady Denham's.' – 'Upon second thoughts Mary,' said her husband, 'I will not trouble you to speak about the Mullin's. – I will take an opportunity of seeing Lady D. myself. – *I* know how little it suits you to be pressing matters upon a Mind at all unwilling.' – *His* application thus withdrawn, his sister could say no more in support of hers, which was his object, as he felt all their impropriety and all the certainty of their ill effect upon his own better claim. – Mrs. P. was delighted at this release, and set off very happy with her friend and her little girl, on this walk to Sanditon House. – It was a close, misty morning, and when they reached the brow of the Hill, they could not for some time make out what sort of Carriage it was, which they saw coming up. It appeared at different moments to be every-thing from the Gig to the Pheaton,[1] – from one horse to four; and just as they were concluding in favour of a Tandem, little Mary's young eyes distinguished the Coachman and she eagerly called out, 'T'is Uncle Sidney Mama, it is indeed.' And so it proved. – Mr. Sidney Parker driving his Servant in a very neat Carriage was soon opposite to them, and they all stopped for a few minutes. The manners of the Parkers were always pleasant among themselves – and it was a very friendly meeting between Sidney and his sister-in-law, who was most kindly taking it for granted that he was on his way to Trafalgar House. This he declined however. 'He was just come from Eastbourne, proposing to spend two or three days, as it might happen, at Sanditon – but the Hotel must be his Quarters – He was expecting to be joined there by a friend or two.' – The rest was common enquiries and remarks, with kind notice of little Mary, and a very well-bred Bow and proper address to Miss Heywood on her being named to him – and they parted, to meet again within a few hours. – Sidney Parker was about seven or eight and twenty, very good-looking, with a decided air of Ease and Fashion, and a lively countenance. – This adventure afforded agreable discussion for some time. Mrs. P. entered into all her Husband's joy on the occasion, and exulted in the credit which Sidney's arrival would

give to the place. The road to Sanditon H. was a broad, handsome, planted approach, between fields, and conducting at the
end of a quarter of a mile through second Gates into the Grounds,
which though not extensive had all the Beauty and Respecta-
bility which an abundance of very fine Timber could give. –
These Entrance Gates were so much in a corner of the Grounds
or Paddock, so near one of its Boundaries, that an outside fence
was at first almost pressing on the road – till an angle *here*, and a
curve *there* threw them to a better distance. The Fence was a
proper Park paling in excellent condition; with clusters of fine
Elms, or rows of old Thorns following its line almost every
where. – *Almost* must be stipulated – for there were vacant
spaces – and through one of these, Charlotte as soon as they
entered the Enclosure, caught a glimpse over the pales of something White and Womanish in the field on the other side; – it
was something which immediately brought Miss B. into her
head – and stepping to the pales, she saw indeed – and very
decidedly, in spite of the Mist; Miss B— seated, not far before
her, at the foot of the bank which sloped down from the outside
of the Paling and which a narrow Path seemed to skirt along; –
Miss Brereton seated, apparently very composedly – and Sir
E. D. by her side. – They were sitting so near each other and
appeared so closely engaged in gentle conversation, that Charlotte
instantly felt she had nothing to do but to step back again, and
say not a word. – Privacy was certainly their object. – It could
not but strike her rather unfavourably with regard to Clara; –
but hers was a situation which must not be judged with severity.
– She was glad to perceive that nothing had been discerned by
Mrs Parker; If Charlotte had not been considerably the tallest
of the two, Miss B.'s white ribbons might not have fallen within
the ken of *her* more observant eyes. – Among other points of
moralising reflection which the sight of this Tete a Tete produced,
Charlotte could not but think of the extreme difficulty which
secret Lovers must have in finding a proper spot for their stolen
Interveiws. – Here perhaps they had thought themselves so
perfectly secure from observation – the whole field open before
them – a steep bank and Pales never crossed by the foot of Man

at their back – and a great thickness of air, in aid –. Yet here, she had seen them. They were really ill-used. – The House was large and handsome; two Servants appeared, to admit them, and every thing had a suitable air of Property and Order. – Lady D. valued herself upon her liberal Establishment, and had great enjoyment in the order and the Importance of her style of living. – They were shewn into the usual sitting room, well-proportioned and well-furnished; – tho' it was Furniture rather originally good and extremely well kept, than new or shewey – and as Lady D. was not there, Charlotte had leisure to look about, and to be told by Mrs. P. that the whole-length Portrait of a stately Gentleman, which placed over the Mantle-peice, caught the eye immediately, was the picture of Sir H. Denham – and that one among many Miniatures in another part of the room, little conspicuous, represented Mr. Hollis. – Poor Mr. Hollis! – It was impossible not to feel him hardly used; to be obliged to stand back in his own House and see the best place by the fire constantly occupied by Sir H. D.

EXPLANATORY NOTES

ABBREVIATIONS

Letters	*Jane Austen's Letters,* ed. R. W. Chapman, second edn. 1952.
Memoir	*A Memoir of Jane Austen,* 1870; second edn. 1871, ed. R. W. Chapman, 1926.
Minor Works	*The Works of Jane Austen,* vi, *Minor Works,* ed. R. W. Chapman, with revisions by B. C. Southam (1969).
O.E.D.	*The Oxford English Dictionary.*
P. & P.	*Pride and Prejudice.*

References to Jane Austen's novels are to the Oxford English Novels editions (reprinted in the World's Classics).

NORTHANGER ABBEY

Page 1. *though his name was Richard*: this may be an Austen family joke. In *Letters,* p. 15, we read 'Mr. Richard Harvey's match is put off till he has got a Better Christian name, of which he has great Hopes' (15 September 1796).

Page 2. (1) *the 'Beggar's Petition'*: a frequently reproduced didactic poem from *Poems on Several Occasions* (Wolverhampton, 1769) by the Revd. Thomas Moss.

(2) '*The Hare and Many Friends*': in Gay's *Fables* (1727). These were often used as schoolroom reading in the late eighteenth century. Mrs. Elton quotes the same fable in *Emma,* p. 412.

(3) *outside of a letter*: on which only the address would have been written. Envelopes were not used in Jane Austen's day.

Page 3. (1) *base ball*: the earliest reference in *O.E.D.* No doubt the game was similar to rounders, which is first cited by *O.E.D.* in 1856.

(2) . . . *how to shoot*: from Pope, *To the Memory of an Unfortunate Lady*: Gray, *Elegy in a Country Churchyard* (Jane Austen misquotes 'fragrance' for 'sweetness' again in *Emma,* p. 254), Thomson, *Spring,* l. 1149:

> Delightful task! to rear the tender thought,
> To teach the young idea how to shoot.

Page 4. (1) *from Shakspeare*: see *Othello*, III. iii. 323; *Measure for Measure*, III. i. 79; *Twelfth Night*, II. iv. 116. The first two are slightly misquoted.

(2) *a sketch of her lover's profile*: Mary Lascelles, *Jane Austen and her Art*, 1939, p. 60, compares Charlotte Smith's *Emmeline, The Orphan of the Castle* (1788) in which the heroine allows the hero to discover her portrait of him.

(3) *amiable youth*: Jane Austen uses this cliché of the sentimental novel in *Love and Friendship*, Letter 5th (*Minor Works*, p. 80).

Page 6. *altering her name*: this affectation is also satirized by Eaton Stannard Barrett in *The Heroine* (1813), in which Cherry Wilkinson adopts the name Cherubina de Willoughby.

Page 7. *Upper Rooms*: opened in 1771. Jane Austen describes an evening there in *Letters*, p. 127 (12 May 1801).

Page 9. *my head*: an arrangement of pomaded hair dressed with gauze and ribbon (*O.E.D.*).

Page 10. *called a divinity*: an unwelcome partner calls Evelina an angel (*Evelina*, 1778, Letter XIII).

Page 13. *Mr King*: James King, M.C. of the Lower Rooms from 1785 to 1805, when he became M.C. of the Upper Rooms.

Page 15. *before the gentleman's love is declared*: in *Rambler* No. 97 Richardson wrote 'That a young lady should be in love, and the love of the young gentleman undeclared, is an heterodoxy which prudence, and even policy, must not allow.'

Page 16. *despair . . . our point would gain*: not traced.

Page 19. *attornies*: privately appointed agents to look after business and legal matters.

Page 21. *the History of England*: perhaps Goldsmith's *History of England* (1771); an *Abridgement* was published in 1774.

Page 22. *Cecilia, or Camilla, or Belinda*: *Cecilia* (1782) and *Camilla* (1796) by Fanny Burney; *Belinda* (1801) by Maria Edgeworth.

Page 23. (1) *coquelicot*: poppy-coloured. Cf. *Letters*, p. 37, 'Coquelicot is to be all the fashion this winter' (18 December 1798).

(2) *the Italian*: Mrs Radcliffe's *The Italian, or the Confessional of the Black Penitents* (1797).

Page 24. Castle of Wolfenbach . . . Horrid Mysteries: Gothic novels by (respectively) Mrs. Parsons (1793), Regina Maria Roche (1798), Mrs. Parsons again (1796), Peter Teuthold (1794), Francis Lathom (1798). Eleanor Sleath (1798), Peter Will (1796). See M. Sadleir, 'The Northanger Novels', *English Association Pamphlet No. 68* (1927), and his introduction to *Northanger Abbey*, World's Classics, 1930.

Page 27. Union-passage: this was probably not so named until the opening of the parallel Union Street in 1807. (It was previously known as Cock Lane.)

Page 28. a whole scrape: an awkward *leg* accompanying a bow.

Page 29. forehand: that part of a horse which is before the rider (*O.E.D.*).

Page 30. splashing-board: a guard or screen in front of the driver's seat (*O.E.D.*).

Page 32. (1) *the Monk*: the famous Gothic novel *The Monk* (1796) by Matthew Gregory Lewis (1775–1818).

(2) *playing at see-saw and learning Latin*: these are not major episodes in Fanny Burney's *Camilla* (1796); but they occur in Book I, ch. 3 and 4, and the implication is that John Thorpe has not read beyond the first few pages.

Page 34. the Octagon Room: apparently a frequently chosen meeting place in Bath. Cf *Persuasion*, p. 389 (p. 171 World's Classics).

Page 42. at noon: this phrase may be loosely used, since Catherine was resolved to read until one. The Pump-room was most frequented while the band played, and this, according to Pierce Egan's *Walks through Bath* (1819), was between the hours of one and half-past three.

Page 46. tittuppy: unsteady, shaky.

Page 54. (1) *tamboured*: embroidered on a tambour or circular frame (*O.E.D.*).

(2) *the mull or the jackonet*: mull (originally 'mulmull') was a thin variety of plain muslin, and jackonet a heavier cotton fabric, originally imported from India.

Page 62. the night that poor St. Aubin died: St Aubin should be St Aubert. See *The Mysteries of Udolpho* (1794), ch. 8.

Page 67. commerce: a popular card-game, usually played for small stakes. Jane Austen makes several references to playing the game herself in *Letters*.

Page 73. (1) *the Bedford*: a well-known coffee-house at the north-east corner of the Piazza, Covent Garden.

(2) *touch*: strictly, a turn or 'go' in a game (*O.E.D.*).

Page 79. *a quarter of an hour*: the time required by etiquette for a visit of this kind.

Page 83. (1) *Julias and Louisas*: common names for novel-heroines in the late eighteenth century, the former perhaps in imitation of the Julie of Rousseau's *La Nouvelle Héloïse* (1761).

(2) *The nicest*: Henry Tilney's condemnation of this particular abusage may originate with Jane Austen's brothers for, in No. 9 of *The Loiterer* – the undergraduate paper edited and mainly written by James and Henry Austen at Oxford in 1789 and 1790 – the word 'nice' is deliberately misused when a pretended correspondent, Sophia Sentiment, calls for the inclusion of some 'nice affecting stories' in the paper.

(3) *Blair*: Hugh Blair (1718–1800), preacher and first professor of rhetoric at Edinburgh, author of *Lectures on Rhetoric and Belles Letters* (1783).

Page 85. *Mr. Hume or Mr. Robertson*: the four-volume *History of Great Britain* by the philosopher David Hume (1711–76) appeared between 1754 and 1761; William Robertson (1721–93) was author of a *History of Scotland during the Reigns of Queen Mary and of James VI* (1759) and a *History of Charles V* (1769).

Page 86. *a sister author*: Fanny Burney, the beautiful girl being Indiana in *Camilla*.

Page 87. *fore-grounds . . . lights and shades*: these technical terms in the appreciation of the picturesque were no doubt culled from the works of Gilpin.

Page 88. (1) *St. George's Fields*: an assembly point in the Gordon Riots of 1780.

(2) *Northampton*: where soldiers were often stationed; cavalry barracks were built in 1796.

Page 91. *spars*: lustrous minerals, often fashioned into ornaments for sale. Cf. *P. & P.*, p. 212.

Page 93. *sarsenet*: a very fine and soft silk material.

Page 96. (1) *tickets*: visiting cards.

(2) *hoop rings*: finger rings encircled with stone in a cut-down setting (*O.E.D.*).

Page 97. Devizes: travellers between Bath and London usually stopped for a meal at Devizes. Cf. Christopher Anstey, *The New Bath Guide* (1766) Letter II:

> What tho' at *Devizes* I fed pretty hearty
> And made a good meal, like the rest of the party

Page 98. one great fortune looking out for another: W. A. Craik, *Jane Austen: the Six Novels* (1965), p. 20 n., suggests that this passage recalls one in Congreve, *Love for Love* (1965), I. viii.

Page 103. I cannot speak well enough to be unintelligible: Catherine Morland's innocently brilliant remark may derive from Henry Mackenzie's *Mirror* (the periodical approved by Mrs. Morland, p. 196): 'many great personages contrive to be unintelligible in order to be respected.' (The resemblance was pointed out by W. H. Helm, *Jane Austen and Her Country-House Comedy*, 1909, p. 80.)

Page 113. But where am I wandering to?: this, together with the blush, suggests that Isabella now envisages Catherine and herself becoming sisters-in-law by marrying the two Tilneys.

Page 122. Petty-France: a small village recorded on Taylor's map of Gloucestershire in 1777. See A. H. Smith, *Place Names of Gloucestershire* 1964, iii, 33.

Page 124. Dorothy the ancient housekeeper: a housekeeper called Dorothée appears in *The Mysteries of Udolpho*.

Page 128. a Rumford: a fireplace of the latest and best type, named after its designer Count von Rumford (1753–1814).

Page 137. (1) hair-powder: a scented powder made of fine flour or starch (*O.E.D.*).

(2) *breeches-ball*: a ball of composition for cleaning breeches (*O.E.D.*).

Page 142. (1) pinery: the earliest use recorded in *O.E.D.* is in 1758, though pineapples were known in this country before then.

(2) *succession-houses*: forcing-houses having regularly graded temperatures into which plants are moved in succession (*O.E.D.*).

Page 145. anti-chamber: Dr Johnson remarked that the word was 'generally written, improperly, antichamber'.

Page 150. Montoni: the villain of *The Mysteries of Udolpho*.

Page 155. dimity: a stout cotton fabric, woven with raised stripes or fancy figures; usually employed undyed for beds and bedroom hangings (*O.E.D.*).

Page 169. *parish meeting*: this may have been either the Easter Vestry or a meeting for poor-law purposes. See Chapman's Appendix on the 'Chronology of *Northanger Abbey*', p. 300.

Page 171. *a well-connected Parsonage*: this is more likely to refer to the convenient arrangement of the rooms in the parsonage than to the social standing attached to the living or to the neighbourhood.

Page 196. '*The Mirror*': a periodical edited during 1779 and 1780 by Henry Mackenzie (1745–1831). Mrs. Morland probably has in mind No. XII, 'Consequence to little folks of intimacy with great ones, in a letter from John Homespun.'

LADY SUSAN

Page 219. *entailed*: a landed estate which was entailed had its succession settled thereby. In other words, Mrs. Johnson believes that Sir Reginald could not disinherit his son whatever he might think of an association with Lady Susan.

Page 227. *common candour*: ordinary disinterested judgement.

Page 238. *the Rattle*: a stock eighteenth-century type, the idle and sometimes boastful gossip. One of the human empty vessels who make the most sound.

Page 240. *consciousness*: almost our 'self-consciousness'.

Page 255. *highly unadvisable for them to meet*: Mrs. Johnson may be warning of the possibility of a duel.

Page 272. *finessed*: skilfully manoeuvred or, as *O.E.D.* (which quotes this context) puts it, 'conducted by artifice'.

THE WATSONS

Page 275. (1) *Town of D.*: Jane Austen seems to have had Dorking in mind.

(2) *the old chair*: a chair was a light chaise drawn by one horse. Jane Austen gives clues to circumstance and sometimes even to character by her descriptions of carriages, much as a modern novelist might do in describing the motor cars used by his characters.

Page 281. *sweep*: an elegantly curved drive.

Page 287. *8 or 900£ a year*: readers who wish to understand the relative value of sums of money in Jane Austen's world should consult

Sense and Sensibility, which is particularly well stocked with references to income. The sum mentioned here approaches that which Elinor Dashwood, in vol. I ch.xvii of that novel, regards as 'wealth', but is less than half of Marianne's 'competence'.

Page 289. *interesting*: in Jane Austen's period, this means attracting strong emotional sympathy, not simply curiosity.

Page 294. *Negus*: a drink named after its inventor Colonel Negus (d.1732), and consisting of port, hot water, sugar, and spices.

Page 296. *a neat Curricle*: built for speed, a curricle was a light two-wheeled carriage which was usually drawn by two horses abreast.

Page 298. (1) *not critically handsome*: not precisely handsome, or 'not exactly beautiful', at least to the eye of the purist.

(2) *thing of*: presumably a slip in the manuscript for 'think of'.

Page 300. *manners . . . address*: manners are the general bearing in conversation, address is the way of speaking.

Page 307. *endite*: indict.

Page 311. *Speculation*: a round game which involved the buying and selling of trump cards. It is played in *Mansfield Park* (Vol.II, ch.vii) and Jane Austen herself enjoyed the game (*Letters*, pp. 229, 247 – 24 October 1808 and 10 January 1809).

Page 312. (1) *Pembroke Table*: a partly folding table, which had four fixed legs and two hinged flaps, one at either side.

(2) *the Bedford*: a coffee-house in Covent Garden, where John Thorpe had met General Tilney (*Northanger Abbey* p. 73).

Page 314. (1) *fish*: pieces of bone or ivory, sometimes as the name implies fish-shaped, which were used in place of money in card games.

(2) *beaufit*: a sideboard or side-table (the more familiar form of the word is 'buffet').

SANDITON

Page 323. *the Morning Post and the Kentish Gazette:* the *Morning Post* began publication at London in 1772 and the *Kentish Gazette* at Canterbury in 1768.

Page 324. *Saline air and immersion*: the medicinal properties of both had had their advocates for some time. See Sarah Howell, *The Seaside* (1974), for a study of the relevant social history.

Page 326. line of the Poet Cowper: in his poem 'Truth', published in 1782, Cowper contrasts an obscure peasant, happy in her simple religious faith, with the brilliant and famous Voltaire, ultimately unhappy because of his scepticism:

> Just knows, and knows no more, her Bible true –
> A truth the brilliant Frenchman never knew; . . .
> O happy peasant! O unhappy bard!
> His the mere tinsel, hers the rich reward;
> He praise'd, perhaps, for ages yet to come;
> She never heard of half a mile from home.
> (ll.327 ff.)

Page 329. anti-spasmodic: effective against spasms or convulsions.

Page 333. Cottage Ornèe: an artificial architectural attempt to capture the picturesque charm of a cottage while doubtless embodying more comforts.

Page 340. Venetian window: a Venetian window had three apertures, the two side ones being narrow.

Page 343. (1) *West Indian*: not native West Indian stock, but a family whose fortune had been made or enhanced after emigration to the West Indies.

(2) *Camberwell*: by the time when *Sanditon* was written, 'Camberwell's popularity as a handy and sanitary retreat from the polluting city had become well established'. H. J. Dyos, *Victorian Suburb: A Study of the Growth of Camberwell* (1961), p. 31.

Page 345. Camilla's Youth: the subtitle of Fanny Burney's *Camilla* (1796) was 'A Picture of Youth'.

Page 348. Chamber-Horse: it is not clear exactly what this would be like, but its use was an alternative to riding a real horse out of doors.

Page 349. Sisters': this, like the phrase indicated by the next note, is one of several instances in which Jane Austen misplaced an apostrophe in the manuscript.

Page 351. (1) *either of Scotts' Poems*: the conversation seems to turn on *Marmion* (1808) and *The Lady of the Lake* (1810), from both of which Sir Edward quotes (*Marmion* vi.30 and *The Lady of the Lake* ii.22).

Page 352. Burns . . . Campbell: Sir Edward could have formed his opinions by dipping into the *Edinburgh Review* or the *Quarterly Review*, which noticed all of the poets mentioned. Many early nineteenth-century editions of Burns contained biographical material, so there is nothing surprising in Charlotte's reply.

Page 355. a Co–: a co-heiress.

Page 357. Eleemosynary: charitable.

Page 358. Lovelaces: Lovelace is the compelling rakish villain of Richardson's *Clarissa Harlowe* (1748).

Page 359. Tombuctoo: contemporary readers might have been aware of the contrast between the Timbuctoo of romance and that of reality. See F. P. Lock, ' "The Neighbourhood of Tombuctoo": A Note on *Sanditon'*, *Notes and Queries* ccxvii (1972).

Page 365. Projector: a speculator.

Page 369. all in a Bath: perspiring profusely.

Page 373. half Mulatto, chilly and tender: with the perception of a fellow-novelist, Margaret Drabble comments interestingly on this unexpected and evocative phrase in her edition of *Lady Susan, The Watsons, and Sanditon* (1974), pp. 221–2.

Page 377. the Gig to the Pheaton: a gig was a light two-wheeled carriage drawn by one horse, whereas a phaeton was a four-wheeled open carriage, also of light construction, drawn by at least one pair of horses.

THE WORLD'S CLASSICS

A Select List

Charles Dickens: David Copperfield
Edited by Nina Burgis

Dombey and Son
Edited by Alan Horsman

Little Dorrit
Edited by Harvey Peter Sucksmith

Martin Chuzzlewit
Edited by Margaret Cardwell

The Mystery of Edwin Drood
Edited by Margaret Cardwell

Oliver Twist
Edited by Kathleen Tillotson

Sikes and Nancy and Other Public Readings
Edited by Philip Collins

Arthur Conan Doyle:
Sherlock Holmes: Selected Stories
With an introduction by S. C. Roberts

A complete list of Oxford Paperbacks, including The World's Classics, Twentieth-Century Classics, OPUS, Past Masters, Oxford Authors, Oxford Shakespeare, and Oxford Paperback Reference, is available in the UK from the General Publicity Department (JH), Oxford University Press, Walton Street, Oxford OX2 6DP.

In the USA, complete lists are available from the Paperbacks Marketing Manager, Oxford University Press, 200 Madison Avenue, New York, NY 10016.

Oxford Paperbacks are available from all good bookshops. In case of difficulty, customers in the UK can order direct from Oxford University Press Bookshop, Freepost, 116 High Street, Oxford, OX1 4BR, enclosing full payment. Please add 10 per cent of published price for postage and packing.